A Student's Dictionary of
Language and Linguistics

A Student's Dictionary of
Language and Linguistics

R. L. Trask
School of Cognitive and Computing Sciences, University of Sussex

A member of the Hodder Headline Group
LONDON • NEW YORK • SYDNEY • AUCKLAND

First published in Great Britain in 1997 by
Arnold, a member of the Hodder Headline Group
338 Euston Road, London NW1 3BH

Co-published in the United States of America by
Oxford University Press Inc.,
198 Madison Avenue, New York NY10016

British Library Cataloguing in Publication Data
A catalogue record for this book is available from the British Library

Library of Congress Cataloging-in-Publication Data
A catalog record for this book is available from the Library of Congress

ISBN 0 340 65267 5 (Hb)
ISBN 0 340 65266 7 (Pb)

3 4 5 6 7 8 9 10

Typeset in 9/10½ pt Plantin by J&L Composition Ltd, Filey, North Yorkshire
Printed and bound in Great Britain by J W Arrowsmith Ltd, Bristol

Notes to the Reader

As the title suggests, this is an introductory dictionary for language and linguistics. It is aimed chiefly at students just beginning the study of the subject, at both undergraduate and post-graduate level, though it will be useful to anybody who wants to do some reading in the field.

This dictionary includes virtually every term you are likely to encounter in your first year of linguistics, as well as a number of terms you probably won't meet until later. These terms are of several types.

First, there is particularly careful coverage of the terminology of traditional grammar. All those terms that you probably didn't learn at school are here, such as *noun*, *gender*, *transitive verb*, *indirect object* and *relative clause*.

Second, you will find the basic terms from every area of general linguistics: phonetics (pronunciation), phonology (sound systems), morphology (word-structure), syntax (sentence-structure), semantics (meaning) and pragmatics (language and context). Among these are *velar*, *fricative*, *phoneme*, *complementary distribution*, *morpheme*, *allomorph*, *generative grammar*, *complementizer*, *antonym*, *componential analysis*, *speech act* and *conversational implicature*.

Third, there is abundant coverage of sociolinguistics (language and society), anthropological linguistics (language and culture), neurolinguistics (language and brain), psycholinguistics (language and mind), child language acquisition and disability. Among the terms treated here are *social network*, *social stratification*, *kinship terms*, *sexism*, *Broca's aphasia*, *synaesthesia*, *perceptual strategy*, *garden-path sentence*, *babbling*, *wug test*, *gavagai problem*, *Williams syndrome* and *Specific Language Impairment*.

Fourth, the dictionary provides good coverage of the terminology of language change, historical linguistics and philology, with terms like *dissimilation*, *reanalysis*, *systematic correspondence*, *merger*, *change from below*, *onomastics*, *codex* and *apparent time*.

Fifth, there is unusually good coverage of the increasingly important field of the origin and evolution of language; among the terms treated are *African Eve hypothesis*, *protolanguage*, *spandrel*, *emergent* and *gossip theory*.

Sixth, the basic terms of computational linguistics are included, such as *parser*, *natural-language processing* and *LISP*.

Seventh, the dictionary exceptionally explains the everyday terms of professional academics, such as *conference*, *journal*, *Festschrift*, *working papers* and *referee*.

Eighth, the book explains the most important terms encountered in using the Internet, such as *Web site*, *newsgroup*, *list*, *virtual library* and *database*.

Ninth, the most prominent languages and language families are identified, including *Indo-European*, *Algonquian*, *Sino-Tibetan*, *Bantu*, *Irish*, *Arabic*, *Sumerian* and *Zulu*.

Finally, the dictionary includes brief biographical entries for a number of prominent people in linguistics and related fields, both from the past (*Grimm*, *Saussure*, *Jones*, *Jespersen*, *Bloomfield*, *Lévi-Strauss*) and the present (*Chomsky*, *Bellugi*, *Labov*, *Searle*, *Greenberg*).

The dictionary is fully up to date; some of the terms included have only recently been introduced and are just beginning to find their way into the textbooks: *exaptation*, *Bill Peters effect*, *coach test*, *Minimalist Programme*, *throwing madonna hypothesis*, *Relevance Theory*.

I have been at pains to correct some widespread misconceptions about language and languages; see for example the entries for *primitive language, old language, Eskimo-Aleut, gender* and *language change*.

Within entries, boldface is used to refer the reader to other, directly relevant entries in the dictionary (only the first appearance within an entry is in bold). Italic denotes glosses, foreign words and any significant term that does not have an entry of its own. Single quotes are used for linguistic items and double quotes for direct quotations or as scare quotes around inappropriate terms.

You might like to try looking a few things up in the dictionary. Here are some sample questions:

- Is Chinese one language or not?
- How does a phonetic transcription differ from a phonemic transcription?
- How do Chomsky and Piaget differ in their views about the way children acquire their first language?
- Are sign languages real languages?
- Which languages are most closely related to English?
- What's the difference between a pidgin and a creole?
- What is a split infinitive? Is it really a bad thing?
- How did the Marxists Bakhtin and Gramsci differ in their views of language policy in education?
- Who are Genie, Isabelle and Chelsea, and what can we learn from their tragic cases?
- Where do they speak Xhosa? Basque? Tok Pisin?

At the end of the book you will find an annotated list of suggested reading in general linguistics and in a number of particular areas.

I hope you find the dictionary useful.

R. L. Trask
School of Cognitive and Computing Sciences
University of Sussex

A

a-, an- A prefix meaning 'without', 'absence of', used in coining names for specific **disabilities**. In principle, this prefix is used only in naming very severe cases, and **dys-** is used for less severe cases, but this distinction is not always carefully observed. The form *a-* is used before a consonant, *an-* before a vowel. Examples include **aphasia** ('absence of speech'), **agrammatism** ('absence of grammar') and **anarthria** ('absence of muscular control').

AAAL See **American Association for Applied Linguistics**.

A-bar A syntactic category which is bigger than an adjective but smaller than an adjective phrase. The adjective phrase *very proud of Lisa* consists of the degree modifier *very* and the A-bar *proud of Lisa*.

abbreviation A conventional short way of writing a word or a phrase, using only letters of the alphabet and sometimes full stops. Examples: *kg* for *kilogramme*, *lb* for *pound*, *e.g.* for *for example*, *i.e.* for *in other words*. Usually, an abbreviation has no distinctive pronunciation of its own, but there are exceptions: for example, *p* for *pence* is sometimes pronounced 'pee'. Do not confuse an abbreviation with a **symbol**, with an **acronym**, with a **contraction**, or with a **clipped form**.

abbreviatory convention Any standard way of using conventional symbols in order to state a linguistic generalization very briefly. In phonology, for example, the statement V[+ high] $\rightarrow$ Ø / V___{C,#}, which conventionally means "a high vowel is deleted when it is both preceded by another vowel and followed either by a consonant or by the end of a word" illustrates several abbreviatory conventions: the use of the symbols V and C for "any vowel" and "any consonant", the use of the symbol $\rightarrow$ for "changes to", the use of Ø for "nothing at all", the use of / for "in the following circumstances", the use of _____ for "in this position", and the use of # for "a word boundary".

abduction A particular type of reasoning, in which a person observes a phenomenon Y, remembers a generalization that can derive Y from X, and concludes that X is therefore true. While logically invalid, this type of reasoning is widely regarded as important both in the **acquisition** of language by children and in producing **language change**. An example is the replacement of the traditional form *There are a lot of people here* by the innovation *There's a lot of people here* in the speech of many speakers. Presumably speakers noted that the word *there* comes first in such sentences, recalled that the subject of a sentence normally comes first, and concluded that the subject in this case must be *there* (and that the verb must therefore agree with *there*, and not with *a lot of people*).

Abercrombie, David A British phonetician (1909–92), prominent as a researcher, a teacher and a writer; he coined a good deal of the terminology of phonetics.

ablative In a language with **case**, that case form which typically expresses the meaning 'out of' or 'away from'. For example, the Turkish noun *ev* 'house' has an ablative *evden* 'from the house', 'out of the house'. In the case of Latin, the label 'ablative' is applied to a case form which has some rather miscellaneous functions.

ablaut (also **apophony, vowel gradation**) The process of producing grammatical changes in words by changing the vowel in the stem, as in *sing ~ sang ~ sung* or *write ~ wrote ~ written*. Ablaut differs from **umlaut** only in its historical source, and the terms are used only by people who know the historical facts.

absolute construction Any phrase which, from the point of view of its meaning, forms a clear part of an utterance but which nevertheless has no grammatical connection to the rest of the utterance. In the following examples, the initial phrases set off by commas are absolute constructions: *The day being cloudy, we decided to postpone our picnic*; *His inheritance squandered, Cecil was forced to look for a job*. Note the difference from the following example: *Having finished her dinner, she reached for her cigarettes*. Here the verb form *having finished* clearly connects the first phrase to the rest of the sentence, and so this phrase is not an absolute construction. Note also that a **parenthetical** differs from an absolute construction in that a parenthetical usually interrupts its sentence and typically has no particular connection with the meaning of the rest of the utterance.

absolute exception An instance in which a normally optional grammatical process is either obligatory or prohibited. For example, most verbs like *consider* can appear in both active and passive constructions: *They consider her to be clever*; *She is considered to be clever*. But *say* is different: *She is said to be clever* is fine, but *They say her to be clever* is impossible. Hence *say* is a 'positive absolute exception' to passivization: it *must* appear in the passive form.

absolute neutralization A phonological analysis in which the analyst sets up an abstract contrast between two sounds at some underlying level, even though there is no such contrast on the surface. For example, some analyses of French posit an underlying consonant /h/ which contrasts with zero; this /h/ is invoked to block certain phonological processes which apply before a vowel, and then /h/ is deleted (it 'merges with zero') to give the correct surface forms.

absolute universal A **universal** which holds true for every single human language without exception, and which can therefore perhaps be regarded as part of the definition of a human language. Examples: every language has both consonants and vowels; every language distinguishes nouns and verbs; no language has a dual unless it also has a plural.

absolutive In an **ergative language**, the case form which is used to mark both subjects of intransitive verbs and direct objects of transitive verbs. In the following Basque sentences, *gizona* 'the man' is the absolutive form: *Gizona dator* 'The man is coming'; *Neskak gizona ikusi zuen* 'The girl saw the man'; but, in *Gizonak neska ikusi zuen* 'The man saw the girl', *gizonak* is not absolutive because it is the subject of a transitive verb (it is in the **ergative** case).

abstract A label applied to any representation or analysis of a linguistic form which is significantly different from what speakers actually say. For example, some linguists would analyse the pronunciation of *sanity* /'sænɪti/ as representing an abstract form /'seɪnɪti/, and some would analyse *Lisa seems to be happy* as representing an abstract form [*Lisa to be happy*] *seems*. All linguistic analysis involves some degree of abstraction, but linguists differ in the degree of abstraction they are prepared to tolerate.

abstract noun A **noun** whose meaning is a general mental concept, rather than a physical object. Examples: *beauty, happiness, deceit, history, size*. This term is also commonly extended to nouns denoting events, like *explosion*, *murder*, and *destruction*. Compare **concrete noun**.

Académie Française The French Academy, an official body in France whose members are charged with overseeing the use and development of the French language. With a largely conservative outlook, the Academy has lent its weight to the maintenance of traditional standards in the written language, but it has little influence over spoken French, which is now very different from the written standard.

accent 1. A particular way of pronouncing a language. It is important to realize that *every* speaker has an accent: it is impossible to speak a language without using some accent. But, in informal or non-technical usage, it is very common to use the term 'accent' merely to mean a kind of accent which is regarded as unfamiliar, or as of low prestige, by the person making the judgement: *a Geordie accent, an American accent, a working-class accent*. Compare **dialect**. 2. An informal name for a **diacritic**.

accentuation Another word for **stress**.

acceptability The degree to which some possible sentence is regarded by native speakers as normal or permissible. A sentence which is constructed in accordance with all the grammatical requirements of the language may still be regarded as unacceptable because it is too long or too difficult to process or merely because it would not be a plausible thing to say in any conceivable circumstances.

acceptance The final stage in **language planning**, in which the newly constructed language comes to be generally used by the community.

accessibility In psycholinguistics, the ability of a speaker to obtain linguistic items from memory. The **tip-of-the-tongue phenomenon** represents an everyday problem of accessibility; **anomia** is a very severe problem of accessibility.

accessibility hierarchy See **NP accessibility hierarchy**.

accidence A very old-fashioned synonym for **inflectional morphology**.

accidental gap In the vocabulary of some language, the absence of a logically possible word which, if it existed, would make the structure of the vocabulary more orderly. For example, English has many sets like *horse / stallion / mare* and *sheep / ram / ewe*, but the set *X / bull / cow* shows a gap: there is no English word meaning 'bovine animal of either sex'.

accommodation 1. (also **coarticulation**) A modification in the articulation of a sound in order to ease the transition to a following sound, as when English /t/ (normally alveolar) is pronounced as a dental before a following dental fricative /θ/, as in *eighth*. 2. (also **convergence**) The behaviour of a speaker who (consciously or unconsciously) adapts her/his speech to the speech of the surrounding people, as when a Scot who moves to the south of England begins to use southern English words and pronunciations.

accommodation theory A sociolinguistic theory which holds that you will adjust your speech towards that of the person you are talking to when you want reduce social distance, show solidarity or get something from that person, but adjust your speech the other way when you want to increase social distance or express your own distinctness.

accusative In a language with **case**, that case form which is typically used to mark the **direct object** of a verb. The Latin noun *puella* 'girl', for example, has an accusative *puellam*, as in *Puellam vidi* 'I saw the girl' (compare *Puella me vidit* 'The girl saw me'). Some people use the term more broadly, and apply it also to the **objective** case of English pronouns; they would say that *me* in the last English sentence was in the accusative. This extended use is not recommended.

accusative and infinitive A traditional name for a particular construction found in Latin, English and some other languages. Example: *He persuaded her to give up smoking*, in which the sequence *her to give up smoking* is the accusative and infinitive.

accusative language A language in which subjects of intransitive verbs and subjects of transitive verbs are treated identically for grammatical purposes while direct objects are treated differently. Most European languages, including English, are accusative. Consider English pronouns: *She arrived safely; She saw us;* but *We saw her.* Compare **ergative language**, **active language**.

acoustic Pertaining to sounds – in phonetics, of course, to speech sounds.

acoustic cue Any acoustic characteristic of a speech sound which aids the hearer in recognizing that sound during speech.

acoustic feature A **distinctive feature** which is related to the acoustic qualities of a speech sound, and not to the articulation of that sound. Acoustic features like [strident], [grave] and [flat] were widely used in the 1950s and '60s, but later they were largely displaced by **articulatory features**.

acoustic phonetics The branch of **phonetics** which studies the properties of the sound waves carrying speech sounds. Acoustic phonetics makes heavy use of instruments for this purpose.

acoustic spectrum A graph, representing the structure of a complex sound, in which **amplitude** is plotted against **frequency** (sense 1). Such a graph shows the relative contribution to the overall sound made by every component frequency. Figure A1 shows the acoustic spectrum of the vowel [i].

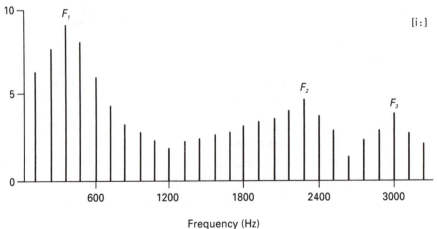

A1 Acoustic spectrum of the vowel [i]

acoustic variance Variation in the nature of the sound waves representing a particular **phoneme**, depending on the neighbouring sounds, the speaker's accent, the rate of speaking, and possibly other factors.

acquired Of a **disability**, not present from birth, but appearing later in life, usually as a result of brain damage or disease. Compare **developmental** (sense 1).

acquisition The entire process by which a young child learns a first language.

acrolect In a **creole**, the most prestigious variety of the creole, the variety which is most similar to the local standard language, or which in some cases *is* the local standard language.

acronym A word or name which is obtained, in the simplest case, by combining the first letters of all the important words in a phrase with the same meaning. Examples: *scuba* (from *self-contained underwater breathing apparatus*), *NATO* (from *North Atlantic Treaty Organization*), *laser* (from *light amplification by the stimulated emission of radiation*). Not all acronyms are quite so neat: the acronym *COBUILD* stands for the *Collins-Birmingham University International Language Database*. Many people would restrict this term to cases in which the result can easily be pronounced as a word; they apply the term **initialism** to cases like *CIA* (from *Central Intelligence Agency*), which must be spelled out letter by letter. This restrictive usage is recommended.

active knowledge The words and grammatical constructions in a certain language which you are able to make use of when speaking that language. Your active knowledge may be rather less than your **passive knowledge**.

active language (also **agentive language**) Any language in which subjects of both transitive and intransitive verbs which are semantically **agents** are treated identically for grammatical purposes, while non-agent subjects and direct objects are treated differently. The following examples from the North American language Eastern Pomo show the use of the two subject pronouns *há:* 'I' (agent) and *wí* 'I' (non-agent): *Há: mi:pal šá:ka* 'I killed him', *Há: wádu:kìya* 'I'm going', *Wí ʔéčkiya* 'I sneezed'.

active voice A construction involving a transitive verb in which the grammatical subject of the verb typically represents the agent performing the action and the direct object represents the entity undergoing the action: *The Mongols invaded China*; *Seward bought Alaska from the Russians*; *I've washed the car*; *Lisa wants a BMW*. In the vast majority of languages, the active voice is the unmarked construction for transitive verbs, involving the simplest form of the verb and the simplest possible marking of other elements in the sentence. In many (not all) languages, the active voice contrasts with a **passive voice**, and sometimes with additional **voices** (sense 1).

actor An extension of the semantic notion of **agent** to include other noun phrases which are not strictly agents but which pattern like agents for grammatical purposes. For example, the subject NP *Lisa* would be considered an actor in each of the following sentences, but only an agent in the first: *Lisa bought a skirt*; *Lisa noticed the incident*; *Lisa received a letter*; *Lisa slept soundly*. Roughly, then, an actor is that noun phrase exercising the highest degree of independent action in the clause.

actuation In language change, the introduction of a change into the language in the first place. Finding out how this happens is one of the most difficult problems in the study of language change. Compare **implementation** (sense 1).

acute accent The diacritic ´, used in various orthographies for various purposes. It is occasionally used in English in writing words of foreign origin, especially French origin: *café*, *élite*.

adaptation The process by which a speaker consciously adjusts her/his speech towards a different variety perceived as more desirable, such as when a British speaker with a regional accent attempts to produce something approximating to **Received Pronunciation**.

address, forms of The different linguistic forms which a speaker might use to address another person. For example, Dr William Robinson might be addressed in various circumstances as *Dr Robinson*, *Doctor*, *sir*, *Mr Robinson*, *William*, *Bill*, *mate*, *Curly*, *darling*, *snuggle-bunny*, or *you*. Languages differ noticeably in the choices they provide and in the rules for using them.

adequacy Any of various criteria which may be invoked for evaluating a proposed linguistic theory.

adjacency pair The minimal unit of conversational interaction, consisting of a single remark followed by a single response of a more-or-less predictable nature. Examples: A: *Are you ready?* B: *Not quite.* A: *How are you?* B: *Fine. How are you?* A: *You're treading mud all over the floor.* B: *Oh, sorry.*

adjectival clause A rather old-fashioned name for a **relative clause**.

adjectival passive The passive participle of a verb functioning as an adjective. Examples: *a ruined city, a newly discovered fossil, well-taught children, He is happily married, a vanished civilization, their long-departed spirits.*

adjective A large **word class** found in English and in many other languages, or a particular word which belongs to this class. In English, a typical adjective like *big* or *beautiful* exhibits the following properties, among others. It can appear in certain positions: *this _____ book; This book is _____; _____ though this book is, it's not very useful.* It can be compared in one of two ways: *big, bigger, biggest; beautiful, more beautiful, most beautiful.* It can take a degree modifier: *very big, too big, fairly big, quite beautiful.* It does not have different singular and plural forms, and it cannot be marked for tense. (Note: some of these properties are also exhibited by other word classes, but only adjectives show all of them.) Some adjectives fail to exhibit a few of these properties, but still show enough of them that we must regard them as adjectives: *asleep, chief, last, topmost.* The meaning of an adjective is most often a quality, but there are lots of exceptions, and, as always, it is very dangerous to try to guess what word class a particular word belongs to merely by looking at its meaning. **Important note:** traditional grammarians often included the **determiners** like *the* and *this* in the Adjective class. This is a grave error, and you should not imitate it, but a few dictionaries of English still do this. **Further note:** in phrases like *a pretty dress, a red dress, a short dress*, the words *pretty, red* and *short* are adjectives; however, in similar-looking phrases like *a cotton dress, a maternity dress, a cocktail dress*, the words *cotton, maternity* and *cocktail* are nouns, as shown by examination of their further behaviour. Do not make the mistake of calling such nouns 'adjectives'.

adjective phrase (**AP** or **AdjP**) An entire **phrase** (sense 2) which behaves just like an **adjective**: it takes the position of an adjective and modifies a noun like an adjective. Examples: *very big, proud of her achievements, more expensive than that one.* An adjective phrase normally contains an adjective as its **head** (here, *big, proud, expensive*). Linguists usually assume that a simple adjective is itself an adjective phrase; this policy makes grammatical analysis simpler.

adjoined relative clause A type of **relative clause** which is placed at the end of the sentence, regardless of where it logically belongs. In the example *A student turned up this morning who'd actually done the reading*, the relative clause *who'd actually done the reading* is adjoined, instead of occurring in its logical position after *student.* In English, the adjoined relative is an option; in some other languages, it is the only possibility.

AdjP An abbreviation for **adjective phrase**.

adjunct Any phrase in a sentence which is not strictly required to make the sentence grammatical. In the example *I saw Lisa in the park yesterday*, the phrases *in the park* and *yesterday* are adjuncts, since *I saw Lisa* would still be a grammatical sentence without them.

adjunction In **transformational grammar**, any procedure for inserting material into a tree. Figure A2 shows three different ways of adjoining the element E into the tree at the left; these are called (1) *sister-adjunction*, (2) *daughter-adjunction* and (3) *Chomsky-adjunction*.

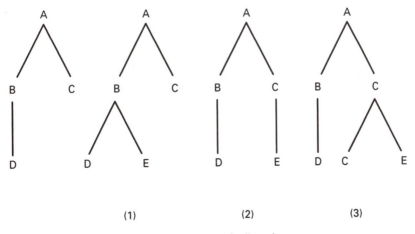

(1)   (2)   (3)

A2   Three types of adjunction

adnominal Any part of a **noun phrase** except for the noun which is the **head** of the NP. In the NP *the young girl in the blue dress who you were talking to*, the adnominals are *the, young, in the blue dress* and *who you were talking to*.

adposition A general label including **prepositions**, **postpositions** and **circumpositions**.

adstrate (or **adstratum**) A neighbouring language which influences some other language but which is neither more nor less prestigious than that other language. Compare **substrate, superstrate**.

advanced tongue root (ATR) In phonology, a **distinctive feature** which is often used to separate the vowels of a language into two groups. In some African languages, the vowels are clearly divided into those pronounced with the root (rear part) of the tongue pushed forward ([+ ATR]) and those in which it is pulled back ([− ATR]). Very often, however, the feature is applied in a somewhat arbitrary way merely to distinguish vowels which are otherwise rather difficult to distinguish, such as the English vowels of *beat* and *bit*; in this usage, the feature [ATR] replaces the older feature [**tense**] (sense 2).

adverb A large **word class** found in English and in many other languages, or a particular word which belongs to this class. In English, a typical adverb like *carefully* exhibits at least the following properties. It can appear in several different positions in a sentence: _____ *she poured the wine; She* _____ *poured the wine; She poured the wine* _____. It can be compared: *carefully, more carefully, most carefully*. It can take a degree modifier: *very carefully, too carefully, fairly carefully*. It does not have different singular and plural forms, and it cannot be marked for tense. Some adverbs, like *yesterday* and *here*, fail to show all of the typical adverb properties, but are still best regarded as adverbs. Some adverbs, the **sentence adverbs**, have certain rather special properties. **Important note:** traditional grammarians tended to use the category Adverb as a dustbin for all the words they didn't know what to do with, such as **degree modifiers** and a number of words showing rather miscellaneous and often unique behaviour, such as *not, please*, the *even* of *Even Lisa enjoyed the lecture*, and the first *as* of *as big as a house*. This is a terrible procedure, and you should not imitate it, but note that many dictionaries of English continue this practice.

adverb fronting Another name for **adverb preposing**.

adverbial Any phrase in a sentence which is functionally similar to an **adverb** in that it modifies the action in respect of time, manner, place or circumstance. In the example *She polished the table lovingly and with great care before she went home*, all three of *lovingly, with great care* and *before she went home* are adverbials, though only the first is an adverb.

adverbial clause Any **subordinate clause** which is semantically related to the rest of its sentence just like an adverb, in that it expresses some adverbial notion like time, manner, place, concession, purpose or cause. In English, an adverbial clause is introduced by a **subordinating conjunction** such as *when, after, while, although, if* and *because*. In the sentence *After Lisa got up, she had a shower*, the sequence *after Lisa got up* is an adverbial clause.

adverbial participle An **adverbial** headed by a **participle**. In the examples *Arriving a little early, she decided to take a stroll* and *Encouraged by her success, she persevered*, the phrases before the commas are adverbial participles.

adverb phrase A complete **phrase** (sense 2) which behaves just like a simple **adverb**, such as *very carefully* or *more slowly than Lisa*. Linguists usually assume that a simple adverb is itself an adverb phrase, since this policy makes grammatical analysis easier.

adverb preposing (also **adverb fronting**) The construction in which an **adverb** which might more usually occur in the middle of the sentence comes at the beginning. Examples: *Carefully she decanted the wine; Eagerly she tore open the letter*.

adversative A word which introduces a contrast, such as *but* or *however*.

aerodynamic myoelastic theory of phonation A theory of how the **vocal folds** work in order to produce **voicing** (sense 1). It holds that the pressure of the air flowing up from the lungs pushes the vocal folds apart, allowing air to flow through; the drop in pressure caused by **Bernoulli's principle** then causes the vocal folds to snap back together, and this sequence is repeated many times per second. This theory is now universally accepted.

aerometry In phonetics, a technique for measuring airflow through the mouth and nose during speech.

affective filter Difficulty in learning a foreign language (or indeed anything else) resulting from self-consciousness and fear of failure. Young children seem not to suffer from this, though most adults do.

affective meaning That part of the meaning of a linguistic form which expresses the speaker's attitude toward it, often an emotional attitude. For example, *rabbit* and *bunny* have the same **conceptual meaning**, but the second contains some affective meaning which is absent from the first.

affirmative A label applied to any form or sentence which is not **negative**.

affix A little piece of grammatical material which cannot stand by itself but which must be attached to something else within a word. Examples include the *re-* of *rewrite*, the *-ness* of *happiness* and the plural marker *-s*, as in *cats*. An affix is usually a single **morpheme**, and of course it is a **bound morpheme**. Note that, when we want to talk about an affix, we write it with a hyphen at the end at which it must be attached to something else. There are several types of affix; see **prefix**, **suffix**, **circumfix**, **infix** and **superfix** for more information.

affricate A complex type of consonant in which a complete closure is made in the mouth and the closure is then released slowly, with friction noise. English has the two affricates [tʃ], as in *church*, and [dʒ], as in *judge*. Other affricates are found in some other languages, such as German [ts] (spelled *z* or *tz*), as in *Zeit* 'time' and *Witz* 'joke'. Compare **plosive**.

African Eve hypothesis (also **mitochondrial Eve hypothesis**) The hypothesis that all human beings now alive, and all members of *Homo sapiens sapiens* who have ever lived, are directly descended from a single tiny population, indeed from a single woman, who lived in sub-Saharan Africa around 200,000 years ago. Based on a comparative study of mitochondrial DNA, this hypothesis is a more specific version of the **out-of-Africa hypothesis**. The African Eve hypothesis requires that the vast majority of early hominids made no genetic contribution to modern humans, and implies that the **Neandertals** cannot be our ancestors; it is obviously compatible with the idea that all attested human languages are derived from a single common ancestor (the **"Proto-World" hypothesis**). In fact, one scholar has seriously suggested that Eve's descendants prospered precisely because they were the first humans to have full-blown language, but few people have taken this **talking Eve hypothesis** seriously.

African languages The indigenous languages of Africa. Numbering perhaps 1500, these languages are classified into just four families: **Afro-Asiatic**, **Nilo-Saharan**, **Niger-Congo** and **Khoisan**.

Afrikaans One of the major languages of South Africa. Afrikaans is descended from the **Dutch** introduced by settlers in the seventeenth century, but it is now significantly different from standard Dutch and must be regarded as a separate language.

Afro-Asiatic A large family of languages covering much of North Africa and the Middle East. It is divided into six branches: ancient **Egyptian, Semitic, Berber, Cushitic, Chadic** and **Omotic**. This family was formerly called the *Hamito-Semitic* family, but the older name is now obsolete.

age-grading In sociolinguistics, the phenomenon in which the speech of every individual changes in a consistent way as the individual grows older, but the speech of the people of any given age remains constant over time. In other words, today's 20-year-olds sound just the way the 20-year-olds sounded 40 years ago, but these older speakers, now 60, sound different from the way they used to. Age-grading is rather rare. Compare **generational change**.

agent The **semantic role** carried by a noun phrase which is perceived as the conscious instigator of an action. The NP *Lisa* is an agent in all of the following examples: *Lisa finished her thesis, Lisa made me peel the potatoes, This picture was painted by Lisa.*

agentive language Another name for an **active language**.

agent phrase In a **passive** sentence, the phrase that expresses the doer of the action. In English, this is done with the preposition *by*, as in *The Moonlight Sonata was written by Beethoven.*

agglutination A type of grammatical structure in which clearly identifiable morphemes are strung together one after another within a word. Example: Swahili *wametulipa* 'they have paid us', consisting of *wa-*'they' + *-me-* Perfect + *-tu-* 'us' + *-lip-* 'pay' + *-a* Indicative.

agglutinative language A language in which **agglutination** is the predominant way of inflecting words, such as Swahili, Turkish, Japanese or Basque.

agnosia A pathological condition in which the sufferer is unable to interpret sensory information properly. There are various types of agnosia, but the linguistically most important one is *auditory verbal agnosia*, the inability to comprehend speech, which occurs, for example, in **Wernicke's aphasia**.

agrammatism Any pathological disorder of speech in which the sufferer is unable to produce speech with ordinary grammatical structure. The sufferer typically loses both the grammatical endings on words (such as plurals and past tenses) and the grammatical words like *the, of* and *to*. Agrammatism is a typical feature of **Broca's aphasia**, but may also occur in other circumstances.

agreement (also **concord**) The grammatical phenomenon in which the *form* of one item forces a second item to appear in some particular form. For example, in the sentence *These books are interesting*, both the determiner *these* and the verb *are* must agree with the noun *books* in number. That is, they must be in their plural forms because *books* is plural: **This books is interesting* is not grammatical. English has only a small amount of agreement, but many other languages have far more of it. Agreement is one type of **local dependency**. Compare **government**.

AI See **artificial intelligence**.

Ainu An **isolated language** spoken by a small number of people in the north of Japan and now in danger of becoming extinct.

airstream mechanism (also **initiation**) Any of several different ways of moving air through the mouth for the purpose of producing speech sounds. Airstreams may be **pulmonic**, **glottalic** or **velaric**, and they may be **egressive** or **ingressive**.

Akkadian An extinct language of the Middle East, a **Semitic** language. Akkadian was the principal language of both the Assyrian and the Babylonian empires; it displaced the earlier **Sumerian** language and was later itself displaced by **Aramaic**. Thousands of inscribed tablets survive, written in a **cuneiform** script; these were deciphered in the nineteenth century.

Albanian A language spoken in and around Albania and constituting a separate branch of the **Indo-European** family all by itself.

alethic modality The type of **modality** which is concerned with the degree of certainty of a proposition. For example, the *must* of *We must have a visitor* expresses alethic modality when it means 'This follows from what we already know'. Compare **epistemic modality** and **deontic modality**.

alexia Another name for **dyslexia**.

Algonquian (or **Algonkian**) A large family of languages spoken in central and eastern North America. The Algonquian languages were the first encountered by English-speaking settlers, who took from them such words as *tomahawk*, *teepee*, *squaw*, *skunk* and *raccoon*. Among the better-known languages are Cree, Ojibwa, Fox, Blackfoot and Cheyenne.

algorithm Any explicit mechanical procedure which, when applied to any problem of some particular type, is guaranteed to produce the right answer. A familiar example is the ordinary procedure for multiplying two numbers on paper.

alienable possession A type of possession in which the thing possessed could in principle be easily separated from the possessor. Examples: *John's car*, *Lisa's cigarettes*, *the dog's dinner*, *Susie's book* (in the sense of 'the book which Susie has'). Compare **inalienable possession**.

allative In a language with **case**, that case-form which typically marks the goal of motion. In Basque, for example, *etxera* 'to the house' is the allative of *etxe* 'house'.

allegro form A brief or reduced form which is typical of rapid or casual speech, such as *Ta* (= 'Thank you') or *'Cha doin'?* (= 'What are you doing?')

Allen, W. Sidney A British linguist (1918–), perhaps best known for his readable books on the pronunciation of Latin and ancient Greek.

alliteration The repetition of the same sound at the beginnings of several words in a phrase. Example: *The burghers of Brighton bundled the belligerent boatmen back to Brest.*

allomorph Any one of the different forms which can be assumed by a single **morpheme** in varying circumstances. For example, the morpheme {sane} has the allomorph /seɪn/ in both *sane* and *insane*, but the allomorph /sæn/ in *sanity*.

allophone Any one of the phonetically different forms which can be assumed by a single **phoneme** in some language in different circumstances. For example, the English phoneme /t/ is realized as aspirated [tʰ] in *till*, but as unaspirated [t$^=$] in *still*; it may also be nasally released [t^n] in *button* and laterally released [t^l] in *bottle*. In some accents, it may further be unreleased [t$^\urcorner$] or glottalized [ʔt] in *hit*, or tapped [ɾ] in *water*. All of these which occur in one accent are the allophones of /t/ in that accent.

alphabet A type of writing system in which, in principle at least, each individual character represents a single speech sound of the language which is being represented. The individual characters of an alphabet are called *letters*. Among the most important alphabets currently in use are the **Roman, Greek, Cyrillic, Arabic, Hebrew, Han'gŭl** and **Nagari** alphabets. Compare **syllabary, logographic script**.

alpha notation In phonology, an **abbreviatory convention** which allows the analyst to combine two rules into a single statement when the rules differ only in the values of certain features. The convention uses a Greek letter as a variable, and that letter must have the same value (plus or minus) in any one reading of the combined statement. For example, rules (1) and (2) below can be combined into (3):

(1)   [− cont, − nas, − voi] → [+ voi, − cont]
(2)   [− cont, − nas, + voi] → [+ voi, + cont]
(3)   [− cont, − nas, α voi] → [+ voi, α cont]

Altaic A family of languages including the **Turkic, Mongolian** and **Tungusic** languages. Some scholars would add **Japanese** and **Korean** to the family, but this is very controversial. Indeed, the very existence of the Altaic family has sometimes been controversial, but at present Altaic seems to be widely accepted as a genuine family.

alternation A systematic variation between one form and another, depending upon the neighbouring sounds or upon the neighbouring morphemes. For example, the English plural marker appears variously as /s/ (as in *cats*), as /z/ (as in *dogs*) or as /ɪz/ (as in *foxes*), depending upon the preceding sound. In certain cases, English /k/ alternates with /s/, depending upon which other morphemes are present, as in *electric/electricity*.

alveolar (A speech sound) produced by putting some part of the tongue on or near the **alveolar ridge**. In English, [t], [d], [n], [s] and [l] are usually alveolar. Where necessary, we distinguish *apico-alveolar* sounds (involving the tip of the tongue) from *lamino-alveolar* sounds (involving the blade of the tongue). The English sounds are lamino-alveolar for most speakers, but apico-alveolar for some.

alveolar ridge The bump just above and behind the upper teeth. In English and other languages, many consonants are produced by placing the tongue against or close to the alveolar ridge; these are the **alveolar** sounds.

alveolo-palatal A label applied to a consonant which is pronounced slightly further back than a **palato-alveolar** consonant. The Polish consonants spelled <ś> and <ź> are alveolo-palatal. **Note:** some people use this term to mean **palato-alveolar**; this is not good usage.

ambiguity The presence in a single string of words of two or more sharply distinct meanings. An ambiguity may be a **lexical ambiguity** (present merely within a single word), as in *This is a lovely port*, or it may be a **structural ambiguity** (resulting from assigning different structures to the string of words), as in *Young boys and girls are easily frightened*, *Visiting relatives can be a nuisance* and *Anne likes horses more than Mark*. Complex cases are possible, such as *Janet made the robot fast*.

ambiguity test Any test proposed for distinguishing true **ambiguity** from mere vagueness. For example, the word *dog* can mean either 'canine' or 'male canine'. We can say *That dog isn't a dog – it's a bitch* without contradiction, showing that *dog* is ambiguous. But *girl* can mean either 'non-adult female' or 'female child', yet we can't sensibly say *That girl isn't a girl – she's a child*, showing that *girl* is not ambiguous, but merely vague. This is the *contradiction test*.

ambiguous Of a word, a string of words or a sentence, possessing an **ambiguity**.

ambisyllabic Belonging to two syllables at the same time. For example, the *t* in *petrol* is ambisyllabic: the vowel of the first syllable can only appear in a syllable which ends in a consonant (hence *t* must be in the first syllable), but the *r* is partially devoiced (hence *t* must be in the second syllable: compare *rat race*, in which the *t* belongs only to the first syllable).

amelioration (also **melioration**) The historical process by which the meaning of a word changes to something more attractive or impressive than formerly. For example, *queen* formerly meant just 'woman', and *knight* formerly meant just 'boy'. The opposite is **pejoration**.

American Association for Applied Linguistics (**AAAL**) The professional association in the USA for practitioners of **applied linguistics**.

American Sign Language (**ASL**, **Ameslan**) The version of **sign language** used in the United States. ASL is descended from a French sign language, and is not mutually comprehensible with **British Sign Language**.

American structuralism The name given to one of the most important and influential approaches to linguistic theory and description. The American structuralists drew their inspiration from the work of Leonard **Bloomfield**, and hence they are sometimes called the **post-Bloomfieldians**. Their approach, which dominated American linguistics in the 1940s and 1950s, was characterized by a healthy respect for the messy facts of real languages and by a distaste for fancy armchair theorizing. Many American structuralists were excellent fieldworkers, and they provided a large number of descriptions and analyses of languages, very often languages which had never been investigated before, especially native American languages. The structuralists developed efficient techniques for recording and describing languages, and their descriptions sometimes achieved unparalleled explicitness. Unfortunately, they also developed some exceedingly dogmatic views about proper procedure; these views were eventually shown to be untenable, and American structuralism gave way in the 1960s to the newer approach called **generative grammar**. Among the leading structuralists were Bernard **Bloch**, Yuen-Ren **Chao**, Charles **Fries**, Robert **Hall**, Zellig **Harris**, Archibald **Hill**, Charles **Hockett**, Martin Joos, Eugene **Nida**, Kenneth **Pike**, Henry **Smith**, Morris **Swadesh**, George **Trager**, W. Freeman **Twaddell** and Rulon Wells, though Hockett and Pike differed from their colleagues in some respects, and Pike was often regarded as a maverick.

American transcription A **phonetic alphabet** used in the USA. This system uses many different symbols from the **International Phonetic Alphabet** (such as [š] for [ʃ] and [ü] for [y]). Many American textbooks use this system instead of IPA.

Amerind A proposed family of languages including *all* the languages of North and South America except the **Eskimo-Aleut** and **Na-Déné** languages. Recently put forward by the American linguist Joseph **Greenberg**, this proposal is extremely controversial and has so far won little support.

Ameslan See **American Sign Language**.

ampersand The character **&** used as a symbol for 'and' in certain contexts, especially in names of companies.

amplitude In a wave (such as a sound wave), the size of the maximal displacement from the zero value. The larger the amplitude of a sound wave, the louder the sound, though the relationship is not linear (that is, doubling the amplitude does not in general double the volume of the sound).

anacoluthon Breaking off a sentence before completing it, in order to say something else. Example: *You know, I'd really like to – oh, look, there's Julie.*

anagram One of two or more words or phrases constructed by putting the same letters in different orders: *seminar / marines / remains*; *the aristocracy / a rich Tory caste*; *Clint Eastwood / Old West action.*

analogical change Another name for **analogy**.

analogical levelling A type of language change in which the grammatical forms of certain words are changed so as to make the whole set of forms more regular. For example, regular phonological change had produced in Old French sets of verb-forms like those for the verb meaning 'love' in the present tense: *aim, aimes, aimet, amons, amez, aiment*. Here the verb-stem fluctuates between *am-* and *aim-*, and this variation was levelled to give the modern forms *aime, aimes, aime, aimons, aimez, aiment*, in which the verb-stem is uniformly *aim-*.

analogy (also **analogical change**) Any type of language change in which forms are altered by speakers so as to make them more similar to other forms. For example, the medieval English plurals *kine, shoon, eyen* and *eyren* were changed to *cows, shoes, eyes* and *eggs* by analogy with the other plurals in *-s*.

analysis by synthesis A procedure by which a machine or a human brain analyses the structure of an incoming signal by guessing how that signal might be constructed, constructing its own signal in line with the guess, and comparing the result with the incoming signal.

analytic A label applied to a grammatical form which is constructed by adding additional words to the word being inflected. For example, English *eat* has the analytic forms *is eating* and *has eaten*; compare the **synthetic** forms *eats* and *ate*.

analytic language Another name for an **isolating language**.

anaphor (also **pro-form**) An item with little or no meaning or reference of its own which takes its interpretation from another item in the same sentence or discourse, its **antecedent**. For example, in *I asked Lisa to check the proofs, and she did it*, the items *she* and *did it* are anaphors, taking their meaning from *Lisa* and *check the proofs*. The use of anaphors is called *anaphora*.

anaptyxis (also **svarabhakti**) The insertion of a vowel between two consonants, as when *Henry* is pronounced *Ennery* or *film* is pronounced *fillum*. The vowel inserted is called an *anaptyctic vowel*, a *svarabhakti vowel* or a *parasite vowel*. Anaptyxis is one kind of **epenthesis**.

anarthria (also **dysarthria**) Difficulty in speaking resulting from poor control over the muscles of speech. There is no problem with the language faculty; the sufferer merely cannot move the organs of speech normally.

Anatolian A group of languages, all of them long extinct, formerly spoken in what is now Turkey and forming one branch of the **Indo-European** family. The most important Anatolian language is **Hittite**.

Anderson, Stephen An American linguist (1943–), a major contributor to the theory of **phonology**.

androcentrism The practice of taking the tastes, values and viewpoints of men as primary or central, while relegating those of women to inferior status. Linguistically, this shows up in various ways, some of them deeply embedded in the language: *Has everyone handed in his essay?* (addressing a mixed group), *a man-eating tiger, The pioneers trekked across the prairies with their cattle, their seed-corn and their wives.* Other androcentric positions include the view that four-letter words are normal for men but vulgar when used by women, and Dr Johnson's practice of labelling as 'female cant' those words in his dictionary which he considered to be more typical of women, such as *frightfully*.

angle brackets In phonology, an **abbreviatory convention** used to state that two feature specifications must be either both present or both absent. Example:

$$
\begin{bmatrix} - \text{ syll} \\ <+ \text{ cor}> \end{bmatrix} \rightarrow \begin{bmatrix} + \text{ high} \\ <- \text{ ant}> \end{bmatrix} \quad / \underline{\quad} \quad \begin{bmatrix} + \text{ syll} \\ + \text{ high} \\ - \text{ back} \end{bmatrix}
$$

Here the specifications [+ cor] and [− ant] are both present in one reading and both absent in the other.

anglicization Pronouncing a foreign word or name in a way that makes it sound like English.

Anglo-Norman The variety of **Norman French** which developed in England after the Norman Conquest.

anglophone English-speaking.

Anglo-Saxon Another name for **Old English**.

angma (also **eng**) The symbol [ŋ] for the velar nasal, as in English *singing*.

animacy hierarchy (also **chain-of-being hierarchy**) A ranking of nouns (and sometimes also pronouns) in which nouns denoting human beings come first, followed by nouns denoting animals, and finally by nouns denoting non-living things. In many languages, this hierarchy is grammatically important: higher-ranking classes may make more distinctions than others, or it may be impossible for a lower-ranking noun to precede a higher-ranking one in a sentence. Some such languages make further distinctions, with first- and second-person pronouns and proper names outranking everything else.

animal communication The entire body of techniques used by non-human animals for communicating with other members of their own species. Though the signalling systems of some species have proved to have remarkable characteristics, no other species is so far known to have anything remotely approximating to human language.

animate A label applied to a noun or a noun phrase which denotes a human being or a higher animal. Examples: *teacher, dog, me, the President of France, the remaining Siberian tigers*. The opposite is **inanimate**.

anomalous A label applied to a linguistic form which does not conform to the usual rules, which is in some way irregular, unexpected, or impossible to interpret.

anomaly, semantic Total incompatibility of meaning among the elements in a single phrase or sentence, rendering it uninterpretable. The example #*Jezebel murdered Ahab, but Ahab didn't die* is semantically anomalous, assuming only one Ahab is involved, since *Ahab died* is an intrinsic part of the meaning of (somebody) *murdered Ahab*. The hash mark # is often used to mark something as semantically anomalous.

anomia Unusually severe difficulty in finding the words one wants while speaking. Anomia usually results from brain damage, and is a common symptom in many types of **aphasia**.

antecedent The phrase from which an **anaphor** or **pro-form** takes its meaning. In the most obvious reading of *After Lisa got up, she had a shower*, Lisa is the antecedent of *she*, which is interpreted as meaning *Lisa*.

antepenult In a word, the third syllable from the end, such as *kang* in *kangaroo* and *bol* in *diabolical*. Compare **penult, ultima**.

anterior In phonology, a **distinctive feature** used to classify consonants. A consonant made further forward than the palato-alveolar region (such as [s], [t], [v] or [m]) is [+ anterior]; all others (including [ʧ]) are [− anterior]. Part of the *SPE* **feature system**, this feature is widely regarded as unsatisfactory.

anthropological linguistics (also **linguistic anthropology**) The discipline which combines the concepts and techniques of linguistics and anthropology in order to examine the relations between language and culture. Anthropological linguists typically look at such phenomena as **kinship terms** and methods of constructing personal names and place names.

anticipation 1. The type of **assimilation** in which a sound is assimilated to a following sound, as when *ten pence* is pronounced *te*[m] *pence*. 2. A **speech error** in which a sound is inserted too early, as when *bed and breakfast* is pronounced as 'bread and breakfast'.

antipassive A construction found in some languages in which an essentially transitive verb is used intransitively with an oblique object instead of a direct object. This construction is not well developed in English, but note the example *John struck at Bill* (compare *John struck Bill*) and the archaic *He ate of the meat* (compare *He ate the meat*).

antonym (also **contrary**) One of two words which, in some sense, have opposite meanings. Not all pairs of antonyms are related in the same way: *dead* and *alive* represent an absolute either–or choice (they are *non-gradable antonyms,* or a *complementary pair*), while *hot* and *cold* merely represent extremes along a continuum of possibilities (they are *gradable antonyms*). The term may also be applied to **reversives** like *raise* and *lower,* and it is sometimes also applied to *converse pairs* like *husband* and *wife* (see under **converse**). As you can see, an antonym of a word X is not necessarily a negation of X.

aorist A traditional label applied to certain verb forms in some languages, often in a highly inconsistent manner. Most usually, the term is applied to simple past-tense forms with no marking for **aspect**, but the use of the term is so variable that, whenever you encounter it, you will need to check carefully to find out how it is being used.

AP An abbreviation for **adjective phrase**.

ape experiments A series of experiments in which investigators have attempted to teach apes (usually chimpanzees) to use some version of language. The earliest and most famous experiments used **sign language**; others have involved magnetic pieces of coloured plastic or shapes displayed on a computer screen. Many of the earlier experiments were so poorly done that their positive results can be dismissed as meaningless; some recent experiments have been more carefully done, and their positive results have persuaded at least some observers that apes have some (limited) capacity to learn and use language under experimental conditions, but critics remain who are unconvinced.

aphaeresis The loss or omission of one or more sounds from the beginning of a word. Examples include the reduction of *opossum* to *possum* and of *especial* to *special,* as well as the loss of the earlier [k] in *knife*. Some people apply the term *aphesis* to the particular case of the loss of an initial vowel (as in my first two examples), but this is not usual. Some people also extend the term to cases of **clipping** like the reduction of *alligator* to *gator*.

aphasia (also **dysphasia**) Language disability resulting from damage to the language areas in the brain. Such damage is most usually caused by wounds to the head or by strokes, but may also result from other causes, such as carbon monoxide poisoning. Depending on the location and the extent of the damage, sufferers exhibit a wide variety of symptoms: difficulty in understanding speech, difficulty in finding words, difficulty in producing grammatical structures, and others. With some reliability, damage to particular areas tends to produce predictable sets of symptoms, and such labels as **Broca's aphasia, conduction aphasia** and **Wernicke's aphasia** are given to specific sets of symptoms resulting from damage to particular areas of the brain.

apical A label applied to any speech sound which is made with the tip of the tongue, instead of with some part of the upper surface of the tongue. Most English-speakers do not use any apical sounds (we use **laminals**), though some of us do use them, and such sounds are common in some other languages.

apocope The loss or omission of one or more sounds from the end of a word. Examples include the reduction of earlier *singan* and *mine* to *sing* and *my*. Some people would extend the term to cases of **clipping** like the reduction of *margarine* and *passion* to *marge* and *pash*.

apodosis (also **consequent**) In a sentence of the *if . . .* (*then*) type, the part which follows the *then*. Example (in brackets): *If I drink any more wine, (then)* [*I'll have a hangover.*] The part after the *if* is the **protasis**.

Apollonius Dyscolus A Greek grammarian (AD *c.* 110–175). His are the earliest European grammatical writings of any length of which any volumes still survive; his book on Greek syntax is especially important.

apophony A less usual term for **ablaut**.

apostrophe The punctuation mark ', used for various purposes. In English, it is chiefly used in writing **contractions** (like *can't*) and in marking the possessive suffix -*'s* (as in *Lisa's book*) — but NOT in the possessives *its* and *whose*.

apparent time Any systematic differences observed between the speech of younger and older people in a single community. Such differences may represent a linguistic change in progress (younger speakers have acquired innovations which were absent when the older speakers were learning their language), or they may merely represent **age-grading**.

Appendix Probi An anonymous document, written in the sixth or seventh century AD, listing common errors in the writing of Latin, and therefore providing us with information about the spoken Latin of the day.

applied linguistics The application of the ideas and methods of linguistics to any of a number of practical problems which have something to do with language. Most familiarly, the term is applied to the analysis of second-language teaching, but it can also be applied to the use of linguistics in such fields as mother-tongue teaching, dictionary writing, translation, and the analysis and treatment of disorders of language.

appositive A noun phrase which immediately follows another noun phrase and refers to the same entity as that other noun phrase. Typically an appositive is not required to identify the entity being referred to, but serves only to add extra information. The phrase set off by commas in the following example is an appositive: *The Great Wall of China, the largest structure ever built by human beings, is visible from the moon.* An *appositive clause* is a **non-restrictive relative clause**.

approximant (also **frictionless continuant**) A consonant sound which is produced without severely obstructing the flow of air in the mouth. English examples include [w] (as in *wine*), [j] (the *y*-sound, as in *yes*) and most realizations of /r/ (as in *red*).

apraxia A pathological condition in which, as a result of brain damage, a sufferer is unable to carry out purposeful movements in a normal manner. Linguistically important is *verbal apraxia*, in which the sufferer produces laboured and distorted speech, as commonly occurs in **Broca's aphasia**.

Arabic A major language of northern Africa and the Middle East, also widely used elsewhere as a second language and as a religious language. For purposes of writing, the Arabs have traditionally used what is essentially the language of the Koran, written over 1100 years ago; this variety is called *classical Arabic*. The modern spoken varieties of Arabic, known collectively as *colloquial Arabic*, differ greatly from classical Arabic and from one another. Arabic is a **Semitic** language.

Arabic alphabet An important **alphabet**, devised originally for the writing of

Arabic, but also frequently used to write many other languages used in areas in which Islam is influential. In spite of its great beauty, the Arabic alphabet is not well suited to the writing of non-Semitic languages, particularly because it lacks vowel letters; consequently, it has variously been modified or even replaced by other alphabets for writing these other languages.

Arabic numerals Our familiar system of writing **cardinal numerals**, using the special characters 0 to 9 combined in a way involving both multiplication and addition. For example, the date 1996 means $(1 \times 1000) + (9 \times 100) + (9 \times 10)$ + 6. Invented in India, these numerals were taken up by the Arabs and passed on by them to Europe, where they displaced the earlier **Roman numerals**.

Aramaic A Middle Eastern language belonging to the **Semitic** family. Aramaic was very widely used as a **lingua franca** in the ancient Middle East, and is believed to have been the mother tongue of Jesus Christ and of most of the disciples. Later largely displaced by **Arabic**, Aramaic is still spoken by a significant number of people, especially in Iraq and Iran (where it is sometimes called *Assyrian*); a western dialect, called *Syriac*, is used as a liturgical language by Syrian Christians.

arbitrariness The property of human languages by which there is no *necessary* connection between the form of a word and its meaning. There is no particular reason why a large snouted animal should be called a *pig*; any name will do, so long as speakers agree about it, and of course speakers of other languages than English have all reached different agreements: French *cochon*, German *Schwein*, Spanish *cerdo*, Welsh *mochyn* and Basque *txerri* all denote the same animal. It is arbitrariness which makes a **universal translator** impossible.

archaic Exhibiting characteristics which were lost later. When we say that Mycenaean Greek is an archaic form of Greek, or that Hittite is an archaic Indo-European language, we mean only that Mycenaean retains ancestral features which were later lost in Greek and that Hittite retains ancestral features that were lost in all related languages that are recorded.

archaism An old word, phrase or grammatical form which is no longer in everyday use but which can still be found in older literature and perhaps in certain special contexts, or which is used for special effect. Archaisms abound in Shakespeare and in the King James Bible: *Male and female created he them*; *Yond' Cassius has a lean and hungry look*; *They called his name Ishmael*. The first telegraphic message transmitted across the Atlantic was *What hath God wrought?*, which contains the archaism *hath*.

archiphoneme In the **Prague School** analysis, the result of a **neutralization**. For example, since /p/ and /b/ do not contrast in English after a syllable-initial /s/, the sound spelled *p* in *spit* would be regarded as representing an archiphoneme, rather than the phoneme /p/.

Arc Pair Grammar A particular theory of grammar, devised by David Johnson and Paul Postal, which operates chiefly in terms of **grammatical relations** like *subject* and *direct object*. Arc Pair Grammar is essentially an elaborated and formalized version of **Relational Grammar**.

arcuate fasciculus A J-shaped bundle of nerve fibres which connects **Wernicke's area** to **Broca's area** in the brain. Damage to it produces **conduction aphasia**.

areal feature Any linguistic characteristic which is found in a number of languages in some particular part of the world, even though those languages are not all related. For example, most languages of southeast Asia have tones; most languages of the Caucasus area have ejective consonants and ergative morphology; most Australian languages have no fricative consonants; many languages in the Balkans have definite articles that follow the noun.

areal linguistics The study of the languages of some particular geographical area, especially when these languages show important characteristics in common.

argot (also **cant**) Special vocabulary used by a secretive or close-knit group, either to hide its conversation from outsiders or merely to demonstrate membership of the group.

argument Any noun phrase which bears some **grammatical relation** to the verb in its sentence and which must be present for the verb to be used grammatically. The verb *smile* requires only one argument (its subject); *destroy* requires two (a subject and an object); *give* requires three (subject and two objects). An **adjunct** is not an argument.

Armenian A language spoken in and around Armenia and constituting a separate branch of the **Indo-European** family all by itself.

Aronoff, Mark An American linguist (1949–), a leading morphologist who has been described as the father of modern morphology.

article 1. A special type of **determiner** found in some languages which typically expresses the degree of specificity or definiteness assigned to the noun phrase containing it. English has two of these: the "definite article" *the* and the "indefinite article" *a(n)*. A speaker who says *I'm looking for the book* is assuming that the addressee knows which book is meant; *I'm looking for a book* carries no such assumption. Note that the second has two interpretations: specific ('I'm looking for a particular book') and non-specific ('I'm looking for any old book'); this difference is not regularly expressed in English. Other languages have different systems, and many languages have no articles at all. 2. A piece of scholarly work, usually much shorter than a book and published in a **journal**.

articulation The process of producing a particular speech sound, or a sequence of speech sounds, by manipulating the organs of speech.

articulatory feature A **distinctive feature** which relates to some aspect of articulation, such as [nasal], [high], [coronal] or [voice].

articulatory phonetics The branch of **phonetics** which studies the organs of speech and their use in producing speech sounds.

articulatory setting An overall tendency to keep the organs of speech in some particular positions throughout speech. For example, some Americans keep the velum persistently low, producing a "nasal twang"; some Texans keep the back of the tongue persistently high, producing the stereotypical "Howdy, pahdnuh" speech of Hollywood westerns; some Britons keep the jaw fixed, the lips spread and the tongue pulled back, producing "plummy" speech.

artificial intelligence (**AI**) The construction and use of computer programs which can imitate the behaviour of human beings. *Weak AI* tries only to develop programs which can perform human-like tasks in any convenient manner; *strong*

AI attempts to construct programs which genuinely mimic human mental processes.

artificial language A language which is invented from scratch by some person or people, and which is usually intended to be used as an auxiliary language between people with different mother tongues. The most famous artificial language is **Esperanto**, but dozens of others exist. An artificial language is not a **natural language**, except for those people (if any exist) who learn it as their mother tongue.

Aryan 1. An obsolete name for the **Indo-European** languages. This purely linguistic label was given an indefensible racist interpretation by the Nazis. 2. See **Indo-Aryan**.

arytenoid cartilages The two triangular cartilages attached to the back of the **vocal folds**; movement of these cartilages opens and closes the **glottis**.

Ascoli, Graziadio An Italian linguist (1829–1907), a specialist in Indo-European and Romance languages, and one of the outstanding comparative linguists of his day.

ascriptive sentence A sentence, especially one with a **copula**, which asserts that some entity has a certain property, such as *Susie is pretty*, *Lisa is a translator*, or *Spaghetti is fattening*. Compare **equational sentence**.

ash The letter æ, used in writing Old English and modern Icelandic and as a phonetic symbol for the vowel of *cat*.

ASL See **American Sign Language**.

aspect A **grammatical category** which deals with distinctions in the way in which an action or a situation is regarded as being distributed in time – in other words, with its internal structure. Consider the following English examples, all of which are in the past tense. In *I drank vodka* (which shows *perfective* aspect), the action is viewed as a whole, with no internal structure. In *I was drinking vodka* (which shows *continuous* aspect), the action is viewed as being spread out over a period of time. In *I had drunk vodka* (which shows *perfect* aspect), the action is viewed as both preceding and affecting some particular moment which the speaker is thinking of. In *I used to drink vodka* (which shows *habitual* aspect), the action is viewed as a usual or habitual one. In *I kept drinking vodka* (which shows *iterative* aspect), the action is viewed as a repeated sequence of individual acts. Aspect is widespread in the world's languages, and many languages have elaborate grammatical apparatus for marking distinctions morphologically in the verb; English, as you can see, uses various **periphrastic** constructions instead. **Important note:** traditional grammarians often confused aspect with **tense** (sense 1), but the two are quite distinct. All of my examples above have present-tense counterparts, except that *I drank vodka* and *I used to drink vodka* have the same present-tense partner: *I drink vodka*, which most often has the habitual interpretation.

Aspects model The particular version of **transformational grammar** proposed in Noam Chomsky's 1965 book *Aspects of the Theory of Syntax*. The term **Standard Theory** (of TG) means about the same.

aspectual verb A verb which does not itself denote any particular activity or state, but merely serves to indicate an aspect of some other named activity. English examples include *start*, *continue* and *finish*.

aspiration 1. The puff of breath which follows certain consonants, such as the *p* of *pit* and the *t* of *tin*. 2. A name for the consonant [h].

assemblage error (also **movement error, shift error**) Any type of **speech error** in which the right elements are selected but put together in the wrong order; examples are **anticipation, perseveration** and **transposition**. Compare **selection error**.

assimilation Any phonetic or phonological process in which a particular sound becomes more similar to some other nearby sound. For example, when *ten pence* is pronounced as *te*[m] *pence*, the /n/ has been assimilated to the following bilabial /p/. The opposite is **dissimilation**.

associative meaning That part of the meaning of a word which is not intrinsic to the word but which results from our experience of the circumstances in which the word is used. For example, the word *whisky* might suggest to you any number of things, such as 'Scotland', 'elegant living', 'immorality', 'manliness', 'hangover', 'nausea', or 'western saloons'.

asterisk The symbol *, which has two quite different functions in linguistics. 1. It is used to mark a form as ungrammatical, as in the example **She has writing her thesis*. 2. It is used in historical linguistics to mark a word or form which is nowhere recorded but which has been reconstructed (that is, linguists have concluded from some evidence that it must have existed once). Thus, for example, specialists are convinced that the Spanish word *aguijada* 'goad' must be derived from a Latin word *aquileāta* 'sharpened', even though no such Latin word is recorded anywhere.

atelic A label applied to an activity, or to a linguistic form (especially a **verb**) expressing that activity, which has no recognizable goal. Examples: *Janet is sleeping*; *Lisa speaks excellent French*. Compare **telic**.

Athabaskan (also **Athapaskan**) A group of languages spoken in western North America, forming the largest group of the **Na-Déné** family. The Athabaskan languages are famous for their unbelievably complex verbal morphology, which is entirely prefixing; two of the best-known Athabaskan languages are Navaho and Apache.

ATN See **augmented transition network**.

ATR See **advanced tongue root**.

attested form A particular word or form, in some language, which is recorded as having been used by a speaker of that language, either in speech or in writing. Compare **reconstructed form**.

attributive position The position occupied by a modifier which immediately precedes the noun it modifies, as in *a* _____ *dress*. Attributive position may be occupied by an adjective (*new, red*) or by a noun (*cotton, maternity*). Adjectives and nouns used in this position are *attributive adjectives* and *attributive nouns*. Note that attributive nouns are NOT adjectives. Compare **predicate position**.

attrition The loss of grammatical inflections, especially endings. For example, Old English *singan, ic singe, wē singað* have undergone attrition to yield the modern forms *(to) sing, I sing, we sing*.

audience design A sociolinguistic theory which holds that you adjust your speech according to who you are talking to – for example, by using more prestige features when talking to educated people and fewer when talking to uneducated people.

audiolingual method A method of learning a foreign language, involving long hours spent in a **language laboratory** mechanically repeating bits of the foreign language heard on tape.

auditory Pertaining to hearing, including the actions of ears and brain.

auditory discrimination In phonetics, the ability to distinguish speech sounds.

auditory feedback Your ability to hear your own speech by means of sound waves travelling through the air and through the bones of your head. Such feedback is important in monitoring your speech.

auditory memory The very short period of time during which you can still "hear" what someone has just said within your head.

auditory ossicles Three small bones in the middle ear, the *hammer* (or *malleus*), the *anvil* (or *incus*) and the *stirrup* (or *stapes*). These bones transmit sound from the eardrum to the inner ear and amplify it.

auditory phonetics The branch of **phonetics** which studies the way in which speech sounds are processed by the ears and the brain.

augmentative A derivational affix added to a word to express large size or excessiveness, or a word formed in this way. Spanish examples include *ricachón* 'stinking rich' (from *rico* 'rich'), *favorzote* 'a heck of a favour' (from *favor* 'favour') and *ginebrazo* 'bloody great shot of gin' (from *ginebra* 'gin').

augmented transition network (**ATN**) A type of **transition network** which is supplemented by a memory and by devices for referring to that memory; this allows the network to handle **dependencies**. Until recently, ATNs were widely used in constructing **parsers**.

Auraicept na nÉces ('The Scholars' Primer') An important Old Irish text dealing with the Irish language, dating perhaps from the seventh century AD; the work laid the foundations for the study of Irish grammar.

aureate word Another name for an **inkhorn term**.

Aurignacian culture A distinctive human culture which appeared in eastern Europe about 45,000 years ago and spread across the continent with the **Cro-Magnon** people. This culture was distinguished by numerous and dramatic innovations in toolmaking, art and social organization, and some specialists believe these people were the first in Europe to speak a full-blown language.

Austin, J. L. A British philosopher (1911–60), best known for introducing **speech acts** into linguistics. His famous book is called *How to Do Things with Words*.

Australian languages The indigenous languages of Australia. At the time of the European settlement, it is thought that between 200 and 250 distinct languages were spoken in Australia; many are now extinct, and most of the others are now spoken only by a handful of people, though a few remain vigorous. The largest part of the continent is (or was) occupied by the **Pama-Nyungan** languages, and most specialists believe that all Australian languages are probably related.

Australopithecus The genus name of several species of early hominids attested in Africa between roughly five million and two million years ago. At least five species have been recognized: *A. ramidus*, *A. afarensis*, *A. africanus*, *A. robustus* and *A. boisei*. (Some specialists assign the last two to a different genus, *Paranthropus*.) All of them (except possibly the first) had fully erect posture but very small brains (and therefore possibly no language). Some of the Australopithecines are undoubtedly ancestral to the genus *Homo* and hence to our own species, but the details are controversial.

Austric A proposed language family linking all of **Austronesian, Austro-Asiatic, Kadai** and **Miao-Yao**. This proposal is deeply controversial.

Austro-Asiatic A family of languages spoken mostly in southeast Asia, divided into **Mon-Khmer, Munda** and some smaller groups.

Austronesian A huge family of languages extending from Madagascar to the Pacific, and including Malagasy (in Madagascar), all the Philippine languages, the indigenous languages of Taiwan, Malay-Indonesian and nearly all the languages of Indonesia and the Pacific (Hawaiian, Fijian, Samoan, and many others). The family was formerly called *Malayo-Polynesian*, but this name is now little used.

Autolexical Syntax A theory of grammar, developed by Jerrold Sadock, in which the structure of a sentence is viewed as the sum of three independent structures: morphological, syntactic and semantic.

automatic alternation Any **alternation** which is completely predictable.

automaton An abstract mathematical device which is capable of performing certain computations. The most powerful type of automaton is the **Turing machine**.

autonomous speech variety (also **idioglossia**) An invented language which is understood only by its inventors. The most famous cases are the ones invented by twin children to talk to each other.

autonomy, principle of A principle of **cognitive science** which holds that the information-processing states of an organism can be characterized without reference to their meaning or to their connection to the external world.

autonomy of language The hypothesis that the human language capacity is an independent part of our mental faculties, and not merely a reflection of our general cognitive abilities. This hypothesis is one of the most central and controversial ideas in linguistics and in cognitive science generally. Two particularly strong versions of it are the **innateness hypothesis** and the **bioprogram hypothesis**.

autonomy of syntax The doctrine that syntax can and should be studied in isolation from other aspects of language structure, most especially from semantics.

autonym Another term for a **self-designation**.

Autosegmental Phonology A major contemporary theory of phonology in which the phonological structure of a word or phrase is viewed as consisting of a number of parallel sequences called *tiers*, with the elements on the different tiers being bound together by *association lines*.

AUX 1. An abbreviation of **auxiliary**. 2. In some theories of grammar, an abstract category which is assumed to be universally present in all sentences and in all languages, regardless of whether an auxiliary is overtly present or not. This AUX is typically assumed to be the element which carries such features as **tense** (sense 1) at an abstract level of representation.

auxiliary (**AUX**) A grammatical item which typically carries markings for such categories as tense, aspect, mood and agreement. Auxiliaries may be specialized verbs (as in English) or they may be entirely distinct from all other parts of speech (as in some Australian languages).

Avestan A very early **Iranian** language, attested from the sixth century BC; this is the language of the Zoroastrian scriptures.

avoidance language (also **mother-in-law language**) A particular style of speaking which, in some speech communities, is used (and often must be used) in the presence of certain people, most commonly the speaker's in-laws. The avoidance language uses different words from the everyday language; sometimes only a few words are different, while in other cases the entire vocabulary is different. The most famous avoidance languages are found in Australia.

Ayer, A. J. A British philosopher (1910–89), a leading exponent of **logical positivism**.

Aztec-Tanoan A language family of the western USA and western Mexico; it is divided into **Uto-Aztecan** and **Tanoan** branches.

B

BAAL See **British Association of Applied Linguistics**.

babbling The sounds typically produced by an infant just before it begins to produce recognizable words. Babbling consists of sequences of repeated syllables, such as [baba] and [dadada].

Babel, Tower of See **Tower of Babel**.

baby-talk An informal name for any greatly simplified type of speech, such as that used by young children or that used by adults addressing young children or other adults in intimate situations.

back Another name for the **dorsum** of the tongue.

back-formation A word formed by the removal of an *apparent* affix from another word, or the process of forming a word in such a way. Examples: *edit* from *editor*, *televise* from *television*, *pea* from original (singular) *pease*, *baby-sit* from *baby-sitter* (originally a compound of *baby* and *sitter*).

background knowledge Knowledge of the world which we make use of in understanding utterances. For example, if you hear *Jimmy was on his way to school*, you probably assume that Jimmy is a schoolboy (and not, say, a middle-aged accountant) and that he is walking or taking the bus (and not, say, flying or swimming), since these are among the things your experience of the world leads you to expect.

background noise In **comparative linguistics**, the existence of chance similarities between languages which may or may not be related. Background noise makes it difficult to identify evidence of remote genetic relations between languages.

backness One of the chief phonetic characteristics of a vowel. In a **back vowel**, the highest point of the tongue is about as far back as it can go; in a **front vowel**, it is about as far forward as it can go; in a **central vowel**, it is somewhere in between.

back slang A type of wordplay in which a word is derived by pronouncing another word as though it were spelled backwards. Example: *yob* from *boy*.

back vowel Any vowel which is pronounced with the back of the tongue raised higher than any other part, such as [u], [o] or [ɔ].

bahuvrihi (also **exocentric compound**) A type of **compound word** which does not overtly express the kind of thing it refers to. For example, a *skinhead* is not a type of head, a *hatchback* is not a type of back, and a *scarecrow* is not a type of crow.

Bakhtin, Mikhail A Russian literary critic (1895–1975); an avowed Marxist, he maintained that language could not be usefully studied in isolation from social and political factors, and he argued for the value of linguistic diversity and pluralism. Compare **Gramsci**.

ballistic movement A rapid movement by an organ of speech (most often the tongue), during which it briefly strikes another organ of speech. Ballistic movements are involved in the production of **taps** and **flaps**.

Bally, Charles A French linguist (1865–1947), one of **Saussure**'s students and one of the leading members of the **Geneva School**. He is best known for founding the discipline of **stylistics** (sense 1).

Baltic A small group of related languages consisting of Latvian and Lithuanian plus several extinct languages, notably Old Prussian. The Baltic languages form a branch of the **Indo-European** family.

Balto-Slavic A name given to the **Baltic** and **Slavic** languages taken together, when they are considered to form a single group within **Indo-European**. Specialists are not certain whether this is the right view or not.

Bank of English A project, based at the University of Birmingham, which is assembling a vast **corpus** of contemporary English (spoken and written).

Bantu A vast group of languages, forming the single largest branch of the **Niger-Congo** family, and including almost all the languages of central, eastern and southern Africa, including Swahili, Zulu, Xhosa, Shona, Luganda, Tswana, Chicheŵa, and many others. Bantu languages are distinguished by their very heavy use of prefixes and by their large number of gender classes (up to two dozen).

bare infinitive (also **base form**) In English, the basic form of a verb, with no grammatical marking of any kind, such as *drink* and *buy* in *You shouldn't drink so* *much* and *Can you buy some potatoes?* This is the form of a verb which is entered in a dictionary, and it is the form which is properly the English infinitive. Compare **to-infinitive**.

bare-NP adverbial An **adverbial** which consists of a noun phrase unaccompanied by a preposition. Examples (in brackets): *I did it* [*the same way*]; *Do it* [*this minute*]; *I've seen that* [*everywhere I've been*].

Barthes, Roland An influential French critic and semiologist (1915–80), a leading exponent of post-structuralist and deconstructivist ideas.

Bàrtoli, Matteo An Italian linguist (1873–1946), a specialist in Romance languages and an advocate of the slogan "Every word has its own history".

Barwise, Jon An American logician (1942–), a leading figure in the development of **formal semantics**.

base 1. In morphology, the item to which an affix is added to derive another form. Thus, *happy* is the base for both *unhappy* and *happily*, while *unhappy* is the base for both *unhappily* and *unhappiness*. 2. In **transformational grammar**, that part of the grammar which is responsible for generating underlying representations (deep structures) of sentences, which are then modified by transformational rules to produce surface structures. The base consists of a set of **context-free rules** and a **lexicon** (sense 2).

base form Another name for the **bare infinitive**.

basic colour terms In a particular language, the names for colours which are not varieties of other colours, which are not constructed from other colour terms, and which can be applied to any kind of object. In English, *red, green, white* and *brown* are among the (eleven) basic colour terms, but *scarlet, yellowish, blue-green* and *blonde* are not. Languages differ in the number of basic colour terms they have, from a minimum of two to a maximum of 11 or 12.

Basic English A specially designed version of English with a vocabulary of only 850 words, intended to be learned quickly by foreigners and used for basic communication. Published in 1930 by the British scholar Charles **Ogden**, Basic English was a popular idea for a while, but it now appears to be almost dead.

basic-level category A semantic category which is the most natural one for naming objects. A single creature might be at the same time an *animal*, a *mammal*, a *carnivore*, a *dog*, a *hound* and a *beagle*, but we would usually call it a *dog*: this is the basic-level category.

basic vocabulary Certain words in a language which are learned early by children and which are very frequent. Among them are the personal pronouns like *me* and *you*, the lower numerals like *one* and *two*, kinship terms like *mother* and *brother*, common verbs like *come* and *die*, common adjectives like *big* and *red*, and names of natural phenomena like *sun* and *rain*. Such words are of interest in historical linguistics, because they are often thought to be replaced much more slowly than other words, and hence to be especially useful in comparing languages. The **Swadesh word list** is based upon such words.

basic word order The ordinary, most usual order of elements in sentences in a particular language, usually expressed in terms of the ordering of Subject (S), Object (O) and Verb (V). English, for example, has SVO order, as in *Napoleon* *invaded Russia.* All six possible basic word orders are attested, with SOV being the most frequent.

basilect In a **creole**, that variety of the creole which is the furthest removed from educated speech and which is hence the least prestigious variety.

Basque A language spoken by about 660,000 people at the western end of the Pyrenees. Basque cannot be shown to be related to any other living language, and it is the last survivor of the languages spoken in western Europe before the arrival of the **Indo-European** languages several thousand years ago. The Aquitanian language of ancient Gaul was an ancestral form of Basque.

bathtub phenomenon In psycholinguistics, the phenomenon by which someone trying to remember a forgotten word or name finds it easier to recall the beginning and the end than to recall the middle.

Baudouin de Courtenay, Jan A Polish linguist (1845–1929), a member of the **Kazan School** who largely laid the foundations of phonology.

BBC English An informal name for **Received Pronunciation**.

bee dance Any of the several remarkable manoeuvres performed in the hive by honeybees which have discovered a source of nectar. Bee dances can express the direction of the nectar, the distance to it, and the quantity; they represent a rare non-human example of **displacement**.

behaviourism An approach to psychology which holds that psychologists should study only observable and measurable phenomena, and should not appeal to unobservable things like 'minds' and 'intentions'. Leonard **Bloomfield** and the **American structuralists** were much influenced by behaviourist ideas, but, ever since Noam **Chomsky**'s devastating critique of B. F. **Skinner**'s behaviourist account of language **acquisition**, linguists have generally rejected behaviourism in favour of **mentalism**.

Bell, Alexander Melville A British phonetician (1819–1905). Bell is best known for his work on developing practical applications for phonetics and for his invention of Visible Speech, a technique for representing speech on paper.

Bellugi, Ursula An American linguist (1931–), best known for her pioneering work on **American Sign Language**.

Belorussian The chief language of Belarus, a **Slavic** language.

beneficiary The **semantic role** identifying the person for whose benefit something is done, such as *Lisa* in *I'm checking the proofs for Lisa.* Some **case** languages have a particular case-form to express this function, called the *benefactive.*

Bengali The principal language of Bangladesh and of adjacent areas of India. Bengali is an **Indo-Aryan** language.

Benue-Congo The largest branch of the **Niger-Congo** family of languages, including the **Bantu** languages and some West African languages.

Benveniste, Émile A Syrian-born French linguist (1902–76); he made major contributions to general and comparative linguistics, and is best known for his work on Indo-European language and society.

Berber A language spoken in North Africa, in several distinct regional varieties, and forming one major branch of the **Afro-Asiatic** family. Tuareg and Tamazight are two of the better-known dialects of Berber.

Berkeley Linguistic Society (**BLS**) An organization, based at the University of California at Berkeley and largely run by students, which holds an annual conference whose proceedings are published as the *BLS* series.

Bernoulli's principle (also **Bernoulli effect**) The physical principle by which the sideways air pressure on a solid body is reduced when the air is flowing past that body. This principle is of crucial importance in the production of **voicing**.

Bernstein, Basil A British educational theorist (1924–) who proposed and defended the **deficit hypothesis** of educational achievement.

BEV See **Black English Vernacular**.

Bickerton, Derek A British-born American linguist (1926–); he is largely responsible for making the study of **creoles** a central part of linguistics, and he is the originator of the **bioprogram hypothesis** and of the concept of **protolanguage**.

bidialectalism Fluency in two different dialects of a language. For example, a Scot who can switch back and forth between **Scots** and **standard English** is bidialectal.

Big Bang An informal name for the idea that language is an **emergent** phenomenon – that is, that it did not evolve slowly and gradually, but that it suddenly burst into existence.

bilabial (A speech sound) produced by putting the two lips together, such as [m], [p] or [b].

bilingualism The ability to speak two languages. Bilingualism may be the property of an individual or of a whole community.

binary feature A **distinctive feature** which can only assume one of two possible values; the two values are commonly represented as [+] and [−]. For example, the feature [nasal] is usually regarded as binary. Binary features are preferred by phonologists because they are easy to manipulate, but they are unrealistic for treating such parameters as **place of articulation** and vowel **height**. Compare **scalar feature**.

binding The relation between two **coreferential** noun phrases in a sentence, an **anaphor** and its **antecedent**; the anaphor is bound by its antecedent (that is, it receives the same interpretation as that antecedent). In *Janet hates herself*, *herself* must be bound by *Janet*; in *Fred asked Bill to see him*, *him* cannot be bound by *Bill* but may be bound by *Fred*.

binding theory In **Government-and-Binding Theory**, that **module** which is responsible for treating **binding** relations in sentences.

biolinguistics (also **biological linguistics**) The study of the biological underpinnings of human language. It addresses the structure and evolution of those parts of the brain and nervous system dealing with language, with the biological aspects of the development of language in children, and with the biological basis of disorders of language and speech.

biological schedule The timetable which is typically observed in the emergence of **maturationally controlled behaviour**, such as learning a first language in childhood.

bioprogram hypothesis The proposal that we are programmed from birth with a "default" structure for language, and that children will therefore construct their language according to this default unless they find themselves surrounded by a language with different properties. This hypothesis, put forward by the linguist Derek **Bickerton**, attempts to explain why the world's **creoles** are so similar to one another: in this view, children who hear only the surrounding **pidgin** will use their innate bioprogram to construct a creole according to the default principles. The idea is highly controversial.

bird song The familiar but highly distinctive sequences of musical notes produced by many species of birds (in most species, only by the males). Bird songs are unusual in the non-human world in that they arguably contain an element of **duality of patterning**.

bisyllable Another name for a **disyllable**.

biuniqueness The requirement that a **phonemic transcription** of a language should have the property that a reader should be able to convert it unambiguously into a detailed **phonetic transcription** and vice versa – that is, that the two types of transcription should be mechanically interconvertible. Maintained by the **American structuralists**, the biuniqueness requirement renders impossible a number of otherwise appealing analyses, particularly those involving **neutralization**, and it has been generally rejected in more recent work, most of which requires only that a phonemic transcription should be convertible into a phonetic one, and not vice versa.

Black English Vernacular (**BEV**) The distinctive variety of English spoken by many black people in American cities. BEV differs from standard English in a number of respects, perhaps most strikingly in its verbal system, which makes grammatical distinctions unknown in standard English.

black-letter writing (also **Gothic script**) A very ornate style of writing and printing used in medieval Europe. It was used for printing German until the 1930s and is still occasionally used in English for special effect.

blade The part of the upper surface of the tongue extending about 1 cm behind the tip. The blade is used by most English speakers in producing many consonants, such as [n]. Consonants produced with the blade are called **laminal**.

blasphemy Any piece of speech or writing which is regarded by believers as deeply offensive to prevailing religious beliefs.

blend 1. A word which is formed by combining pieces of other words, such as *smog* (*smoke* + *fog*), *guesstimate* (*guess* + *estimate*) and *Oxbridge* (*Oxford* + *Cambridge*). The process of forming such a word is **blending**. 2. A **speech error** in which pieces of two words or phrases are combined, such as *dreeze* (produced by a speaker hesitating between *draught* and *breeze*) or *Posties* (for intended *Post Toasties*).

blending The creation of **blends** (sense 1).

Bloch, Bernard An American linguist (1907–65), one of the most prominent and influential of the **American structuralists** and for many years the editor of *Language*, the world's leading linguistics journal.

Bloch and Trager system An earlier version of the **Trager-Smith system** for analysing and transcribing the vowels of American English.

block language The special type of language used for such purposes as public notices and book titles, consisting only of words and phrases, with no complete sentences. Examples: *No left turn*; *War and Peace*.

Bloomfield, Leonard A distinguished and influential American linguist (1887–1949). Trained in historical linguistics, Bloomfield did important work on Germanic and Austronesian languages, and his famous work on Algonquian languages pioneered the application of the comparative method to native American languages. His 1933 book *Language* revolutionized linguistic thinking, and his ideas were developed by his colleagues and successors into **American structuralism**, which dominated the American linguistic scene until about 1960.

BLS See **Berkeley Linguistic Society**.

Boas, Franz An influential German-born American anthropologist and linguist (1858–1942). Boas was largely responsible for initiating the study of native American languages and cultures, and also for giving American linguistics the anthropological orientation which it long retained; he founded the *International Journal of American Linguistics*. Edward **Sapir** was his student.

body language An informal synonym for **non-verbal communication**.

boldface Thick black letters, like those used for the headwords in this dictionary.

Bolinger, Dwight An American linguist (1907–92). With a background in music and the humanities, Bolinger took little interest in the fashionable theories of his day. He was fascinated by the messiness of real speech, and is best known for his work on the neglected topic of intonation. A kindly and generous man, Bolinger was much loved, and he was one of the finest writers in all of linguistics.

bootstrapping In some views of **acquisition**, the procedure by which a child uses its knowledge of syntax to help interpret the meanings of the words it hears.

Bopp, Franz A German linguist (1791–1867), generally regarded as the founder of Indo-European comparative linguistics.

borrowing The process by which a word which exists in one language is copied into another language. For example, English has borrowed *castle* from Norman French, *ballet* from modern French, *vanilla* from Spanish, *soprano* from Italian and *kayak* from Eskimo. Such borrowings are called **loan words**.

bottom-up A label applied to any type of processing which begins with the smallest elements and combines them into increasingly larger elements until the whole message has been processed. The opposite is **top-down**.

boundary Any point in a piece of language at which a linguistic element begins or ends. For example, the phrase *such unhappiness* contains a **word** boundary, while the word *unhappiness* contains two **morpheme** boundaries.

bounding theory In **Government-and-Binding Theory**, that **module** which is responsible for putting limits on the distance over which elements of a sentence can be moved.

bound morpheme Any **morpheme** which cannot stand alone to make a word, but which must always be combined with something else within a word. English examples include the *re-* of *rewrite*, the *step-* of *stepmother*, the *-ing* of *reading*, the *-ful* of *powerful*, and the past-tense marker *-ed* of *played*. As the examples show, a bound morpheme is always represented with a hyphen at the end at which it is bound.

boustrophedon A style of writing in which the lines alternate between left-to-right and right-to-left. No modern language is normally written in this way, but boustrophedon writing is frequent in early written texts from the Middle East and from Greece.

bow-wow theory The conjecture that language arose in imitation of natural sounds, particularly animal sounds. There is no evidence to support this conjecture.

braces (also **curly brackets**) An **abbreviatory convention** for collapsing two or more rules into a single **rule schema** when they contain different elements at one point but are otherwise identical. For example, the rule [+ obstr] → [− voice] / _____ [− voice] (an obstruent is voiceless before another voiceless sound) and the similar rule [+ obstr] → [− voice] / _____ # (an obstruent is voiceless when word-final) can be collapsed as [+ obstr] → [− voice] / _____ {[− voice], #}. Compare **parentheses**.

bracketing A graphical device for representing the grammatical structure of a word, a phrase or a sentence by using square brackets to enclose grammatical units. For example, the word *unhappiness* can be bracketed as [[un[happy]]ness], while the sentence *Lisa bought a red skirt* would be [[Lisa][[bought][[a][[red] [skirt]]]]]. If category labels are added to the brackets, the result is a **labelled bracketing**.

braille A system of printing for blind people, in which each letter or other character is represented by a distinct arrangement of raised dots which can be felt with the fingers.

brain The large organ in the head, consisting of nervous tissue and divided into several distinct parts. The largest part, the *cerebrum*, is divided into two *hemispheres* and covered with a thick layer called the *cerebral cortex*; this cortex appears to be the seat of most of our cognitive abilities, including language. See **lateralization**, **localization** and the **language areas**.

branching node In a **tree structure**, any **node** which has two or more **daughters**.

breaking of the voice Another name for **voice mutation**.

Bréal, Michel A French linguist (1832–1915); he made major contributions to general and comparative linguistics, but is perhaps best known for introducing **semantics** into linguistics.

breath A simple **phonation type** in which air flows through the open **glottis**, producing an audible sighing noise. Breath is not as noisy as **whisper**.

breath group A stretch of utterance produced with a single expiration of breath.

breathy voice 1. A voice quality characterized by relaxed vocal folds and a high rate of airflow, producing a "sighing" quality; breathy voice is quite noticeable in the speech of some individuals. 2. A widespread but erroneous synonym for **whispery voice**. Many textbooks use this term inappropriately.

Bresnan, Joan An American linguist (1945–), an influential grammatical theorist and one of the creators of **Lexical-Functional Grammar**.

Breton A language spoken in western Brittany (in France), a member of the **Brythonic** branch of **Celtic**.

British Association of Applied Linguistics (**BAAL**) The professional organization in Britain of the practitioners of **applied linguistics**.

British National Corpus A corpus of about 100 million words of contemporary British English, both spoken and written, compiled by a consortium of universities and publishers. The corpus is held on a computer at Oxford University, and all the words in it are tagged for their grammatical class.

British Sign Language (**BSL**) The version of **sign language** used in Britain.

Brittonic Another spelling of **Brythonic**.

broad *a* An informal name for the vowel sound of *father* and *car*.

broadening A change in the meaning of a word by which the word becomes applicable to more cases than formerly. For example, the ancestor of English *arrive* meant only 'come to shore', but today this word means 'come to a place' (in general). The opposite is **narrowing**.

broad transcription A type of **transcription** which does not attempt to represent phonetic detail, but which only represents those phonetic differences which are significant in distinguishing words. In most cases, this is simply another name for **phonemic transcription**.

Broca, Paul A French surgeon (1824–80), the first to identify **Broca's aphasia** and **Broca's area**.

Broca's aphasia (rarely also **motor aphasia**) A particular type of **aphasia**, characterized by painfully slow and laboured speech, loss of intonation and rhythm, slightly slurred pronunciation, and above all by the disruption of grammar: sufferers cannot produce grammatical structures, and have difficulty in understanding grammatically complex sentences, though understanding is otherwise fairly normal. Broca's aphasia typically results from damage to **Broca's area**.

Broca's area A particular small region of the outer surface of the brain, located just behind the left temple, which is of crucial importance in language processing. Damage to it typically produces the symptoms of **Broca's aphasia**.

Brown, Roger An American linguist (1925–), best known for his work on language **acquisition** by children.

Brown University Corpus of American English A corpus of about one million words of American English, drawn from published sources and consisting of about 500 individual running texts.

Brugmann, Karl A German linguist (1849–1919); he was one of the leading **Neogrammarians**, and he made important contributions to the comparative phonology and morphology of Indo-European languages.

Bruner, Jerome An American psychologist (1915–), a leading proponent of the view that language can be entirely explained by the general cognitive abilities of human beings, and hence an opponent of the **autonomy of language** and of Chomsky's **innateness hypothesis**.

Brythonic (also **Brittonic**) The branch of **Celtic** including Welsh, Breton and Cornish, also called *P-Celtic*.

BSL See **British Sign Language**.

buccal voice Speech produced within the cavity of the cheeks, as in the speech of Donald Duck.

Buck, Carl D. An American historical linguist (1866–1955), a specialist in **Indo-European** and the author of a famous compilation of vocabulary in Indo-European languages.

Bühler, Karl An Austrian psychologist (1879–1963), the originator of **functionalism** in linguistics.

Bulgarian The major language of Bulgaria, a **Slavic** language.

Bullock Report A 1975 report into the teaching of English in British schools. Formally titled *A Language for Life*, it advocated an emphasis upon English right across the whole curriculum.

bunching A label applied to any tongue position in which the body of the tongue is held high in the mouth, as it is during the articulation of the vowel [i] and of the American **molar r**.

Burmese The principal language of Burma, belonging to the **Tibeto-Burman** branch of **Sino-Tibetan**.

burst The sudden peak in energy occurring when a **plosive** is released.

Burushaski An **isolated language** spoken in two valleys in Kashmir, near the disputed border between India and Pakistan.

C

C A symbol for **consonant** in phonology.

CA An abbreviation for any of **componential analysis**, **conversation analysis** or **contrastive analysis**.

cacophony Harsh or unpleasant sounds.

Caddoan A small family of languages in the western USA. Caddoan languages are remarkable for their small phoneme inventories and complex morphophonology.

caesura A pause or break within a line of verse: *To err is human,//to forgive, divine.*

call Any one of the vocal signals used by some species of animal to which a consistent meaning is attached. Most species have only three to six such calls, though vervet monkeys have over twenty.

CALL A short form for **computer-assisted language learning**.

calligraphy The art of beautiful handwriting.

calque (also **loan translation**) A word or phrase constructed by using a word or phrase in another language as a model and translating it piece by piece. For example, the Ancient Greek word for 'sympathy' or 'compassion' was *sympathia*, formed from *syn* 'with' and *pathia* 'suffering'. The Romans calqued this Greek word into Latin as *compassio*, from *con* 'with' and *passio* 'suffering'. German has in turn calqued the Latin word as *Mitleid*, from *mit* 'with' and *Leid* 'suffering', 'grief'. If we were to calque one of these into English, we would get something like *withgrief; in fact, of course, we have simply borrowed the Greek and Latin words. Calques are rare in English, but we have a few, such as *it goes without saying*, calqued on French *il va sans dire*. Some other languages make heavy use of calques.

canonical form The most typical or most general pattern for the linguistic items in some class. In some languages, for example, the canonical form of syllables is CV(C).

canonical sentoid strategy A **processing strategy**, used by speakers of languages with fixed word order and little morphological marking, in which the first string of words that could possibly be a sentence is assumed to be a sentence. It is this strategy that makes **garden-path sentences** like *The horse shot from the stable fell down* so difficult to process, since the hearer assumes that *The horse shot from the stable* is a sentence and is left floundering.

cant Another word for **argot**.

Cantonese The variety of **Chinese** spoken in southeastern China, including the city of Canton and the territory of Hong Kong. Cantonese is also widely spoken by Chinese in southeast Asia, and is the variety spoken by most Chinese in Britain and the USA.

CAP See **control agreement principle**.

cardinal numeral A counting number like *one, two, three*, or *twenty-seven*. Compare **ordinal numeral**.

cardinal vowels A certain set of arbitrarily chosen vowel sounds. Arranged in a kind of grid, the cardinal vowels serve as points of reference for identifying real vowels in actual languages, in roughly the same way that lines of latitude and longitude serve as points of reference on a map.

caregiver speech (also **motherese, child-directed language**) The type of speech used by adults in addressing small children for whom they are responsible.

Carnap, Rudolf A German philosopher (1891–1970), a leading exponent of **logical positivism** and one of the developers of **truth-conditional semantics**.

case Any one of the forms which a noun or a noun phrase may assume in order to represent its grammatical or semantic relation to the rest of the sentence. For example, the Turkish noun *ev* 'house' has several case forms: Nominative *ev* (subject), Definite Accusative *evi* (direct object), Dative *eve* 'to the house', Locative *evde* 'in the house', Ablative *evden* 'out of the house' and Genitive *evin* 'of the house'. Some languages have dozens of cases; others have none at all.

Case In **Government-and-Binding Theory**, one of a set of abstract properties assigned to noun phrases to mark their position within the structure of a sentence.

case grammar An approach to grammatical description which is based on a set of **semantic roles** ("deep cases") like Agent, Patient, Experiencer, Beneficiary, Location and Goal.

Case theory In **Government-and-Binding Theory**, the **module** which deals with the principles governing the assignment of **Case**.

Catalan A **Romance** language spoken in eastern Spain (including Barcelona) and in a small area of southern France.

cataphor A label sometimes applied to an **anaphor** which precedes its **antecedent**. In the obvious reading of *After she got up, Lisa had a shower*, *she* is a cataphor referring to *Lisa*. This term is rarely used today.

categorical perception of speech The marked tendency of speakers to hear speech sounds, or at least consonants, as belonging definitely to the particular phonemes of their language. For example, any synthetic sound lying between [ba] and [da] in its acoustic characteristics will be heard either as [ba] or as [da], with nothing in between.

categorial grammar A particular theory of grammar which is formulated in terms of a small number of basic categories, a larger number of derived categories which are defined in terms of the basic ones, and a set of rules for combining these categories into syntactic structures. For example, if Sentence (S) and Noun (N) are taken as the basic categories, then an intransitive verb is (S/N), meaning that it combines with a noun to produce a sentence, while a transitive verb is ((S/N)/N), meaning that it combines with a noun to produce an intransitive verb.

category Any class of linguistic objects having properties in common. See especially **syntactic category** and **grammatical category**.

catenative verb Another name for a **control verb**.

CAT scanner A sophisticated type of X-ray machine which can map the soft tissues of the body in detail by photographing a series of thin slices through the body. Neurolinguists use it to map the brains of subjects. The initials stand for *computerized axial tomography*.

Caucasian A group of about 38 languages spoken in and near the Caucasus mountains. There are two northern groups, *Northeast Caucasian* and *Northwest Caucasian*, which are possibly (but not certainly) related, plus a southern (or **Kartvelian**) group, which does not appear to be related to the others. Some Caucasian languages have huge numbers of consonants and very few vowels (the extinct Ubykh had 80 and two, respectively). The best-known Caucasian language is the Kartvelian language **Georgian**.

causative A construction which expresses the notion "make somebody do something". The sentence *I washed the car* has a corresponding causative *Lisa made me wash the car*.

Cavalli-Sforza, Luigi Luca An Italian-born American geneticist (1922–), who has claimed to have found important correlations between genes and languages in a number of populations, most notably in the Americas. Though deeply controversial, his work has been interpreted as providing evidence for ancient movements of peoples.

cavity Any identifiable open space, especially in the vocal tract, such as the **oral cavity** or the **nasal cavity**.

Caxton, William An English merchant (1415–91), the first person to print books in English and a major figure in the standardization of English. He was also a distinguished translator and language teacher.

c-command A particular relation which may hold between two nodes in a **tree structure**. A particular node A c-commands another node B if and only if you can start at A, go up the tree until you reach the *first* node from which there is a different path downward, and go down that other path until you arrive at B. In Figure C1, the V node c-commands each of the four circled nodes, but nothing else, and the V node is itself c-commanded by *both* NP nodes, but not by any of the other nodes. The term was originally short for *constituent command*, but this longer form is no longer used.

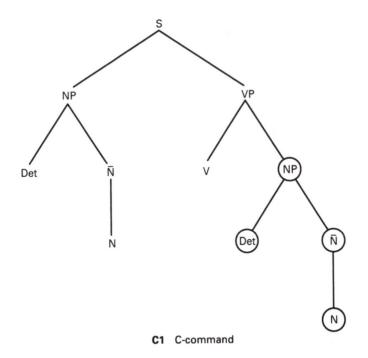

C1 C-command

cedilla The diacritic ₎, used in various orthographies for various purposes. It is occasionally used in English in writing words borrowed from French, as in *façade*, where it shows that the *c* is to be pronounced "soft" (as an [s]), rather than "hard" (as a [k]).

Celtic A major branch of the **Indo-European** family of languages. Once predominant across much of Europe, the Celtic languages are now confined to the western edges of the continent. They are divided into two groups: **Goidelic** (*Gaelic*, or *Q-Celtic*), including **Irish**, **Manx** and **Scottish Gaelic**, and **Brythonic** (*Brittonic*, or *P-Celtic*), including **Welsh**, **Cornish**, **Breton** and possibly ancient **Gaulish**. **Note:** the name was formerly spelled *Keltic*, which represents the pronunciation more directly.

Center for Applied Linguistics An American organization for the promotion of applied linguistics, based in Washington, DC.

Center for the Study of Language and Information (**CSLI**) A privately funded institute, based at Stanford University in California, which supports work in linguistics, logic, computational linguistics and information theory, and which frequently publishes work in these areas.

centralization The pronunciation of a vowel closer to the centre of the mouth than some reference position. For example, [ë] represents a vowel resembling [e] but pronounced closer to the centre of the mouth.

central vowel A vowel which is neither **front** nor **back**, which is pronounced with the highest part of the tongue near the centre of the mouth, such as [ɨ] or [ə].

centre-embedding Any grammatical construction in which a constituent is interrupted by another constituent of the same type. The example *The man who my sister is going out with is filthy rich* illustrates the embedding of the clause *who my sister is going out with* inside another clause. Multiple centre-embeddings are notoriously difficult to process: *The book the professor the students who are doing well like recommended is good.*

centrifugal force In a language or a speech community, any factor which tends to increase diversity of speech.

centripetal force In a language or a speech community, any factor which tends to increase standardization and homogeneity of speech.

centum language Any ancient **Indo-European** language in which velar plosives like /k/ and /g/ were *not* palatalized to something like /s/ or /dʒ/ before the front vowels /i/ and /e/. The difference between centum languages and **satem languages** was once considered important; today it is regarded as trivial, since such palatalization is a frequent and natural process in languages: even many of the daughters of ancient centum languages have become satem languages.

cerebrum The large, walnut-shaped part of the brain. The grey, wrinkled outer layer of the cerebrum, the *cerebral cortex*, is the location of all higher cognitive faculties, including language.

CFG See **context-free grammar**.

Chadic A group of languages in western Africa, one branch of the **Afro-Asiatic** family. The best-known Chadic language is Hausa.

chain-of-being hierarchy Another name for the **animacy hierarchy**.

chain shift A type of phonological change in which several sounds (usually vowels) change their pronunciations in such a way that one moves into the space vacated by another. Two types are distinguished: **push chains**, in which the shift begins when one sound moves too close to another, and **drag chains**, in which the shift begins when one sound moves away from the others.

Champollion, Jean-François A French scholar (1790–1832), the decipherer of the ancient Egyptian **hieroglyphs**.

chance resemblance A striking similarity in form and meaning between words in different languages which results purely from coincidence, and not from any historical connection. For example, Spanish *mucho* 'much', *día* 'day' and *haber* 'have' look very similar to their English counterparts, but the words are not related at all, even though English and Spanish are distantly related: these are chance resemblances. Chance resemblances between arbitrary languages are vastly more frequent than our naive expectations would suggest, and they constitute a headache in looking for remote **genetic relationships**.

change from above A type of language change in which an innovation is consciously introduced by educated speakers and then takes hold in the language.

change from below A type of language change in which an innovation is introduced by uneducated speakers, is at first strongly stigmatized, but eventually spreads also to the speech of educated speakers.

Chao, Yuen-Ren A Chinese-born American linguist (1892–1982), one of the leading **American structuralists** and a pioneer in the linguistic study of Chinese; he was influential in introducing Chinese language and scholarship to the west.

character A single written symbol which forms part of a system for representing language, especially one which is not a letter of an alphabet. We speak of "Chinese characters" or sometimes of "phonetic characters" in the IPA.

chart parser A type of **parser** that uses a particular data structure, a *chart*, to keep track of the current state of the parse. Chart parsers are at present widely used in **natural-language processing**.

chatterbox syndrome (also **cocktail party syndrome**) A certain disability. The sufferer is severely mentally retarded, but can speak rapidly and effortlessly; the output is generally quite grammatical, apart from a few faulty word-forms, but it generally makes no sense. This syndrome provides support for the **autonomy of language**.

Chatterji, Suniti Kumar An Indian linguist (1890–1977), a specialist in modern **Indo-Aryan** languages (especially **Bengali**), and perhaps the most famous Indian linguist of the twentieth century.

checked vowel 1. A vowel which occurs in a syllable closed by one or more consonants, such as the /e/ in *bed*. 2. A vowel which can only occur in this position, such as English /e/.

Chelsea An American woman who was born deaf, who was wrongly diagnosed as subnormal, and who consequently grew up without language. Correctly diagnosed at the age of 31 and given a hearing aid, she succeeded in learning enough English to live in the world and even to hold down a job, but she has never acquired anything like a normal command of language. Her sad case provides striking support for the **critical period hypothesis**.

chereme In some analyses of **sign language**, one of the small number of meaningless units (positions, hand configurations, movements) into which the meaningful **signs** can be decomposed.

cherology The analysis of the nature of **signs** in **sign language**.

chest pulse A single contraction of the muscles used in expelling air from the lungs during speech.

Chibchan A large family of languages extending from Honduras to Colombia.

Chicago Linguistic Society (**CLS**) An organization, based at the University of Chicago and largely run by students, which holds a famous annual meeting whose proceedings are published as the *CLS* series.

Chicheŵa (also *Chewa*, *Nyanja*) A major language of Malaŵi, a **Bantu** language.

child-directed language Another name for **caregiver speech**.

CHILDES A system for transcribing tape recordings of child speech directly into computers, where the recordings can be consulted by anyone with access. The name stands for *Child Language Data Exchange System*.

child language The distinctive type of speech produced by young children who have not yet mastered their first language.

Chimpsky, Nim See **Nim Chimpsky**.

Chinese A language, or more accurately a group of related languages, spoken by about one billion people in China, Taiwan and Hong Kong and by Chinese expatriates throughout southeast Asia and much of the world. The seven major varieties of Chinese are mutually incomprehensible and by any normal standard are distinct languages, but they are traditionally referred to by the Chinese as "dialects". The **logographic script** of Chinese does not represent pronunciations at all (see this last entry for some important remarks), but it is nevertheless not true that all Chinese languages are written identically. Before the twentieth century, no spoken form of Chinese was normally written at all; the only written language was the classical Chinese of 2000 years ago, which does not resemble any modern spoken form and which is pronounced very differently by speakers of different Chinese languages. The most important Chinese language is **Mandarin**, spoken by perhaps 700 million people. Two slightly different versions of Mandarin are the official languages of China and of Taiwan; the version used in China is called *Putonghua*, that in Taiwan *Guoyu*. Other major Chinese languages include Wu, with over 50 million speakers (including the city of Shanghai) and **Cantonese**, with over 30 million speakers. Chinese forms the **Sinitic** branch of the **Sino-Tibetan** family.

Chinese room A hypothetical experiment proposed by the philosopher John **Searle**. In it, a person who knows no Chinese none the less succeeds in translating Chinese texts into English merely by following a set of mechanical rules which direct him to copy out English words selected from a card file. Searle's point is that a computer program can perform prodigious feats that mimic the action of human intelligence without having anything we could properly call comprehension or awareness of what it is doing, and hence that hopes for **artificial intelligence** are misguided.

Chinook Jargon An important **pidgin** formerly widely used on the northwest coast of North America, an area with an extraordinary number of different indigenous languages.

chirography A fancy word for *handwriting*.

chômeur In **Relational Grammar**, a noun phrase which has been "ousted" from an **argument** position without disappearing from the sentence. In a passive like *Sodium was discovered by Davy*, *Davy* is a chômeur.

Chomsky, Noam An American linguist (1928–), the most famous and influential linguist of modern times. Beginning in the 1950s, Chomsky revolutionized the field of linguistics, and his contributions are many and various. He introduced the notion of **generative grammar** and proposed and developed **transformational grammar**, which became the most influential of all theories of grammar; with Morris **Halle**, he also developed **generative phonology**. His savage review of B. F. **Skinner**'s behaviourist account of language **acquisition** was influential in removing linguistics from the grip of **behaviourism** and in turning the field firmly toward **mentalism**. With his advancement of the **innateness hypothesis** of language acquisition, Chomsky argued for close connections between language, mind and brain; his ideas, though very controversial, strongly influenced the development of **psycholinguistics**, and have helped to embed linguistics firmly within the new field of **cognitive science**. Chomsky has continued to develop his ideas; for example, in the 1980s he greatly revised his earlier grammatical ideas in the construction of **Government-and-Binding theory**, and in the 1990s he radically revised his ideas again in formulating the **Minimalist Programme**. Based at **MIT**, where he has spent virtually his entire career, Chomsky continues to be a major figure today, and he has also become known as a devastating critic of American foreign policy.

Chomsky adjunction See under **adjunction**.

Chomsky hierarchy A ranking of different kinds of **formal grammars** from the least to the most powerful. The idea is to compare the properties of the formal languages defined by each class of grammars with the observed properties of natural languages, in order to determine what type of grammar might be most appropriate for describing natural languages.

Christopher A British man, a **savant** who is incapable of looking after himself but who none the less displays a prodigious talent for learning languages: he has learned over two dozen languages, ranging from French to Berber, some from reading grammar books, others by talking to native speakers. Cases like Christopher's provide support for the **autonomy of language**.

chroneme In some analyses, a **phoneme** which consists merely of a unit of length added to a segment. In a language with /i/ and /iː/, the second may be analysed as /i/ plus a chroneme /ː/.

Chukchi-Kamchatkan A family of languages spoken in northeastern Siberia. The most important language in the family is Chukchi, with about 15,000 speakers.

cineradiography A technique for making X-ray films of the vocal tract during speech.

cipher A secret code.

circumfix An **affix** which comes in two pieces, one of which goes at the beginning and the other at the end. An example is Tigrinya *bi-* . . . *-gize* 'at the time when', which is "wrapped around" the word it is affixed to.

circumflex accent The diacritic ˆ, used for various purposes in various ortho-

graphies and transcriptions. It is occasionally used in writing English words borrowed from French, as in *bête noire* and occasionally in *rôle*.

circumlocution A roundabout way of saying something.

circumposition An **adposition** which comes in two pieces, one preceding the object and the other following. Mandarin Chinese has the circumposition *dào . . . li* 'into' as in *dào guòn li* 'into the can'.

citation In scholarly work, an acknowledgement of earlier work which is being made use of or referred to. Failure to provide such citations is considered at best incompetent and at worst dishonest.

citation form That form of a lexical item which is used in naming it, talking about it or entering it in a dictionary: *dog*, *big*, *go*.

class 1. See **natural class**. 2. See **social class**.

classical language A dead language, or an ancient form of a modern language, which is regarded as representing a kind of pinnacle of perfection (usually because it was the vehicle of important literary or religious texts), and which continues both to be studied and to serve as a source of learnèd vocabulary. Examples include ancient **Greek**, **Latin**, **Sanskrit** and classical **Arabic**.

classifier In some languages, a grammatical word which must accompany a noun in certain circumstances, most often in counting. In Malay, for example, animal names cannot be counted directly, but must take the classifier *ekor* 'tail': hence 'two rats' is not *dua tikus* but *dua ekor tikus* 'two tail rat'.

clause A grammatical unit containing a subject and a predicate. There are two types: **main clauses** and **subordinate clauses**. Every sentence contains at least one main clause. The sentence *Larry cleared the table* has only one main clause; *Larry cleared the table and Esther washed the dishes* has two main clauses; *After Larry had cleared the table, Esther washed the dishes* has a subordinate clause and a main clause. **Important note:** Chomskyan linguists use this term more broadly: for them, every **lexical verb** must belong to a separate clause. For Chomskyans, then, the sentence *Having finished the dishes, she decided to wash the car* has three clauses; for everyone else it has only one, since there is only one overt subject.

clause chaining A type of sentence structure found in certain languages, in which only one clause (usually the last) has a fully inflected verb, all other clauses containing only a reduced verb-form (a **converb**) marked merely to indicate a different subject or tense from the fully inflected verb.

clause union A construction in which the objects of a complement verb are apparently expressed as objects of the main verb. In Spanish, for example, 'I want to show you them' can be expressed either as *Quiero mostrartelos* (literally 'I-want show-you-them') or as *Te los quiero mostrar* (literally 'you them I-want show'); the second shows clause union, since the objects of *mostrar* have apparently become objects of *quiero*.

clausemate Either of two elements in a sentence which belong to the same simple clause.

clear-cases principle The idea that, in cases in which native speakers are not sure whether something is grammatical in their language or not, a grammar should be written to handle other, clear cases and the resulting grammar should then determine the status of the doubtful cases. This idea has proved to be much less helpful than once hoped.

clear *l* A variety of [l] which is pronounced with the front of the tongue held high and the back kept low, producing a characteristic high-pitched timbre. Most speakers in England use a clear *l* only before a vowel, as in *leaf* or *feeling*. Many speakers in Wales and Ireland use a clear *l* everywhere, even in words like *feel* and *field*; this pronunciation is very prominent to English ears. Most speakers in Scotland and North America never use a clear *l* at all. Compare **dark *l***.

cleft palate A permanent opening in the roof of the mouth, allowing air to flow from the mouth out through the nose even when the **velum** is closed. The result is permanent **nasalization** of speech.

cleft sentence A particular sort of sentence structure used to put some element into **focus**. For example, the ordinary English sentence *John bought a car yesterday* has several clefted counterparts, such as *It was John who bought a car yesterday* and *It was yesterday that John bought a car*. Compare **pseudo-cleft sentence**. **Note:** some people use the term 'cleft sentence' more generally, to include ordinary clefts (*it*-clefts) and pseudo-clefts (*WH*-clefts).

clever Hans effect The ability of non-human animals to perform seemingly impressive stunts, such as arithmetic, by picking up subtle clues from their trainers. This effect is a constant problem in evaluating the various attempts to teach animals to handle human languages.

cliché A once-colourful phrase which has lost its force through overuse, such as *Football is a game of two halves*.

click A consonant produced with a **velaric ingressive airstream mechanism**. Clicks are used as ordinary consonants only in some languages of southern Africa (especially the **Khoisan** languages); elsewhere, they occur only in some aspect of **paralanguage**, as in the English *tsk, tsk* noise.

click experiment In psycholinguistics, an experimental technique in which subjects listen to recordings of speech upon which brief noises ('clicks') have been superimposed; such experiments are performed for various purposes.

CLIE See the **Committee for Linguistics in Education**.

cline A one-dimensional scale expressing some characteristic which a relevant object may possess to any degree between zero and 100 per cent. For example, we might posit a 'birdiness' cline, with sparrows, eagles, albatrosses, chickens, ostriches and penguins all being 'birdy' to varying degrees. The notion is used in some "fuzzy" theories of grammar, in which, for example, some element may be a noun to a greater or lesser degree.

clinical linguistics The application of the ideas and methods of linguistics to the analysis and treatment of disorders of language.

clipped form A word which is derived by chopping a piece off from a longer word or phrase, usually one with the same meaning: *gym* from *gymnasium*, *flu* from *influenza*, *phone* from *telephone*, *sitcom* from *situation comedy*. The process of forming a word in this way is called **clipping**. Note that a clipped form is a real word, and not an **abbreviation**.

clipping The process of creating a **clipped form**.

clitic A grammatical item which appears to be less than a word but more than an affix. English examples include the *'ll* of *She'll do it* and the possessive *'s*. In a French sentence like *Je te le donnerai* 'I'll give it to you', the pronouns *je* 'I', *te* 'you' and *le* 'it' are all clitics.

close vowel Another name for a **high vowel**.

closed class A **word class** which has only a small number of members and which rarely gains new members. English examples include **determiner**, **preposition** and **pronoun**. Compare **open class**.

closed syllable A **syllable** which ends in a consonant. Both syllables of *minstrel* are closed, as are the first, second and fourth syllables of *contemptible*. Compare **open syllable**.

closure That part of the articulation of a **stop** consonant during which airflow is completely blocked off.

cloze test A technique used in testing reading comprehension, often that of foreign learners of a language, in which certain words are omitted from a printed text and replaced by blanks. It is a subject's ability to fill the blanks with well-chosen words which is tested.

CLS See **Chicago Linguistic Society**.

cluster See **consonant cluster**.

coach test A procedure for testing whether subjects can distinguish potential **minimal pairs**. A story is constructed in which either of the two key items could be sensibly used at one point but the two possibilities lead to radically different interpretations of the story; a subject hears the story with one or the other item at the crucial point and is then questioned to find out what has been understood.

coalescence A phonological change in which a sequence of two segments is converted to a single segment, such as when the [tj] of *can't you* becomes a single segment [ʧ]. The opposite is **unpacking**.

coarticulation 1. Any articulation involving two simultaneous constrictions in the vocal tract, such as the consonant [gb] in the language name *Igbo* or the glide [w], both of which require both labial and velar constrictions. 2. Another name for **accommodation** (sense 1).

COBUILD In full, the Collins-Birmingham University International Language Database, a vast (20 million words) **corpus** of English held at Birmingham University and used in the production of reference books and English-teaching materials. The *Collins COBUILD* dictionaries for advanced foreign learners are particularly noteworthy for their numerous innovations.

Cockney The traditional name for the distinctive working-class speech of the metropolitan London area.

cocktail party effect The phenomenon by which a person in a noisy crowd can selectively "tune in" to the speech of one other person, ignoring the speech of others in the vicinity.

cocktail party syndrome Another name for the **chatterbox syndrome**.

coda The final part of a **syllable**, after the vowel. In the syllable *sand*, the coda is *nd*.

code 1. In **semiotics**, any single system of communication. 2. In **sociolinguistics**, any distinguishable language or speech variety.

code-switching Using two different languages or language varieties in the same conversation. Code-switching is common in bilingual communities.

codex A volume containing copies of ancient documents.

codification In **language planning**, the business of developing a single standard form for a language which previously lacked one.

cognate A word in a particular language which is related to another word in a genetically related language, in that both represent direct continuations of a word in the common ancestor of both languages, with no **borrowing**. For example, English *foot* and *father* are cognate with German *Fuss* 'foot' and *Vater* 'father', and the English and German words are more distantly cognate with French *pied* 'foot' and *père* 'father'. Occasionally the term 'cognate' is extended to words which have a common origin but which have been borrowed into at least some of the languages in question. For example, an unrecorded Latin word **caveola* 'small enclosed place' is the source of English *jail*, Old French *jaiole* 'jail', Spanish *jaula* 'cage, cell' and Basque *txabola* 'hut'; we may speak of all these as cognate, even though only the Old French and Spanish words are directly descended from their common ancestor, while the English and Basque words have been borrowed from neighbouring languages.

cognate object A **direct object** which merely repeats the meaning of the verb, such as *dream* and *thoughts* in *I dreamed an amazing dream* and *She's thinking terrible thoughts*.

cognition The totality of the mental processes by which knowledge is acquired, including perception, intuition and reasoning.

cognitive abilities The totality of our capacity to perceive, understand, learn, reason and make judgements. Specialists do not agree on whether human language is merely a by-product of our general cognitive abilities or whether it is something entirely distinct.

cognitive development The emergence of **cognitive abilities** in children.

cognitive grammar Any approach to the study of grammar which tries to be consistent with what we know about human mental processes.

cognitive linguistics 1. Broadly, linguistics conceived as an integral part of **cognitive science**. 2. Narrowly, a particular approach to the study of language which tries to interpret linguistic structures and categories in terms of our perception and experience of the world.

cognitive science The scientific study of the human mind, including such aspects as perception, intuition, acquisition of knowledge, reasoning and speaking. Cognitive science is an interdisciplinary field combining contributions from linguistics, psychology, philosophy, computer science and artificial intelligence.

coherence The degree to which a particular piece of discourse is easy for you to understand in terms of your knowledge of the world – that is, the degree to which a piece of language "makes sense". Compare **cohesion**.

cohesion The presence in a text of explicit linguistic links between the various parts of the text which help to give the whole thing a clear structure. Among the English items commonly used to provide cohesion are *he, she, they, this, after, therefore* and *but*. Compare **coherence**.

cohort model A theory of **word recognition** which holds that a person who hears the beginning of a word in speech immediately considers *all* possible words with that beginning as possibly being the word being produced. For example, an English-speaker hearing [bæ-] supposedly considers *bad, bat, back, bag, batter, basil, battery,* and all other such words as possibilities, only narrowing down the choice as further speech sounds are heard. This theory clearly contains some truth, but it is surely too unconstrained.

coinage Another word for **neologism**.

coindexing A notational device (usually subscript letters) for indicating that two noun phrases in a sentence refer to the same thing. In *Janet$_i$ lost her$_i$ book, Janet* and *her* are coindexed, meaning that Janet has lost her own book; in *Janet$_i$ lost her$_j$ book*, these words are not coindexed, and so Janet has lost somebody else's book.

collapsing Writing two or more distinct rules in a single statement (a **rule schema**) by using **abbreviatory conventions**. See the example under this last entry.

collective noun A noun which denotes a group of individuals, such as *committee, board* (of directors), *cabinet* (of ministers) or *Liverpool* (the football team). Collective nouns in British English are notable for their ability to take plural verb forms even when singular: *The government have announced a new proposal; Liverpool are looking for a new midfield player*. This is not possible in American English.

colligation The grouping together of words with similar grammatical behaviour.

collocation The tendency of certain words to occur together, such as *grill* (or *broil*) with *meat* and *toast* with *bread*.

colloquial speech Relaxed, informal speech. Such speech typically contains words and forms which would not be used in formal speech or in formal writing; these are called *colloquialisms*. *Do not* confuse colloquialisms with **slang** or with **non-standard** language: colloquial speech is used by all normal speakers, and a speaker who used only formal speech in all circumstances would be virtually pathological.

combining form 1. In some languages, a special form assumed by a word when it forms the first element in a longer word. For example, Latin *judex* 'judge' has a combining form *judic-* in derivatives like *judicare* '(to) judge', *judicamentum* 'judgement' and *judicialis* 'judicial'. 2. In English, an element of Greek or Latin origin which can only exist as part of a larger word, such as *techno-* in *technology, technocrat* and *technobabble*.

come-into-my-bower theory A conjecture about the origin of language; it holds that language originated in sexual displays and attempts to find a mate. There is no evidence to support this conjecture.

comitative A **case** form expressing the meaning '(together) with', such as Basque *Anarekin* 'with Ana'.

command 1. The force of a sentence which expresses an order: *Put that vase down!* 2. Any of various structural relations which may hold between elements in a sentence, most importantly **c-command**.

comment In some analyses of sentence structure, that part of a sentence which expresses new information, the rest being the **topic**.

Committee for Linguistics in Education (**CLIE**) A professional organization in Britain which investigates and advises on linguistic matters at all levels of education.

common case A name sometimes given to that form of an English pronoun which is used for all purposes other than the subject of a sentence, such as *me* or *them*. This form is also called the **objective** or **accusative** case.

common core The characteristics shared by all varieties of a single language.

common gender 1. In a **gender** language, the property of a noun which can take more than one gender, with a predictable difference in meaning. For example, French *prof* 'teacher' and *collègue* 'colleague' are masculine when referring to men but feminine when referring to women. 2. In some languages, such as Dutch and Swedish, the name given to the single gender class resulting from the merger of the historical masculine and feminine genders and still contrasting with the historical neuter.

common noun A **noun** which is not the name of any particular entity and which can be applied to any item in the appropriate class, such as *dog*, *wine* or *beauty*. Compare **proper noun**.

communal change A type of **language change** in which all or most speakers acquire the change at roughly the same time. For example, when the new word *CD* entered English, it was quickly learned and used by almost all speakers.

communication The transmission or exchange of messages between people.

communication theory An approach to the study of communication, including speech, derived from communications engineering. In this approach, a source encodes and transmits a message along a channel; the message reaches its destination, is decoded and then produces its effect. Compare **information theory**.

communicative competence The ability to use a language appropriately in social situations: knowing how to begin and end conversations, when and how to be polite, how to address people, and so on (this is called *sociolinguistic competence*), and how to organize a piece of speech in an effective manner and to spot and compensate for any misunderstandings or other difficulties (this is *strategic competence*). Often the term is used more widely to include all these things plus knowledge of purely linguistic factors like pronunciation, grammar and vocabulary (*linguistic competence*).

commutation Another name for **contrastive distribution**.

commutation test A procedure for demonstrating that two speech sounds contrast in a language. In English, [pæd] and [bæd] clearly have different meanings, and so [p] and [b] *commute* (contrast) in English, and must be assigned to different phonemes.

COMP In **Government-and-Binding Theory,** an abstract node which is posited as being present in every clause of every sentence. Most obviously, this node is the location of a **complementizer,** but the COMP node also serves other purposes in the framework.

comparative A form of an adjective or an adverb which can be used with a following *than*, such as *bigger, more beautiful, more slowly*, or a similar form in another language.

comparative linguistics The branch of linguistics which deals with the identification of **genetic relationships** among languages.

comparative method In historical linguistics, a procedure for figuring out the forms of words in an unrecorded ancestral language by comparing the forms of the words in the daughter languages.

comparative philology An older name for **comparative linguistics.**

comparative reconstruction The use of the **comparative method** to figure out what unrecorded ancient languages looked like.

comparison Variation in the form of a word to express different degrees of some quality: *big, bigger, biggest; good, better, best; slowly, more slowly, most slowly.*

competence An abstract idealization of a speaker's knowledge of her/his language, excluding such factors as slips of the tongue, memory limitations and distractions. Compare **performance.**

competition model A theory of the **acquisition** of a first language by children which holds that each language provides a variety of (possibly conflicting) clues as to the structure and meaning of utterances, and that children learn to attach particular weight to particular clues – say, to word order in English or to word-endings in Russian. The theory is especially defended by opponents of the **innateness hypothesis.**

complement A general term for some part of a sentence whose presence is required by something else in the sentence, especially by a verb. In the examples *Esther put the beans in the pot, Lisa is a translator* and *He called me a fool*, the elements *the beans, in the pot, a translator, me* and *a fool* are all complements of one sort or another.

complement clause A **clause** which forms a grammatical unit with a lexical item. Here are some examples with the complement clauses bracketed: *I've heard a report* [*that troops are massing on the border*] (a *noun-complement clause* attached to *report*); *She decided* [*that she would buy it*] (a *verb-complement clause* attached to *decided*); *She is certain* [*that she can do it*] (an *adjective-complement clause* attached to *certain*); *I don't know* [*whether she's coming*] (a verb-complement clause attached to *know*).

complementary distribution The relation between two linguistic forms which can never occur in the same environment. For example, most speakers in England have **clear** *l* only before a vowel and **dark** *l* only everywhere else. Two speech sounds which are in complementary distribution, providing they are phonetically similar, may be assigned to a single **phoneme.** Compare **contrastive distribution.**

complementizer A word which introduces a **complement clause,** such as *that* or *whether* in *Lisa said that she would come* and *I don't know whether Susie can drive.*

complementizer-gap constraint A **constraint** in English that disallows an overt **complementizer** immediately followed by a **gap.** Compare **Who do you think that* e *is coming?* with *Who do you think* e *is coming?*

completion point A point in a conversation at which you indicate that you have finished your **turn** and that someone else may now speak. There are various ways of doing this, such as pausing and asking a question.

complex preposition A single **preposition** consisting of two or three words: *out of, up till, in spite of, in front of.*

complex sentence A sentence which contains at least one **subordinate clause.** Compare **compound sentence.**

complex symbol Another name for a **feature matrix.**

complexity theory A branch of computational mathematics which investigates the difficulty of solving different classes of problems in terms of the amount of computer time and storage space required.

component 1. Any one of the several subsystems posited in certain theories of grammar; a **module.** 2. Another name for a **semantic feature.**

componential analysis An approach to studying the meanings of words. The meaning of a word is assumed to consist of a number of **semantic features** (or **semantic components**); for example, *stallion* might be analysed as [horse +, adult +, female −].

composition Another word for **compounding.**

compositionality, principle of An important principle of **semantics.** It says: the meaning of a sentence is derived from the meanings of the words it contains in a completely regular way which depends only on the grammatical structure of the sentence.

compounding (also **composition**) The formation of a **compound word.**

compound sentence A sentence which contains two or more **main clauses.** Example: *Susie waved her broom and the bear slouched off.*

compound word A word formed by combining two (or more) smaller words: *redhead, hatchback, scarecrow, overthrow, forget-me-not, five-pound note.* Some compounds contain an additional affix: *blue-eyed, over-represented.*

comprehension The entire process of understanding speech or writing.

computational linguistics The use of computers to perform various tasks involving language – most often, **natural-language processing.**

computer-assisted language learning (**CALL**) Using a computer to learn a language. Most typically, the computer sets you exercises and then marks your work and perhaps awards you a score.

computer language A highly specialized set of instructions used to program a computer.

conative 1. That function of language by which the speaker tries to get somebody else to do something. 2. A verbal **aspect** expressing the sense 'attempted but not finished'.

concatenation Stringing things together in a linear sequence.

conceptualism The view that the meaning of a generic word like *dog* is not something in the external world but rather a mental concept which relates the word to the world. Compare **nominalism** (sense 2), **realism**, **Platonism**.

conceptual meaning (also **denotation**) The most central part of the meaning of a word or other linguistic object; that part of its meaning which is intrinsic to it and which is always present, independent of context and free of associations.

conceptual structure The form in which our thoughts are couched.

concessive clause A subordinate clause which begins with *although* or *(even) though*, or a similar clause in another language, such as the first clause in *Although it had been raining for days, the cricket pitch was in good condition*. The use of a concessive clause implies that the following clause is somewhat unexpected.

concord Another name for **agreement**.

concordance A reference book that lists in alphabetical order all the significant words in some literary work or works (for example, the plays of Shakespeare), with the location of each occurrence of each word and often with the passage in which it occurs in each case.

concrete noun A noun which denotes some kind of physical object, such as *dog*, *child*, *tree*, *house* or *iron*. Compare **abstract noun**.

Condillac, Étienne de A French philosopher (1714–80), one of the first scholars to stress the connection between language and mind.

conditional A distinctive set of verb forms found in some languages and used in forming **conditional sentences** and sometimes more generally in expressing implied conditions, suppositions or approximations. An example is Spanish *él sabría* 'he would know'.

conditional sentence A sentence containing an *if*-clause, or a similar sentence in another language. There are various types of conditional sentence, the main distinction being between *open* conditionals (like *If you wash the dishes, I'll dry*) and *unreal* or *counterfactual* conditionals (like *If I spoke better French, I could get a job in Paris*). (Note that the *if* that means *whether* doesn't count: *I don't know if Lisa is coming* is not a conditional sentence.)

conditioning Systematic variation in the form of a linguistic unit depending on what it occurs next to. For example, the three regular variants of the English plural morpheme, as in *cats* (/s/), *dogs* (/z/) and *foxes* (/ɪz/), are conditioned by the phonetic nature of the preceding sound, and the presence or absence of aspiration in English /p t k/, as in *pit, spit, slipper, tip*, is conditioned both by the position of the stress and the nature of the neighbouring sounds.

conduction aphasia A type of **aphasia** resulting from damage to the **arcuate fasciculus**, which connects **Wernicke's area** to **Broca's area**. The victim cannot find words, but can understand speech.

conference A meeting at which scholars get together to present and discuss their latest work. A particularly large and important conference is often called a *congress*.

configurational language A language in which sentences normally have **constituent structure** – that is, a language in which the structure of a sentence is well represented by a **tree structure** of the familiar kind. Most languages appear to be like this, including English, but see **non-configurational language**.

configurational structure Another name for **constituent structure**.

congenital Present from birth.

congruence For some linguistic unit, the degree of agreement in defining it by different criteria. A **sentence** is usually highly congruent: phonological, morphological, syntactic and semantic criteria all tend to pick out the sentence as a unit. A **word** may be less congruent: the various criteria may not agree in deciding what is or is not a word. For example, the contraction *hasn't* is a single word by some criteria but not by others.

Conj The abbreviation for **conjunction** (sense 1).

conjoining Combining two or more words, phrases or sentences in a **coordinate structure**.

conjugation 1. The full set of inflected forms of a single verb in some language. 2. A class of verbs all of which inflect in the same way.

conjunct Any one of the items that are connected in a **coordinate structure**.

conjunction 1. In modern linguistics, a little word that connects two (or more) linguistic units of the same kind, such as *and* or *or*, or the class of such words. Traditional grammarians call these **coordinating conjunctions**. 2. In traditional grammar, a much larger class of words including the (coordinating) conjunctions of sense 1, the **subordinating conjunctions** like *if* and *although*, and the **complementizers** like *whether* and *that*. This broad sense is not normal in linguistics. 3. Another name for **coordination**.

connected speech Ordinary speech consisting of a series of utterances, as opposed to single sentences, phrases or words considered in isolation.

connectionism (also *parallel distributed processing*) An approach to **cognitive science** which is inspired by the architecture of the brain and which therefore involves building models in which large numbers of elements are interconnected in complex ways, just as the neurons in the brain are interconnected. There have been attempts to model certain aspects of language behaviour in this way.

connective A broad label applied to any word which serves to connect sentences or parts of sentences in some fashion. Examples include *and*, *or*, *but*, *therefore*, *hence* and *nevertheless*.

connotation That part of the significance of a word which goes beyond its strict linguistic meaning and includes all of its associations, whether personal or communal. For example, the word *rugby* might connote to you any or all of 'athleticism', 'manliness', 'large men' or 'boorishness and bawdiness'; it might remind you of your pride in the achievements of your local or national side; it might even remind you of a present or former boyfriend. All of these are part of the connotation of the word. The term means about the same as **associative meaning**, though this last usually excludes **affective meaning**. Compare **conceptual meaning** (also called **denotation**).

consequent See **apodosis**.

consonant 1. In phonetics, any speech sound whose articulation involves a significant obstruction of the airstream, such as [p], [l], [s] or [m]. 2. In phonology, any speech sound which forms (part of) the margin of a syllable (the beginning or the end), and not its central part, or **nucleus**. The opposite term in both cases is **vowel**. **Note:** These definitions are not equivalent. For example, the "*y*-sound" ([j]) of *yes* is a vowel by definition 1, but a consonant by definition 2. **Note:** some people prefer to use the term **contoid** for sense 1, reserving 'consonant' for sense 2.

consonantal 1. Pertaining to **consonants**. 2. A **distinctive feature** which has the value [+] for obstruents, nasals and liquids and [−] for vowels and glides.

consonant cluster Two or more **consonants** in a row within a single word. Note that this term applies to pronunciation, not to spelling: thus, *string* starts with a cluster of three consonants but ends with only one consonant, while *thread* starts with a cluster of only two consonants, and *scythe* does not contain any clusters at all (compare *side*).

consonant harmony A restriction on the **consonants** which are allowed to occur within a single word. For example, in Basque, which has contrasting laminal and apical sibilants, a word may contain only one or the other. Compare **vowel harmony**.

conspiracy The state of affairs in which an analyst finds that several formally distinct rules set up as part of the description of a language combine to produce a generalization which is stated by none of them.

constituency test Any of various criteria which can be invoked to help decide whether some string of words in a sentence is a **constituent** or not. Examples: can it be moved as a unit; can it be deleted; can it be interrupted; can it be conjoined with another similar string in a coordinate structure; can it be the antecedent of a pro-form?

constituent Any piece of a sentence, of whatever size, which forms a single grammatical unit within that sentence. In a **tree structure** for the sentence, each constituent will appear as a single branch with a labelled **node** at its top to identify the type of constituent it is.

constituent structure (also **configurational structure**) A type of sentence structure in which a sentence consists of a small number of smaller grammatical pieces, each of which consists of still smaller pieces, each of which in turn consists of even smaller pieces, and so on, down to the smallest grammatical units available. This is the kind of hierarchical structure shown in a typical **tree structure** for a sentence. A language in which sentences have such structure is a **configurational language**; a language in which they don't is a **non-configurational language**. Most languages appear to be configurational.

constraint Any statement in the description of a language (or of languages generally) which says that something must *not* happen: for example, that a rule must not apply in certain circumstances, or that a particular sequence of sounds must not occur.

constriction In the articulation of a **consonant** (sense 1), the point at which the vocal tract is narrowest, and hence the point at which airflow is most severely obstructed.

construct state In certain languages, a special form assumed by a noun to show that it is possessed. For example, in Hebrew, 'the scarf' is *ha-tsaʿif* and 'the girl' is *ha-yalda*, but 'the girl's scarf' is *tsəʿif ha-yalda*, in which the word for 'scarf' appears in its construct state.

construction Any grammatical structure which appears systematically in some language, or any particular instance of it.

constructional homonymy (also **constructional homonymity**) Another name for **structural ambiguity**.

construe 1. To analyse the grammatical structure of; to parse. 2. In the phrase *to be construed*, to form part of a grammatical construction (with something else). For example, in *She turned the light on*, the particle *on* must be construed with the verb *turn*.

consultant Another word for **informant**, preferred by some because of the unfortunate resemblance between *informant* and *informer*.

contact See **language contact**.

content The **meaning** of a linguistic element, often especially a **morpheme** or a **word**. Compare **form** and **function**.

content/process controversy A dispute over whether children "contain" linguistic knowledge at birth or whether they merely possess the ability to "process" linguistic input. The first position is the **innateness hypothesis**; the second denies this hypothesis and sees language acquisition as resulting only from general cognitive abilities.

content word (also **full word**) A word which has dictionary meaning, such as *girl, green, enjoy* or *above*. Compare **grammatical word**.

context Either of two factors which provide a kind of background within which an utterance is interpreted. The *linguistic context* (or *co-text*) consists of what has already been said; the *extralinguistic context* consists of the topic of conversation, the participants' expectations, their knowledge of the world, their surroundings, and the relationship between them.

context-free grammar (CFG) A **formal grammar** consisting entirely of **context-free rules**. Context-free grammars can provide good descriptions of almost all grammatical phenomena in almost all languages, but there are a few unusual constructions which they can't handle, notably **cross-serial dependencies**.

context-free language A **formal language** which is generated by a **context-free grammar**.

context-free rule A rule of grammar which states that a single category can be rewritten as a string of any number of categories, from zero on up. Examples: $NP \rightarrow e$ (where *e* means 'nothing'); $NP \rightarrow Det\ N'$; $S \rightarrow NP[+WH]\ V[+AUX, +FIN]\ VP[-FIN]$. See the discussion under **phrase-structure grammar**.

context of situation Another name for the *extralinguistic context* of an utterance; see under **context**.

context-sensitive grammar (CSG) A formal grammar which contains **context-sensitive rules** but nothing more powerful. Such grammars are far too powerful to serve as models of natural-language grammars.

context-sensitive language A **formal language** which is generated by a **context-sensitive grammar**.

context-sensitive rule In a **formal grammar**, a rule which has the general form $A \rightarrow B / C$ _____ D, where A is a single category but B, C and D may be strings of any length, including zero. That is, such a rule allows a category A to be rewritten as a string B *if and only if* A is immediately preceded and/or followed by certain other things. For example, the rule $V \rightarrow Vt /$ _____ NP says that the category Verb may be rewritten as the category Transitive Verb if and only if it is followed by a noun phrase. Such rules are rarely used in linguistics.

contextual variation Another name for **stylistic variation**.

continuant Any speech sound during whose articulation the flow of air through the mouth is never completely blocked, such as [a], [s] or [l]. "Officially", nasals like [m] are not continuants, but, since air continues to flow through the nasal cavity, some linguists prefer to class nasals as continuants.

continuity hypothesis 1. The view that the sounds of **babbling** develop directly into speech sounds during **acquisition**. This view is controversial. 2. The conjecture that human language is directly descended from the **calls** used by non-human species. This view has few supporters among linguists today, since most linguists see human language as something utterly different from animal signals. **Note:** in each case, the opposing view is called the **discontinuity hypothesis**.

continuous Another name for the **progressive**.

contoid A synonym for **consonant** in the phonetic sense of that term (sense 1): a speech sound whose pronunciation involves a significant obstruction of the airflow in the mouth. Compare **vocoid**.

contour tone A **tone** which necessarily involves a change in pitch, such as a fall, a rise or a fall-rise.

contraction A short way of pronouncing a word or a sequence of words. Examples: *can't* for *can not*, *she'll* for *she will*, *won't* for *will not*, *she'd've* for *she would have*, *o'er* for *over*.

contradictory 1. Either of two statements which cannot be both true or both false. Example: *Susie is married*; *Susie is unmarried*. 2. The relation in meaning between two words which cannot both be properly applied to the same thing at the same time, such as *married* and *single*.

contrary 1. Either of two statements which cannot be both true, though they can be both false. Example: *Garfield is a dog*; *Garfield is a cat*. 2. Another name for an **antonym**.

contrast 1. Another term for **contrastive distribution**. 2. The relation between two syllables in the same word which differ in **stress** or **pitch**.

contrast, principle of (also **uniqueness**) The principle of "one form, one meaning" – that is, that there should not be two different forms with the same meaning. This principle appears to be important in child language acquisition, since children seem very reluctant to accept that two different words, or two different grammatical forms, can have the same meaning.

contrastive analysis (**CA**) (also **contrastive linguistics**) The systematic comparison of two language systems, or of specified parts of those systems. CA is particularly important in second-language teaching.

contrastive distribution (also **commutation**) The relation between two speech sounds in a language which behave as follows: replacing one of them by the other one in a given word or utterance gives a completely different meaning, at least in some cases. Speech sounds which are in contrastive distribution must be assigned to different **phonemes**. For example, if we replace [f] by [v] in English [fæt] *fat*, we get [væt], which is clearly a different word, *vat*. Hence [f] and [v] must belong to different phonemes in English. The same was not true of Old English, in which [v] occurred only between vowels and [f] occurred only in other positions; in Old English, [f] and [v] were in **complementary distribution**, and in fact they belonged to a single phoneme, usually represented as /f/.

contrastive linguistics Another name for **contrastive analysis**.

contrastive stress Stress placed upon some item to draw an explicit contrast with something else: *I said ACcept, not EXcept.*

control The relationship which holds between an overt noun phrase and an "empty" noun phrase in the same sentence. For example, in *Larry promised Jackie to wash the car*, the empty subject of *wash* is controlled by *Larry* (it is Larry doing the washing), but, in *Larry persuaded Jackie to wash the car*, the empty subject is controlled by *Jackie* (it is Jackie doing the washing).

control agreement principle (**CAP**) A proposed principle governing the occurrence of **agreement**. The full statement is technical, but very roughly it says this: a word may agree with a sister which is a noun, an N-bar or a noun phrase.

control theory In **Government-and-Binding Theory**, that **module** which is responsible for treating **control** relations.

control verb (also **catenative verb**, **equi-verb**) A **verb** which can appear at the beginning of a **control** construction, such as *promise*, *persuade* or *want*.

convention 1. Any notational device used in some system, such as an **abbreviatory convention**. 2. Any once-and-for-all statement made in some analytical system, so that a certain operation or state of affairs automatically has certain consequences, which therefore need not be spelled out repeatedly.

converb In **clause chaining**, any one of the special verb forms which occur in clauses not containing a fully inflected verb.

convergence 1. The situation in which two or more different languages independently undergo the same changes or acquire very similar characteristics. Convergence can be a nuisance in historical linguistics: if some languages have characteristics in common, it may be difficult to determine whether they have all inherited those characteristics from a common ancestor or whether they have merely converged. 2. Another name for **accommodation** (sense 2).

conversational implicature A conclusion which is not asserted by a speaker but which is nevertheless drawn by the listener on the ground that, if the conclusion were not true, the speaker would have said something different. For instance, if

I tell you "Not many Americans speak French", you will draw the conclusion "A few Americans speak French" (the implicature), since, if this were not true, I would surely have said something different in the first place. Compare **entailment, presupposition**.

conversational maxims See **maxims of conversation**.

conversation analysis An approach to studying the structure of ordinary conversations which is based on empirical methods – that is, observation comes first, and principles are extracted from observation. Compare **discourse analysis**.

converse Either of two words A and B (a *converse pair*) whose meaning is related in the following way: if I am connected to you by A, you are connected to me by B. Examples: *wife/husband*; *above/below*; *buy/sell*; *teacher/student*.

conversion (also **zero-derivation, functional shift**) A type of language change in which a word is moved from one part of speech to another, without any modification or affixation. This is very common in English: the adjective *brown* has become a verb, as in *You must first brown the meat*; the noun *access* has become a verb, as in *That utility can be accessed from the main menu*; and the verb *drink* has become a noun, as in *She had a quick drink*.

cooccurrence The relation between two linguistic objects which are both present in the same syllable, morpheme, word, phrase or sentence.

cooccurrence restriction Any limitation on the ability of linguistic objects to be both present within a larger unit. For example, English /s/ cannot be directly followed by any of /b d g/ in the same syllable; the intransitive verb *smile* may not be directly followed by a noun phrase; the mass noun *dissatisfaction* may not be preceded by the article *a*.

cooing The earliest identifiable stage in infant vocalization, consisting chiefly of vowel-like sounds. Cooing is followed by **babbling**.

cooperative principle A proposed major principle of conversation. It says this: make your contribution such as is required, at the stage at which it occurs, by the accepted purpose or direction of the talk exchange in which you are engaged. This principle is decomposed into a number of **maxims of conversation**.

coordinate structure (also **coordination, conjunction**) A syntactic structure in which two or more grammatical units, usually of the same type, are joined ("conjoined"), usually by a connecting word (a **conjunction**) like *and, or* or *but*. Examples: *Esther and her sister are here* (conjoined NPs); *You must pass your exams or leave the university* (conjoined VPs); *Rain started to fall, but the match continued* (conjoined Ss).

coordinate structure constraint The statement that a **coordinate structure** is a syntactic **island** – that is, a syntactic process cannot "reach inside" a coordinate structure. For example, though we can say *The Italians drink wine but the Danes prefer beer*, we cannot ask **What do the Italians drink wine but the Danes prefer?*

coordinating conjunction A traditional name for a word which connects things in a **coordinate structure**, such as *and* or *or*. Today these words are usually just called **conjunctions**.

coordination Another name for a **coordinate structure**.

Copenhagen School The name given to a group of Danish linguists who, in the 1930s, '40s and '50s, developed the approach to linguistics called **Glossematics**. Their principal theorist was Louis **Hjelmslev**.

coprolalia A pathological condition in which the sufferer utters a constant stream of obscenities.

Coptic The name given to the later stages of the ancient **Egyptian** language. Displaced by **Arabic**, Coptic finally died out as a spoken language, but is still used as a liturgical language by Coptic Christians.

copula A grammatical item, most often a verb, which serves to indicate *either* that two things are identical *or* that some entity belongs to a certain class or has a certain property. The English copula is *be*, and the two uses are illustrated by the examples *Paris is the capital of France* and *Lisa is very charming*. Not all languages have a copula.

core 1. See **common core**. 2. See **core grammar**.

coreference The relation between two noun phrases which refer to the same person or thing. Such noun phrases are **coreferential**. Coreference is shown in writing by **referential indices**; see the example under that entry.

core grammar In **Government-and-Binding Theory**, that part of the grammar of a language which is determined by universal principles. Compare **periphery**.

Cornish The **Celtic** language formerly spoken in Cornwall, like its close relative **Welsh** a later form of the ancient language of the British displaced by English. Cornish died out as a mother tongue around 1800, but some people have learned it as a second language.

Corominas, Juan (in Catalan, *Joan Coromines*) A Catalan historical linguist and philologist (1905–97), known above all for his great etymological dictionary of Spanish.

coronal A consonant which is pronounced with the blade of the tongue raised, such as [θ], [s], [d], [n] or [ʃ].

corpus (plural **corpora**) A body of spoken or written texts in a language which was produced by native speakers and which is available for linguistic analysis. Nowadays corpora are very often stored on computers for ease of processing.

corpus callosum A hard, fibrous body which provides the only connection between the two hemispheres of the brain. When it is severed (as is sometimes done to relieve the symptoms of epilepsy), the result is a **split brain**.

corpus linguistics Any approach to linguistic description which depends crucially on the use of corpora. The availability of computers has made this an increasingly important aspect of the subject.

correction See **negative evidence** (sense 2).

correspondence See **systematic correspondence**.

correspondence fallacy The view that there is some kind of direct, non-arbitrary relation between a linguistic form and its meaning. This view is universally rejected today because of the overwhelming evidence that **arbitrariness** is the norm in language, in spite of the presence of a certain degree of **iconicity**.

correspondence hypothesis The hypothesis that the mental processes by which a speaker constructs a sentence are identical to the formal processes by which a sentence is generated in **transformational grammar**. Obviously wrong, this idea quickly gave way to the **derivational theory of complexity**.

corruption A term which, except in very limited circumstances, has no place in the study of language. Neither regular changes (like the change of Old English *hlaford* to *lord*) nor irregular ones (like the reduction of *May God blind me!* to *Gorblimey!*), nor even changes applied to borrowed words (like the borrowing of English *football* as Basque *fubor*), are properly described as "corruptions". They are merely changes, and neither the word nor the language is any more "corrupt" as a result of the change. A rare use of this term in language studies occurs with ancient written documents which have been copied and re-copied by a sequence of scribes, each of whom has introduced some errors; the final result, which may be very different from the original, is said to be *corrupt*.

cortex The grey layer covering the outside of the **cerebrum**, the largest part of the brain. The cerebral cortex is the site of most of our higher cognitive faculties, including language.

Coseriu, Eugenio A Romanian linguist (1921–), known for his wide-ranging contributions to all areas of linguistics, but perhaps especially for his work on Romance languages.

cost The opposite of **economy** in describing languages. The cost of a description is increased every time we add more categories, more rules, more exceptions, rules which are less natural, less general or more powerful, and so on. Deciding which of several analyses is least costly, and hence most economical, is not a trivial exercise.

count(able) noun A **noun** which denotes something which can be counted, such as *dog*, *girl*, *table*, *cup*, *size* or *colour*. Compare **mass noun**.

counterexample A single piece of linguistic data which appears to be straightforwardly inconsistent with some proposed rule, principle or universal.

counterfactual An *if*-sentence which refers to a non-existent state of affairs: *If I spoke French, I could get a job in Paris*; *If McClellan had attacked Lee at once, the American Civil War might have ended two years earlier*.

counter-intuitive Conflicting with the immediate reactions of native speakers. For example, one analysis of the English infinitival *to* (as in *I want to go home*) classes it as a verb; this analysis in fact works extremely well, but most speakers find it counter-intuitive.

Coustenoble, Hélène A French phonetician (1894–1962); a student of Daniel **Jones**, she spent her entire career in London and was noted for her outstanding teaching.

cover symbol Any symbol used as an informal shorthand for representing some class of objects, such as *C* for 'any consonant'.

covert category A class of objects in a language which is not overtly marked in any way but which serves as the basis of some generalization. An example is the class of English verbs which can take the prefix *un-*, such as *tie*, *zip*, *dress*, *fasten* and *lock*.

covert prestige The property of certain speech forms which are publicly regarded by the community as a whole as being of low prestige but which are none the less vital in expressing and maintaining one's membership in a particular social group. For example, a working-class Londoner who tried to abandon his "Cockney" speech forms in favour of standard English might quickly find himself rejected by his friends and neighbours, since the use of those Cockney forms carries the message "I regard myself as a member of your group". Compare **overt prestige**.

Cowgill, Warren An American historical linguist (1929–85), a leading specialist in **Indo-European**.

CP In **Government-and-Binding Theory**, an abstract node posited as the highest node in every sentence (and every clause).

cranberry morpheme A **bound morpheme** which uniquely occurs in only a single word, such as the *cran-* of *cranberry*, the *twi-* of *twilight* or the *-art* of *braggart*.

creak A particular **phonation type** in which the vocal folds open and close so slowly that the individual openings can be separately heard; the result sounds rather like a creaking gate. Creak can sometimes be heard from male British speakers with "posh" accents at the end of an utterance, when the pitch of the voice falls.

creaky voice (also **laryngealization**) A complex **phonation type** in which part of the vocal folds produces **creak** while another part produces ordinary **voicing** (sense 1). Creaky voice can sometimes be heard in English in the same circumstances as pure creak, and it is used contrastively in some other languages.

creativity 1. Another name for **open-endedness**. 2. Our ability to use language in novel ways that bend or break the ordinary rules, as is done, for example, in poetry.

creole A natural language which develops from an earlier **pidgin** when that pidgin becomes the mother tongue of some group of people. Especially when a creole is spoken alongside a local prestige language, there may be a continuum of different varieties of the creole, ranging from the **basilect** (the variety most remote from the prestige language) through various **mesolects** (intermediate varieties) to the **acrolect** (the variety most similar to the prestige language).

creolization The process in which an earlier **pidgin** is converted into a new natural language, a **creole**. This requires the grammar of the pidgin to be fixed and extended and its vocabulary to be greatly enlarged.

criteria Any of various means by which a linguistic analysis may be evaluated, such as economy (using the smallest possible number of categories and rules), simplicity, completeness, consistency, or harmony with proposed **universals**.

critical linguistics The application of linguistics to the examination of political and ideological issues, sometimes particularly to the use of language for persuasion, intimidation and propaganda.

critical period hypothesis The hypothesis that first-language acquisition by human beings is only possible during the first few years of life, after which the language-learning faculties are "shut down" by the body's genetic programming. There is abundant evidence that this view is correct: see, for example, **Chelsea**, **Genie** and **Isabelle**.

Croce, Benedetto An Italian philosopher (1866–1952), the outstanding Italian intellectual of his day and a leading anti-Fascist. He stressed the creative, aesthetic, diverse and ever-changing nature of language and coined the slogan "language is perpetual creation".

Cro-Magnon The name given to the first modern humans (*Homo sapiens*) in western Europe, where they are attested about 35,000 years ago.

cross-categorial generalization A generalization which applies to more than one **word class**, such as the observation that both nouns and adjectives inflect for case in German, Russian or Latin.

crossover A label applied to a somewhat diverse set of facts involving the impossibility of certain orderings of noun phrases in a sentence. An example is **Who$_i$ did he$_i$ say Jackie kissed?*, which is impossible when *who* and *he* denote the same person; compare *Who$_i$ said Jackie kissed him$_i$?*, which is fine.

cross-sectional study A study of child language acquisition in which a number of different children of the same age are compared. Compare **longitudinal study**.

cross-serial dependency A rare type of construction in which two sequences of items in a single sentence are grammatically linked in pairs in the manner shown in Figure C2.

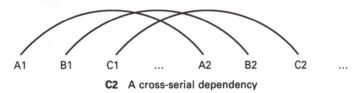

C2   A cross-serial dependency

Such constructions are very difficult to handle in a formal grammar. Swiss German is a language that has such constructions. Compare **nested dependency**.

Crowther, (Bishop) Samuel A Nigerian clergyman and applied linguist (?1806–91). The first black African bishop in the Church of England, Crowther was a pioneer in African linguistics; he is particularly noted for his work in standardizing, describing and teaching the Yoruba language.

Crystal, David A British linguist (1941–). Having earlier worked chiefly in **clinical linguistics**, Crystal has more recently become widely known as the author of a number of popular books on language, as the editor of a series of reference books, and as a radio commentator on language matters.

CSG See **context-sensitive grammar**.

CSLI See **Center for the Study of Language and Information**.

cued speech A technique for aiding deaf people in understanding speech; it uses hand gestures near the face to distinguish similar sounds.

cueing In testing the linguistic or cognitive abilities of animals, the inadvertent giving of clues as to what an animal is supposed to do, resulting in greater success than the animal could have achieved in a properly conducted test: the **clever Hans effect**.

Culioli, Antoine A French linguist (1924–), the leading proponent of a highly formalized version of **cognitive linguistics** (sense 2).

cultural transmission The property of language by which a child must learn a language from adults who already know it. That is, particular languages are not innate, though it is still possible that important properties of human languages generally *are* innate.

cumulative exponence A type of morphology in which two or more grammatical categories are simultaneously marked by a single unanalysable morph. For example, a certain class of Latin nouns has nominative singular *-us*, nominative plural *-i*, genitive singular *-i*, genitive plural *-orum*, dative singular *-o*, dative plural *-is*, and so on: neither case nor number is separately marked in any way.

cuneiform A type of writing using wedge-shaped strokes pressed into a soft clay tablet with an angled reed stylus. Cuneiform writing was used in the Middle East for several thousand years for writing **logographic scripts, syllabaries** and **alphabets**; among the languages commonly written in this way were **Sumerian, Akkadian** and **Hittite**. See Figure C3.

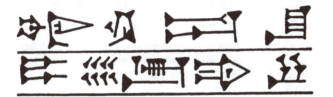

C3 A sample of cuneiform writing

curly brackets Another name for **braces**.

cursive Any form of handwriting in which the letters are joined together; "joined-up writing".

Curtius, Georg A German linguist (1820–85), known especially for his application of the **comparative method** to Latin and Greek.

Cushitic A group of languages spoken in east Africa and forming one branch of the **Afro-Asiatic** family. The best-known Cushitic language is Somali.

cutoff age The age after which acquisition of a first language becomes impossible; see the **critical period hypothesis**.

cycle In many theories of phonology and grammar, an analytical procedure by which certain rules are applied first to the smallest part of a linguistic form, then again and again to ever-larger parts, until the rules are finally applied to the entire form. The cycle has proved to be a valuable and powerful device in constructing linguistic descriptions.

Cyrillic alphabet An important **alphabet** derived from the **Greek alphabet** and originally devised for writing the **Slavic** languages. It is still used today for writing Russian and some other Slavic languages, and it has sometimes also been used for writing other languages spoken in the former USSR.

Czech The principal language of the Czech Republic, a **Slavic** language.

D

dactyl A metrical **foot** (sense 1) consisting of a stressed syllable followed by two unstressed ones, as in *capital* or *murmuring*.

Daic Another name for **Kadai**.

Dalgarno, George A Scottish philosopher (*c.* 1619–87), a leading figure in the development of a special language for philosophical use.

dangling participle A participial phrase which is not grammatically connected to the rest of its sentence. In the following examples, the bracketed phrases are dangling participles: [*Driving down the road,*] *a dog leapt out in front of me*; [*Having said that,*] *there's another interpretation.* Dangling participles are condemned by prescriptivists and are often regarded as ill-formed by linguists.

Danish The principal language of Denmark, one of the **Germanic** languages.

Dardic A group of **Indo-Iranian** languages spoken in and around Kashmir. Their precise position within Indo-Iranian is unclear, but they are most often regarded as distinct from both the **Indo-Aryan** and **Iranian** groups. The best-known Dardic language is Kashmiri.

dark *l* A variety of [l] pronounced with the back of the tongue raised, producing a characteristic low-pitched timbre. In England, dark *l* is normally used before a consonant or a pause, as in *feel* or *field* (except by those speakers who use [w] instead). Speakers in Wales and Ireland typically do not use dark *l* at all, while most Scottish and North American speakers use dark *l* in all positions, including before a vowel, as in *lily.* Compare **clear *l*.**

data Material serving as a direct source of information about the structure of a language. This may take several forms: texts written in the language, recordings or transcriptions of utterances produced by native speakers, answers to questions put to native speakers, or a native speaker's intuitions about the facts of the language. Linguists differ substantially in the weight they attach to these various forms of data.

database A (usually large) collection of data stored on a computer or on a CD-ROM which allows the user to find things quickly and to obtain answers to questions about the data. For example, the CD-ROM edition of the *Oxford English Dictionary* can be used as a database, since the user can get answers to questions like 'Which words entered the language between 1500 and 1600?' The availability of databases makes **corpus linguistics** possible. Some language databases are accessible on the Internet; others can be purchased on CD-ROMs.

dative In a **case** language, that case which is typically used to mark an **indirect**

object. In Basque *Liburua Anari eman diot* 'I gave Ana the book', *Anari* is the dative of *Ana*.

daughter (also **immediate constituent**) A relationship which may hold between two **nodes** in a **tree structure** for a sentence. If node A is immediately above node B, then B is a daughter of A.

Daughter-Dependency Grammar (**DDG**) A theory of grammar, developed by the British linguist Richard Hudson in the 1970s, which combines **constituent structure** and **dependency grammar** in a single representation.

daughter language Any one of several languages which have developed from a single earlier language by the ordinary processes of linguistic change. For example, Spanish, French and Italian are all daughters of **Vulgar Latin**, the Latin spoken in the Roman Empire.

Dauzat, Albert A French linguist (1877–1955), best known for his series of **dialect atlases** of France.

Davidson, Donald A British philosopher (1917–), a leading figure in the development of the **formal semantics** of natural languages.

dB The abbreviation for **decibel(s)**.

DDG See **Daughter-Dependency Grammar**.

dead language A label which is applied to two quite different sorts of cases, which you should be careful to distinguish. 1. A language which was formerly spoken but which has died out completely as a mother tongue, having been abandoned by its last speakers. Examples include **Sumerian**, **Etruscan** and **Cornish**. 2. An earlier stage of a language which has never ceased to be spoken but whose modern forms are very different from it. **Latin** is a dead language in this sense: it has never ceased to be used as a mother tongue, but its modern forms, such as French, Spanish and Italian, are so different from the language of the Romans, and from one another, that we no longer find it convenient to call them 'Latin'.

deafness Partial or total loss of hearing.

decibel The standard unit for expressing the **intensity** of a sound, and hence its **loudness**. The decibel scale is logarithmic, so a sound at 20 decibels is ten times as intense as one at 10 decibels, and one at 30 decibels is 100 times as intense.

decipherment The process of figuring out how to read ancient written texts which were formerly unintelligible. Sometimes the term is applied more specifically to the business of working out the writing system, independently of whether the language can be understood.

declarative Another term for **indicative**.

declension 1. The complete set of inflected forms assumed by a particular noun in a particular language. 2. Any one of the several different classes into which nouns are divided by their inflection in some languages.

declination The gradual lowering of the **pitch** of the voice during an utterance.

decoding A metaphorical label for the **comprehension** of speech.

deconstruction An approach to textual criticism which seeks to get behind the author's evident intentions and to expose the hidden assumptions, prejudices and purposes which are concealed in a text.

decreolization The process in which a **creole** changes so as to become more similar to the natural language from which it was originally derived. This process usually results in a **post-creole continuum**.

***de dicto/ de re* distinction** A difference in the way certain expressions may be interpreted. Consider the example 'Susie believes that all philosophers are eccentric.' Suppose the following is the case: of all the people who really are philosophers, Susie indeed considers them eccentric, but Susie also believes (mistakenly) that the linguist Chomsky is a philosopher, and she does not consider him eccentric. So: is the example statement true or false? In the *de dicto* interpretation, it is false: if you ask Susie if the statement is true, she will reply "No – Chomsky is not eccentric." But, in the *de re* interpretation, it is true: for every person who is a philosopher, Susie indeed believes that person to be eccentric.

deep case Another name for a **semantic role**.

deep dyslexia A severe type of **dyslexia** in which the sufferer replaces a printed word with one related in meaning but utterly different in form, for example by reading *heat* as *fire*.

deep structure In **transformational grammar**, an abstract underlying representation of the grammatical structure of a sentence which is posited in order to allow the analyst to state certain generalizations more easily. The conception of deep structure has changed frequently and dramatically over the years, and recently the term **D-structure** has been preferred. Note that deep structure is an analytical artefact and that it is grammatical in nature, *not* semantic (though see **Generative Semantics**), nor do most linguists assign any kind of mental reality to it (though there are exceptions). Compare **surface structure**.

deep-structure ambiguity A **structural ambiguity** which has the property that, in a particular theory of grammar, both interpretations correspond to identical **tree structures** at the surface level. The string *Anne likes horses more than Mark* is an example in any theory of grammar in which **gaps** are not overtly marked in the tree structure. Compare **surface-structure ambiguity**.

default In some theories of grammar, a value which is automatically assigned to something whenever there is no explicit statement requiring a different value. For example, since most noun phrases are third-person, we might allow third person to be assigned by default to any NP which is not explicitly marked as first- or second-person. Defaults can greatly reduce the number of individual statements which have to be made.

defective A label applied to a lexical item which lacks some of the forms typically exhibited by members of its class. For example, *beware* is a defective verb: we can say *Beware of the dog!*, but not **John bewared of the dog* or **John always bewares of the dog*.

defective distribution The property of a **phoneme** which cannot appear in all the positions typically occupied by other members of its class. For example, English /ŋ/ has defective distribution, since, unlike the other nasals /m/ and /n/, it cannot appear word-initially or after /s/.

defective *r* The pronunciation of English /r/ as a labio-dental approximant [ʋ], often wrongly perceived as a [w]. This type of pronunciation is rather common among British males; it is used by such public figures as Roy Jenkins and Jonathan Ross.

deficit hypothesis The hypothesis that many children from working-class or immigrant backgrounds have inadequate command of grammar and vocabulary to express complex ideas and hence that they cannot succeed in school. Compare **difference hypothesis**.

definite article A **determiner**, such as English *the*, which is most typically attached to a noun phrase to indicate that that noun phrase refers to something already known to the hearer. Compare **indefinite article**.

definite description A **noun phrase** which is not a name but which is sufficiently explicit to pick out a unique thing or a unique class of things, such as *my mother, the capital of France*, or *these books*.

definiteness The property which distinguishes **definite descriptions** and **proper names** from other noun phrases: picking out a unique thing or a unique class of things.

definition A statement which identifies the meaning of a term in sufficient detail to allow a reader to decide exactly when that term may be correctly applied to something.

degree The **grammatical category** which expresses the extent to which some quality is present, as in *big, bigger, biggest*.

degree modifier (also **intensifier**) A word which qualifies the degree to which some property is present, such as *very, extremely, fairly, scarcely, too* or *sort of*, as in *very big* or *too big*.

deictic category Any **grammatical category** which primarily makes distinctions based on the identity of the speaker or the time and place of speaking. Among the deictic categories are **person, deictic position** and **tense**.

deictic position The **grammatical category** which serves to express differing locations in space, normally with respect to the speaker. English has a simple system contrasting only *this* with *that* and *here* with *there*; some other languages have more elaborate systems.

deixis Linguistic pointing: the use of grammatical items like *this* and *that, here* and *there, now* and *then, I, you* and *they*, and tense-marking.

Delattre, Pierre A French-born American phonetician and applied linguist (1903–69), best known for his work on the teaching of French pronunciation and on the development of **acoustic phonetics**.

delayed auditory feedback The laboratory technique in which you hear your own voice, not directly, but via a tape recording which has been deliberately delayed by a fraction of a second. The effect of this on your speech is usually devastating.

delayed release A conventional but inaccurate label for the feature which distinguishes an **affricate** from a **plosive**; it would be more accurately called *frictional release*. The opposite is **instantaneous release**.

Delbrück, Berthold A German linguist (1842–1922), a leading **Neogrammarian**; he is best known for his work on comparative Indo-European syntax.

deletion Any change in pronunciation in which some speech sound disappears entirely, as when the initial [k] disappeared from English words like *knife* and *knot*.

delicacy In **Systemic Linguistics**, the degree of detail in which some linguistic object is characterized at some point in the overall analysis.

delineation A deliberate attempt to give distinctiveness and autonomy to a regional variety of a language, such as Australian English, to turn it into a badge of identity, especially national identity.

demonstrative A **determiner** which expresses location in space, such as English *this/these* and *that/those*.

demotic Popular; not learnèd or official; sometimes (but not always) uneducated. Demotic speech is the ordinary speech of most people. In ancient Egypt, demotic writing was the type of writing used by educated people for everyday purposes, as opposed to the **hieroglyphs** used by priests and scribes for important official purposes.

demotion In **Relational Grammar**, any syntactic process which 'moves' a noun phrase from a more prominent to a less prominent position in a sentence, such as when the subject of a transitive verb is converted by passivization to an agent phrase or even removed from the sentence altogether.

denotation Another name for **conceptual meaning**.

dental Any consonant which is pronounced by putting the tongue on or near the teeth, such as English [θ] (as in *thin*) and French [t].

deontic modality The type of **modality** involving obligation and permission, exemplified by *Susie must be here* when this means 'Susie is obliged to be here'. Compare **alethic modality**, **epistemic modality**.

dependency Any relation between two items in a sentence such that the presence, absence or form of one of them is linked to the presence, absence or form of the other. The example *Who is Susie talking to?* illustrates several dependencies: the verb *is* must agree with the subject *Susie*; the preposition *to* requires an object (*who*); the fronted position of *who* requires a gap to follow the preposition *to*.

dependency grammar An approach to grammatical description which does not recognize **constituent structure**. Instead, sentence structure is seen as a set of links between individual words: each word is linked to some other word, and all words are ultimately linked to one central word, usually the verb.

dependency phonology An approach to phonology in which a **segment** is analysed into a set of smaller elements called *components*, some of which may be more prominent than others. For example, a vowel system might be analysed into the components |i a u|, so that, for example, [e] is |i;a| but [ɛ] is |a;i|, where the semicolon indicates that the first element is dominant.

dependent clause Another name for a **subordinate clause**.

dependent-marking A grammatical pattern in which the connection between a **head** and something which depends on that head is marked on the dependent, not on the head. An example is the pattern in which the relation between a verb and its noun phrase arguments is expressed by case-marking of the NPs, and not by agreement in the verb. Compare **head-marking**.

deponent verb In Latin, a verb which takes only passive forms but which none the less behaves like an active verb, such as *uti* 'use'. Sometimes the term is extended to other cases of verbs whose morphology is at odds with their syntax.

depth hypothesis The hypothesis that **left-branching** structures require more mental processing than **right-branching** structures.

derailment A **speech error** in which a speaker produces a wrong word which is similar in its beginning to the intended one, such as saying *fire engine* for *fire escape*.

derivation 1. The process of obtaining words from other words by adding **affixes**, as when *prehistory* and *historical* are derived from *history*. 2. In certain theories of grammar, notably **transformational grammar**, the entire series of steps by which an underlying structure (or **deep structure**) is converted by rules into a **surface structure**.

derivational morphology That part of **morphology** which is concerned with constructing words (lexical items) from other words – for example, by adding prefixes or suffixes, as when *rewrite* and *booklet* are derived from *write* or *book*. Compare **inflectional morphology**.

derivational theory of complexity The hypothesis that the difficulty of processing a sentence is directly proportional to the length and complexity of its **derivation** (sense 2) within a **transformational grammar**. Once popular, this idea attracts little interest today.

Descartes, René A major French philosopher (1596–1650). The foremost advocate of **mind–body dualism**, he stressed the importance of language in distinguishing human beings from all other creatures. Impressed by Descartes' emphasis on the creative, non-mechanical nature of language, the linguist Noam **Chomsky** has declared himself the intellectual heir of Descartes, and has applied the label *Cartesian linguistics* to the tradition which he sees his own work as continuing.

descriptivism The approach to language description in which the observed facts of the usage of native speakers are described as they are found to exist. Almost all serious linguistic work is descriptivist. Compare **prescriptivism**.

design features A list of characteristics which appear to be common to all human languages. Lists vary, but all include **arbitrariness, displacement, duality of patterning, open-endedness** and **stimulus-freedom**.

Det An abbreviation for **determiner**.

determiner A word class, or a member of this class, which serves to specify the degree of applicability of a noun phrase. English determiners include *the, a, this, that*, and the **quantifiers** like *some, all, many* and *no*.

determinism, linguistic See **linguistic determinism**.

Devanagari See **Nagari alphabet**.

developmental 1. Of a language disorder, present from early childhood, and not resulting from later brain damage; an example is *developmental dyslexia*. The opposite is **acquired**. 2. Pertaining to the way in which children acquire their first language, or to the study of this.

developmental linguistics The linguistic study of the **acquisition** of a first language by children.

deviant A very general label applied to any linguistic form which has something wrong with it – for example, to an ungrammatical sentence or to an abnormal utterance produced by someone with a disability.

devoicing Any process in which a voiced segment becomes voiceless. A segment which has undergone devoicing is *devoiced*; note that it is an error to use 'devoiced' in the sense of **voiceless**.

Devoto, Giacomo An Italian linguist (1897–1974). A specialist in Romance languages, Devoto is known for his attempts at reconstructing **Proto-Romance** and for his work in **stylistics**.

diachronic Pertaining to language change over time. Compare **synchronic**.

diacritic A mark written above, below, next to or on top of a letter or character to indicate something about its pronunciation, as in *é, ô, ç, ü, ñ* or *ø* in various languages.

diacritic feature A **distinctive feature** or **syntactic feature** with no phonetic or linguistic content which is introduced merely to mark something as behaving in an exceptional way.

diaeresis The diacritic ¨, used for various purposes in various orthographies and transcriptions. In the IPA, it represents a centralized vowel, so that [ë] represents a centralized variety of [e]. In American transcription, it represents a reversal of backness, so that [ü] represents the front counterpart of [u], *i.e.* [y]. In English, the diaeresis is occasionally used to show that two vowels are to be pronounced separately, as in the name *Zoë*. In German, this diacritic is used to mark a vowel which has undergone **umlaut**, as in *Männer* 'men' (compare *Mann* 'man').

dialect A particular variety of a language spoken by the people in some geographical area (a *regional dialect*) or in a particular social group (a *social dialect*, or *sociolect*). British usage regards dialects as differing only in vocabulary and grammar, while differences in pronunciation are treated under the separate heading of **accent**; American usage regards differences in accent as part of the differences in dialect. **Note:** in everyday speech, the term *dialect* is sometimes applied to a regional language of low prestige, but the term is never so used in linguistics.

dialect atlas A book of maps, each of which shows in detail the regional variation on some point of pronunciation, vocabulary or grammar.

dialect continuum A state of affairs in which the local form of a language changes gradually as you travel across the area in which the language is spoken, and sharp boundaries between one **dialect** and another do not generally exist. This is the normal state of affairs, and we can draw lines between dialects only arbitrarily, or at best by locating **isogloss bundles**.

dialect geography The study of regional **dialects** – that is, of the geographical distribution of differing linguistic forms.

dialect levelling Another name for **homogenization**.

dialectology The study of **dialects**, especially regional dialects.

dialect survey An organized investigation of the regional speech-forms in some part of the world. Such a survey is essential in preparing a **dialect atlas**.

dichotic listening An analytical technique in which a subject wears a set of headphones and hears different things in both ears.

diction The choice and use of words, especially from the point of view of the effectiveness of the result.

dictionary A reference book which provides definitions of some set of words. Some dictionaries provide such additional information as pronunciations, etymologies, examples of use and advice on good usage; some also include a certain amount of encyclopedic information, such as the names of important people. A *bilingual dictionary* provides translations from one language into another.

Diez, Friedrich A German linguist (1794–1876), generally regarded as the founder of Romance historical linguistics.

difference hypothesis The hypothesis that the speech of working-class children, while different from the standard speech of middle-class speakers and penalized in school, is fully capable of expressing complex ideas. Compare **deficit hypothesis**.

diffusion The gradual spread of a language or of a linguistic feature across a geographical area.

diglossia An unusual state of affairs in which two different languages or language varieties are used in a single speech community, with each variety being largely reserved for certain purposes. In all such cases, one variety (Low, or L) is the mother tongue of most or all speakers, while the other (High, or H) is acquired only by formal education. Typically, L is used for ordinary conversation, folk literature and soap operas (among other things), while H is used for news broadcasts and newspapers, university lectures and serious literature (among other things). The key point is specialization: using the "wrong" variety for a particular function is seen as comical or offensive, and even speakers with a limited command of H prefer to hear H when H is appropriate. **Note:** some linguists, especially in Europe, apply the term 'diglossia' much more loosely and broadly to almost any speech community with two languages, but it is best reserved for the particular situation just described.

digraph A sequence of two letters conventionally used to represent a single sound, such as the <sh> used in English to represent /ʃ/.

diminutive 1. An **affix** added to a word to indicate small size or merely affection. 2. A word formed in this way. Examples: *booklet* (from *book*), *kitchenette* (from *kitchen*), *Tommy* (from *Tom*).

ding-dong theory The conjecture that language arose via **sound symbolism**, so that people produced sounds which somehow mirrored their environment – for example, the word *mama* supposedly reflects the movement of the lips as the child's mouth approaches the breast. There is no evidence to support this conjecture. The **ta-ta theory** is a version of it.

Dionysius Thrax A Greek grammarian (second to first centuries BC), the author of the earliest known grammar of Greek. His grammar heavily influenced the western grammatical tradition, though his authorship of the entire work is disputed.

diphthong A single vowel which changes its quality noticeably during its pronunciation, such as the [eɪ] of *day* and the [aɪ] of *die*. A more complicated case is a **triphthong**; a vowel that doesn't change at all is a **pure vowel**. **Note** that this term applies only to pronunciation, and has nothing to do with spelling: the <ea> of *bread* represents a pure vowel, not a diphthong.

diphthongization Any process in which a pure vowel changes to a diphthong, as when Middle English /iː/ changed to /aɪ/, as in *fine*.

directive An utterance whose purpose is to get the hearer to do something, such as a request, a question or a command.

direct method A method of language teaching in which all communication between teacher and students takes place in the language being learned, and the teaching of reading, writing and grammar is postponed until students have some fluency in speaking and listening.

direct object The **grammatical relation** borne by a noun phrase which represents the thing most directly affected by the action of a verb. Here are some typical direct objects, in brackets: *John hit [Bill]*; *Susie kissed [Natalie]*; *Mike dropped [the glass]*; *Casanova seduced [half the women in town]*. We also regard as direct objects those noun phrases which behave grammatically in the same way, even though they don't strictly represent things that are affected by the action of the verb: *Susie plays [bridge]*; *Mike loves [cooking]*; *Lisa speaks [French]*; *I have [blue eyes]*. The presence of a direct object is what distinguishes a **transitive verb** from an **intransitive verb**. Direct objects in a given language have identifiable grammatical properties, such as position (in English, usually immediately after the verb), case-marking (not in English, but in German, Russian and Latin a direct object must take the **accusative** case), or capacity to become the subject of a **passive voice**: *Wellington defeated [Napoleon]*; *Napoleon was defeated by Wellington*.

direct speech Reporting another speaker's exact words, as in *She said "I'll come."* Compare **indirect speech**.

disability (also **disorder**) The inability to function normally, resulting from damage to muscles, the nervous system or the brain. A disability may be present at birth, or it may be acquired later through injury.

disambiguation Any procedure for selecting one of the meanings of an **ambiguous** string. For example, the ambiguous string *Visiting relatives can be a nuisance* can be disambiguated by adding a continuation, such as ... *especially when they drop in unexpectedly* or ... *especially when their houses are hard to get to.*

discontinuous constituent A **constituent** which appears in a sentence in two pieces, separated by other material which is not part of the constituent. In [*A student who speaks Abkhaz] has turned up*, the bracketed sequence is obviously a constituent (it's the subject of the sentence), but in *A student has turned up who speaks Abkhaz*, that same constituent is split into two discontinuous pieces.

discontinuity hypothesis The rejection of the **continuity hypothesis**, in either sense of that term.

discourse A continuous stretch of speech (or less commonly writing) which can reasonably be regarded as forming a unit, in that it has some kind of recognizable structure. The clearest examples of discourse are **speech events**, but an ordinary conversation may also be regarded as a discourse.

discourse analysis An approach to studying the structure of **discourse** which involves applying the existing analytical devices of linguistics (phonology, grammar, semantics) and looking for regularities in terms of these. Compare **conversation analysis**.

discovery procedure An explicit mechanical procedure for constructing a grammar from a corpus of data in some language. The **American structuralists** regarded the formulation of a discovery procedure as being a major goal of scientific linguistics; today the idea that such a thing is desirable or even possible is dismissed as a fantasy.

discreteness The property of language by which a piece of speech can be exhaustively chopped up into a sequence of linguistic units with sharp boundaries between them. This can in fact be done at several levels of analysis: an utterance can be chopped into a sequence of speech sounds (phonemes), into a sequence of morphemes, or into a sequence of words, at least.

disjunction 1. A **coordinate structure** involving *or*, as in *Would you prefer [coffee or tea?]* 2. In a linguistic rule, a statement saying "choose one"; see the example under **braces**.

disorder Another word for **disability**.

displacement The property of language which allows us to talk about things other than the here and now: about the past or the future, about places which are far away, even about hypothetical and non-existent states of affairs. With the sole exception of the **bee dance**, displacement appears to be unique to human beings.

dissimilation Any change in pronunciation in which a sound changes so as to become more different from some other nearby sound. For example, Latin *anima* 'soul' was borrowed into Basque, where it was changed to *arima*: the first nasal was dissimilated, making it more different from the second nasal. The opposite is **assimilation**.

dissyllable An old-fashioned spelling of **disyllable**.

distal Far away. The term is applied to the most distant **deictic position**, as represented by items like *that* and *there*. Compare **proximal, mesial**.

distinctive feature One of a set of simpler elements into which any speech sound can be decomposed. For example, the consonant [t] might be decomposed into features as [+ obstruent, − continuant, − friction, + voice, + coronal], meaning that it involves obstruction of the airstream, a complete closure in the mouth, no friction (hence it's a plosive), no voicing, and the raising of the front of the tongue. Several systems of distinctive features have been proposed; the one most widely used is the *SPE* **feature system**. Most (not all) systems are binary: the characteristic named by the feature is either present (+) or absent (−), and there is no third possibility. The great advantage of distinctive features is that they allow us to label **natural classes** easily: for example, the specification [+ nasal] picks out all (and only) nasal sounds, while [+ obstruent, − voice] picks out all (and only) voiceless obstruents.

distribution For a particular linguistic object or class of objects, the list of positions in which it can occur.

disyllable (also **bisyllable** and, formerly, **dissyllable**) A word containing two syllables, like *apple* or *direct*.

ditransitive verb A verb which takes two objects, such as *give*. In *She gave me a kiss*, both *me* and *a kiss* are objects of *gave*.

divergence 1. The process by which genetically related languages (languages which started off as no more than dialects of a single language) undergo different changes over time and hence become ever more different from one another, perhaps eventually to the extent that we can no longer detect their common ancestry. 2. Adjusting your speech away from that of the person you are talking to, in order to show social distance.

divine origin The conjecture that human language originated as a gift from God. No scholar takes this idea seriously today.

DO See **direct object**.

Doke, Clement A British-born South African linguist (1893–1980). Doke was a pioneer in African linguistics; he rejected much of the traditional European grammatical terminology in favour of new terms more suited to the Bantu languages he worked on.

domain 1. Of a rule, the set of structures to which that rule applies. 2. Of a node in a syntactic tree, the part of the tree lying below that node.

dominance A relation that may hold between two nodes in a syntactic tree. Node A *dominates* node B if and only if there is a continuous downward path from A to B that follows the lines in the tree – in other words, if B is a part of the constituent named by A. By convention, a node dominates itself.

Donatus A Roman grammarian (fourth century AD). His extremely influential grammars of Latin established a descriptive tradition that lasted for centuries.

donkey sentence Any sentence which contains a pronoun which can only refer to something unidentified whose existence is not even guaranteed. The classic example is *Any man who owns a donkey beats it*, in which *it* can only refer to *a donkey*, but no donkey has been identified. Such sentences present extraordinary difficulties of analysis.

dorsal A consonant articulated with the back of the tongue, such as [k] or [g].

dorsum The **back** of the tongue, the part that touches the roof of the mouth when you pronounce a [k]. **Note:** some people apply the term 'dorsum' to almost the entire upper surface of the tongue.

do-**support** The phenomenon in English of inserting the "dummy" auxiliary *do* into a sentence which has no other auxiliary but needs one. For example, the statement *She smokes* has no auxiliary, and *do* must be inserted into both the negative *She doesn't smoke* and the question *Does she smoke?*

double articulation Another name for **duality of patterning**.

double-bar category Another name for a **phrasal category**.

double-base transformation (also **generalized transformation**) In the earliest theory of **transformational grammar**, a special type of transformation which combined two smaller sentences into one larger sentence. Such transformations were abandoned from the *Aspects* **model** onwards.

double negative The popular name for what linguists call **negative concord**.

double-object construction A construction in which a single verb has two objects, as in *She gave me a kiss*.

doublet A pair of words in the same language which are both borrowed (at different times) from the same source. For example, English *castle* and *château* are both borrowed from the same French word. Larger sets exist: *hospital / hostel / hotel*; *gentile / genteel / gentle / jaunty*.

downdrift The tendency in some **tone languages** for the pitch of high tones to be lowered slightly after a low tone, so that the difference between high and low tones becomes steadily smaller during an utterance.

downgrading The use of a larger linguistic unit in a position in which a smaller one would be expected, as in the phrase *his damn-your-eyes attitude*, in which the complete sentence *damn your eyes* occurs where a lexical adjective would be expected.

drag chain One type of **chain shift**; see that entry.

Dravidian A major language family in southern India and Sri Lanka. Its best-known members are **Kannada, Malayalam, Tamil** and **Telugu**.

drift The process by which a language continues to change in the same direction over many generations.

D-structure In **Government-and-Binding theory**, the name given to the abstract underlying level of representation formerly called **deep structure**.

dual A grammatical form, found in some languages, serving to express exactly two of something and contrasting with both a singular (one) and a plural (three or more), and rarely with other forms. Classical Arabic has, for example, singular *malikun* 'a king', dual *malikani* 'two kings' and *malikuna* '(three or more) kings'. In English, the dual exists only very marginally, in such forms as *both* and *neither* (compare plural *all* and *none*).

dualism 1. A view of **semantics** which holds that there is a direct connection between linguistic forms and the non-linguistic entities and events they refer to (their **referents**). Today this view is universally rejected in favour of approaches in which the connection between forms and referents is mediated by **sense**. 2. See **mind–body dualism**.

duality of patterning (also **double articulation**) A fundamental property of human language, by which a small number of meaningless elements (the consonant and vowel **phonemes**) are variously arranged into a much larger number of meaningful elements (**morphemes** and **words**). For example, the four meaningless English phonemes /p/, /t/, /k/ and /æ/ can be arranged into /æt/ *at*, /pæt/ *pat*, /kæt/ *cat*, /tæp/ *tap*, /tæk/ *tack*, /tæt/ *tat*, /æpt/ *apt*, /ækt/ *act*, /tækt/ *tact* or *tacked*, /kæp/ *cap*, /kæpt/ *capped*, /pækt/ *pact* or *packed*, and several other items. This property is crucial, since, if every speech sound had its own meaning, we would not be able to produce more different meanings than we can produce speech sounds. Animal signalling systems generally lack this property, though **bird songs** and **whale songs** arguably contain an element of duality.

Dumézil, Georges A French linguist (1898–1986), a specialist in Indo-European and Caucasian languages and in Indo-European mythology. His famous interpretations of early Indo-European society, especially its proposed division into priests, warriors and workers, have been influential but controversial.

Dummett, Michael An English philosopher (1925–), a major contributor to the theory of meaning in language.

dummy (also **expletive**) A meaningless grammatical element which, in some language, must be inserted in certain positions to produce a well-formed result. English has at least two: the *it* of *It's raining* and *It's obvious she likes him*, and the *there* of *There's a wasp on your back*.

duration The time taken to pronounce a speech sound. The linguistic use of duration is **length**.

durative An **aspect** category which expresses an action or state perceived as lasting for some length of time.

Dutch The principal language of the Netherlands and of northern Belgium, one of the **Germanic** languages. The Belgian dialects of Dutch are sometimes called **Flemish**.

dvandva A type of compound word in which both elements are **heads** and neither modifies the other: *Austria-Hungary, tragicomic*.

dynamic tone In some **tone languages**, a **tone** which is realized by something more complex than a pitch level, such as a **contour tone** or one involving variation in duration or intensity.

dynamic verb A verb which denotes an action or an event, such as *go, kill, kiss* or *explode*. Compare **stative verb**.

dys- A prefix added to a suitable Greek root in order to name some kind of **disability**. In principle, a name coined with *dys-* represents a lesser degree of disability than one formed with **a-**, but this distinction is not always maintained.

dysarthria Another name for **anarthria**.

dyslexia (also **alexia, word blindness**) A specific type of reading disability, in which the sufferer has difficulty in recognizing and distinguishing letters and also in perceiving the order of the letters. People who exhibit this problem in childhood have *developmental dyslexia*; those who acquire it from a brain injury have *acquired dyslexia*. Dyslexia is often accompanied by *dysgraphia*, similar difficulties in writing.

dysphasia Another name for **aphasia**.

E

Early Modern English The name given to a particular period in the history of English, conventionally dated from 1450 or 1500 to 1700.

ear training The process by which students of phonetics learn to recognize and characterize speech sounds by listening to them.

Eblaite A **Semitic** language spoken in northwest Syria in the third millennium BC; written records exist from the twenty-fourth century BC, and Eblaite is one of the earliest languages for which we have written texts.

echo question A question which is a response to another utterance and which largely repeats part of that utterance. Here's an example. Susie: *I bought a Mac yesterday.* Mike: *You bought* what?

echolalia A pathological condition in which the sufferer repeats, usually without comprehension, part or all of whatever somebody else says.

economy Any of various criteria which may be invoked to evaluate a particular linguistic analysis, all of them involving a notion of 'fewness', such as using fewer phonemes, or using fewer rules, or requiring fewer exceptions, than other conceivable analyses. Economy is considered desirable. The opposing notion is **cost**.

ECP See **empty category principle**.

edition A published version of an ancient text, often with notes and comments added by the editor, and sometimes also with suggested corrections and additions, if the text used is corrupt or defective.

educational linguistics A broad label covering the scrutiny, planning and reform of all aspects of language in education in the light of the insights of those trained in linguistics, including such topics as the teaching and learning of both the mother tongue and foreign languages and the structure and content of language and linguistics degrees and their suitability for particular vocations and post-graduate programmes.

EFL See **TEFL**.

egocentrism 1. The inability to recognize that other individuals are distinct from oneself and hence that cooperative behaviour is necessary. This is said to be a characteristic of very young children, who are therefore obliged to learn, among other things, how to conduct a conversation. 2. The property of a **deictic system** by which the reference points are always the speaker and the moment of speaking.

egressive airstream mechanism Any way of producing a stream of air for speaking in which the air flows out of the mouth. The **pulmonic, glottalic** and **velaric airstream mechanisms** can all produce egressive air, but only the first and second are known to be used for linguistic purposes.

Egyptian The language of the ancient Kingdom of Egypt, constituting a separate branch of the **Afro-Asiatic** family. Egyptian is abundantly recorded from about 3000 BC, and is one of the very first languages for which we have written texts.

The language was written in a remarkable system called **hieroglyphs**; since its decipherment by **Champollion** in the nineteenth century, we have been able to read the texts. The language survived well into the Christian era, its later forms being called **Coptic**.

ejective A consonant produced with a **glottalic egressive airstream mechanism**, such as [k']. Such consonants are rare in Europe, but common in some languages of the Caucasus and of North America.

elaborated code A style of language which uses a wide range of grammatical structures, which is capable of a very great degree of explicitness, which is highly effective in communicating with others with whom one has little experience in common, and which is acquired only through extensive formal education. According to the **deficit hypothesis**, use of this style is confined to middle-class and upper-class speakers, and is denied to working-class speakers. Compare **restricted code**.

elaboration (also **language development**) Taking a language which has previously been used only for certain purposes and introducing changes (such as new vocabulary) that will allow it to be used for a much wider range of purposes, such as (for example) writing laws and trying court cases, talking about car engines, and writing about physics and linguistics. This is usually a central part of **language planning**.

Elamite An extinct language formerly spoken in southwestern Iran and attested in writing from about the twenty-third to the fourth century BC. We can read the texts. Elamite is usually regarded as related to no other languages, though some have argued vigorously for connecting it to **Dravidian**.

E-language A language regarded as a set of possible sentences. Compare **I-language**.

elative In certain **case** languages, a case expressing the meaning 'out of'.

elicitation The process of gaining information about an unfamiliar language by asking native speakers questions which are carefully designed to bring out the required information.

elision The omission of sounds in connected speech, as when *fish and chips* is reduced to *fish 'n' chips*.

ELIZA A famous computer program which makes apparently sensible responses to questions and statements typed in in English by a human user, so that the user almost seems to be discussing things with the program.

ellipsis The omission from an utterance of some material which is strictly required to complete the sentence but which can be recovered from the context. In the exchange *Seems we have a problem. – Yes, we have*, the first utterance shows ellipsis of *it* and the second of *a problem*.

elocution The art of effective public speaking, or training in this.

embedded question (also **indirect question**) A **question** which is not being asked directly, but which is a smaller part of a larger sentence. Examples (in brackets): *I don't know [where she is]*; *Try to find out [if anybody has seen her]*. Compare **headless relative clause**.

embedding Any structure in which a constituent is contained within a larger constituent of the same kind. For example, the noun phrase *the book on the table* contains the smaller noun phrase *the table* embedded within it.

Emeneau, Murray A Canadian-born American linguist (1904–). A student of Edward **Sapir**, Emeneau has made substantial contributions to many areas, including Sanskrit, Indo-European, Dravidian and native American languages; he is particularly known for his work on **linguistic areas**.

emergence In child language acquisition, the first appearance of a form or structure, which may be long before that form or structure is mastered fully and used consistently.

emergent Not evolving from simpler early stages in the usual way; appearing suddenly in its fully developed form when certain critical requirements are in place. Life itself is often thought to be an emergent property, and there are people who maintain that language is an emergent characteristic which suddenly appeared when the organization of the brain had reached a critical stage, instead of developing from simple beginnings through stages of increasing complexity.

emic Of a description, focusing on the relations existing between the elements in a system. For example, an emic account of English [b] would note that [b] contrasts with various other speech sounds, such as [p], [d] and [m]. Compare **etic**.

empty category principle (**ECP**) A fundamental principle of **Government-and-Binding Theory**; it states: a trace must be properly governed. In practice, the ECP places heavy restrictions on the ability of parts of a sentence to be moved to other positions, and thus it prevents the grammar from generating large amounts of rubbish.

empty morph A piece of morphological material which has no identifiable meaning or function. For example, in Basque *mendietan* 'in the mountains', *mendi* is 'mountain', *-e-* is the plural marker, and *-n* is 'in', leaving *-ta-* unassigned as an empty morph.

empty word Another name for a **grammatical word**.

enclitic A **clitic** which is phonologically attached to what precedes it, such as *-n't* in *couldn't*. Compare **proclitic**.

encoding A metaphor for the **production** of speech.

endangered language A language which, because of political and social pressures and/or a small number of speakers, is in danger of becoming extinct in the near future. It is thought that over 3000 of the world's 6500 or so languages will become extinct in the course of the twenty-first century.

endearment A word or phrase intended to show affection, such as *darling* or *sweetie*.

endocentric Of a constituent, having a distribution similar to that of its own **head**, at least in principle. For example, the noun phrase *these new books* is endocentric, since it has a similar distribution to that of *books*: *Books are expensive*; *These new books are expensive*. Compare **exocentric**.

eng Another name for **angma**.

English The principal language of Britain, Ireland, Canada, the USA, Australia,

New Zealand and parts of the West Indies, also widely spoken in South Africa, the Indian subcontinent, all the former British and American colonies and elsewhere. With around 350 million native speakers and an unknown but huge number of people who speak it as a second language, English ranks only behind Mandarin Chinese in numbers, but it is unquestionably the world's premier language for diplomacy, business, science, technology, navigation and air traffic control, popular culture, and almost everything else. English is a **Germanic** language which developed originally from the speech of the Anglo-Saxons who invaded Britain from the Continent around the fifth century AD, but it has been heavily influenced by French and Latin and it has undergone some dramatic changes in pronunciation, vocabulary and grammar; consequently, it is now rather atypical among the Germanic languages and among European languages generally.

English First A political movement in the USA which seeks to make English the sole official language of the country and to deny non-speakers of English the right to use their own languages in all or most official contexts or in education. Few linguists have any sympathy with the movement.

entailment A possible relation between two statements. When we say "A entails B", we mean that, if A is true, then B must be true. For example, the statement *Booth assassinated Lincoln* entails both *Somebody killed Lincoln* and *Lincoln is dead*. Entailment does not survive negation: the negated sentence *Booth did not assassinate Lincoln* does not entail either of these things. Compare **presupposition, conversational implicature**.

environment For any piece of speech, the other pieces of speech which immediately precede and follow it. For example, the /p/ in *spit* is preceded by an /s/ in the same syllable and followed by a stressed vowel; this is (a large part of) its environment.

EPD (in full, the *English Pronouncing Dictionary*) A **pronouncing dictionary** of British English, edited by Daniel **Jones** and appearing in many editions; it has since been supplanted by **LPD**. The particular system of transcription used in the book is called the *EPD transcription*; this has given way to the revised version developed by A. C. **Gimson**.

epenthesis The insertion of a segment into the middle of a word, as when Old English *æmtig* became *empty*, or when *prince* is pronounced like *prints* or *film* as 'fillum'. When the segment inserted is a vowel, we speak of **anaptyxis** or **svarabhakti**.

epiglottis A spoon-shaped cartilage below and behind the tongue; in most other mammals, it serves to seal off the windpipe during eating and drinking, but the human epiglottis is ineffectual at this.

epigraphy The study of ancient inscriptions on hard materials like stone and metal. Compare **palaeography**.

epiphenomenon A phenomenon which, on the surface, looks like a single unitary phenomenon, but which is actually the more-or-less accidental result of the interaction of several independent principles. **Chomsky** has suggested that any given human language is an epiphenomenon, being nothing more than the result of the interaction of the principles of **universal grammar** plus some **parameter** settings.

epistemic modality The type of **modality** concerned with knowledge and belief, exemplified by *Susie must be here* when this means 'No other conclusion is possible'. Compare **alethic modality, deontic modality**.

epithet A descriptive word or phrase added to a person's name, as in *William the Conqueror, King John Lackland* or *Richard Lionheart*. Many **surnames** derive from medieval epithets like *Brown* and *Miller*. Compare **sobriquet**.

eponym The name of a person whose name is given to a place, or of a character whose name is given to a literary work. The name of the emperor *Constantine* is the eponym of *Constantinople*, and *Tristram Shandy* is the eponymous hero of the novel of the same name.

equational sentence A sentence which asserts that something is identical to something else: *Paris is the capital of France*; *The Sinclair Spectrum was the first commercial personal computer*; *Boris Yeltsin is the president of Russia*. An equational sentence can be turned round: *The capital of France is Paris*. Compare **ascriptive sentence**.

equi-NP deletion Another name for a construction involving **control**.

equi-verb Another name for a **control verb**.

ergative In an **ergative language**, the **case** used to mark the subject of a transitive verb. See the examples under **absolutive**.

ergative language A language in which **ergativity** is prominent, such as Basque, the Eskimo languages, and many of the languages of the Caucasus, New Guinea, Australia and the Pacific.

ergative verb A verb which can be used either intransitively, with a patient as subject, or transitively, with a patient as object and an agent as subject. An example is *sink*, as in *The boat sank* and *The sub sank the boat*; others are *melt, open, boil* and *blow up*. **Note:** this term is inaccurate and objectionable, but it is widely used.

ergativity A grammatical system in which the subjects of intransitive verbs and the direct objects of transitive verbs are treated identically, while the subjects of transitive verbs are treated differently. Ergativity may be *morphological* (expressed in case-marking or verbal agreement) or *syntactic* (expressed in such syntactic phenomena as the ability of noun phrases to be coordinated or their ability to participate in **control**).

error analysis The study of the systematic errors which are made by a person learning a foreign language as a result of imperfect knowledge of that language.

error data The data available to linguists from the examination of **speech errors**, and also from errors of reading, writing and comprehending.

-ese A suffix used to label a distinctive way of speaking or writing. Some languages are named this way, like *Chinese* and *Japanese*, but we speak also of *motherese* (the kind of speech used by mothers talking to babies) and *journalese* (the style of language used by journalists). Compare **-speak**.

Eskimo-Aleut A language family occupying Greenland, northern Canada, much of Alaska and the eastern tip of Siberia. There are two Eskimo languages, *Inuit* and *Yupik*, both with considerable dialectal variation, while *Aleut* is more distantly related. All these languages exhibit a great deal of **incorporation**, and hence they are **polysynthetic languages** (in the broad sense of the term). The popular notion that the Eskimo languages have vast numbers of words for different kinds of snow is quite false.

ESL See **TESL**.

esophagic Another spelling of **oesophagic**.

esophagus Another spelling of **oesophagus**.

ESP (in full, *English for Special Purposes*) An approach to the teaching of English as a foreign language which focuses on teaching the kind of English required for a particular professional purpose, such as law, medicine or aviation.

Esperanto The best-known **artificial language**, invented and published in 1887 by Dr L. L. Zamenhof, a Polish oculist. Esperanto has an absolutely regular morphology; otherwise, it has a fairly typical European grammatical structure, except that it has no grammatical gender and no classes of nouns or verbs. The oft-repeated statement that the language has "only sixteen grammatical rules" is quite false. An international organization promotes the use of Esperanto as an auxiliary language among the peoples of the world.

essive In some **case** languages, a case-form expressing the temporary state or character of some entity, such as Finnish *poikana* 'as a boy' (*poika* 'boy').

EST See **Extended Standard Theory**.

Estonian The major language of Estonia, a **Finno-Ugric** language closely related to Finnish.

Estuary English A range of accents heard in southeastern England and falling somewhere between **Cockney** and **Received Pronunciation**.

eth The character ð, used to represent a voiced dental fricative in the IPA and in the orthography of Icelandic (where its capital version is Ð); it was also sometimes used in Old English to write the (single) dental fricative, but it has been replaced by th. Compare **theta**.

ethnography of speaking An anthropological approach to speech which focuses upon the social role of speech in a community or within a particular social group. Proponents examine such issues as the social functions of speech and the manner in which social roles are expressed in speaking.

ethnomethodology A variety of sociology which avoids appeals to pre-existing theoretical concepts and which instead focuses on the techniques ("methods") used by people engaging in social interaction. Its chief linguistic application is **conversation analysis**.

etic Of a description, focusing on the physical form of linguistic units. For example, an etic description of English [b] might note that it is a voiced bilabial plosive. Compare **emic**.

Etruscan A dead language formerly spoken in northern Italy and recorded in texts from about the seventh to the first centuries BC. Written in an offshoot of the Greek alphabet, the Etruscan texts are mostly brief and repetitive, and we can read them only to a limited extent. There is no evidence that Etruscan is related to any other language at all. The language was displaced by **Latin** after its speakers were incorporated into the Roman state.

etymological dictionary A book which lists the words of a language together with explanations of their origins. The most important such dictionaries of English are those of Partridge, of Onions and of Klein.

etymological fallacy The mistaken belief that the "true" meaning of a word is what it meant long ago, rather than what it means now. For example, *impertinent* formerly meant 'irrelevant', but today it means 'impudent, insolent', and it is a fallacy to claim that the "real" meaning of the word is 'irrelevant'.

etymology 1. The origin and history of a particular word. 2. The branch of linguistics dealing with the origins and histories of words.

etymon (plural **etyma**) An ancestral form of a word. For example, English *knee* derives from Old English *cnēo*, which derives from Proto-Germanic **kniwam*, which derives from Proto-Indo-European **gneu-*; any one of these older forms is an etymon of *knee*. Compare **reflex**.

euphemism A polite and rather indirect expression used in place of a more direct expression which is considered vulgar or painful: *make love* for 'copulate', *pass away* for 'die', *powder one's nose* for 'urinate'.

euphony Attractiveness of sound.

Eurasiatic A hypothetical super-family of languages recently proposed by Joseph **Greenberg** and including the Indo-European, Uralic, Altaic, Chukchi-Kamchatkan and Eskimo-Aleut families plus Korean, Japanese, Ainu and Gilyak. Greenberg has not yet published his evidence, but the proposal is already deeply controversial. The proposed Eurasiatic family largely overlaps the **Nostratic hypothesis** proposed by other scholars, and a few linguists use the two names interchangeably, which is unwise.

Eve hypothesis Another name for the **African Eve hypothesis**.

Evenki A major language of Siberia, belonging to the **Tungusic** branch of the **Altaic** family. Evenki was formerly called *Tungus*.

evidential A (usually obligatory) grammatical marker found in some languages which expresses the evidence which the speaker has for making a statement. In such a language, English *She came home last night* may have several different translations, each carrying additional information such as "I saw her myself", "Somebody told me" or "I have inferred this from evidence".

evolution of language 1. The almost completely unknown series of stages by which the (presumably very primitive) earliest ancestral speech developed into the elaborate language abilities of modern humans. 2. In the view called **stadialism**, the series of stages through which every language supposedly passes. 3. A term occasionally applied to **language change**, or at least to the more gradual types of change.

Ewe An important language of west Africa, a **Kwa** language.

exaptation A type of language change in which some (especially morphological) material which has lost its former function acquires a new function. For example, when the old Basque ablative case-suffix *-ik* was replaced by new ablative formations, *-ik* did not disappear from the language but was instead pressed into service as a partitive marker.

exception A particular item or construction which is inconsistent with some rule. For example, *men* is an exception to the rule that English nouns form their plurals in -*s*, and *go* is an exception to the rule that intransitive verbs cannot be passivized: *She is gone*.

exchange error Another name for a **transposition**.

exclamation An utterance which chiefly serves to express emotion, such as *What a pity!*, *No way!* or *How lucky you are!* In English, an exclamation which is a complete sentence, like the last example, has a distinctive grammatical form.

exclusive first person A pronoun or verb form, found in some languages, which means 'I and somebody else, not including you'. Compare **inclusive first person**.

excrescence The addition of a consonant to the end of a word, as when *vermin* becomes *varmint* or *no* becomes *nope*.

existential sentence A type of sentence in which the existence or non-existence of something is asserted, either in general or in a specified location: *There are no unicorns*; *There's a wasp on your back*. Many languages use a special construction for this purpose, as does English, with its *there is* construction.

exocentric Of a constituent, having a distribution very different from that of its own **head**. For example, the category *sentence* is exocentric, since its head (variously taken in different frameworks as its verb or as an abstract category) does not appear in the positions in which a sentence can appear. Compare **endocentric**.

exocentric compound Another name for a **bahuvrihi**.

exotic language A language which is, superficially at least, very different in structure from your own language. To an English-speaker, the languages of the Amazon or of Australia might seem very exotic, but of course to speakers of these other languages it is English which is exotic. As the linguist John Lyons once remarked, "Every language is exotic."

expansion 1. The process of separating a **rule schema** into the several different rules it abbreviates. 2. An adult's enlarged version of a child's utterance, as when the child's *Daddy shoe* is expanded to *Yes, Daddy is putting his shoes on*. Compare **recast**.

experiencer The **semantic role** expressed by a noun phrase representing a person who undergoes a mental or emotional experience, such as *Lisa* in *Lisa has a headache* and *Lisa is happy*.

experimental paradox A problem affecting experimental work in linguistics and psychology: the more realistic the setting of the experiment is, the more factors are beyond control; the tighter the control of the experiment, the less realistic it is.

expletive 1. Another name for a **dummy**. 2. A swear word.

expletive infixation The curious process in English by which a swear word is inserted into the middle of another word, as in *fan-fuckin-tastic* and the classic *down in Tumba-bloody-Rumba shootin' kanga-bloody-roos*.

exponent A piece of morphological material which expresses some grammatical information. For example, the -*ed* of *walked* is an exponent of past tense.

expression Another name for **form**. Compare **content**.

expressive Pertaining to the expression of an individual's emotions or personality.

expressive aphasia Any type of **aphasia** which primarily affects speech **production**. Compare **receptive aphasia**.

Extended Standard Theory (**EST**) The version of **transformational grammar** which was current around 1972–7, replacing the earlier **Standard Theory** and giving way in turn to the **Revised Extended Standard Theory**.

extension The set of all objects in the real or conceptual world to which some linguistic expression may refer. For example, the extension of *cow* is the set of all cows. Compare **intension**.

external evidence In studying the history of a language, evidence which is not linguistic in nature: archaeological data, comments about the language in historical documents written in another language, and so on. Compare **internal evidence**.

external history For a particular language, a historical account of its origins, of when, where and by whom it was spoken, and of the nature of the written records available in it, sometimes accompanied by a history of its speakers and of the social and political forces to which the language has been subjected. Compare **internal history**.

extraction Moving some element of a sentence out of its normal or logical position into some other position, particularly when this results in an **unbounded dependency**; see the examples under this last entry.

extralinguistic Pertaining to any aspect of the world other than language.

extraposition Any construction in which some constituent of a sentence which "logically" belongs somewhere else is put at the end of the sentence. Thus, *I bought a book about hamsters this morning* has an extraposed form *I bought a book this morning about hamsters*, and *A friend who I hadn't seen for years turned up this morning* has an extraposed form *A friend turned up this morning who I hadn't seen for years*.

extrinsic ordering In a linguist's description of a language, a statement that certain rules must apply in a certain order which is asserted by the linguist purely in order to get the right result, without invoking any general principles. Compare **intrinsic ordering**.

eye dialect In writing, the use of non-standard spellings to indicate the use of non-standard speech: *wuz* for *was*, *sez* for *says*, *massa* for *master*.

eye rhyme Two words which look as if they ought to rhyme, but don't: *move/love*, *great/meat*.

F

face Your public self-image. Face is what you lose when you are embarrassed or humiliated in public. We can distinguish your *positive face* (your need to maintain your membership of a social group) from your *negative face* (your need to be individual and independent). A *face-threatening act* is any piece of behaviour (including speech) which can easily make another person lose face; a *face-saving act* is any piece of behaviour which lessens or removes the threat of losing face. **Politeness** is largely a linguistic technique for preserving face.

factive verb A verb which presupposes the truth of what follows it, such as *realize*. The sentence *Susie realizes that Cecil is married* only makes sense if Cecil is married.

false friends (also *faux amis*) Two words in different languages which have similar forms but different meanings, such as English *library* and French *librairie* 'bookshop'.

falsetto A distinctive **phonation type**, in which the vocal folds are stretched tightly and the pitch of the voice is much higher than normal.

family of languages See **language family**.

family resemblance The connection among the various meanings of a single word, especially when there seems to be no possibility of writing a single definition that will cover all of them. Consider *lose*, for example: *She lost her toothbrush/temper/balance/parents/virginity/game of chess*.

family tree A diagram, in the form of a tree, representing the structure of a **language family**. The languages which are most closely related are grouped together as branches of the tree.

Fant, Gunnar A Swedish speech scientist (1919–), best known for his work on speech synthesis, on the acoustic theory of speech production, and, with Morris **Halle** and Roman **Jakobson**, on the development of **distinctive features**.

Faroese The **Germanic** language of the Faroe Islands, closely related to Icelandic.

Farsi Another name for **Persian**.

faux amis Another name for **false friends**.

feature See **distinctive feature**.

feature matrix (also **complex symbol**) A combination of **distinctive features** (in phonology) or of **syntactic features** (in syntax), with **values** assigned. For example, the matrix [+ vowel, − back] can be used to pick out the set of **front vowels** in a language, while [+ vowel, − back, + high, − round] might be used to pick out the vowel /i/ in a language which also has /y/ (hence the need for the feature specification [− round]).

feedback The process by which you can hear your own speech through the air and through the bones of the head. Feedback is essential in maintaining proper control over speech.

felicity conditions The conditions which must be satisfied for a particular utterance to be appropriate and effective. For example, the utterance *I now pronounce you husband and wife* has no effect unless a number of obvious conditions are met.

feminine In certain languages with **gender**, a conventional name for a gender class showing some degree of correlation with female sex. Not all gender languages have such a gender class.

feral child (also **wild child**) A child whose childhood has largely been spent in isolation from ordinary human contact and especially from human language, such as **Victor** or **Genie**.

Ferguson, Charles An American linguist (1921–). Ferguson has made major contributions to several areas, including east Asian languages, child language acquisition, applied linguistics and sociolinguistics; perhaps his single best-known innovation is the the concept of **diglossia**.

Festschrift A book published to commemorate the achievements of a distinguished scholar and containing scholarly papers contributed by the honouree's former students and colleagues.

Fick, August A German linguist (1833–1916), known for his work on the phonology and etymology of the Indo-European languages.

fieldwork The activity of collecting data on a language from its native speakers on their home ground.

figure of speech The use of language in a non-literal way, often in order to draw a comparison. Many different types are recognized, such as **simile**, **metaphor**, **metonymy** and **synecdoche**.

filter 1. Any device which allows certain frequencies of sound to pass through while blocking the passage of other frequencies. 2. In some theories of grammar, a formal device which "checks" the sentences generated by the grammar to see if they satisfy a certain requirement and rejects as ungrammatical any which do not.

filtered speech Speech which has been passed through a **filter** (sense 1), thereby removing certain frequencies from it. For example, speech heard over a telephone line is filtered, since the telephone line removes the higher frequencies.

fine-tuning hypothesis The hypothesis that adults speaking to children carefully use only grammatical structures which the children can cope with. This hypothesis is now rejected.

finger spelling Any of various systems for spelling out words one letter at a time by using different arrangements of the fingers to represent the letters of the alphabet. Compare **sign language**.

finite (also **tensed**) A label applied to a **verb** which is fully marked for whatever **tense** and **agreement** is typical of the language under discussion, or to a **clause** containing such a verb. English, with its sparse **inflectional morphology**, is not the ideal language for illustrating the distinction between finite and **non-finite** verb-forms, but consider these examples: *Susie smokes*; *Susie enjoys smoking*; *Susie started to smoke when she was fifteen*. Here *smokes*, *enjoys* and *started* (and also *was*) are finite forms, while *smoking* and *smoke* are non-finite. The problem with English is that finite and non-finite forms are often identical: in

Most of my friends smoke, the verb *smoke* is finite, but in *Most of my friends don't smoke*, the form *smoke* is non-finite (the finite form here is the *do* of *don't*).

finite-state grammar (also **regular grammar**) A very simple type of **formal grammar** which is exactly equivalent to a **transition network**.

Finnish The major language of Finland, a **Finno-Ugric** language.

Finno-Ugric The largest branch of the **Uralic** family of languages, divided into the *Finnic* languages like Finnish, Estonian and Saami and the *Ugric* languages like Hungarian.

First Germanic Consonant Shift The formal name for **Grimm's Law**.

First Grammatical Treatise A grammatical study of Old Icelandic written in the twelfth century AD; its anonymous author, known as the *First Grammarian*, displayed some remarkably advanced views on phonology.

first person The category of **person** including reference to the speaker and possibly others associated with the speaker. The English first-person pronouns are *I* and *we*. See **inclusive** and **exclusive first person**.

Firth, J. R. An influential British linguist (1890–1960), the holder of the first chair in linguistics in Britain. Firth's contributions were mainly in semantics, where he developed the notion of **context of situation**, and in phonology, in which he introduced **Prosodic Analysis**. Firth's influence upon British linguistics has been profound; his ideas have been greatly elaborated by M. A. K. **Halliday**.

Fishman, Joshua An American sociolinguist (1926–), widely regarded as the founder of the sociology of language.

fis phenomenon (also *wabbit* **phenomenon**) The phenomenon in which a young child who cannot pronounce a word in the adult manner none the less rejects imitations of her/his own pronunciation by adults. Thus, a child who says *fis* or *wabbit* for 'fish' or 'rabbit' will refuse to accept the same pronunciation from adults. This observation is commonly believed to show that the child's perception is ahead of its production.

fixed reference A property of all known systems of **animal communication**: each individual **call** has a fixed meaning, which cannot be altered or modified in any way, and two calls cannot be combined to produce a new or more complex meaning. Human languages are not like this at all.

flap A consonant produced by moving the tongue or the lower lip rapidly from one position to another, so that it briefly strikes something else along the way. Compare **tap**. **Note:** many people use the terms 'flap' and 'tap' interchangeably; this is not recommended.

Flemish A name sometimes given to the non-standard dialects of **Dutch** spoken in Belgium and northern France. **Note:** this label was formerly applied to the Dutch of Belgium generally, but no longer.

flexion Another form of **inflection**.

flouting the maxims Violating the **maxims of conversation** at a superficial level in order to be cooperative at a deeper level. For example, if a prospective employer asks Mike's PhD supervisor "What kind of scholar is Mike?", and the supervisor replies "Well, he's a very nice fellow and everyone likes him", the supervisor is flouting the maxims of Relevance (he's apparently not answering the question) and Quantity (he's apparently not providing enough information), but he is still communicating effectively.

fluency Smooth and rapid use of language, especially speech.

fluent aphasia Any type of **aphasia** in which speech is rapid and effortless (though not necessarily sensible), such as **Wernicke's aphasia** or **jargon aphasia**.

focus Special prominence which is given to some element in a sentence to mark it as expressing the most important new information or to contrast it with something else. In English, we do this either by stressing the focused element (*I met my wife IN LONDON*) or by using a **cleft sentence** (*It was in London that I met my wife*). Some other languages use word order for this purpose.

focusing A reduction in **variation** in the language of a speech community which results, not from official intervention or formal **language planning**, but only from the spontaneous preferences of speakers.

Fodor, Jerry An American linguist and philosopher (1935–), best known for his work on the relation between language and mind.

folk etymology An arbitrary change in the form of a word to make it seem more transparent or more familiar, as when French *écrevisse* was changed into English *crayfish*, or when *asparagus* is changed into *sparrowgrass*.

folk linguistics Uninformed speculation or mythology about the origin and nature of human language or of one's own language, or of its place in human affairs. The **Tower of Babel** myth is a famous example.

folk taxonomy The conventional and (in principle) unscientific classification of animals and plants (and sometimes other things) into categories in some particular language or language variety.

foot 1. The basic unit of rhythm in poetry, generally consisting of two or more syllables of which one bears the main stress. 2. A somewhat similar unit of rhythm in speech, recognized by some theories of phonology.

foregrounding Any process for making something into the most central and prominent figure during a certain stretch of discourse.

foreign accent syndrome An informal label for a pathological condition in which a person who has suffered a head injury begins speaking her/his native language with what sounds to listeners like an identifiable foreign accent – for English-speakers, most often a German or Scandinavian accent. Research has shown, however, that such people do not have true foreign accents, but only mild disturbances of their pronunciation which remind others of particular foreign accents.

foreigner talk The rather distinctive style of speech you use in talking to a foreigner who does not speak your language very well.

forensic phonetics The use of phonetics in criminal investigations, especially in trying to identify the sex, age and geographical background of a person whose voice is recorded and hence in identifying the speaker.

form (also **expression**) The physical shape assumed by a linguistic unit, as opposed to its **content** or **function**.

formal 1. Pertaining to linguistic forms, and not to their meanings or functions. 2. Fully explicit and mechanical; leaving nothing to be filled in by human beings. This is the sense of the term in phrases like **formal grammar** and **formal semantics**. 3. A label applied to a style of language which is considered appropriate in situations in which we are being highly conscious of the impression we are making on other people, such as when we are writing an essay or being interviewed for a job.

formal grammar A fully explicit device which specifies, for a given initial set of elements (the 'vocabulary' or 'alphabet'), the complete set of strings of those elements which are in the language defined by the grammar. This is the form normally taken by a **generative grammar**, in the traditional and restrictive sense of this term.

formalization The process of expressing a description or analysis of language data as a **formal grammar**, or as a part of one.

formal language A language generated by a **formal grammar**.

formal logic Any system which provides exact mathematical representations for (some of) the sentences of a language and rules for manipulating these so as to allow valid conclusions to be drawn. The simplest such system is *propositional logic*; a somewhat more elaborate system is *predicate logic*.

formal semantics Any approach to **semantics** which provides an explicit mechanical procedure for determining the meanings of complex linguistic expressions (such as sentences) in terms of the meanings of the simpler expressions of which it is composed (such as words). The most influential type of formal semantics is **Montague semantics**.

formal universal A **universal** of language which says something about the form a grammar can take. Compare **substantive universal**.

formant A narrow band of frequencies in which the vocal tract, when it is in some particular configuration, resonates strongly, so that those frequencies are prominent in the resulting speech sound. Formants show up as dark bands in a sound spectrogram and are very useful in identifying the speech sounds being produced. They are most prominent with vowels, less prominent with nasals and resonants, and more or less invisible with obstruents.

formative A **morpheme**, sometimes especially one which plays a part in syntax, such as the English possessive marker -'s.

form class Any class of items in a language which have common morphological characteristics – for example, the class of English nouns, or the class of Spanish verbs with stems in -a-.

form word Another name for a **grammatical word**.

fortis Of a speech sound, articulated with greater force or muscular tension than another speech sound which is otherwise similar. The opposite is **lenis**.

fortition (also **strengthening**) Any phonological process in which some segment becomes more "consonant-like". An example is the strengthening of the glide [j] into some kind of fricative, affricate or plosive in most varieties of Basque. The opposite is **lenition**.

fossilized form A particular word or construction in a language which preserves an ancient linguistic feature which has otherwise been generally lost from the language, but which is nevertheless in everyday use and not regarded as an **archaism**. English examples include *if I were you*, *so be it*, and *she is gone*.

Foucault, Michel A French philosopher and sociologist (1926–84) who wrote extensively about language; he is perhaps especially known for developing the concept of a "fellowship of discourse" among the members of a social group.

Foundation for Endangered Languages An international organization, based in Britain, which offers support to small linguistic communities and combats prejudice toward **minority languages**.

founder effect The widespread occurrence of some linguistic feature in the languages of some area, resulting from the fact that that feature was prominent in the language(s) spoken by the small group of people who originally settled the area. Some people have also suggested that all languages might retain founder effects from the ancestral speech of all humankind, "frozen accidents" which are not cognitively necessary but which have simply persisted.

Fowler, Henry An English grammarian and lexicographer (1858–1933), best known for his 1926 book *Modern English Usage*, long considered the bible of good English usage.

frame 1. A sentence with a blank space in it, used in a **slot-and-filler** approach to describing languages; see the examples under that entry. 2. A mental picture of some area of knowledge. For example, if you hear the word *car*, you immediately activate your mental picture of a typical car, and so you can easily make sense of an utterance like *Susie's car has a rear engine*. Compare **script** (sense 2).

francophone French-speaking.

Franglais An informal label for a style of French which is very heavily influenced by English.

free morpheme A **morpheme** which can stand alone to make a word by itself, such as *girl*, *happy*, *this*, *with* or *explain*. Note that a free morpheme may be combined with other morphemes in a single word: *girls*, *happier*, *explained*.

free relative clause Another name for a **headless relative clause**.

free variation The state of affairs in which either of two (or more) sounds or forms may be used in a particular position without changing the meaning and without producing anything strange. For example, the final /p/ of *Stop!* may be glottalized or not, and unreleased or not: it makes no difference. The word *economics* may be pronounced with /i: / or /e/ in the first syllable. The comparative of *common* may be *commoner* or *more common*.

free word order 1. The phenomenon, occurring in certain languages, by which the individual words in a sentence or a clause may be placed in any order whatever, without changing the meaning and without producing an ungrammatical result. 2. A similar phenomenon, occurring in certain languages, by which the individual *phrases* may be placed in any order. This second case is more properly called *free phrase order*, but 'free word order' is unfortunately usual.

Frege, Gottlob A German philosopher and logician (1848–1925), the founder of formal logic and a major influence upon the development of **semantics**.

French The chief language of France, of Luxembourg, of parts of Belgium and Switzerland and of Quebec, also widely spoken in the former French colonies and elsewhere. Until a few decades ago, French was the world's premier language for diplomacy and high culture, but it has now been largely displaced from these roles by English, though English itself makes heavy use of French words and phrases in these areas. French is a **Romance** language which was substantially influenced by the Germanic language of the Franks, who conquered Gaul (France) in the early Middle Ages.

frequency 1. The number of complete cycles (oscillations) performed by a given wave per unit of time, commonly expressed in Hertz (cycles per second). The higher the frequency of a sound wave, the higher the **pitch** perceived, though the relation is not linear (doubling the frequency does not double the pitch). A speech sound, of course, consists of a mixture of frequencies, some more prominent than others. 2. The number of times some linguistic unit occurs in speech in comparison with other units. For example, /d/ is far more frequent in English than is /ð/.

frequency effect The observation that, during the comprehension of speech or writing, more frequent words are recognized more quickly than less frequent ones.

frequentative Another name for **iterative**.

Freudian slip A **speech error** with overt sexual content, such as *white Anglo-Saxon prostitute* for 'white Anglo-Saxon Protestant', or *Your thesis needs orgasmic unity* (intended 'organic unity'). The label derives from an idea of the psychoanalyst Sigmund Freud that such slips reveal underlying sexual anxieties; this interpretation is controversial.

fricative A speech sound which is produced by forcing the airstream through a small aperture somewhere in the vocal tract, usually in the mouth; the obstruction produces friction noise. Examples are [f], [v], [θ], [s] and [z]. The voiceless vowel [h] is sometimes classed as a fricative.

friction Noise produced when the air passing out of the mouth during speech encounters some kind of obstacle.

frictionless continuant An older name for an **approximant**.

Fries, Charles An American linguist (1887–1967), a prominent member of the **American structuralists**. He worked on English grammar, lexicography and language teaching, but he is particularly known for his attacks on **prescriptivism** and for the highly original description of English grammar presented in his book *The Structure of English*.

Frisian A **Germanic** language spoken in the northern Netherlands, in north-western Germany and on several islands along the North Sea coast. Frisian is sometimes said to be the closest relative of English.

Friulian A **Rhaeto-Romance** language spoken in northeastern Italy.

Fromkin, Victoria An American linguist and phonetician (1923–). Coming to linguistics late, Fromkin is known for her work in phonetics and phonology, on neuroscience and above all on speech errors; she was also deeply involved with **Genie**. Co-author of the world's most successful introductory textbook of linguistics, she is a prominent and forceful spokesperson for the subject.

front The forward part of the upper surface of the tongue, usually (but not always) excluding the **tip** and the **blade**.

fronting 1. Any change in pronunciation in which a vowel moves forward in the mouth, as when [u] becomes [y]. 2. Another term for **preposing**.

front vowel A vowel during whose production the highest part of the tongue lies toward the front of the mouth, such as [i], [y], [e] or [a].

Fry, D. B. A British phonetician (1907–83). A student of Daniel **Jones**, Fry is well known for his work in acoustic and instrumental phonetics, in speech science generally and in educating the deaf.

Fula (also **Fulani**) A major language of several west African countries, a **Niger-Congo** language.

full word Another name for a **content word**.

function The job done by a linguistic element. The term is most often applied to the effect of a **grammatical morpheme** or **grammatical word** such as the connecting word *of* and the *-ing* which goes on to verbs in English. These things chiefly provide the grammatical "glue" which gives structure to sentences, but they don't have meanings in the sense that **lexical morphemes** like *green* and *woman* have meanings. Compare **form**.

functionalism An approach to the description of languages which attaches great importance to the uses to which language is put. In practice, this term is applied to a wide variety of different approaches, some of which are 'functional' only in a very vague sense.

functional load The number of words (especially common words) which are distinguished in pronunciation only by the contrast between two particular phonemes. For example, the /p/–/b/ contrast has a high functional load in English, since dozens of word pairs are distinguished by it: *pare/bare, pit/bit, pack/back, maple/Mabel, copper/cobber, scrapple/scrabble, nipple/nibble, lap/lab, tap/tab, cup/cub*, and many others. But the /d/–/ð/ contrast has a low functional load, since it distinguishes only a few pairs of words: *den/then, udder/other, side/scythe*, and a very few others.

functional morpheme Another name for a **grammatical morpheme**.

functional sentence perspective An approach to the description of sentence structure which attaches great importance to the **thematic structure** (information structure) of sentences – that is, to the way in which old and new information is organized and presented. Developed by some of the later **Prague School** linguists, this approach has been moderately influential.

functional shift Another name for **conversion**.

function word A word which has little or no meaning of its own but which has a grammatical function, such as English *the, of, and* or the auxiliary *have* (as in *I have seen her*).

fundamental frequency The **frequency** (sense 1) at which a body vibrates when it vibrates in the simplest manner possible.

fusion The morphological phenomenon in which a word consists of several morphemes but cannot be neatly chopped up into a sequence of morphemes. English examples include *feet* (*foot* + Plural) and *took* (*take* + Past).

fusional language A language in which **fusion** is prominent.

futhark (or **futhork**) Another name for the **runic alphabet**, derived from its first six letters.

future In some languages, a **tense** category which correlates chiefly with future time. English has no future tense; we have only a number of "present" (non-past) forms which can be used to refer to future time, each one expressing some particular view of the future.

future-in-the-past A verb form indicating that some event was, at some time in the past, seen as lying in the future, as in *I was going to buy a car.*

future perfect A verb form indicating that some event which has not yet occurred will, at some time in the future, be in the past, as in *I will have finished this job by Friday.*

G

Gabelentz, Georg von der A German linguist (1840–93). Apart from his work on Chinese, Gabelentz made important contributions to philology, descriptive linguistics and theoretical linguistics; in many respects he anticipated **Saussure**, who may have been influenced by him. Far in advance of his time, he was long forgotten and has been rediscovered only fairly recently.

Gaelic Another name for the **Goidelic** branch of **Celtic**. The name (pronounced GAY-lik) was formerly applied specifically to **Irish**; pronounced GALL-ik (rhymes with *italic*), it is also the name of the Celtic language of Scotland.

Gage, Phineas An American construction worker through whose head and brain a long, thick iron bar was driven by an explosion in 1848. Gage's language and speech were unaffected by the accident, thus providing early evidence for the **localization** of the **language areas** in the brain.

Galician A **Romance** language spoken in northwestern Spain.

gap A point in a sentence at which something should logically be present but nothing is. Examples (gaps marked by e): *What do you want e?; The woman you were talking to e is my sister; Rod gave the museum a T-shirt and Elton e e a pair of glasses.*

garden-path sentence A sentence so constructed that it appears to make perfect sense up to some point, after which the remaining words will not fit the meaning already settled on, even though the whole sentence has a quite different and sensible interpretation, such as *The horse shot from the stable fell over.*

Gardiner, Sir Alan A British theoretical linguist and Egyptologist (1879–1963), author of the classic *Egyptian Grammar.*

Gauchat, Louis A Swiss dialectologist (1866–1942), one of the founding fathers of dialectology.

Gaulish The **Celtic** language spoken in most of Gaul (France) at the time of the Roman conquest; it is long extinct.

gavagai problem A logical problem faced by a child learning its first language: how does the child know what a new utterance means? If an adult points at a bounding rabbit and says "*Gavagai*", how does the child know whether *gavagai* means 'rabbit', or a particular colour or variety of rabbit, or 'running rabbit', or any of a trillion other things? Is it the name of that particular rabbit? Does it perhaps mean 'Look at him go', or 'Beware!', or 'He's pretty', or something else? Children's ability to solve such problems must tell us something about the nature of the human language faculty.

Gazzaniga, Michael An American neuroscientist (1939–) who has done important work on the relation between language and brain.

GB See **Government-and-Binding Theory**.

Geach, Peter A British philosopher and logician (1916–), known for introducing the celebrated **donkey sentences** into logical discourse.

Ge'ez The classical **Semitic** language of Ethiopia, introduced from southern Arabia and attested from the fourth to the fourteenth centuries AD. The ancestor of Amharic and other Ethiopian languages, Ge'ez is still used as a liturgical language by Ethiopian Christians.

gender 1. A grammatical phenomenon found in certain languages, by which nouns are grammatically divided into two or more classes requiring different kinds of **agreement** on other words which are grammatically connected, such as determiners, adjectives or verbs. For example, French *livre* 'book' and *maison* 'house' belong to different genders, and hence 'an old book' is *un vieux livre*, but 'an old house' is *une vieille maison*. The number of gender classes may vary widely: French has two, German has three, the Australian language Dyirbal has four, Swahili has eight, Navaho has about a dozen and some African languages have perhaps two dozen or more (it is not always easy to count genders). Depending on the language, the gender of a noun may correlate strongly with meaning, or only weakly, or not at all; the same is true of gender and the form of a noun. **Note** in particular that grammatical gender does not necessarily have anything to do with sex: in Tamil, there is a strong correlation between gender and sex; in French, only a weak one; in Swahili and Navaho none at all. Sex is just one of many semantic factors which may or may not be correlated with gender assignment; others include animacy, humanness, shape, size, physical state (solid or liquid), stiffness or floppiness, edibility and danger. English, it is worth pointing out, has *no* grammatical gender: we have only some sex-marked pronouns. 2. A person's biological sex, particularly when this is considered from the point of view of differing social roles. In various societies, gender differences in this sense may be reflected in such social differences as clothing, hairdos, types of work, and the allowability of smoking, swearing or wearing makeup; there are almost always noticeable differences in the use of language, and in a few cases these can be dramatic.

General American The type of accent used by Americans in the Midwest and the West, the areas which have been settled too recently for distinctive local characteristics to appear.

Generalized Phrase Structure Grammar (GPSG) A theory of grammar developed by Gerald Gazdar and others in the early 1980s. GPSG is a sophisticated version of **phrase-structure grammar**, with no transformations or derivations, and it represents a return to the explicit generative grammars of the 1950s.

generalized transformation Another name for a **double-base transformation**.

generational change A type of linguistic change in which a change begins in a small way in one generation and then gradually extends its effect over succeeding generations of speakers, so that younger speakers consistently show a greater degree of divergence from the original state of affairs than do older speakers. This appears to be a common type of change.

generative grammar 1. A particular grammar of a particular language which, in a purely mechanical way, is capable of enumerating all and only the grammatical sentences of that language. Generative grammar in this sense was introduced by Noam **Chomsky** in the 1950s. 2. Any theory of grammar which has as its goal the construction of such grammars. 3. The enterprise of constructing such theories of grammar. 4. A label applied very loosely to work done within the **Government-and-Binding** framework or within the **Minimalist Programme**, even though such work is expressly not generative in the original sense.

Generative Linguists in the Old World (**GLOW**) An organization of European linguists devoted to research in Chomskyan linguistics.

generative phonology 1. A particular theory of phonology, developed in the 1960s, in which highly abstract underlying representations are acted upon by a (possibly long) sequence of phonological rules to produce surface forms (pronunciations). 2. A collective term for the various contemporary theories of phonology which see themselves as continuing the tradition of the earlier work; prominent examples are **Autosegmental Phonology** and **Metrical Phonology**, but others exist.

Generative Semantics A distinctive version of **transformational grammar** developed in the late 1960s and early 1970s. It differed from the then-current **Standard Theory** in a number of respects, but most obviously in its positing of exceedingly abstract **deep structures** which were typically equated with the semantic structures of sentences, and hence in its rejection of the distinction between syntax and semantics. The programme proved to be impossibly ambitious, but it has had a lasting influence.

generic A **noun** or a **noun phrase** which denotes a large class of entities, such as *dog*, *tree*, *linguists* or *the French*.

genetic algorithm A computer program which is modelled on Darwinian natural selection and which has the capacity to evolve. The program is started with a problem and with a diverse set of candidate solutions to that problem. These are first tested and ranked in order of their "fitness" (their success in solving the problem). The solutions are then "mated" (combined) to produce "offspring" (new solutions consisting of a random mixture of the properties of their 'parents'); fitter solutions have a higher chance of mating successfully than less fit ones. "Mutations" (minor changes) are then introduced into the offspring at random. The new set of solutions is again tested and ranked in order of fitness. This process is repeated as many times as the investigator chooses. Such programs have proved to be remarkably successful at finding good solutions to certain types of problem, and they are now being applied to certain problems in linguistics, such as the evolution of language.

genetic density The number of distinct **language families** per unit area in some part of the world. The world average is about 6.0 families per million square miles, but regional averages vary from 1.6 in Siberia to 273.3 in New Guinea. Compare **linguistic diversity**.

Genetic Hypothesis of Language The hypothesis that the human language faculty is rooted in our biology, that it is a genetic characteristic of the human species which we have evolved over time, just like our opposable thumb and our upright posture. According to this view, language just *grows* in children, much as their teeth grow, except that language learning requires exposure to speech. A strong version of the **innateness hypothesis**, this idea is increasingly influential among linguists, and it appears to be supported by a growing body of evidence; it is none the less controversial.

genetic relationship The relationship between two or more languages which are all descended from a single common ancestral language – that is, the languages started off long ago as nothing more than regional dialects of that ancestral language but have diverged over time into distinct languages. English, for example, is genetically related to Dutch, German and Swedish, with which it shares a common ancestor dating back about 2500 years, and more distantly to French, Russian, Greek and Hindi, with which it shares a common ancestor dating back perhaps 6000 years. The *genetic classification* of languages is a major goal of historical linguistics.

Geneva School The name given to the linguistic work done by a number of students and successors of **Saussure** in Switzerland, most of them based in Geneva. Charles **Bally** is perhaps the best-known figure.

Genie An American girl who was kept locked up by her psychopathic parents throughout most of her childhood, prevented from hearing any language and punished if she made a sound. Discovered only at age 13 and unsurprisingly found to be mentally subnormal, she was placed in care; in spite of significant progress in mental development, she acquired English only to the level of an average two-and-a-half-year-old. Her sad case possibly provides support for the **critical period hypothesis**, but almost everything about Genie's condition, circumstances and treatment after discovery is deeply controversial.

genitive In a language with **case**, that case which marks a possessor, such as Basque *-en*, as in *Jonen ama* 'Jon's mother'.

Geordie The distinctive variety of English spoken in and around the English city of Newcastle.

Georgian The chief language of the Republic of Georgia, a **Kartvelian** language.

German The principal language of Germany, Austria and much of Switzerland; a member of the **Germanic** branch of **Indo-European**. German is divided into a number of regional dialects; those in the north are collectively called *Low German*, those in the south, *High German*. The standard language, also called *High German*, is based on the southern dialects.

Germanic A group of languages, mainly spoken in northern Europe and constituting one branch of the **Indo-European** family. Among the Germanic languages are English, Frisian, Dutch, Afrikaans, German, Yiddish, Icelandic, Faroese, Norwegian, Swedish, Danish, and the extinct Gothic and Norn; ancestral forms of some of these are recorded. All are descended from an ancestor which we call *Proto-Germanic*, probably spoken in southern Scandinavia around 500 BC.

gerund A form of a **verb** which exhibits all or most of the ordinary properties of a verb but which allows the **verb phrase** containing it to function as a **noun phrase** within a sentence. The English gerund marker is *-ing*. Consider the sentence *Deliberately collapsing the scrum is a foul in rugby*. Here *collapsing* is a gerund: it takes an object (*the scrum*) and an adverb (*deliberately*), but the whole VP *deliberately collapsing the scrum* behaves as an NP (it is the subject of the sentence). Compare *This deliberate collapsing of the scrum has to stop*. This time *collapsing* is not a gerund but a **verbal noun**: it takes no object and no adverb, but it allows a determiner (*this*), an adjective (*deliberate*) and a prepositional phrase in place of an object, properties exhibited by nouns, not by verbs.

Geschwind, Norman An American neurologist (1926–84); he revived and elaborated the conception of the brain as consisting of specialized areas with interconnections, and he was largely responsible for the recognition and classification of the various types of **aphasia**.

gestural theory The hypothesis that language arose out of gestures. Though vigorously defended by a few enthusiasts, this hypothesis has found limited support among linguists generally.

ghost word A word which does not exist but which has been entered in a dictionary by mistake, because of a misunderstanding.

Gilliéron, Jules A Swiss dialectologist (1854–1926). Widely regarded as the father of modern dialectology, Gilliéron was a prominent foe of the **Neogrammarians** and an advocate of the slogan "every word has its own history".

Gimbutas, Marija A Lithuanian-American archaeologist (1921–94), the leading advocate of the identification of the **Kurgan culture** with the speakers of **Proto-Indo-European**.

Gimson, A. C. A British phonetician (1917–85), a specialist in the pronunciation of English and the author of a standard book on the subject. A student of Daniel **Jones** and Jones's successor in London, "Gim" introduced many of the ideas, terms and notational devices of the **American structuralists** into the British tradition, and his revision of the *EPD* transcription used by Jones has been the standard system for transcribing **Received Pronunciation** ever since.

given-new distinction A way of dividing up an utterance according to its information content: *given* information is already obvious from the context, while *new* information is being provided for the first time.

glide (also **semi-vowel**) A speech sound which patterns like a consonant but is phonetically a brief vowel, such as [w] in *we* or [j] in *yes*.

global aphasia A particularly severe form of **aphasia** in which both speech and comprehension are largely destroyed.

gloss A brief translation of some expression in a foreign language, intended only as a rough guide to its meaning, function or structure. There is a standard procedure for citing glosses, which you should stick to. For a single word, we write, for example, Basque *etxe* 'house'. For longer expressions, we do this: Basque *Gizon-a-k ikus-i n-a-u-Ø* man-Det-Erg see-PerfPart 1SgDO-Pres-Aux-3SgSubj 'The man has seen me' (the hyphens are inserted by the analyst to separate morphemes; the symbol Ø represents a zero element; the abbreviations for grammatical morphemes like Determiner, Ergative, Perfective Participle, First Singular, Direct Object, and so on, should be explained separately).

glossary A (usually brief) list of foreign words or technical terms with translations or definitions.

Glossematics The name given to an approach to linguistic theory and description developed in Denmark in the 1930s, '40s and '50s, chiefly by Louis **Hjelmslev**. The framework is highly abstract and it uses a great deal of unfamiliar terminology; consequently, it has perhaps been less influential than it deserves.

glossogenetics An approach to the study of the **origin and evolution of language** which focuses upon the purely biological aspects. This is one type of **biolinguistics**.

glossolalia The technical name for **speaking in tongues**.

glottalic airstream mechanism One way of producing a flow of air for speaking. The **glottis** is closed, and then the entire **larynx** is moved up or down in the throat like a piston, thereby changing the air pressure in the mouth. Moving the larynx up forces air out of the mouth (it produces an **egressive** airstream), while moving it down pulls air into the mouth (it produces an **ingressive** airstream). Both of these airstreams are used linguistically in certain languages; the first gives **ejective** consonants, the second gives **implosive** ones.

glottal stop A consonant produced by closing the glottis completely for a moment. Represented by the symbol [ʔ], it is not a phoneme in English but occurs phonetically in certain circumstances: for example, in the famous Cockney pronunciation of *butter* and in everyone's speech in a careful pronunciation of the negative *uh-uh*.

glottis The opening between the **vocal folds**, through which air passes during speech whenever the glottis is not closed.

glottochronology A technique applied to two or more languages in **genetic relationship** in order to estimate how long ago they diverged. Certain standard vocabulary items are compared (usually the **Swadesh word list**) to find out what proportion of the words is different in the languages being compared; the greater this proportion, the longer ago the languages separated. To make this approach work, of course, we have to have an estimate of how fast vocabulary changes, and this is the difficult and controversial part of the technique. Compare **lexicostatistics**.

GLOW See **Generative Linguists in the Old World**.

goal The **semantic role** which expresses the person or place towards which motion is directed, such as *Lisa* and *London* in *I sent Lisa the books* and *I'm travelling to London*. Compare **source**.

God's truth The view that every language has a real, identifiable structure, and that the business of linguists is merely to find and describe that structure. Compare **hocus-pocus**.

Goidelic (also **Gaelic**) One branch of the **Celtic** family, including Irish, Manx and Scots Gaelic; Goidelic is sometimes called *Q-Celtic*.

gossip theory The conjecture that language developed out of a need for groups of people to bond together by keeping track of one another. This conjecture is currently defended by a number of investigators. One version holds that the chief driving force was a need for males returning from hunting to find out what their mates had been up to! (Given the tradition of conferring playful names on conjectures about language origin, perhaps we should dub this one the *yenta theory*.)

Gothic An extinct **Germanic** language spoken by many of the Germanic barbarians who overran the Roman Empire. The sole substantial surviving text in Gothic is a fourth-century Bible translation by the Gothic bishop Wulfila. A variety of Gothic was found to be still spoken in the Crimea in the sixteenth century, but it died out soon after.

Gothic script Another name for **black-letter writing**.

government A grammatical relation between two items in a sentence in which the *presence* of the first item determines the *form* of the second. For example, prepositions often govern objects in particular case-forms. The German prepositions *für* 'for' and *mit* 'with' govern different cases: *für mich* 'for me' (accusative object) but *mit mir* 'with me' (dative object). Verbs also commonly govern particular forms of their objects: Basque *ikusi* 'see' requires an object in the absolutive case, while *eutsi* 'grab' takes a dative object and *gogoratu* 'remember' takes an instrumental object. In the **Government-and-Binding** framework, the notion of government has been generalized and extended in important ways.

Government-and-Binding Theory (**GB**) (also **Principles-and-Parameters Approach**) A theory of grammar developed by Noam **Chomsky** and his associates in the 1980s, the direct descendant of the various earlier versions of **transformational grammar**. GB still has transformations, but it is very different from the earlier frameworks. GB has recently been the single most influential theory of grammar, but it is now giving way to a radically different successor, the **Minimalist Programme**.

GPSG See **Generalized Phrase Structure Grammar**.

graffiti (plural; the singular is **graffito**) Informal writing scrawled by somebody in a public place. Graffiti are occasionally important in **historical linguistics**; for example, the graffiti preserved at Pompeii, entombed by volcanic ash in AD 79, give us useful information about the spoken **Latin** of the day. **Note** the spelling.

grammar 1. Narrowly, that part of the structure of a language which includes sentence structure (**syntax**) and word structure (**morphology**). A linguist who specializes in the study of grammar in this sense is a *grammarian*. 2. Broadly, the entire structure of a language, including not only its syntax and morphology but also its phonology and semantics, and possibly also its pragmatics. 3. A particular description of a language, or a book containing it.

grammar-translation method A very traditional way of teaching a foreign language; the student must memorize grammatical rules and lists of words and then translate written passages out of or into the language being learned.

Possibly useful for learning a **dead language** like **Latin**, this method is hopelessly inadequate for learning to use a living language effectively.

grammatical category Any one of various categories which may be present in particular languages and which, when present, oblige all the words in a relevant class always to appear in one of two or more distinct grammatical forms, depending on the grammatical environment. For example, English has the category of **number** for nouns, and so every noun must always appear in either a *singular* or a *plural* form; there is no possibility of avoiding the choice. Apart from number, common grammatical categories include **aspect, gender, mood person, tense**, and **voice** (sense 1), though others occur in some languages. Of those just named, only person appears to be universally present in languages.

grammaticality Another name for **well-formedness**.

grammaticalization Any change in a language in which a word or a construction loses its original meaning and becomes a grammatical marker. An example is the English *be going to* construction, which has acquired the grammatical function of marking a future intention: formerly *I am going to visit Mrs Smith* could only mean 'I am now on my way to Mrs Smith's house', but today it usually means 'I intend to visit Mrs Smith'.

grammatical morpheme (also **functional morpheme**) A **morpheme** which has a purely grammatical function, such as English *of*, plural *-s* or the *-ing* which goes on to verbs. Compare **lexical morpheme**.

grammatical relation Any one of several ways in which a noun phrase may be connected grammatically to the rest of its sentence, and especially to the verb: **subject, direct object, indirect object, oblique object**, and possibly others.

grammatical word (also **empty word, form word**) A word which has a purely grammatical function, such as *of*, *the*, the auxiliary verb *have* or the *to* of *Give it to me*. Compare **content word**.

Gramsci, Antonio An Italian Communist politician and theoretician (1891–1937); he stressed the importance of language in establishing cultural hegemony and advocated the prescriptivist teaching of prestigious forms of language to workers and peasants in order to empower them. Compare **Bakhtin**.

grapheme One of the minimal units in a writing system – in an alphabet, a **letter**, like <a> or <s>. Graphemes are usually cited within angle brackets.

grapheme–phoneme conversion The process of turning written letters or characters into pronunciations. This is necessary when reading aloud, but it is not usually done in reading silently.

Grassmann, Hermann A German mathematician and amateur linguist (1809–77); he did important descriptive work on **Sanskrit**, but is best known for discovering **Grassmann's Law**.

Grassmann's Law In Sanskrit and ancient Greek, a constraint which prohibits aspiration from occurring in two consecutive syllables, as illustrated by Greek *thriks* 'hair' but genitive *trikhós* (from earlier **thrikhós*). The law is affectionately known to students as the 'ha-ha rule'.

Great Vowel Shift A dramatic series of changes in the pronunciation of the long vowels of English which took place mainly during the fifteenth and sixteenth centuries. The Great Vowel Shift was a **chain shift**; it is the reason that the vowel letters in English often have such different values from their values in other European languages, and it is also a major part of the explanation of **alternations** like those in *sane/sanity*, *clean/cleanliness* and *crime/criminal*.

Greek The chief language of Greece, sometimes spoken also in neighbouring areas. Greek constitutes a branch of **Indo-European** all by itself, and it is attested almost continuously since the late second millennium BC. *Mycenaean Greek* is an archaic variety recorded in the **Linear B** texts of ancient Crete; *Homeric Greek* is the pre-classical language of the *Iliad* and the *Odyssey*; *classical Greek* (or *ancient Greek*) is the language of the great literary works written around the fifth century BC; *Hellenistic Greek* is the Greek used in the empire of Alexander the Great; *New Testament Greek* is the post-classical variety in which the New Testament is written; *Byzantine Greek* is the language of the Byzantine Empire; *modern Greek* is the contemporary language of Greece. Until recently, Greek had two competing standard varieties called *katharévusa* and *dhimotiki*, but a compromise standard has been agreed on which favours the second.

Greek alphabet The distinctive **alphabet** used for writing **Greek** for over 2500 years, sometimes used also for writing other languages. It was derived from the **Phoenician alphabet** and was apparently the first alphabet ever to contain vowel letters.

Greenberg, Joseph An American linguist (1915–). Greenberg has contributed substantially to many areas of linguistics, but he is best known for making the study of **typology** and **universals** a central part of linguistics and for his work on **genetic relationships**. His classification of **African languages** into just four families is now universally accepted, but his more recent classification of American languages into just three families, including a single vast **Amerind** family, has been received with considerable hostility.

Grice, Paul A British philosopher (1913–88), best known for introducing the **cooperative principle** and the **maxims of conversation**.

Grimm, Jacob A German linguist and folklorist (1785–1863). He and his brother Wilhelm are well known to the general public for their collection of fairy tales; as a linguist, Jacob is best known for his monumental work on the history and prehistory of the **Germanic** languages, and in particular for formulating **Grimm's Law**. He also introduced a great deal of the terminology of historical linguistics.

Grimm's Law (also **First Germanic Consonant Shift**) A series of related phonological changes which affected a number of consonants in the Proto-Germanic ancestor of the **Germanic** languages. For example, the ancestral **p* changed to *f*, so that the Germanic language English has forms like *foot*, *father*, *fish* and *for*, compared to its distant relative Latin, which did not undergo the change and has *ped-*, *pater*, *piscis* and *pro* for the same meanings.

groove fricative A **fricative** whose production involves a lengthwise groove along the upper surface of the tongue, such as [s]. Compare **slit fricative**.

group genitive The English construction in which a possessive -*'s* is added to a large noun phrase, as in *The Wife of Bath's Tale* and *the woman you were talking to's husband*.

grue A colour term which covers the range covered by English *blue* and *green* (at least). Many languages have such a word.

guided learning A type of learning which is partly controlled by innate biological principles of learning. It is now widely thought that guided learning is the norm for human beings and probably for other creatures; the **innateness hypothesis** may be seen as representing the application of guided learning to language.

Guillaume, Gustave A French linguist (1883–1960). A student of Antoine **Meillet,** he championed the cognitive view of language. His voluminous lectures are still only partly published.

Gujarati (also **Gujerati**) An **Indo-Aryan** language spoken in western India and also by many people in Britain.

Gur (also **Voltaic**) A group of more than eighty languages spoken in west Africa and constituting one branch of the **Niger-Congo** family.

Guthrie, Malcolm A British linguist (1903–72), a pioneer in the comparative study of the **Bantu** languages.

Gyarmathi, Sámuel A Hungarian (Transylvanian) physician and amateur linguist (1751–1830); he published the first comparative study of the **Finno-Ugric** languages.

H

Haas, Mary An American linguist (1910–96), best known for her descriptive and (especially) comparative work on native American languages.

habitation name The name of a city, town or village.

habitual The **aspect** category which expresses a usual or habitual action. English has a special form for this in the past tense only, the *used to* construction, as in *She used to smoke.* In the present tense, we use the simple present for the same purpose: *She smokes.*

Hall, Robert An American linguist (1911–). One of the most prominent of the **American structuralists,** Hall has contributed to a wide range of topics, including creoles, language teaching and especially Romance languages; his is the major attempt at reconstructing **Proto-Romance,** the ancestor of the **Romance** languages. Hall has been a vigorous defender of the data-oriented approach to linguistic description and an equally vigorous critic both of **prescriptivism** and of the theoretical ideas of Noam **Chomsky** and his followers, which he sees as excessively theoretical at the expense of data.

Halle, Morris A Latvian-born American linguist (1923–), best known for his contributions to phonology and morphology. He was one of the originators of **distinctive features,** and he was the prime mover behind the development of **generative phonology,** which, with his colleague and protégé Noam **Chomsky,** he developed into its classical form in *SPE*.

Halliday, Michael A. K. A British linguist (1925–), the intellectual heir of **Firth** and the creator of **Systemic Linguistics**. Halliday is particularly well known for his work on the analysis of texts.

Hamito-Semitic An obsolete name for the **Afro-Asiatic** family.

Hamp, Eric An American historical linguist (1920–), a leading specialist in **Indo-European**.

handbook A reference book which presents a great deal of information on some topic, often a particular language or family of languages.

Han'gŭl The indigenous **alphabet** of Korea, sometimes used for writing Korean in preference to Chinese characters. This extraordinary alphabet is unique among the world's alphabets in that its letters are composed of strokes corresponding to distinctive features: all letters for labial consonants contain a square, all letters for alveolars contain an L-shape, all letters for lax unaspirated plosives contain a horizontal bar across the top, and so on.

hapax In an ancient written language, a word which is recorded only once and whose reality is therefore possibly in doubt.

haplology The loss of one of two consecutive syllables which are similar or identical. Basque *sagar* 'apple' plus *ardo* 'wine' should yield **sagar-ardo*, but the form is *sagardo* 'cider', with haplology.

hard consonant An impressionistic label traditionally applied to certain correlations between spelling and pronunciation; see the examples under **soft consonant**.

hard-wiring The permanent and unalterable presence, usually from birth, of some neural structure in the brain, and hence of some mental processes in the mind. All versions of the **innateness hypothesis** require that some aspects of the human language faculty must be hard-wired into our brains.

Harris, James A British philosopher (1709–80), the author of a major philosophical grammar, in which he stressed the connection between language and mind.

Harris, Zellig A Ukrainian-born American linguist (1909–92). A prominent but very distinctive member of the **American structuralists**, Harris worked chiefly on syntax and discourse analysis; he devised increasingly abstract and algebraic approaches to linguistic description, and he was the inventor of **transformations**, which were later developed by his famous student Noam **Chomsky** in a very different direction from Harris's conception.

Hart, John A British phonetician (?1501–74), one of the most outstanding figures in the field before the nineteenth century. He published a magnificent description of the phonetics and phonology of the spoken English of his day.

Harvard children Three children known in the literature as Adam, Eve and Sarah, the subjects of a famous study of language **acquisition** carried out by Roger **Brown**.

Hattori, Shiroo A Japanese linguist (1908–), generally regarded as the founder of scientific linguistics in Japan. He wrote widely on descriptive and theoretical issues, and championed the attachment of Japanese to the **Altaic** family.

Haugen, Einar An American linguist (1906–94), a contemporary of the

American structuralists but perhaps not really one of them. He was one of the founders of sociolinguistics and of contrastive linguistics, and he contributed greatly to the study of language planning, bilingualism and language contact, as well as being a specialist in Scandinavian languages (his first language was Norwegian). He took more interest in European linguistics than most of his American colleagues, and tried to establish a dialogue between the two groups.

Hausa A language spoken in northern Nigeria and adjacent areas, a member of the **Chadic** branch of the **Afro-Asiatic** family. Hausa has more native speakers than any other sub-Saharan African language.

Hawaiian The indigenous **Polynesian** language of Hawaii, now virtually extinct.

Hayyuj, Judah A tenth-century Jewish grammarian, the first important grammarian of Hebrew; he was born in Morocco but spent his career in Spain.

h-dropping An informal name for a type of English accent in which the phoneme /h/ is lost, so that, for example, *hair* and *air* are pronounced identically, as are *harm* and *arm*, *hear* and *ear*, and so on. This type of pronunciation is extremely widespread in England, but it is strongly stigmatized.

head That element of a constituent (syntactic unit) which is grammatically central in that it is chiefly responsible for the nature of the constituent. For example, in the noun phrase *those old books*, it is the presence of the noun *books* as the head which makes the whole thing a noun phrase, while in the adjective phrase *very proud of Lisa*, it is the presence of the adjective *proud* as the head which makes the whole thing an adjective phrase.

Head-Driven Phrase Structure Grammar (**HPSG**) A theory of grammar devised by Carl Pollard and Ivan Sag in the late 1980s. HPSG is an extraordinarily homogeneous framework in which almost all work is done by its unusually elaborate **lexical entries**. The framework is exceptionally convenient for computational work.

headless relative clause (also **free relative clause**) A special type of **relative clause** which forms a complete **noun phrase** all by itself. Example (in brackets): [*Whoever did that*] *is in trouble*. Sometimes a headless relative looks just like an **embedded question**: the sentence *I saw what she put in the bag* contains a headless relative when it means 'I saw the thing that she put in the bag', but an embedded question when it means 'I saw her put something in the bag, and I recognized what it was'.

head-marking Any construction in which the grammatical connection between two items in a phrase is shown by an overt marking on the **head**. For example, the relation between a verb and its subject or object may be shown by marking the verb, rather than by case-marking the subject or object. Compare **dependent-marking**.

headword (also **lemma**) Any one of the words which are entered alphabetically in the left-hand margin of a dictionary and for which definitions are provided.

heavy-NP shift The phenomenon in which a noun phrase which is unusually long is placed at the end of a sentence, instead of in the more normal position for a noun phrase of that particular function. For example, the normal English transitive construction is *I found a picture in a junkshop*; we cannot say *I found in *a junkshop a picture*, but we *can* say *I found in a junkshop one of the finest examples of early Italian Renaissance art I have ever had the pleasure of beholding*, with heavy-NP shift.

heavy syllable A syllable which takes longer to pronounce than some other syllables because it contains a long vowel, a diphthong, or a final consonant cluster. The difference between heavy syllables and **light syllables** is important in the phonology of some languages, though not all of them draw the line in exactly the same place. See **mora**.

Hebrew The ancient and modern language of Israel. Ancient Hebrew, the language of most of the Old Testament and of other important Jewish religious writings, died out as a mother tongue long ago, but a modified form of it has been revived in modern Israel, where it is now the mother tongue of most native-born Israeli Jews. This is the only case on record in which a dead language has been successfully revived.

Hebrew alphabet The **alphabet** traditionally used to write **Hebrew,** and also **Yiddish**. Like most **Semitic alphabets**, it lacks vowel letters.

hedge A phrase which you can add to an utterance to reduce the degree of your commitment to what you are saying: *I suspect, I would guess, it seems to me*.

height One of the primary phonetic characteristics of a vowel. In a **high vowel,** the highest point of the tongue is about as high as it can go; in a **low vowel,** it is about as low as it can go; in a **mid vowel,** it is somewhere in between.

Hellenic A name sometimes given to the branch of **Indo-European** which includes only **Greek** and possibly also ancient **Macedonian** (sense 1).

hemisphere Either of the two roughly symmetric halves of the brain, or more particularly of the cerebral cortex.

Henderson, Eugénie A British phonetician and phonologist (1914–89), a specialist in southeast Asian languages and one of the foremost proponents of **Prosodic Analysis**.

Herder, Johann A German writer (1744–1803); he is known to linguists for his book on language origins, which stresses his view of language as an organism subject to growth and decay.

hesitation marker A noise like *um* or *er*.

Hiberno-English The English of Ireland.

hieroglyphs The writing system used for official purposes by the ancient Egyptians, an extraordinarily complex mixture of **logograms** and phonetic characters. The system was deciphered by **Champollion** after the discovery of the **Rosetta Stone**. This name is occasionally extended to other writing systems of similar nature or appearance.

High German 1. A collective name for the dialects of German spoken in southern Germany, Austria and Switzerland. Compare **Low German**. 2. The standard form of German, which is based on the southern dialects.

high vowel (also **close vowel**) A **vowel** which is produced with the high part of the tongue about as high as it can go, such as [i] or [u].

Hill, Archibald A. An American linguist (1902–92), a prominent **American**

structuralist who contributed to both theoretical and (especially) applied linguistics.

Hindi The major language of northern India, a member of the **Indo-Aryan** family. At the spoken level, Hindi is the same language as **Urdu**, from which it differs in using a different alphabet and in having different abstract and technical vocabulary.

Hiri Motu A pidginized form of the **Papuan** language Motu, widely used as a **lingua franca** in Papua New Guinea, where it has official status. It is also called *police Motu*.

Hispanist A specialist in **Spanish**, or in the languages of the Iberian Peninsula.

historical linguistics The branch of linguistics which studies the ways in which languages change and the consequences of those changes, which works backward to reconstruct ancient and unrecorded languages (and unrecorded stages of particular languages), and which tries to establish historical connections between languages, especially **genetic relationships**.

history of linguistics The study of the historical development of linguistics as a discipline. (**Note:** do not confuse this with the preceding item.)

Hittite An extinct language spoken in the second millennium BC in central Anatolia (modern Turkey), the chief language of the powerful Hittite Empire. Hittite belongs to the **Anatolian** branch of the **Indo-European** family, and its discovery and decipherment in the early twentieth century revolutionized Indo-European studies.

Hjelmslev, Louis A Danish linguist (1899–1965), the prime developer of **Glossematics**.

Hockett, Charles An American linguist (1916–). Hockett was one of the most important and most original of the **American structuralists**. Though he worked in a number of areas, including language teaching and grammatical description, he is perhaps best known for his development of phonology, in which he elaborated the **phoneme** principle and largely initiated the study of **phoneme systems**. The author of a major textbook of linguistics, he was also a prolific coiner of linguistic terms, most of which are still in regular use today, and he became a stern critic of what he saw as the excesses of Noam **Chomsky** and his followers. He introduced the concept of the **design features** of language, and he examined the issue of the **origin and evolution of language**.

hocus-pocus The view that a language has no single identifiable structure, that a description of it by a linguist is largely just the linguist's own ideas superimposed on the data, and hence that many quite different descriptions may be more or less equally valid. Compare **God's truth**.

Hoijer, Harry An American anthropological linguist (1904–76), a student of Edward **Sapir** and a leading figure in the description and classification of native American languages. He is especially known for his work in reconstructing *Proto-Athabaskan*, the ancestor of the **Athabaskan** languages.

Hokan The name given to a highly speculative proposal to link genetically a large number of small families and isolated languages in the southwestern USA, Mexico and Central America. The Hokan idea is still more a research programme than a language family, but considerable progress has been made in deciding which of the various languages are or are not genuinely related.

holophrase In the early stages of child language, a single word which is apparently intended to convey the meaning of a complete sentence, such as *juice* for 'I want some juice' or *shoe* for 'This is my shoe'.

home sign A **sign language** which is invented by deaf children who have no exposure to an established sign language. It appears that deaf children in this position almost always invent a home sign system, providing powerful evidence for the **language instinct**.

Homo The genus to which our own species belongs, whose members are collectively called *hominids*. The earliest member of the genus was *H. habilis*, which lived in Africa about 2.4 million years ago. This was followed by *H. erectus*, which arose in Africa about 1.8 million years ago and later spread out over much of the Old World. Around 400,000 years ago there appeared a distinct population variously classified as *H. heidelbergensis* or as "archaic" *H. sapiens*; the precise relation of the **Neandertals** to *H. sapiens* is disputed. Fully modern humans, *Homo sapiens sapiens*, appeared just over 100,000 years ago. The manner in which our species arose is disputed; see the **out-of-Africa hypothesis** and the **parallel evolution hypothesis**. The language capabilities, if any, of the various hominids is also disputed. (Some specialists recognize two or three additional hominid species transitional between those cited.)

homogenization (also **dialect levelling**) The process by which a group of people with different linguistic backgrounds, possibly over a very large area, come to have virtually uniform speech. This has happened in the USA and in Australia.

homograph One of two (or more) words which have different meanings and pronunciations but which are written identically: *lead* (the metal) and *lead* (the verb); *entrance* ('way in') and *entrance* ('bewitch').

homonym A general term covering both **homographs** and **homophones**.

homophone Either of two or more words which have different meanings but which are pronounced identically. (It doesn't matter if they are spelled identically or differently.) Examples: *flour* and *flower*; *great* and *grate*; *pear*, *pare* and *pair*; *bear* (the animal) and *bear* (the verb meaning 'tolerate'). Since there are many accents of English, not all speakers have the same homophones. All of the following are homophones for some speakers but not for others: *horse* and *hoarse*; *threw* and *through*; *dew* and *do*; *nose* and *knows*; *pull* and *pool*; *poor* and *pour*; *whine* and *wine*; *winter* and *winner*; *court* and *caught*; *caught* and *cot*; *farther* and *father*; *god* and *guard*; *hair* and *air*; *three* and *free*; *stir* and *stare*; *buck* and *book*; *higher* and *hire*; *marry*, *merry* and *Mary*.

honorific A distinctive form used by a speaker to express respect toward someone else. For example, the ordinary Japanese word for 'pretty' is *kirei*, but a speaker addressing or talking about someone toward whom he or she wishes to show respect will use *o-kirei*, in which the prefix *o-* is an honorific.

Hopi A **Uto-Aztecan** language spoken in the southwestern USA; it was famously studied by **Whorf**.

Hornby, A. S. A British applied linguist (1898–1978), one of the most celebrated figures in the teaching of English as a foreign language and author of a famous dictionary of English for foreign learners.

Householder, Fred An American linguist and classicist (1913–94). One of the most remarkable figures in twentieth-century linguistics, Householder seems to have worked on everything, from the ancient Greek grammarians to computational linguistics. An outstandingly knowledgeable and fair-minded critic, he criticized equally the excesses of the **American structuralists** and of Noam **Chomsky** and his followers. Householder is an exceptionally fine writer, and his lively and fascinating essays should be read by all linguists.

HPSG See **Head-Driven Phrase Structure Grammar**.

Hrozný, Bedřich A Czech linguist (1879–1952); he successfully deciphered the **Hittite** texts and showed that the language was **Indo-European**.

Humboldt, Wilhelm von A German statesman, diplomat, linguist and philosopher of language (1767–1835). Brother of the famous explorer Alexander von Humboldt, Wilhelm somehow found time during a long and busy political career to acquire a knowledge of an astounding number of languages: Latin, Greek, Sanskrit, Basque, Chinese, Pacific languages, North American languages. Though he published many descriptive studies, he is best known for his famous system of morphological **typology** and for his voluminous essays on the relations among language, mind and culture.

Hungarian (also **Magyar**) The principal language of Hungary, also spoken in adjacent areas. Hungarian belongs to the **Finno-Ugric** languages.

Hurrian A dead language spoken in northern Mesopotamia (Iraq) and adjoining areas in the late third and second millennia BC. Some scholars think that Hurrian, and its relative *Urartian*, may belong to one of the **Caucasian** families.

hydronym The name of a body of water, such as a river or a lake.

hyoid bone A small V-shaped bone lying at the top of the throat, connected to no other bone and held in place by an array of muscles. The **larynx** is suspended from the hyoid bone.

hyperbole Overstatement; exaggeration, as in *I've told you a million times*.

hypercorrection 1. An error resulting from a confused attempt at avoiding another error. For example, an American who pronounces *dew* as [du:] and who tries to acquire the British pronunciation [dju:] might overdo it and also pronounce *do* (wrongly) as [dju:]; this is a hypercorrection. 2. In sociolinguistics, the phenomenon in which the members of a particular social class, in very formal contexts, produce a higher frequency of prestige variants than the social class above them.

hypocorism A **diminutive** (sense 2), especially one used to mark affection or as a **euphemism**, such as *Mikey*, *undies* or *hanky*.

hyponym A word whose meaning is a special case of some more general word (its **superordinate**). For example, *rose* and *tulip* are hyponyms of *flower*, while *spaniel* is a hyponym of *dog* and *dog* is a hyponym of *animal*.

hypotaxis The use of **subordinate clauses**. Example: *After she got up, she had a shower*. Compare **parataxis**.

I A common abbreviation for **INFL**.

IA See **item-and-arrangement**.

iamb A metrical foot consisting of one unstressed syllable followed by one stressed one, as in *contain, below* or *the book*. Iambic metre is exceptionally common in English poetry: *The curfew tolls the knell of parting day; The turtle lives 'twixt plated decks which practically conceal its sex*.

iambic reversal (also **thirteen-men rule**) The phenomenon in English by which a stress which normally falls on the last syllable of a word is shifted to a preceding syllable when another stress follows: *thirtéen* but *thirteen mén*.

Iberian An extinct language recorded in a number of inscriptions in eastern and southern Spain and southern France from about the sixth to the first centuries BC. Mostly written in an indigenous script, the inscriptions can be read at the phonological level (the sounds), but we cannot make any sense of them. Iberian does not appear to be related to any other language; suggestions that it is related to **Basque** are dismissed by specialists.

Ibn Janah (also **R. Yonah**) A Jewish grammarian (*c.* 990–1050), born in Spain; the author of the first complete grammar of biblical Hebrew.

Ibn Jinnī An Arab linguist (†1200), author of important works on the phonology and grammar of Arabic.

Ibn Madā' al-Qurtubī An Arab linguist (1120–96); interested in the teaching of Arabic, he stressed an empirical approach to describing the language in place of speculative accounts.

Ibo Another spelling of **Igbo**.

-ic A suffix commonly used to form a name for a family of languages, as in *Celtic, Slavic* and *Afro-Asiatic*. Note that *Turkish* is the name of a language, while *Turkic* is the name of a family. Compare **-ish**.

Icelandic The principal (and sole) language of Iceland, a member of the **Germanic** family introduced there by the Vikings. Icelandic is remarkable for its extreme conservatism.

icon A **symbol** which resembles the thing it represents, such as an outline of a leaping deer on a road sign to warn drivers of deer crossing the road. **Pictograms**, and to a lesser extent **ideograms**, are a linguistic use of icons.

iconicity A direct connection between the form of a word and its meaning. The most familiar type is **onomatopoeia**, in which the sound of the word represents a non-linguistic sound with some directness: *boom, meow, clink, whiz*. But other types exist: for example, the light and fluttery sound of the Basque word *tximeleta* (roughly, chee-may-LAY-tah) seems to represent the light and fluttery appearance of the creature it denotes, a butterfly. Iconicity is not rare in languages, but its opposite, **arbitrariness**, is none the less the norm.

ictus The position of the rhythmical beat in a foot or a line of verse.

ideational function That part of language use involving information, evaluation and judgements. Compare **interpersonal function**.

ideogram A **logogram**, often particularly one which is more abstract than a **pictogram** but which still has a recognizable visual connection with its meaning, such as a picture of a hand to represent the verb *take*.

idioglossia A technical name for an **autonomous speech variety**.

idiolect The speech of a particular individual.

idiom An expression whose meaning cannot be straightforwardly guessed from the meanings of the words in it, such as *let the cat out of the bag, not get to first base, a pig in a poke* or *turn the other cheek*.

Igbo (also **Ibo**) The major language of southeastern Nigeria, a member of the **Kwa** branch of the **Niger-Congo** family.

Ijo (also **Ijaw**) A major language of southeastern Nigeria, a member of the **Kwa** branch of the **Niger-Congo** family.

I-language A language seen as a set of rules and principles in the mind of a speaker; **competence**. Compare **E-language**.

illative In some **case** languages, a case which expresses the sense of 'into', as in Finnish *taloon* 'into the house' (*talo* 'house').

ill-formedess Ungrammaticality. An ill-formed string (loosely called an 'ill-formed sentence') is one which fails to conform to the grammatical rules of the language. The opposite is **well-formedness**.

illiteracy Inability to read and write. An illiterate individual is one who has failed to master the reading and writing skills which are normal in that individual's society. An entire society which lacks a recognized writing system is usually said to be *aliterate*, or sometimes in a historical context *preliterate*.

illocutionary act A particular instance of doing something by speaking: ordering, asserting, requesting, promising, sentencing to jail, and so on. The purpose of such an act is its *illocutionary force*.

image schema A **metaphor**, especially one based on space or direction, which pervades a language. In English, for example, 'up' is metaphorically both 'more' and 'good', while 'down' is both 'less' and 'bad': *Unemployment is up again; Susie is going up in the world; The crime rate is falling; Natalie is feeling really low.*

imitation Copying, especially the copying of adult speech by young children learning a language. It is perfectly clear that learning a language involves far more than imitation, but specialists do not agree on just how important imitation is.

immediate constituent In a syntactic **tree structure**, another term for **daughter**.

immediate constituent analysis Dividing a sentence up into **immediate constituents**. This is much the same as constructing a syntactic **tree structure**, but the term 'IC analysis' is commonly applied only in cases in which we do not bother to identify the type of each constituent with a node label.

immediate dominance The relation that holds in a syntactic **tree structure**

between a **mother** and its **daughters**: the mother immediately dominates its daughters.

immersion A technique for learning a foreign language. The student is surrounded by the language being learned, hears nothing else, and is expected to communicate in that language.

immigrant language A language which is spoken in some country by a sizeable group of people who have recently immigrated into that country, such as Arabic in France or Bengali in Britain. Compare **minority language**.

imperative A verb form used in a direct command. English uses its **infinitive** for this purpose, as in *Wait for me!* or *Be careful!*, but some other languages use distinct forms for this purpose. The imperative is commonly classified as a **mood**.

imperfect A particular verb form found in some languages, notably the **Romance** languages like French, Spanish and Italian, which chiefly serves to express an action spread out over time in the past; it is **past** in tense and **imperfective** in aspect. There is no single English equivalent.

imperfective An **aspect** category which assigns internal structure to an activity. The imperfective has several subcategories, such as **progressive**, **habitual** and **iterative**. The English past-tense forms *She was playing tennis* and *She used to play tennis* are both imperfective (progressive and habitual, respectively), while *She played tennis* is **perfective**. **Note:** do not confuse the imperfective with the **imperfect**.

impersonal A label applied to any of several constructions in which the grammatical subject is an empty "dummy", or at least something other than an (unstated) agent: *It's raining, It is thought that* . . . , German *Es hungert mich* 'I'm hungry' (literally, 'It hungers me'), *Tears have been shed.*

implementation 1. The spread of a language change through a speech community. Compare **actuation**. 2. In **language planning**, official attempts at persuading people to use the new form of the language.

implicational universal Any **universal** of the following form: if a language has property P, then it has property Q. An example: if a language has front rounded vowels, then it has back rounded vowels.

implicature See **conversational implicature**.

implosive A consonant produced while the larynx is being lowered, so that air is drawn into the mouth.

impressionistic transcription A **phonetic transcription** obtained merely by listening to a speaker, with no use of instruments.

inalienable possession A type of possession in which the item possessed cannot, in principle, be separated from the possessor: *Susie's eyes, Barbara's name, Mike's family, Susie's book* (in the sense of 'the book that Susie wrote'). Some languages use a special construction for such cases. Compare **alienable possession**.

inanimate A label applied to any noun or noun phrase which denotes something other than a human being or an animal: *book, stone, explosion, dandelions, most* *investigations, the Amazon, all the tea in China.* Note that plants are inanimate. The opposite is **animate**.

inchoative A distinctive **aspect** form found in some languages and expressing the beginning of an activity.

inclusive first person A pronoun or verb form, found in some languages, which means 'I and you (and possibly others)'. Compare **exclusive first person**.

incompatibility A relation in meaning which holds between two words which cannot both be applied to the same thing. For example, *cat* and *dog* are incompatible, since *Gilbert is a cat* and *Gilbert is a dog* cannot both be true (though they can both be false).

incorporation The grammatical phenomenon in which a single inflected word contains two or more lexical roots. English has this only marginally, as in *I'm baby-sitting tonight*, in which the noun *baby* has been incorporated into the verb, but in some other languages such incorporation is a frequent and fully productive process.

indefinite article A **determiner**, such as English *a(n)*, which is most typically attached to a noun phrase to indicate that that noun phrase refers to something not already known to the hearer. Compare **definite article**.

indefiniteness The property of a noun phrase which does not pick out a unique thing, such as *a book, some friends of mine* or *many people*.

index See **referential index**.

indicative (also **declarative**) The **mood** category associated with the uttering of a statement which the speaker believes to be true, as in *The cat wants to go out*. In perhaps all languages, the indicative mood is expressed by using the simplest possible verb-forms.

indigenous Present in a particular place since a very long time ago. The *indigenous language* of a place is the language which is (or was) spoken there from such an early date that we have no knowledge of any earlier languages. An *indigenous writing system* is one which appears to have been created in the place where it is used, and not introduced from outside.

indirect object The **grammatical relation** borne by the noun phrase expressing the person who receives something, when this is grammatically distinct from the **direct object**. Traditional grammarians would classify *Lisa* as an indirect object in both *I sent the books to Lisa* and *I sent Lisa the books*, but not all linguists agree: some regard *Lisa* as an indirect object only in the first, others only in the second, while still others maintain that English has no indirect objects at all.

indirect question Another name for an **embedded question**.

indirect speech Reporting what a speaker has said without using the speaker's exact words, as in *She said that she would come*. Compare **direct speech**.

indirect speech act An utterance whose primary purpose bears no simple or direct relation to its linguistic form or content. For example, a request to close the door may take many forms which do not have the linguistic form of a request and which may not even mention closing the door, such as *You ought to close the door*, *Were you born in a barn?* or *Watch it! The hamster's out of his cage!*

Indo-Aryan A huge group of languages spoken in the north and centre of the Indian subcontinent and in Sri Lanka; among them are Hindi, Urdu, Bengali, Gujarati, Panjabi, Marathi and Sinhalese. All of them are descended from the ancient **Sanskrit** language of India, and they make up one group of the **Indo-Iranian** branch of **Indo-European**.

Indo-European An enormous family of languages, containing more known languages, living and dead, than any other established family. Before the European expansion of a few centuries ago, IE languages were spoken in an almost uninterrupted area extending from India to western Europe (hence the name), and we know that IE languages were formerly spoken also in central Asia and in Anatolia, though they have since disappeared from there. Since the European expansion, IE languages now dominate in North and South America and the Caribbean, in Australia and New Zealand, and in northern Asia; they are also widely spoken in Africa, in southeast Asia and in the Pacific. The major branches of the family are **Celtic**, **Germanic**, **Italic** (which includes **Romance**), **Albanian** (possibly a survivor of the *Illyrian* branch), **Greek** (the sole survivor of the *Hellenic* branch), **Baltic**, **Slavic** (these last two are sometimes grouped together), **Armenian** (probably the last survivor of the *Thraco-Phrygian* branch) and **Indo-Iranian**, plus the two extinct branches of **Anatolian** and **Tocharian**. Several minor branches are also recognized, consisting only of dead and poorly attested languages. The ancestor of the IE languages is **Proto-Indo-European**; see that entry.

Indo-European homeland problem The problem of determining the area in which **Proto-Indo-European** was spoken. The range of proposals is very large, and there is no consensus, though southern Russia or Ukraine is probably the single most popular choice. See **Kurgan culture**.

Indo-Germanic An obsolete name for **Indo-European**.

Indo-Hittite hypothesis The hypothesis that the ancestor of the **Anatolian** languages, including Hittite, was not a daughter of **Proto-Indo-European**, as is commonly thought, but was instead a sister of it – in other words, that Anatolian is the most distantly related branch of the whole family. Proposed by **Sturtevant**, this idea has been generally rejected but has recently found some support.

Indo-Iranian A vast group of languages making up one main branch of the **Indo-European** family and chiefly spoken in southern Asia. The group is divided into three subgroups: **Indo-Aryan**, **Iranian** and **Dardic**.

Indonesian The principal language of Indonesia, properly called *Bahasa Indonesia*. A member of the **Austronesian** family, Indonesian is the same language as **Malay** but it represents a distinctive standard form.

Indo-Pacific A proposed language family linking the **Papuan** languages of New Guinea with the isolated language of the Andaman Islands and with the extinct languages of Tasmania. This proposal is accepted by few specialists.

Indus Valley script An ancient and highly distinctive writing system used by the Indus Valley civilization, in what is now Pakistan, about 2500–1900 BC. The script has not been deciphered, and we don't know what language the texts are written in, though a favourite conjecture is that it was a **Dravidian** language.

inessive In some **case** languages, a case which expresses the meaning 'in', as in Finnish *talossa* 'in the house' (*talo* 'house').

inference Any conclusion which you may reasonably draw from an utterance you hear. Three important types are **entailment, presupposition** and **conversational implicature**.

infinitive A **non-finite** verb-form occurring in some (not all) languages which carries the minimum of morphological marking and which typically carries no meaning beyond the meaning of the verb itself. In English, the infinitive (sometimes called the **bare infinitive**) is simply the stem of the verb, the form entered in a dictionary, such as *go, take, consider* or *be*. The so-called **to-infinitive** is not properly an infinitive at all, nor even a verb-form.

infix An **affix** which interrupts another single morpheme. In Tagalog, for example, the verbal root *sulat* 'write' (a single morpheme) exhibits inflected forms like *sinulat* and *sumulat*, with infixes *-in-* and *-um-*. **Note:** it is very common to see the label 'infix' applied to an affix which merely occurs between another affix and the root, but this usage is objectionable.

INFL (**I**) In some theories of grammar, an abstract element which is posited as present in every sentence and which usually carries markers of **tense** and **agreement**.

inflecting language A language whose morphology is chiefly characterized by **inflection**, that is, by the direct modification of words for grammatical purposes. For this purpose, we do not count **agglutination** as a type of inflection. Typical examples are Latin, Russian and German.

inflection (also **inflexion, flexion**) 1. Variation in the form of a single **lexical item** for grammatical purposes, as in *dog/dogs* or *take/took*. 2. Any one of the several forms exhibited by a lexical item which inflects, such as *dogs* for *dog*. 3. A particular **affix** used for inflection, such as the English plural inflection *-s*.

inflectional morpheme A **morpheme** which plays a part in **inflectional morphology**, such as English plural *-s* or the *-ing* which goes on to verbs.

inflectional morphology That part of **morphology** which is concerned with modifying the forms of words for grammatical purposes, as in English *dog/dogs, take/takes/took/taken/taking*, or *big/bigger/biggest*. Compare **derivational morphology**.

inflexion Another name for **inflection**.

informal The opposite of **formal** (senses 2 and 3).

informant A native speaker of a language who provides information about the language to a linguist studying it. Some linguists object to this term as demeaning and prefer **consultant**, but this term too is open to criticism.

information structure The structure of a sentence from the point of view of which parts of it represent information already known to the hearer ("old" or "given" information), and which parts represent information being presented for the first time ("new" information). The concepts of **topic**, **focus** and **contrastive stress** are all relevant to information structure.

information theory A mathematical theory of communication. It is concerned exclusively with the transmission of data in one direction, and it takes no account of the person receiving the communication; compare **communication theory**.

Ingvaeonic The name given to a group of **Germanic** dialects spoken on the North Sea coast of Europe in the early centuries AD; **English** is descended from the Ingvaeonic speech introduced into Britain in the fifth century.

ingressive airstream mechanism Any way of producing a stream of air for speaking in which the air flows into the mouth. The **pulmonic, glottalic** and **velaric airstream mechanisms** can all produce ingressive air, but only the second and third are known to be used for linguistic purposes.

initial Occurring at the beginning of a word, or sometimes of a syllable.

initialism A word formed by combining the initial letters of a phrase, with a result that cannot be pronounced as a word but must be spelled out letter-by-letter: *FBI* (*Federal Bureau of Investigation*), *BBC* (*British Broadcasting Corporation*). Some people do not distinguish an initialism from an **acronym**, but it seems helpful to do so.

initial symbol In a **generative grammar**, the category which must be given before any rules can be applied to generate anything. This is usually S, for *sentence*.

Initial Teaching Alphabet (i.t.a.) A specially modified form of the Roman alphabet, with 44 letters, used for teaching young children to read; after a while, they transfer to the ordinary spelling.

initiation Another term for **airstream mechanism**.

inkhorn term (also **aureate word**) A very fancy word, usually one taken from Latin or Greek, which is not in normal use but which is occasionally used by a writer trying to make an impression, such as *commixtion* 'blending together' or *disgregation* 'separation'.

innate In-born; present from birth; not learned or acquired through experience.

innateness hypothesis The hypothesis that we are born with important knowledge about the nature of human language already built into our brains. Put forward by **Chomsky**, this hypothesis attempts to explain how children manage to learn a first language so rapidly and accurately and why they seemingly never make certain types of mistakes. It is deeply controversial, but it is defended with enthusiasm by many linguists.

inscription A written text carved on to a hard material such as stone or metal.

instantaneous release The property of a **plosive** which distinguishes it from an **affricate**. The opposite is **delayed release**.

institutional linguistics The study of language use or **language policy** in official or professional contexts such as the courts, the medical and legal professions and schools.

instrument The **semantic role** representing the thing used to do something, such as *pencil* in *I wrote it down with a pencil*.

instrumental In some **case** languages, a case-form used to mark the instrument with which something is done. For example, Basque *luma* 'pen' has the instrumental form *lumaz* in *Lumaz idatzi dut* 'I wrote it with a pen'.

instrumental phonetics Any approach to **phonetics** involving the use of instruments. These days the instruments are usually electronic, and the data obtained are often analysed by computers.

intensifier Another name for a **degree modifier**.

intension For a given word, the set of properties which something must have before that word can be applied to it. For example, the intension of *cow* might be something like 'large adult female bovine, gives milk, moos, has horns . . .' Compare **extension**.

intensity The amount of energy carried by a sound wave, commonly measured in **decibels**. Intensity correlates with perceived loudness, but doubling the intensity does not double the loudness.

intentional stance Another name for **theory of mind**.

interactional function The use of language for purely social purposes, such as forming and maintaining bonds and conveying emotions. Compare **transactional function**.

interactive activation model A model of **word recognition** and **word retrieval** which suggests that hearing any word, or even part of a word, immediately "activates" *all* words of similar form or related meaning, and that each of these in turn activates further words, including the very ones which activated *them*, so that activation "flows" back and forth in the brain for a while. Compare the **spreading activation model**.

interchangeability The ability of speakers and hearers of a language to exchange roles with complete freedom.

interdental (A speech sound) produced by putting the tongue between the teeth, such as English /θ/ (in *think*) or /ð/ (in *this*) for most speakers (though not for all).

interference Carrying features of your first language over into a second language – for example, speaking with a foreign accent or using articles in a non-native way.

interjection A word or phrase which has no grammatical connection with anything else and which typically expresses emotion: *Ouch!*, *Hooray!*, *Shit!*, *Bloody hell!*

interlanguage A language system created by someone learning a foreign language, typically a reduced version of the foreign language with many features carried over from the learner's mother tongue.

interlevel Any level of representation posited in some analysis as lying between two other levels whose existence is more firmly established.

interlocutor The person you are talking to.

internal evidence Evidence about the historical development of a language obtained from the form of the language itself, particularly from its phonology, grammar and vocabulary, but sometimes also from old documents written in the language. Compare **external evidence**.

internal history A historical account of the changes which have affected a particular language over time – that is, changes in phonology, grammar, vocabulary and word meaning. Compare **external history**.

internal inflection A type of **inflection** which is carried out by modifying the shape of a root, rather than by adding **affixes**. For example, the Arabic root *ktb* 'write' has inflected forms like *katab* 'he wrote', *kutib* 'it was written', *aktub* 'he writes' and *uktab* 'it is written'.

internal reconstruction A technique used in **historical linguistics** to discover facts about an unrecorded earlier stage of a single language. The method works solely with data from a recorded stage of that language, especially **alternations**, with no appeal to the facts of related but distinct languages or varieties. Compare **comparative reconstruction**.

internalization The process of acquiring a knowledge of the grammar of a language, especially of a first language by a child.

International Computer Archive of Modern English A corpus of contemporary English stored on computer in Bergen (Norway) and available to scholars for study.

International Corpus of English A corpus of written and spoken English from all the English-speaking countries of the world, stored on computer in London; its purpose is to permit the comparison of regional varieties of English.

international language A language which is widely used, in various parts of the world and for a variety of purposes, by people for whom it is not a mother tongue. At various times, Latin, French and Arabic have all been used as international languages, but today the position of English as the world's premier international language is unchallenged.

International Phonetic Alphabet (**IPA**) An internationally agreed set of characters and diacritics for representing speech sounds. The alphabet was devised by the **International Phonetic Association** and is modified from time to time. The IPA makes heavy use of specially designed characters, which makes it awkward to print, but it is almost universally used by phoneticians and linguists, except in the USA, where **American transcription** continues to be widely used, and sometimes among specialists in particular languages, who often have their own traditional conventions.

International Phonetic Association (**IPA**) The international professional body of phoneticians (specialists in phonetics); it created the **International Phonetic Alphabet** and modifies this alphabet from time to time.

interpersonal function That part of language use involving interactions with other people: greeting, persuading, ordering, and the like. Compare **ideational function**.

interpretation Assigning a meaning to something you hear or read.

interpreting The art of listening to a person speaking in one language and then immediately after (or even simultaneously) producing a spoken equivalent in a different language. Compare **translation**.

interpretive semantics The characteristic of a **formal grammar** in which the syntactic component builds complete syntactic structures, and only then does the semantic component look at these and assign semantic interpretations. Compare **Generative Semantics**.

interrogative The **mood** category attached to a question. Some languages have a distinct grammatical form for this.

intervocalic Occurring between vowels, such as the /t/s in *water* and *city*.

intonation The **pitch** pattern of an utterance, the way the voice goes up and down during an utterance. Speaking without intonation is pathological and gives an inhuman "robotic" quality to speech.

intransitive verb A **verb** which does not take a **direct object**, such as *arrive*, *smile*, *grumble* or *meditate*. We can say *She arrived*, *She arrived late* or *She arrived at the party*, but not **She arrived the party*. Compare **transitive verb** and see the remarks there.

intrinsic ordering In a linguist's description of a language, a particular ordering for some sequence of rules which comes about because of general principles, and therefore does not have to be stated by the linguist. Compare **extrinsic ordering**.

intrusive r A non-historical /r/ which, in certain **non-rhotic accents** of English, appears between vowels in certain circumstances: *law*[r] *and order*, *this bra*[r] *is nice*, *Lisa*[r] *Opie*, *India*[r] *and China*, *the Philadelphia*[r] *Eagles*, and sometimes even *draw*[r]*ing*.

intuition A judgement which you make about your own language: about whether something is grammatical or not, about what it means, about whether it is ambiguous or not, about how it is related to something else, and so on.

inversion Any construction in which the usual order of two items is reversed. The most familiar English example is *subject–verb inversion*, in which the subject follows its verb instead of (as is normal) preceding it: *Can you see it?*; *What are you doing?*

Iordan, Iorgu A Romanian linguist (1888–1986), a specialist in **Romance** linguistics and author of a famous book on the subject.

IP See **item-and-process**.

IPA 1. See **International Phonetic Association**. 2. See **International Phonetic Alphabet**.

Iranian A group of languages spoken in southwestern Asia, making up one branch of the **Indo-Iranian** branch of **Indo-European**. Among them are Persian, Kurdish and Pashto. Two ancient Iranian languages, **Avestan** and **Old Persian**, are abundantly recorded and of great linguistic importance.

Irish The indigenous language of Ireland, belonging to the **Goidelic** branch of the **Celtic** languages. Irish is attested in fragments from the fifth century AD and in substantial texts from the seventh century; specialists distinguish several different historical stages. The language is now in danger of extinction.

Iroquoian A major family of languages spoken in eastern North America, mostly around the Great Lakes. Among them are Seneca, Cayuga and Tuscarora. The Iroquoian languages are now believed to be distantly related to the **Siouan** languages.

irrealis A label often applied in a somewhat unsystematic way to a set of verb forms, in some language, having some kind of connection with unreality.

irregular Of a linguistic form, not constructed according to the usual rules for its class: *feet, took, worse*. The opposite is **regular**.

Isabelle A French girl who was deprived of exposure to language until she was six years old. Rescued at that age and placed in normal surroundings, she began learning French rapidly, and within a year she was almost indistinguishable from other children. Comparison of cases like Isabelle's with cases like those of **Victor**, **Genie** and **Chelsea** provides support for the **critical period hypothesis**.

-ish A suffix often used in forming a name for a language, as in *Spanish, English* and *Kurdish*. Compare **-ic**.

island A part of a sentence which many syntactic processes cannot "reach into". For example, a relative clause is an island in English: corresponding to a statement like *The guests who arrived in a car are ready to go home*, we cannot ask a question like **Which car are the guests who arrived in ready to go home?*, because the question is trying to "reach into" the island.

isochrony A type of speech rhythm in which each unit of a certain type tends to be produced at regular intervals of time. Two common types are **stress-timing** and **syllable-timing**.

isogloss A line drawn on a map which shows the approximate boundary between two different linguistic forms used in different areas by speakers of a single language.

isogloss bundle A group of **isoglosses** which fall in roughly the same place. Such a bundle is often taken as marking a significant dialect boundary.

isolated language A language which has no known genetic relatives, or at least no living relatives. Famous examples are **Basque** in Europe and **Burushaski** in Asia; **Japanese** and **Korean** are also widely regarded as isolates, though not all agree.

isolating language (also **analytic language**) A language in which every word consists of a single morpheme, such as Vietnamese or classical Chinese (modern Chinese is different). Such a language has no morphology.

isolation aphasia A rare type of **aphasia** in which a freakish injury leaves the language areas of the brain intact but disconnected from the rest of the brain. A sufferer can neither speak normally nor understand speech, but tends to repeat mechanically anything said to her.

isomorphism A one-to-one matching between the items in two different systems. For example, the colour terms of two languages would be isomorphic if each single term in one language had a single exact equivalent in the other.

-ist The suffix usually used to coin a term for a specialist in a particular language or language family. Thus, a *Celticist* is a specialist in **Celtic**, and a *Hispanist* is a specialist in **Spanish** or the Hispanic languages generally.

i.t.a. See **Initial Teaching Alphabet**.

Italian The principal language of Italy, one of the **Romance** languages.

Italic A group of languages making up one branch of **Indo-European**, including **Latin** (and its **Romance** descendants) and several extinct languages:

Faliscan, Oscan, Umbrian, and a number of sparsely attested others, all of them anciently spoken in Italy.

italics Slanted type, *like this*. Italics are widely used for emphasis and for citing titles; in linguistics, we use them for citing linguistic forms, as when we speak of the English word *dog* or of the Basque word *etxe* 'house'.

item-and-arrangement (**IA**) A label applied to an approach to describing languages in which the investigator identifies classes of words, morphemes or other grammatical objects and gives rules stating which of these things can be combined and in what order; there are no abstract underlying representations, and no rules converting these into surface forms. This approach was much favoured by the **American structuralists**.

item-and-process (**IP**) A label applied to an approach to describing languages in which abstract underlying representations are posited by the investigator in order to express certain generalizations, and these underlying forms are then acted upon by a series of rules to change them into surface forms. This label was particularly attached to the early versions of **transformational grammar**, in which the IP idea was taken to an extreme; it is rarely heard today.

iterative (also **frequentative**) An **aspect** category expressing repeated action. English has no specific verb-form for this, and we have to say something like *She kept (on) trying*, but some other languages do have a specific verb-form for this purpose.

J

Jaberg, Karl An important Swiss dialectologist (1877–1959).

Jackendoff, Ray An American linguist and cognitive scientist (1945–); he has contributed both to grammatical theory and to the study of language and mind.

Jackson, Kenneth H. A British linguist (1909–91), an outstanding specialist in **Celtic** languages.

Jakobson, Roman A Russian linguist (1896–1982) who spent much of his career in Prague and in the USA. One of the most wide-ranging and influential figures in the history of linguistics, he worked on phonology, literary theory, language acquisition, aphasia, and Slavic languages. He was largely responsible for introducing **Prague School** ideas to the USA and for introducing **distinctive features** into phonology; he also championed the notion of **markedness** and initiated work on **universals**.

Jakobson-Halle feature system A system of **distinctive features** devised in the 1950s by Roman **Jakobson** and Morris **Halle**. The first complete set of features to be proposed, the J-H system used acoustic features representing the characteristics of speech sounds which showed up in a sound spectrogram, like [flat] and [grave]. The system was eventually displaced by the *SPE feature system*.

Japanese The principal language of Japan. Japanese is not known to be related to any other language, though some linguists believe it may be remotely related both to **Korean** and to the **Altaic** languages. The Japanese writing system is of extraordinary complexity, consisting of a mixture of Chinese characters (*kanji*) and two sets of syllabic characters (*kana*).

Japhetic 1. An archaic name for the **Indo-European** family of languages. 2. A hypothetical language family proposed by the eccentric Georgian linguist Nikolai **Marr**; at various times he included in it virtually all of the known non-Indo-European languages of Europe and western Asia, and even **Celtic** and some American languages. Marr maintained that Japhetic had been the ancestral language of Europe, that its speakers had formed a classless communistic society, and that it had been displaced by the speakers of Indo-European, who had introduced imperialism and capitalism. These ideas have long been dismissed as absurd fantasies.

jargon 1. The distinctive technical terminology of a specialist discipline, such as evolutionary theory, law or linguistics. The term is sometimes extended to the distinctive vocabulary of any social group, such as truck-drivers or radio hams. 2. Non-existent and unintelligible words used by some sufferers from **aphasia** or other language disorders.

jargon aphasia A type of **aphasia** in which the sufferer's speech consists entirely, or nearly so, of incomprehensible nonsense words. Rhythm and intonation are often quite normal, though comprehension is usually destroyed.

Jespersen, Otto A Danish linguist (1860–1943), a specialist in the grammar and history of English and known especially for his seven-volume history of English grammar.

jocular formation A word or expression created deliberately for humorous effect, such as *wasm* 'an outdated doctrine'.

Johnson, (Dr) Samuel A British scholar (1709–84), author of a famous and influential dictionary of English (1755).

Jones, Daniel A British phonetician (1881–1967). Jones studied under **Passy** and **Sweet**; learning of the **phoneme** concept from the **Kazan school,** he was the first to use the term 'phoneme' in English. He became head of the first department of phonetics in Britain, at the University of London, and he published several classic books, including *The Pronunciation of English* (1909), *EPD* (first edition 1917), *An Outline of English Pronunciation* (first edition 1918), and *The Phoneme* (first edition 1950). Almost all the British phoneticians of the twentieth century were taught by Jones or by his students.

Jones, Sir William A British judge in India (1746–94). A distinguished amateur phonetician and linguist, Jones is known above all for his famous remark in 1786 that Sanskrit must be related to Greek and Latin; this is commonly regarded as having initiated the discovery and study of the **Indo-European** language family.

journal A periodical publication devoted to scholarly articles in some discipline. There are dozens of journals devoted to linguistics and language studies; some deal with general linguistics, others with specialist areas like sociolinguistics, historical linguistics or language acquisition, still others with particular languages or language families. Among the major journals of general linguistics are *Language* (USA), the *Journal of Linguistics* (UK) and *Lingua* (Netherlands).

Specialist journals include the *Journal of Child Language*, the *International Journal of the Sociology of Language* (sociolinguistics), *Diachronica* (historical linguistics), the *Journal of French Linguistics*, and *Linguistic Inquiry* (Chomskyan linguistics).

Jud, Jakob An important Swiss dialectologist (1882–1952).

Judaeo-Spanish (also **Ladino**) A **Romance** language spoken by Jews in the Middle East, especially in Turkey; these are the descendants of the Jews expelled from Spain in 1492.

juncture Any phonetic feature whose presence signals the presence of a grammatical boundary. Differences in juncture account for the differences in pronunciation between *nitrate* and *night rate*, and between *white shoes* and *why choose*.

Junius, Franciscus A German-born Dutch linguist (1591–1677) who mostly worked in England; he is regarded as the founder of the historical study of the **Germanic** languages.

jussive A command directed at someone other than the addressee, a "third-person imperative", as in Marie Antoinette's *Let them eat cake!*

K

Kadai (also **Daic**) A language family of southeast Asia, including **Tai** and some smaller languages.

Kannada A major language of southern India, a **Dravidian** language.

Kanzi A bonobo (pygmy chimpanzee) who has been taught to use a version of **sign language** and who has reportedly achieved much greater success than the chimps used in earlier experiments.

Karen A group of languages belonging to the **Tibeto-Burman** family, widely spoken in Burma and Thailand.

Karlgren, Bernhard A Swedish linguist (1889–1978). He was the first to apply the **comparative method** to the **Chinese** languages and to reconstruct an ancient form of Chinese.

Kartvelian A small family of languages spoken in the Caucasus, also called *South Caucasian*. The best-known Kartvelian language is Georgian.

Kashmiri The principal language of Kashmir, a member of the **Dardic** branch of **Indo-Iranian**.

Katz, Jerrold An American linguist and philosopher of language (1932–). Though he made important contributions to the early development of **transformational grammar**, Katz is best known for his Platonistic view of language, in which linguistic objects are purely abstract (not of this world), from which it follows that linguistics is not an empirical science but an abstract discipline like mathematics.

Katz-Postal hypothesis In **transformational grammar**, the principle that a transformation may not change the meaning of a sentence to which it applies. The earliest (*Syntactic Structures*) version of TG had allowed transformations to change meaning (for example, by introducing negation), but the K-P hypothesis, which appeared in 1964, was accepted as a cornerstone in the *Aspects model* and in all later versions of TG.

Kazan School The name given to the work of the two Polish linguists Jan **Baudouin de Courtenay** and Mikołaj **Kruszewski**, who worked at Kazan in Russia in the late nineteenth century. They introduced the notion of the **phoneme** and anticipated many of the ideas of **Saussure**.

Keltic An old-fashioned spelling of **Celtic**.

Kenyon and Knott system An analysis of American English vowels which has been widely used in American textbooks and dictionaries.

kernel sentence In the earliest (*Syntactic Structures*) version of **transformational grammar**, a sentence whose derivation involves no optional transformations: in practice, an affirmative declarative sentence containing only a single clause. In this model, all other types of sentence are derived from kernel sentences by optional transformations. The idea of kernel sentences was scrapped in the 1965 *Aspects model*.

Ket A language spoken in Siberia, the last survivor of the **Yeniseian** family.

key The tone or spirit of a spoken interaction, which may range from intimate to frostily formal.

Khoisan A group of languages spoken in southern Africa, mostly in and near the Kalahari Desert, consisting of two main groups: Bushman and Nama (formerly called *Hottentot*). These languages are famous for the extraordinary number of **clicks** found in their consonant systems. It is not certain that they form a single genetic family.

kinesics The use of gestures and expressions during speech in order to add meaning or to modify the import of spoken language, or the study of this.

King's English See **Queen's English**.

kinship terms The set of words in a particular language for naming family members and relatives, such as *mother, brother, uncle* and *granddaughter*. Kinship terminology is usually highly structured, and there are interesting differences among languages. Anthropological linguists typically take great interest in kinship terms.

Kiparsky, Paul A Finnish-American linguist (1941–), a major contributor to phonological theory and to the study of phonological change.

koiné A more-or-less uniform spoken language which is used as the ordinary vehicle of communication over a sizeable area, usually by a number of people for whom it is not the mother tongue. The term was originally applied to the variety of Greek which spread throughout the empire of Alexander the Great.

Koko A gorilla who was taught to use a version of **sign language**. The degree of success achieved by Koko is deeply controversial.

Kordofanian A group of languages spoken in Sudan; their genetic affiliation is disputed, some linguists favouring **Nilo-Saharan**, others **Niger-Congo**.

Korean The principal language of Korea, an **isolated language**. Some linguists think Korean may be related to **Japanese** and to the **Altaic** languages. Korean is written both with Chinese characters and with the indigenous **Han'gŭl** alphabet.

Krio An English-based **creole** used in several parts of west Africa, especially in Sierra Leone.

Kripke, Saul An American philosopher and logician (1940–), the chief developer of **modal logic**; his work led directly to **possible-worlds semantics** and then to **Montague semantics**.

Kroeber, A(rthur) L. An American anthropologist (1876–1960), a student of North American languages and a pioneer in anthropological linguistics; he was largely responsible for making linguistics an integral part of American anthropology.

Kru A group of languages spoken in west Africa, a branch of the **Niger-Congo** family.

Kruszewski, Mikołaj A Polish linguist (1851–87), a leading member of the **Kazan school**; he is generally credited with having introduced the notion of the **phoneme** into linguistics.

Kurath, Hans An Austrian-born American dialectologist (1891–1992). The leading figure in American dialectology, Kurath was highly innovative in methodology and presentation, and he was principally responsible for the **dialect atlases** of New England and of the eastern states.

Kurdish A prominent **Iranian** language spoken in parts of Turkey, Iraq, Iran and Syria.

Kurgan culture An ancient culture, uncovered by archaeologists, which flourished on the steppes north of the Black Sea around 6000 years ago and apparently spread out from there. The Kurgan people built no settlements, but their characteristic grave mounds, or *kurgans*, are highly distinctive. A number of specialists have argued that the Kurgan people were the speakers of **Proto-Indo-European**.

Kuryłowicz, Jerzy A Polish linguist (1895–1978), one of the most prominent linguists of the twentieth century. He contributed widely to historical and theoretical linguistics and to the study of Indo-European and Semitic languages, but he is perhaps best known for his "laws" of analogy and for his observation that Hittite preserved some of the PIE **laryngeals** (sense 2).

Kwa A large group of West African languages forming one branch of the **Niger-Congo** family; among them are Igbo, Yoruba and Ewe.

L1 Your mother tongue, as opposed to a language which you are trying to learn, the **L2**.

L2 A second language which you are trying to learn.

labelled bracketing A **bracketing** which includes a label for **syntactic category** on each unit recognized.

labial Pertaining to the lips. Any sound whose production involves the use of the lips, such as [m] or [f], may be described as 'labial', but we often prefer more specific labels like **bilabial** or **labio-dental**.

labialization Lip-rounding accompanying another articulation, as in [kʷ] (a [k] pronounced with lip-rounding).

labio-dental (A speech sound) produced with the upper lip and the lower teeth, such as [f] or [v].

labio-velar A loose label for any sound whose production involves both the lips and (the back of the tongue plus) the **velum**, such as [kʷ] (a *labialized velar*) or [w] (a *labial-velar*).

Labov, William An American sociolinguist (1927–), an enormously original and influential figure who has created much of the methodology of the discipline and uncovered a series of surprising and fascinating phenomena.

Lacan, Jacques A French psychiatrist (1901–81) who stressed the importance of language in psychoanalytic theory; he coined the slogan "it is the world of words that creates the world of things".

LAD The abbreviation for **Language Acquisition Device**.

Ladefoged, Peter An English phonetician (1925–) who works in the USA. Though a major theorist of phonetics, he is best known for his tireless fieldwork in recording the sounds of hundreds of languages.

Ladin A **Rhaeto-Romance** language spoken in northeastern Italy.

Ladino Another name for **Judaeo-Spanish**.

LAGB See the **Linguistics Association of Great Britain**.

la-la theory (also **sing-song theory**) The conjecture that language arose out of song and play. There is no evidence to support this conjecture. The **come-into-my-bower theory** is a version of this.

laminal (A speech sound) produced with the **blade** of the tongue and the **alveolar ridge**, such as [t] or [s] for most (not all) speakers of English.

Lana A chimpanzee trained to communicate by pressing computer keys each of which was marked with an abstract symbol representing a word; her "language" was called **Yerkish**.

Lancaster-Oslo/Bergen Corpus of British English (**LOB Corpus**) A corpus of written British English stored on computer in Norway.

Langacker, Ronald W. An American linguist (1942–), a contributor to syntactic theory and the leading proponent of **cognitive grammar**.

langage In **Saussure**'s classification, the human language faculty.

language The central object of study in linguistics, but one which can be approached from several points of view. The ultimate goal of the discipline is the elucidation of the human **language faculty** (Saussure's *langage*), the cognitive and neurological facts which enable us to learn and use languages. To this end linguists have often found it necessary to distinguish between the abstract mental system of rules, principles and constraints which are shared by speakers (variously called *langue* or **competence**), and the real utterances produced by individual speakers on particular occasions (*parole* or **performance**). A further distinction must be made between the properties shared by all human languages (Chomsky's **universal grammar**), resulting from the nature of our language faculty, and the properties of individual languages, which will be partly accidental. In practice, it is these individual languages which are most easily examined, and it is important to realize that only **natural languages** (mother tongues) strictly count for this purpose, though linguists are none the less sometimes interested in **artificial languages, pidgins** and even **animal communication**. An individual natural language may itself be viewed either as a set of rules and principles in the minds of speakers (Chomsky's **I-language**) or as a set of possible sentences (his **E-language**). A **formal language**, which is always viewed as a set of sentences, is of course not a natural language, but linguists often find it useful to construct formal languages in order to compare their properties with the observed properties of natural languages; a formal language which provides a good match may tell us important things about the structures of human languages generally.

language acquisition   See **acquisition**.

Language Acquisition Device (**LAD**) A hypothetical mental system, supposedly present in our brains at birth, which enables us to learn a first language in childhood. The LAD supposedly consists of three parts: a set of linguistic universals, a device for constructing hypotheses about possible rules of grammar, and a procedure for evaluating these hypotheses. Proposed by **Chomsky**, the LAD idea has now given way in his work to the **parameter-setting model**.

language areas The well-defined regions of the brain which play a crucial role in language production and comprehension, notably **Broca's area** and **Wernicke's area**.

language attrition The gradual loss of a language through lack of use – for example, the loss of a mother tongue by an immigrant to a country where a different language is spoken.

language awareness An educational policy aimed at stimulating curiosity about language and at integrating different approaches to language within the educational system.

language change Change in a language over time. Every language which is spoken as a mother tongue is changing constantly, in pronunciation, in grammar, and in vocabulary; there is no such thing as a living language which fails to change. That fabled village in Derbyshire or the Appalachians where they still speak Elizabethan English does not exist.

language classification Any of various ways of organizing languages into groups. The most familiar type of classification is by **genetic relationship** – classifying languages according to their ancestry. Another important kind of classification is **typology** – grouping languages according to their structural characteristics.

language conflict Any of various kinds of public disagreement about language use and language policy, but most especially those involving the competing claims of different languages in a multilingual society.

language contact The state of affairs in which speakers of different languages have dealings with one another which are sufficiently intense that features of vocabulary, pronunciation or grammar are taken over from one language into another.

language death The disappearance of a language as a mother tongue, usually because its last speakers abandon it in favour of some other language, rarely because its last speakers are all killed.

language development Another name for **elaboration**.

language engineering Another name for **language planning**.

language faculty The totality of the mental, cognitive and neurological faculties which jointly enable us to learn and use languages.

language family A group of languages which are all genetically related – that is, they are all descended from a single common ancestral language, and they began life as no more than dialects of that ancestor. At present about 300 families are recognized, most of them in the Americas, but further work will probably reduce that number by joining some families into larger families.

language for special purposes (**LSP**) Teaching a second language with the goal of enabling learners to function effectively in that language in some specific area, such as air-traffic control or the law.

language game 1. A metaphorical way of looking at language, one which stresses its fluid and flexible nature. This idea has been chiefly developed by **Wittgenstein** as a remedy for traditional ideas, in which a language was often seen as no more than a set of labels for a world of pre-existing and more or less fixed objects and concepts. 2. Any way of playing with spoken language, such as talking backwards or changing the shapes of words in a systematic way; Pig Latin is a familiar example.

language instinct The powerful tendency of children to construct a language on the basis of whatever input is available to them; **creoles** and **home sign** systems provide evidence of the reality of this tendency.

language laboratory A room equipped with instruments like tape recorders, videos and possibly computers and used to assist learners of a foreign language.

language loss The state of affairs in which an individual or a community gradually ceases to use a language, leading eventually to inability to speak it in the case of an individual and **language death** in a community.

language maintenance (also **language loyalty**) The continued use of a language by its speakers, especially in circumstances in which it is under pressure from another language; the opposite of **language loss** or **language death**.

language of thought (also **mentalese**) A hypothetical special language used for thinking and quite distinct from ordinary spoken language. The idea is controversial.

language organ Any of various hypothetical structures in the brain which are assumed to play a crucial role in the learning and use of language.

language pathology The study and treatment of all forms of abnormal linguistic behaviour, typically involving contributions from linguists, neurologists, psychologists and medical practitioners.

language planning (also **language engineering**) Making deliberate decisions about the form of a language, such as choosing among competing forms and inventing new vocabulary. This is most often carried out on some kind of official basis. A large-scale programme of language planning may be divided into **selection, codification, elaboration, implementation** (sense 2) and **acceptance**.

language policy An official government policy regulating the form, teaching or use of one or more languages within the area controlled by that government.

language processing The sum of the mental activities involved in producing and comprehending language.

language shift A change by a group of people from one mother tongue to another, as when speakers of Irish or Hopi abandon their ancestral tongue in favour of English.

language teaching The process of instructing students in the use of a language, either their mother tongue or a foreign language.

langue In **Saussure**'s classification, language regarded as a system shared by a community of speakers, roughly the same as **competence**. Compare *parole*.

Lao The principal language of Laos, a member of the **Tai** family.

Lappish A popular but rather offensive name for **Saami**.

LARSP (in full, *Language Assessment, Remediation and Screening Procedure*) A particular approach to the study and treatment of language disability in children. A profile is constructed of children who develop normally, and this is compared with the profile of a child suffering from a disability in order to try to pinpoint the problem.

laryngeal 1. (A speech sound) articulated in the larynx. 2. One of a set of hypothetical consonants reconstructed for **Proto-Indo-European** on internal grounds and later found (in some cases) to be directly attested in Hittite. The phonetic nature of these sounds is not known with certainty.

laryngealization 1. Another name for **creaky voice**. 2. The use of a **glottalic airstream mechanism**.

laryngectomy Removal of the larynx for medical reasons.

larynx (informally, **voice box**) A complex structure in the throat through which air from the lungs must pass during speech; it contains the **vocal folds**.

late closure, principle of A **perceptual strategy** of speech **comprehension** which says "if possible, put the next word into the phrase you are currently processing". By this principle, if you hear *Susie decided gradually to get rid of her* *teddy bears*, you will associate *gradually* with *decided*, rather than with *to get rid of her teddy bears*.

lateral (A speech sound) produced in such a way that airflow is completely blocked in the midline of the mouth while air flows along one side or both sides, such as [l].

lateralization Specialization of function between the two hemispheres of the brain.

Latin The language of ancient Rome and of the Roman Empire, a member of the **Italic** branch of **Indo-European**. Latin displaced the indigenous languages in much of the empire, and it has never ceased to be spoken, but its modern forms are so different from the language of the Romans, and from one another, that we no longer find it convenient to call them 'Latin'; instead, we gave them names like **Spanish**, **French** and **Italian** (these are the **Romance** languages). The *classical Latin* of the Romans continued to be used as a language of learning in Europe for many centuries, and English and other languages have borrowed thousands of words from it.

Latvian The principal language of Latvia, a **Baltic** language.

Laura (also **Marta**) An American woman who suffers from the **chatterbox syndrome**.

lax The opposite of **tense** (sense 2); see that entry.

learnability problem The problem of how children manage to learn their first language. This is a central problem in modern linguistic theory, especially since there is good reason to believe that children do not receive enough information in order to learn a language from scratch. Consequently, many linguists favour the **innateness hypothesis**, by which we are born knowing what human languages are like.

learnèd form A word which has been borrowed directly into a language from an ancestral form of that language and which hence does not show the normal phonological developments typical of the borrowing language. For example, Latin *strictus* develops regularly into *étroit* 'narrow' in its daughter French, but the Latin word is also borrowed directly as French *strict* 'strict, narrow'; this is a learnèd form.

lect Any distinguishable speech variety.

left-branching A type of syntactic structure in which modifiers precede their heads, so that recursion of the structure, when represented in a **tree structure**, produces a series of branches running down to the left. An English example is that illustrated in *Susie's boyfriend's mother's job*. Left-branching is strongly characteristic of **SOV languages**.

left-dislocation A construction in which a noun phrase is moved to the beginning of a sentence, with its ordinary position being filled by a pronoun, as in *Susie, I like her a lot*. Compare **topicalization**.

left-to-right processing A model of **comprehension** which assumes that a hearer processes a sentence steadily from left to right, from the beginning to the end. This model is almost certainly too simple; see **perceptual strategy**.

Lehiste, Ilse An Estonian-American phonetician and linguist (1922–), best known for her work on **suprasegmentals**.

Lehmann, Winfred P. An American linguist (1916–), a specialist in **Indo-European**. He introduced a number of linguistic concepts and methods into IE studies, but is best known for his reconstruction of PIE syntax.

Leibniz, Gottfried W. A German philosopher and mathematician (1646–1716) who wrote on the origin and development of languages.

lemma 1. The complete set of the inflected forms of a **lexical item**. For example, the lemma *go* includes the forms *go, goes, going, went, gone*. 2. Another name for a **headword**.

length (also **quantity**) The amount of time required to pronounce a speech sound, particularly when this is linguistically important in a particular language. Many languages distinguish long and short vowels and consonants (long segments are marked with a colon): Old English /god/ 'God' and /go:d/ 'good'; Italian /nono/ 'ninth' and /non:o/ 'grandfather'.

lenis The opposite of **fortis**; see that entry.

lenition (also **weakening**) Any phonological process in which a speech sound is changed to another sound which involves a less complete blockage of the airstream, such as the lenition of the [p] when Latin *ripa* 'riverbank' became Spanish *riba* and French *rive*. The opposite is **fortition**.

Lenneberg, Eric An American neurologist (1921–75); he made a number of contributions, but is perhaps best known for formulating the **critical period hypothesis**.

lento speech Speech which is unusually slow and careful. See **allegro form**.

Lepsius, Carl R. A German linguist (1810–84). He did important descriptive work on African and Asian languages, especially Egyptian, but is best known for his 'Standard Alphabet', an early **phonetic alphabet**.

Leskien, August A German linguist (1840–1916), a specialist in Baltic and Slavic languages and a leading **Neogrammarian**.

letter One of the characters in an **alphabet**, such as the *a*, *b*, *c* of the Roman alphabet. This term is not applied to a character in a non-alphabetic writing system.

level In some linguistic theories, one of the several "layers" which are recognized for analytical purposes; usually any recognized linguistic process is confined to applying at some particular level, and often (not always) the levels are arranged in a particular order.

levelling See **analogical levelling**.

Lévi-Strauss, Claude A French anthropologist (1908–). Much influenced by linguistics, especially by **Jakobson,** he introduced the concept of **structuralism** into anthropology, from where it became a major intellectual movement in the social sciences generally.

Lewis, Henry A Welsh philologist (1889–1968), a premier specialist in the **Celtic** languages.

lexeme Another name for a **lexical item**.

lexical Pertaining to words, especially to **lexical items**.

lexical access The first stage of **word recognition**, in which a sequence of speech sounds is compared with possible words in the **mental lexicon**.

lexical ambiguity An **ambiguity** resulting entirely from the multiple meanings of a single word, as in *This splendid old port is mentioned in Captain Cook's diaries* (a type of wine or a city by the sea).

lexical category Another name for **word class**.

lexical decision task An experimental technique in which a subject is asked to decide quickly whether some sequence of sounds or letters is a word or not: *blick, stand, frink*, and so on.

lexical diffusion A type of phonological change in which a newer pronunciation replaces an older one in a few words at a time, gradually spreading to more and more words.

lexical entry In a **formal grammar**, that portion of the **lexicon** (sense 2) detailing the properties of a single **lexical item**: its pronunciation, its meaning, its **word class**, its **subcategorization** behaviour, any grammatical irregularities, and possibly other information.

lexical field theory Another name for **semantic field theory**.

Lexical-Functional Grammar (**LFG**) A theory of grammar developed by Joan Bresnan and Ronald Kaplan. LFG uses elaborate **lexical entries** and represents a sentence as two structures simultaneously, a *c-structure*, which looks like an ordinary syntactic **tree structure**, and an *f-structure*, which includes certain additional types of information.

lexical item (also **lexeme**) A word regarded as a somewhat abstract item which has a more or less constant meaning or function but which can possibly vary in form for grammatical purposes. For example, the lexical item DOG has the grammatical forms *dog* and *dogs*, while the lexical item TAKE has the grammatical forms *take, takes, taking, took* and *taken*. A lexical item is a word in the sense in which a dictionary contains words.

lexicalization 1. Providing a single word to represent a meaning. For example, the meaning 'adult female bovine' is lexicalized in English as *cow*, but there is no English lexicalization for the meaning 'adult bovine (of either sex)'. 2. A change by which something that used to be two or more words becomes a single word, as when English *God be with you* became the word *goodbye*.

lexical morpheme A **morpheme** which has dictionary meaning, such as *dog*, *take, green*, the *step-* of *stepmother* or the *post-* of *post-war*. Compare **grammatical morpheme**.

lexical morphology Another name for **word-formation**.

Lexical Phonology and Morphology A linguistic theory which integrates phonology and morphology and which divides the whole area into a series of levels, with every recognized process confined to applying at some particular level.

lexical relation Another name for a **semantic relation**.

lexical rule 1. In some types of **formal grammar**, a **rule** which inserts **lexical items** into a **tree structure**. An example is N → {*boy, girl, dog, tree*, . . . }, which says 'put one of these items into an N (noun) node in a tree'. 2. In some types of formal grammar, a rule which builds up a syntactic unit from **lexical items** and possibly other material. An example is AdjP → [*un*- + V[transitive] + -*ed* (*by* NP)], which says that an adjective phrase may be constructed as shown, thus yielding sentences like *Her arrival was unnoticed by the crowd*.

lexical semantics The study of the meanings of words, including the way in which some word-meanings are related to others.

lexical verb (also **main verb**) A **verb** which is not an **auxiliary**. Examples: *smile, destroy, begin, want*.

Lexicase A theory of grammar developed by Stanley Starosta in the 1970s, a combination of **dependency grammar** with **case grammar**.

lexicography The writing of dictionaries, or the scholarly study of this activity.

lexicology The study of words, from any point of view.

lexicon 1. The **vocabulary** of a particular language. 2. In a formal grammar, that part of the grammar which includes the **lexical entries**. 3. Another word for a **dictionary**.

lexicostatistics A statistical technique for comparing languages which are known to be in **genetic relationship** and for which **cognates** have been identified. Sample word lists (typically the **Swadesh word list**) for the languages are compared to see how many cognates are still retained by the languages; the fewer cognates retained, the greater the degree of separation. If a time element is introduced, the result is **glottochronology**.

lexis The vocabulary of a language.

LF See **logical form**.

LFG See **Lexical-Functional Grammar**.

Li, Fang-Kuei A Chinese linguist (1902–87) who mostly worked in the USA; he pioneered the study of the non-Chinese languages of China.

liaison Something that happens in French. A word which, in isolation, ends in a vowel may acquire a final consonant before another word beginning with a vowel, as when *petit* 'little' [pti] becomes [ptit] when followed by *ami* 'friend' [ami]: *petit ami* 'little friend' [ptitami]. This is *liaison*.

licensing The appearance of some item in a sentence because it is required or allowed by some other item in that sentence. For example, in *She took her notebook*, the transitive verb *took* licenses the object noun phrase *her notebook*.

Lieberman, Philip An American speech scientist (1934–) known especially for his work on the **vocal tract**.

ligature The joining of two letters, as in æ, used to form the character **ash**, and sometimes also for writing Latin words in English, as in the name *Cæsar*.

light syllable A **syllable** which takes less time to pronounce than some other syllables; see the discussion under **heavy syllable**.

limited scope formula A grammatical pattern used only with a small number of words, particularly by a young child.

Linear A A **syllabary** used by the Minoan civilization of Crete in the second millennium BC; it has never been deciphered, and we don't know what language is concealed in the texts.

Linear B A **syllabary**, derived from **Linear A**, used by the Mycenaean Greeks to write Greek during the Greek Bronze Age (the late second millennium BC). The script was successfully deciphered by the British amateur linguist Michael **Ventris** in 1952.

lingua franca A language which is routinely used in some region for dealings between people who have different mother tongues.

lingual (A speech sound) produced by using the tongue in some way.

linguicide The deliberate destruction of a language by official policy, involving strong persecution of it up to and even including the murder of its speakers.

linguist 1. A practitioner of **linguistics**; a scientist of language. 2. A person who speaks several languages; a polyglot.

linguistic 1. Pertaining to language(s). 2. Pertaining to **linguistics**.

linguistic anthropology Another name for **anthropological linguistics**.

linguistic area (also *Sprachbund*) A geographical region containing several languages which are not closely related but which share a number of structural properties, especially properties which they do not share with their closer relatives elsewhere. A linguistic area results from long and intense contact; a famous example is found in the Balkans.

linguistic determinism The hypothesis that the structure of a particular language, or the structure of human languages generally, strongly influences the way speakers look at the world. The **Sapir-Whorf hypothesis** is a famous version of this, but the notion is more general: for example, some have argued that the universal tendency of languages to distinguish agents and non-agents encourages us to disregard the significance of forests, rivers and oceans.

linguistic diversity The number of different languages spoken in a given area. Such diversity varies greatly; among the most diverse regions of the planet are the Amazon basin, many parts of Africa, the Caucasus, southeast Asia and, above all, New Guinea, where about 1000 languages (15 per cent of the world's total) are spoken in an area the size of Texas. Compare **genetic density**.

linguistic geography The study of the distribution of languages around the planet, including change in that distribution over time.

linguistic imperialism The state of affairs in which a single language or variety becomes so prestigious that others used in the same area are relegated to inferior status and possibly condemned or persecuted.

linguistic palaeontology The use of data from ancient (especially reconstructed) languages to draw conclusions about the culture of their speakers.

linguistic philosophy Another name for **ordinary language philosophy**. **Note:** do not confuse this with **philosophy of language**.

linguistic relativity hypothesis Another name for the **Sapir-Whorf hypothesis**.

linguistics The scientific study of language.

Linguistics Association of Great Britain (**LAGB**) The professional organization of theoretical and general linguists in the UK.

linguistic sign In the work of **Saussure**, the combination of a linguistic form (the *signifiant*) with its meaning or function (the *signifié*).

Linguistic Society of America (**LSA**) The professional organization of theoretical and general linguists in the USA.

linguistic theory The entire body of theoretical work on the nature of human language.

lip-reading A technique for understanding speech by watching the movements of the lips, used by deaf people and by those working in very noisy environments.

lip-rounding Bringing the sides of the lips together, often with some degree of protrusion of the lips, as happens in the production of rounded vowels like [u] and [o], the consonant [w], and (for many speakers) the [s] in *sweet* and the [ʃ] in *sheep*.

liquid A traditional label for any speech sound which is either a **lateral** or a **rhotic**; informally, the class of "L-sounds" and "R-sounds".

lisp Any feature of pronunciation which is perceived as childish, affected or defective. A familiar English example is the use of the dental fricatives [θ] and [ð] in place of [s] and [z].

LISP A computer language which is particularly convenient for performing certain tasks involving language.

list An electronic service linking specialists in a particular discipline by means of the Internet, allowing them to seek advice, discuss controversial issues, announce publications and conferences, and the like. A number of language-based lists exist, the largest being *Linguist*, which deals with general linguistics and has (at the time of writing) over 7000 subscribers worldwide. Lists are aimed at professional specialists but are usually open to everyone. If you join one, be very cautious about joining in the discussion unless you are certain you have something useful to say. Do not ask beginners' questions (a **newsgroup** is the right place for this); do not ask the other members of the list to do your homework for you; and be unfailingly courteous. Breaking these rules will get you expelled from the list very quickly, and you will acquire a worldwide reputation for being ignorant and offensive.

literacy The ability to read and write.

literary language 1. Any language which has been used in the writing of a substantial body of literature. 2. That particular form of a language which is regarded by its speakers as most appropriate for serious writing.

literature 1. Writing of an imaginative nature, such as novels, short stories, plays and poetry. 2. The body of published scholarly work, both books and journal articles, in a particular specialist field. When undertaking work in a particular field, you are expected to be familiar with the literature in that field, if there is any.

Lithuanian The major language of Lithuania, a **Baltic** language. Lithuanian is considered to be the most conservative **Indo-European** language still spoken.

litotes (also **meiosis**) Understatement, such as when we say "not bad" for something outstandingly good.

liturgical language A language used by the members of some religion for religious purposes, particularly as the vehicle of sacred writings, but often also for prayers and ceremonies. Very often a liturgical language is a language which is dead as a mother tongue.

living language Any language which is somebody's mother tongue today.

loan translation Another name for a **calque**.

loan word A word in one language which has been taken over ("borrowed") from another language, such as English *pepper* (from Latin), *skirt* (from Old Norse), *castle* (from Norman French), *amateur* (from modern French), *brandy* (from Dutch) and *kayak* (from an Eskimo language).

LOB Corpus See the **Lancaster-Oslo/Bergen Corpus of British English**.

local dependency A grammatical connection between two points in a sentence which must be contained within a single syntactic unit, such as a noun phrase, a verb phrase or a single clause. **Subcategorization, agreement** and **government** are all types of local dependency. Compare **unbounded dependency**.

localization The occurrence in the brain of small areas with very specific functions. The **language areas** are examples.

locative In some **case** languages, a case which expresses location, corresponding to English 'in, on, at', such as Basque *etxean* 'in the house' (*etxe* 'house').

Locke, John An English philosopher (1632–1704); he emphasized the imperfection of language as a vehicle of communication and as an obstacle to the acquisition of knowledge.

Lodwick, Francis An English phonetician (1619–94), the inventor of an early **phonetic alphabet** and of a sketch for a "universal language".

logical form (**LF**) In **Government-and-Binding Theory**, a level of syntactic representation in which all quantifiers and WH-words are moved to the beginning of the sentence in order to mark their scope; this is required for the sentence to receive a semantic interpretation.

logical positivism An approach to philosophy which holds that the only meaningful statements, apart from those which are true or false by definition, are those which are empirically verifiable; proponents reject as meaningless all versions of metaphysics and theology, and sometimes also ethics.

logogen model A model of **word recognition** in which perceptual information builds up until a critical level is reached, at which point the word being recognized is identified.

logogram A symbol representing a complete word, such as 5 for 'five' or & for 'and'. In a **logographic script**, all or most words are represented by logograms, which means that thousands of symbols are required. Note that the logograms ('characters') of Chinese and Japanese more typically represent **morphemes**, rather than words: for example, the Chinese word *huǒchē* 'train', a compound of *huǒ* 'fire' and *chē* 'vehicle', is written with the two characters for *huǒ* and *chē*.

logographic script A **writing system** which consists of **logograms**. The only fully logographic script in use today is that of Chinese, though some other writing systems, such as that of Japanese, use a mixture of logograms and other characters. **Note:** the logograms of a logographic script represent *words*, not "ideas". No writing system has ever been discovered which represents "ideas" or "thoughts" directly; every system represents the words of a particular language.

logonomic rules In some versions of **social semiotics**, a set of high-level rules governing the social use of language: rules about who is allowed to speak in what circumstances, about what sort of language is appropriate, about who is allowed to issue instructions or to make jokes, about what counts as a joke, about what is considered offensive, and so on.

long Of a speech sound, having a duration which is greater than that of another, otherwise similar, sound, especially when the difference is contrastive in the language; see the examples under **length**. There are several ways of marking a long segment: the long counterpart of /a/ may be given as /aː/ (the IPA system), as /ā/, or as /aa/.

longitudinal study In child language acquisition, the study of one or more children over a substantial period of time, in order to see how their acquisition proceeds. Compare **cross-sectional study**.

lookahead In a model of **comprehension**, the capacity of the model to examine words which occur later than the one currently being processed.

loudness The way the **intensity** of a sound appears to our ears. The more intense the sound, the louder it sounds, but doubling the intensity does not double the loudness.

Lounsbury, Floyd An American anthropological linguist (1914–), a specialist in **Iroquoian** who also contributed to the decipherment of the **Mayan** inscriptions.

Low German A collective label for the varieties of German spoken in the north of Germany. Compare **High German**.

Lowth, Robert An English scholar (1710–87), the author of a famous and influential **grammar** of English.

low vowel (also **open vowel**) A vowel which is produced with the highest part of the tongue as low as it can go in the mouth, such as [a] or [ɑ].

LPD The *Longman Pronunciation Dictionary*, the leading **pronouncing dictionary** of British and American English.

LSA See **Linguistic Society of America**.

LSP See **language for special purposes**.

lucus a non lucendo A bizarre way of guessing the origin of a word, in which a word is (wrongly) derived from an unrelated word of almost opposite meaning. The classic instance is the guess that Latin *lūcus* 'grove of trees' derives from Latin *lūcēre* 'be bright', on the ground that a grove is not bright. Much favoured by some early commentators, this approach has long been dismissed as ridiculous.

Luick, Karl An Austrian linguist (1865–1935), a specialist in the historical phonology of English. He effectively introduced structuralist ideas into his field at a time when **structuralism** had not yet been created.

Luo A major language of east Africa, especially Kenya; it belongs to the **Nilo-Saharan** family.

Lusatian Another name for **Sorbian**.

Luxembourgish (also *Lëtzebuergesch*) The mother tongue of almost all the population of the Grand Duchy of Luxembourg, a highly distinctive variety of **German**. It has some official standing in the country.

Lyons, (Sir) John An English linguist (1932–), best known for his work in semantics and for his popularizations of linguistics.

M

Maasai A major language of Kenya, a **Nilo-Saharan** language.

Macedonian 1. The ancient language of Macedonia, the mother tongue of Alexander the Great. Almost nothing is known about it, but it is thought to have been an **Indo-European** language, possibly closely related to **Greek**. 2. The **Slavic** language of the Republic of Macedonia, closely related to **Bulgarian**.

machine translation The use of computer programs to translate written texts from one language to another.

Magyar Another name for **Hungarian**.

main clause A **clause** which does not form part of a larger clause. Every sentence necessarily contains at least one main clause; a **compound sentence** contains two or more main clauses; a **complex sentence** contains at least one **subordinate clause**.

main verb Another name for a **lexical verb**.

Malagasy The principal language of Madagascar, an **Austronesian** language.

malapropism The use of a wrong word which has a similar sound to the intended one, such as *facilities* for *faculties* or *epitaph* for *epithet*.

Malay A major language of southeast Asia, an **Austronesian** language. It has two slightly different standard forms; that used in Malaysia is *Bahasa Malaysia* or *Malay*, while that used in Indonesia is *Bahasa Indonesia* or *Indonesian*.

Malayalam A major language of southern India, a **Dravidian** language.

Malayo-Polynesian An obsolete name for the **Austronesian** family.

Malinowski, Bronislaw A Polish-born British anthropologist (1884–1942); he stressed the importance of language in anthropological work, influenced **Firth**, and introduced the notion of **phatic communion**.

Malkiel, Yakov A Ukrainian-born American historical linguist (1914–), a specialist in the **Romance** languages and a leading practitioner of **etymology**.

Malmberg, Bertil A Swedish phonetician and linguist (1913–), a wide-ranging scholar best known for his work in **phonetics** and in **Romance** linguistics.

Maltese The chief language of Malta, a distinctive offshoot of **Arabic** much influenced by European languages.

Manchu The former language of Manchuria, the language of the Manchu conquerors of China, today almost extinct. It belongs to the **Tungusic** branch of the **Altaic** family.

Mandarin The most important variety of **Chinese**; see under that entry.

Mande A group of languages spoken in west Africa and forming one branch of the **Niger-Congo** family. The best-known member is Bambara.

manner of articulation (Any one of) the range of different ways of producing a consonant sound in a particular location in the vocal tract. The chief categories are **plosive, affricate, fricative, nasal, trill, tap, flap** and **approximant,** of which the first three are collectively called **obstruents** and the rest **sonorants.** Though the lateral/median contrast is in principle independent of manner, it is conventional to class lateral approximants ("**laterals**") and lateral fricatives and affricates as additional manners of articulation. The informal labels **rhotic** and **liquid** are often used to group certain distinct manners when this is convenient.

Manually Coded English Another name for **Signed English.**

Manx The indigenous language of the Isle of Man, which became extinct in the twentieth century. It belongs to the **Goidelic** branch of **Celtic.**

Maori The indigenous language of New Zealand, a member of the **Polynesian** branch of the **Austronesian** family.

Marathi A major language of northwestern India, an **Indo-Aryan** language.

margin Either end of a **syllable**. In the syllable *strip*, the margins are occupied by the cluster /str/ and the consonant /p/; in *free*, the margins are occupied by /fr/ and zero.

marked form A form or construction which differs from another, competing, form (the **unmarked form**) in any of several respects: it contains more morphological material (*lioness* is marked with respect to *lion*, and *Vietnam was colonized by the French* is marked with respect to *The French colonized Vietnam*), it is of more limited applicability (*brethren* is marked with respect to *brothers*), or it departs more noticeably from the ordinary patterns of the language (*This book I like* is marked with respect to *I like this book*).

markedness The property that distinguishes a **marked form** from an **unmarked form.**

markedness model A theory of **code-switching** which holds that each language is associated with, and expected in, certain contexts.

markedness shift A type of language change in which a formerly **marked form** becomes the **unmarked form** and vice versa. For example, a **passive voice** is normally marked with respect to an **active voice**, but in some Pacific languages the passive has become the normal, unmarked form, while the active is now a less usual marked form.

Marr, Nikolai A Georgian linguist (1864–1934). After some competent early work, he became increasingly eccentric, and introduced both **stadialism** and his **Japhetic** (sense 2) theory; his strange ideas were picked up by Stalin and elevated to linguistic orthodoxy in the Soviet Union, with catastrophic effects on the discipline.

Marta Another name for **Laura**.

Martinet, André A French linguist (1908–), the developer of a distinctive view of language which he called *functionalism*, a view having much in common with the ideas of the **Prague School**. He is best known for his work on phonological change.

masculine In certain languages with **gender**, a conventional name for a gender class showing some degree of correlation with male sex. Not all gender languages have such a gender class.

mass comparison Another name for **multilateral comparison**.

mass noun A **noun** which denotes something that cannot be counted, such as *water, sand* or *happiness*. Compare **count(able) noun**.

matched guise technique An experimental technique used to elicit unconscious social evaluations of speech. Subjects are asked to express opinions about strangers whose voices are heard in recordings; these recordings involve certain individuals speaking the same text more than once using different accents or languages.

mathematical linguistics Any approach to language which makes heavy use of mathematics, but particularly the branch of mathematics which studies **formal grammars**.

Mathesius, Vilém A Czech linguist (1882–1945), the founder of the **Prague School** and a major developer of what we now call **text linguistics**.

matrix clause Any clause which contains another (subordinate) clause embedded within it. In the sentence *After Caroline got up, she had a shower*, the matrix clause is *she had a shower*. Note that a matrix clause does not have to be the main clause in a sentence, since multiple levels of embedding are possible.

matrix language In **code-switching**, the particular language which dominates during some stretch of discourse, within which bits of the other language may occur. The matrix language may change during a single discourse.

maturationally controlled behaviour Behaviour which is biologically controlled and which emerges in all normal individuals in normal circumstances at a particular stage of development, such as walking or sexual activity. Language is now widely thought to be a further example.

maximal projection In the **X-bar system**, the largest category which can be related to a particular *lexical category* (**word class**), such as *noun phrase* for *noun, verb phrase* for *verb*, and *prepositional phrase* for *preposition*: a **phrasal category**. Maximal projections have certain properties in common in English: for example, they alone can undergo **topicalization** or be placed in **focus** in a **clefted sentence**. A maximal projection is simply a formal view of a phrasal category.

maxims of conversation A proposed set of rules governing the behaviour of speakers in conversation; an example is "Say no more than you are in a position to say." Introduced by **Grice**, these maxims are the source of **conversational implicatures**.

Mayan A group of languages spoken in southern Mexico and Central America and forming one branch of **Penutian**. A Mayan language called *classical Mayan* was the language of an important civilization in the first millennium AD; the remarkable Mayan written texts have been deciphered only recently.

McCawley, James D. A Scottish-born American linguist (1938–), a prominent contributor to a wide range of theoretical and descriptive areas, known also for his wit and his bawdy humour.

McDavid, Raven I. An American lexicographer and dialectologist (1911–84) who played a leading role in the preparation of the several American dialect atlases.

McLuhan, Marshall A Canadian communication theorist (1911–80), a critic of what he saw as the stifling effect of written language upon culture; his slogan was "the medium is the message".

meaning A central concept in the study of language, but one which is not easy to pin down. It is clear that words and morphemes typically carry meanings, except that purely grammatical items like *of* and the verbal suffix *-ing* have grammatical functions which are "meanings" only in a loose sense. Larger units like phrases and sentences also have meanings; these depend both on the meanings of the smaller items inside them and on their syntactic structures (*John hit Bill* does not mean the same as *Bill hit John*). The study of the intrinsic meanings of linguistic expressions is **semantics**, and we now distinguish this from **pragmatics**, which is the study of those aspects of meaning that crucially involve the context of an utterance. The study of word meanings is **lexical semantics**, and we need at the very least to distinguish between the irreducible central meaning of a word (its **conceptual meaning**, or **denotation**, or **sense**) and the various other types of associations it may have (its **associative meaning**, its **affective meaning**, and so on). There are very many approaches to the study of meaning; especially prominent in the study of sentence meanings are the various types of **formal semantics**.

meaning postulate In semantics, a statement expressing a relation between the meanings of certain words. For example, *buy* and *sell* are related as follows: if A sells X to B, then B buys X from A.

mean length of utterance (**MLU**) The average length of the utterances produced by a child, usually counted in **morphemes**, not in words, so that *I drinked it* would have a length of 4.

medial Occurring in the middle of a word, such as the /nt/ cluster in *banter*.

median (A speech sound which is) not **lateral**, such as [p], [n] or [r].

mediopassive (also **middle**) A verb form which is active in form but passive in meaning, as in English *My new book is selling well* and *Nylon washes easily*.

medium (plural **media**) The means by which a message is transmitted. The primary medium of language is **speech**, but **sign language** and **writing** represent two other media which may carry language.

Meeussen, Achille Émile A Belgian linguist (1912–78), a wide-ranging scholar best known for his work on the **Bantu** languages, and especially on their tones.

Meillet, Antoine A French linguist (1866–1936), an outstanding and influential practitioner of general and (especially) **comparative linguistics**; he was the greatest historical linguist of his day.

Meinhof, Carl A German cleric (1857–1944), a pioneer in African language classification.

meiosis Another term for **litotes**.

melioration Another name for **amelioration**.

Mencken, H(enry) L. An American journalist (1880–1956), an enthusiastic promoter of American English, whose independence from British English he stressed tirelessly.

Menéndez Pidal, Ramón A Spanish philologist (1869–1968), a specialist in ancient place names and author of a magisterial history of Spanish.

mentalese Another name for the **language of thought**.

mentalism The belief that such unobservable phenomena as minds, thoughts, intentions and mental processes generally are objectively real and hence that they can reasonably be invoked in scientific investigation and even be made the object of study themselves. Mentalism is today the prevailing view in linguistics and in cognitive science generally. Compare **behaviourism**.

mental lexicon The collection of words stored in the human mind.

mental model (also **mental representation**) A representation of something within the human mind. For example, you probably have in your head a model of a *zoo*, one of *Antarctica*, one of a *seduction*, and even one of a *week*. See also **frame** and **script**.

merger A type of change in pronunciation in which the speakers of a language cease to make a distinction between two sounds which were formerly distinguished. This may occur only in certain positions, or it may happen in all positions; in the second case, the number of phonemes in the language is reduced. For example, English formerly had one vowel in words like *toe* and *no* but a different vowel in words like *tow* and *know*. But almost all speakers have now lost this distinction and pronounce all such words with the same vowel: the two original vowels have thus undergone merger.

mesial Neither nearby nor far away, but somewhere in between. The term is applied to a **deictic position** representing such a position. English has no mesial forms, but Spanish does: it has *éste* 'this', *ése* 'that' (just there), and *aquél* 'that' (over yonder). The second form is a mesial; the first and third are **proximal** and **distal**, respectively.

mesolect In a **creole**, any variety of the creole which is noticeably closer to the local standard language than a **basilect** but not as close as an **acrolect**.

metalanguage A language which we use in order to talk about another language (the **object language**). It is perfectly possible to use, say, English to talk about English, but doing so can easily lead to confusion between the English we are talking about and the English we are using to talk about it, and hence philosophers and linguists often prefer to construct their own special metalanguage in order to talk about a natural language.

metanalysis A type of historical change in which a segment is transferred from the end of one word to the beginning of the next, or vice versa, as in the change of *a napron* to *an apron* and of *an ewt* to *a newt*.

metaphony Another name for **umlaut**.

metaphor A **figure of speech** in which something is represented by a linguistic expression which is literally inappropriate, in order to draw attention to a perceived resemblance. Examples: *they were glued to their seats*; *her problems are eating at her*; *she's been mining that particular vein for years*.

metathesis Any change in the form of a word in which one or more segments are moved to different places in the word. For example, Latin *crocodilus* 'crocodile' has become *cocodrilo* in Spanish, with metathesis of the *r*, and English *wasp* has become *wops* in some areas, with metathesis of *p* and *s*.

metonymy Referring to something by naming one of its attributes, as when we say *the Crown* to mean 'the Sovereign', or *Anfield* to mean 'Liverpool Football Club' (whose home ground is Anfield).

metre The rhythmical arrangement of syllables in verse, commonly analysed in terms of **feet**. In some theories of phonology, ordinary speech is also assumed to possess a kind of metre.

Metrical Phonology A major contemporary theory of phonology, designed chiefly to deal with rhythmic (prosodic) phenomena, especially stress. Two different notations are in use, one using *trees*, the other *grids*.

metrics The study of **metre**, either in verse or in speech.

metronymic An additional name carried by a person which indicates the name of his/her mother or another female ancestor. Compare **patronymic**.

Meyer-Lübke, Wilhelm A Swiss linguist (1861–1936), a specialist in **Romance** languages and author of a celebrated **etymological dictionary** of Romance.

Miao-Yao A small group of languages spoken in southeast Asia. Linguists do not agree to which larger family these languages should be assigned, though **Sino-Tibetan** is a favourite candidate.

Michelena, Luis (in Basque, *Koldo Mitxelena*) A Basque linguist (1915–87), the greatest scholar the **Basque** language has ever seen, known above all for his work on the history and prehistory of the language.

middle 1. A distinctive set of verb-forms found in certain languages, notably ancient Greek, serving to indicate that the subject is acting on or for himself/herself. 2. Another name for the **mediopassive**.

Middle English The name given to (late) medieval English, conventionally dated from 1066 or 1100 to 1450 or 1500.

mid vowel A vowel which is neither **high** nor **low**. It is customary to distinguish two mid heights: *high mid* (*half-close, close-mid*), such as [e] and [o], and *low mid* (*half-open, open-mid*), such as [ɛ] and [ɔ].

Mill, John Stuart An English philosopher (1806–73) who attached great importance to names and naming in his writings.

mind–body dualism The philosophical view that a mind is something utterly different from a body, and hence that mental processes like thinking must involve something completely different from mere physical processes like the firing of neurons. Though defended by **Descartes**, such dualism is universally rejected today by linguists and other cognitive scientists.

minimal attachment, principle of A proposed **perceptual strategy** which says "connect each new item you hear in the simplest way possible to what you have already heard". So, for example, when you hear *The horse shot . . .* , you at once assume that *shot* is a verb whose subject is *the horse*; this works fine most of the time, but it leads you into difficulty with **garden-path sentences** like *The horse shot from the stable fell over.*

Minimalist Programme An approach to grammatical theory proposed by **Chomsky** in the 1990s. It seeks to replace the elaborate apparatus of the **Government-and-Binding Theory** with just a few simple and general principles of sentence structure.

minimal pair Two words of distinct meaning which exhibit different segments at one point but identical segments at all other points. The existence of such a minimal pair proves that the two segments which are different must belong to different phonemes. For example, English *fat* and *vat* constitute a minimal pair for the phonemes /f/ and /v/, as do *rifle* and *rival* and *leaf* and *leave*. Larger minimal sets are possible: English *sum, sun, sung* constitute a minimal set for /m/, /n/ and /ŋ/.

Minoan The unknown ancient language concealed in the **Linear A** inscriptions from Crete.

minority language A language which is, and long has been, the first language of some part of the population in a country in which the **national language** is something different. Examples include Welsh and Scots Gaelic in Britain and Dutch, Breton, Basque, Occitan, Catalan, Corsican and Alsatian German in France. Compare **immigrant language**.

MIT The Massachusetts Institute of Technology, a university in Cambridge, Massachusetts, where Noam **Chomsky** has long worked; it is the home of **generative grammar**, of **transformational grammar**, and of Chomskyan linguistics generally.

mitochondrial Eve hypothesis Another name for the **African Eve hypothesis**.

mixed language 1. A hypothetical type of language which originated by combining elements from two (or more) different languages. No such language is known to exist; even a **creole** can usually be traced to a single source language with influences from other languages. 2. A label applied somewhat loosely to any language which has been heavily influenced (especially in its vocabulary) by one or more other languages, such as English (heavy borrowing from French, Latin, Old Norse) or Albanian (from Latin, Greek, Slavic, Turkish).

MLU See **mean length of utterance**.

mnemonic A word, phrase or verse designed specifically to help you remember some longer word, name, list or number(s). An example is **NICE** for the distinctive properties of English auxiliaries.

modal auxiliary An **auxiliary** which expresses some **mood** or **modality**. The

English modals, such as *can, could, must, will* and *might*, exhibit some distinctive grammatical properties.

modality Another name for **mood**, but one often applied more specifically to certain distinctions concerned with the speaker's estimate of the relationship between the actor and the accomplishment of some event. For example, *Susie can drive to London* has at least three interpretations differing in modality: "She knows how to do it"; "She is physically able to do it"; "She is permitted to do it". See **alethic, deontic** and **epistemic modality**.

modal logic A variety of **formal logic** which is capable of treating sentences of the form "It is necessarily the case that . . ." and "It is possible that . . .".

model A representation of some part of a language or of the human language faculty, such as grammar or word recognition. The construction of models is a central part of theorizing about language.

model theory An approach to **formal semantics** which involves the construction of explicit representations resembling miniature universes; the meanings of linguistic expressions are evaluated in terms of these models.

Modern English The most recent stage in the history of English, conventionally dated from 1700 to the present.

modifier Any syntactic unit which forms part of a larger unit and which adds semantic information to the **head** of that larger unit. For example, in the noun phrase *that lovely bottle of wine which Susie brought*, all of *lovely, of wine* and *which Susie brought* are modifiers of *bottle*, the head of the noun phrase. A modifier may be **restrictive** or **non-restrictive**.

Modistae The name given to those medieval grammarians who practised **speculative grammar**.

modularity The property of being composed of several smaller units (**modules**) which are largely independent. Many linguists believe that the human mind is modular with respect to our language faculty, that our language faculty is largely independent of other mental and cognitive abilities, as suggested by those disabilities (like the **Williams syndrome**) which leave language largely intact while severely damaging other mental capabilities. Many linguists further believe that our language faculty is itself modular, that it is composed of several smaller specialized components, as suggested by those types of **aphasia** which damage certain aspects of language while leaving others largely unscathed.

module 1. In some theories of grammar, any one of the separate and distinct components of the theory which are posited to do different jobs. The best-known modular theory is **Government-and-Binding Theory**. 2. In some theories of language, or of the mind or the brain generally, any one of the separate mental or neural structures which are posited as existing and as performing distinct functions. Such disabilities as **aphasia, Specific Language Impairment** and the **Williams syndrome** provide evidence that both language and our mental faculties generally must be in some important way modular.

molar *r* A distinctive pronunciation of English /r/ in which the tongue is bunched up so that its sides touch the molar teeth while the tip is held low behind the lower teeth. This type of /r/ is used by many (not all) Americans and Canadians.

Mongolian A group of closely related languages spoken in central Asia, forming one branch of the **Altaic** family.

monitoring device A hypothetical piece of mental machinery which checks speech being produced to see that it is correct. Such a device clearly exists at some level, since we can quickly correct our own mistakes in speech, but the fact that **speech errors** so often involve real (but wrong) words suggests that another monitor may be operating at a subsconscious level.

Mon-Khmer A group of languages spoken in southeast Asia and forming the largest branch of the **Austro-Asiatic** family. The group includes Khmer (Cambodian) and probably also **Vietnamese** (this is controversial).

monogenesis The hypothesis that all human languages ever spoken are descended from a single common ancestor, the first language of all humankind. Most linguists suspect that this hypothesis is very likely correct, but there appears to be no way we can find out. The opposing view is **polygenesis**. Compare the **"Proto-World" hypothesis**.

monoglot A person who speaks only one language.

monolingual Speaking only one language. This term is perhaps more commonly applied to a speech community than to an individual.

monophthong A pure vowel, such as [a] or [y]. Compare **diphthong**.

monosyllable A word of one syllable, like *cat* or *strength*.

Montague, Richard An American philosopher and logician (1931–71); he pioneered the formal study of the syntax and semantics of natural languages and developed **Montague semantics**.

Montague semantics (also **Montague grammar**) A version of **formal semantics** in which each syntactic rule in the grammar is accompanied by a semantic rule which provides a meaning for the structure built by the syntactic rule (this is the *rule-to-rule hypothesis*). This approach has been enormously influential.

mood The **grammatical category** which expresses the degree or kind of reality assigned to a sentence. Mood is not well developed in English, but many other languages make elaborate grammatical distinctions (often marked in the verb) to distinguish states of affairs which are regarded as certain, probable, possible, doubtful, unreal, or conditional upon something else. Mood shades off imperceptibly into **modality**, and also into **evidential** systems.

mora A phonological unit longer than a single segment but typically shorter than a **syllable**. Most often, a **light syllable** consists of one mora, while a **heavy syllable** consists of two. Moras are important in the phonology of certain languages, such as Japanese.

moribund language A language which now has so few fluent native speakers remaining that its extinction in the near future seems certain.

morph Any piece of morphological material which you want to talk about, without committing yourself to any view of its morphological status. For example, the Basque noun *mendi* 'mountain' has an inflected form *mendietan* 'in the mountains'; you can speak of the morph *-etan* here without committing yourself to any analysis of it.

morpheme The minimal grammatical unit; the smallest unit that plays any part in morphology or syntax. A morpheme is an abstract unit which may or may not be realized by a fairly consistent stretch of phonological material. For example, a noun plural in English typically consists of a sequence of two morphemes, a noun-stem plus a plural morpheme, but the phonological realization of this sequence varies in ways that are both regular and irregular: *cats, dogs, foxes, feet, mice, children, sheep, radii, passers-by*. However, just as we can say that *dogs* is {*dog*} + {Plural}, we can say that *feet* is {*foot*} + {Plural}, and that the plural *sheep* (as in *Those sheep are hungry*) is {*sheep*} + {Plural}. Morphemes may be classified as **free** or **bound**, and as **lexical** or **grammatical**.

morpheme-structure condition A constraint upon the possible phonological shape of morphemes in a language. It is possible for the permitted shapes of morphemes to be different from the permitted shapes of words; for example, Basque permits a morpheme to begin with the consonant /r/, but it does not permit a word to begin with /r/.

morphologization A type of language change in which independent words are reduced to **bound morphemes**, as when Latin phrases like *lenta mente* 'with a slow mind' were converted into single adverbs like Spanish *lentamente* and French *lentement* 'slowly'.

morphology The branch of linguistics dealing with the study of word structure, conventionally divided into **inflectional morphology** and **derivational morphology**.

morphophoneme In some analyses, an abstract phonological unit which is realized as one of two or more different **phonemes** in different circumstances, often especially in **neutralization**. For example, German *Bund* 'union' (with final [t]) has genitive *Bundes* (with [d]); since [t] and [d] generally contrast in German and must be assigned to two different phonemes /t/ and /d/, we might choose to say that *Bund* ends in a morphophoneme (represented T or //t//) which is realized as the phoneme /t/ when final but as the phoneme /d/ otherwise. This type of analysis was particularly favoured by some **American structuralists**; today it would be more usual merely to say that *Bund* ends in /d/ but that /d/ and /t/ are neutralized word-finally.

morphophonemic alternation The appearance of two or more different phonemes in the same position in the same morpheme in different circumstances. Examples: the /s/ ~ /z/ ~ /ɪz/ alternation in the English plural marker, as in *cats/dogs/foxes*; the /k/ ~ /s/ alternation in *electric/electricity*; the /p/ ~ /b/ alternation in Turkish *kitap* 'book', dative *kitaba*.

morphophonology (also **morphophonemics**) The description of **morphophonemic alternations**.

morphosyntax The area of interface between morphology and syntax.

mother A relation which may hold between two **nodes** in a **tree structure**. If a higher node A is directly connected by a line to a lower node B, and there is no other node lying between them, then A is the mother of B.

motherese Another name for **caregiver speech**.

mother-in-law language Another name for **avoidance language**.

mother tongue An individual's first language, the one learned in childhood. It is possible to have more than one mother tongue.

Mother Tongue A label for the hypothetical ancestral language of all human-kind, posited by the proponents of **monogenesis** and of the **"Proto-World" hypothesis**.

motor Pertaining to movements of muscles, or more generally to nervous impulses flowing outward from the brain. Compare **sensory**.

motor theory of speech perception The hypothesis that we can only perceive speech sounds by mentally forming those sounds ourselves.

move alpha The only **transformation** recognized in **Government-and-Binding Theory**, a very general rule which simply says "move something to another place". By itself, of course, this rule would produce huge amounts of ungrammatical output, but its action is severely constrained by the other **modules** of the theory.

movement error Another name for an **assemblage error**.

movement rule In certain theories of grammar, notably **transformational grammar**, a rule which moves something from one location to another in the structure being built up for some sentence.

Müller, Max A German linguist who worked in Britain (1823–1900), a specialist in Asian languages, especially in **Sanskrit**. He was the first Professor of Comparative Philology at Oxford, and he was a successful popularizer of linguistics.

multilateral comparison (also **mass comparison**) A technique for comparing languages, in the hope of identifying **genetic relationships** among some of them. The investigator compares **word lists** taken from the languages of interest and looks for resemblances; languages showing large numbers of resemblances are singled out for further attention. Some element of comparison is a necessary first step in any search for genetic relationships, but Joseph **Greenberg** has recently been arguing that this method, all by itself, is adequate to identify previously unsuspected genetic groupings. His case has generated a furious controversy, and it is so far rejected by most linguists.

multilingualism The ability to speak several languages. This may be a property of an individual or of a speech community.

multiregional hypothesis Another name for the **parallel evolution hypothesis**.

Munda A small group of languages spoken in northeastern India and forming one branch of the **Austro-Asiatic** family.

murmur Another name for **whispery voice**.

Murray, Alexander A Scottish **polyglot** and scholar (1775–1813) who wrote extensively on **language change** with ideas that were at times surprisingly advanced.

Murray, (Sir) James A Scottish lexicographer (1837–1915), the editor of the first edition of the *Oxford English Dictionary*.

Murray, Lindley An American grammarian (1745–1826), the author of some highly prescriptive and enormously influential grammars of English for use in schools.

Muskogean A group of languages spoken in the southeastern USA; its best-known member is Choctaw. Muskogean is now believed to be related to the **Algonquian** family.

mutation A systematic change in certain **consonants** in a word for grammatical reasons. Mutations are typical of the **Celtic** languages; for example, Welsh *pen* 'head' exhibits several mutations in the phrases *dy ben* 'your house', *ei phen* 'her house' and *fy mhen* 'my house'.

N

Na-Déné A family of languages spoken in western and northwestern North America, consisting of the **Athabaskan** group plus a few others.

Nagari alphabet (also **Devanagari**) An **alphabet** used in north India for writing Sanskrit, Hindi and other languages.

Nahuatl The chief language of the Aztec empire, a member of the **Uto-Aztecan** family; it is still spoken today by many Mexicans.

name See **proper name**.

naming insight The crucial realization by young children that words are names for things, typically acquired at around 15 months.

narrative A description of a series of events.

narrowing A change in the meaning of a word by which the word becomes applicable to fewer cases than formerly. For example, English *deer* formerly meant 'animal' (in general), but it has been narrowed to denoting only a particular kind of animal. Compare **broadening**.

narrow transcription Another name for **phonetic transcription**.

nasal (A speech sound) produced with air flowing out through the nose while airflow is blocked in the mouth, such as [m] or [n].

nasal cavity An empty space lying above the mouth and connecting the nostrils to the **pharynx** (the back of the mouth). When the **velum** is lowered, air can flow out through the nasal cavity; when the velum is raised, such airflow is blocked.

nasalization Lowering the **velum**, so that air flows out through the **nasal cavity** while a speech sound is being produced. The IPA represents this with a tilde, so that a nasalized [a] is represented [ã]. **Note:** when you have a bad cold in the head, your speech does *not* become nasalized: it becomes much *less* nasalized than normal, because air cannot easily flow through the nasal cavity when this is blocked.

national language The chief language of a particular country, such as English in the UK and in the USA. Not every country has a national language: multilingual countries like Belgium and Singapore have two or more **official languages** but no national language.

native American languages The indigenous languages of the Americas. Over a thousand probably existed before the European settlement; today perhaps 650 survive, most of them in grave danger of extinction. Specialists recognize anywhere from 140 to 200 distinct families.

native speaker With respect to a given language, a person for whom that language is a mother tongue, a language learned from early childhood.

natural class 1. Formally, any class of linguistic objects which can be characterized using less information than is required to characterize any part of it, such as the class of nasal consonants or the class of verbs. 2. Informally, any class of linguistic objects which behave in the same way and which therefore need to be referred to in a description with a single label. **Note:** one of the goals of linguistic description is to provide a framework that represents natural classes in the second sense as natural classes in the first; failure to do this leads only to the endless and unsystematic labelling of things.

natural gender 1. In a language with **gender**, an arrangement in which the gender of a noun is totally predictable from its meaning. Few gender languages are like this. 2. An inaccurate label sometimes applied to a language which has no grammatical gender, but which has a certain amount of sex-marking, especially in its pronouns, as does English, with its *he/she/it*.

naturalism The view that there is an intrinsic, non-arbitrary connection between the form of a word and its meaning. This view is universally rejected today. The opposite is **nominalism** (sense 1).

natural kind The name of an identifiable class of entities which exists in the world independent of any human efforts, such as *duck, tiger, lemon, oak* or *penguin*. Natural kinds may be contrasted with *cultural kinds* (*cup, knife, bicycle*) and *functional kinds* (*vehicle, weapon, toy*).

natural language 1. Any language which is, or once was, the **mother tongue** of a group of people. 2. By extension, any conceivable language which has all the characteristics of human languages and which therefore might, in principle, serve as a mother tongue.

natural-language processing The use of computers to perform any of a number of tasks involving natural languages, often particularly the construction and use of **parsers**.

Natural Morphology A theory of morphology developed by Wolfgang Dressler and others in the 1980s. It focuses on the idea that certain types of morphological structure are more *natural* than others, and suggests that languages tend to change so as to maximize this naturalness.

Natural Phonology A theory of phonology developed by David Stampe and others in the 1970s. It stresses the importance of rules (processes) which are *natural* – that is, which tend to occur universally in languages – as opposed to processes which are not natural and which have to be learned by children acquiring the language.

natural selection The ordinary mechanism of evolutionary change. In any generation, the individuals in a particular species differ somewhat in their genes, and hence in their physical and cognitive characteristics. Those individuals which are best fitted to their circumstances will, on average, be more successful at surviving and reproducing, and thus more successful at passing their genes, and hence their characteristics, on to the next generation. Many linguists believe that the human **language faculty** arose by natural selection, that individuals with slightly better language capabilities had such an advantage that they steadily crowded out less able speakers, until finally only fully capable language-users survived. This view has the consequence that language must have developed gradually, in small increments. Others reject the selectionist view and prefer to see language as an **emergent** phenomenon.

nature-versus-nurture controversy A long-standing argument over whether language develops automatically in humans, like seeing and walking, or whether it is merely learned, like ice-skating or driving a car.

Navajo (also **Navaho**) An **Athabaskan** language spoken in the southwestern USA. It has more speakers than any other native American language in the USA and is the only one regularly written.

Navarro Tomás, Tomás A Spanish phonetician (1884–1979), the leading phonetician in Spain in the twentieth century.

N-bar A syntactic category which is bigger than a **noun** but smaller than a **noun phrase**; most typically, an N-bar is the thing that combines with a **determiner** to produce a noun phrase. An example is *bottle of wine*, which requires a determiner to make a noun phrase, as in *a bottle of wine*. **Note:** many elementary textbooks decline to recognize N-bars, but they are essential in serious syntax.

Neandertals A distinctive, heavily-built people who inhabited much of Europe until about 35,000 years ago. Their precise relation to us is much debated, as is the question of whether they could speak. **Note:** the older spelling *Neanderthals* is now obsolescent.

near-merger A state of affairs in which a speaker consistently produces a small but real difference between two speech sounds but cannot hear the difference and typically claims that no difference exists.

negation The presence of a **negative** within a linguistic expression, or the addition of such an element, or the effect of that element when present.

negative A grammatical element which, when added to a sentence, converts it from true to false or vice versa. For this purpose, English uses the item *not* and a variety of more complex forms like *doesn't*: *Our teacher is British/Our teacher is not British*; *Susie smokes/Susie doesn't smoke*. The opposite is **affirmative**.

negative concord (also, informally, **double negative**) The grammatical phenomenon in which the presence of a negative word like *not* forces other words in the sentence to take negative forms. Negative concord occurs, for example, in standard Spanish, in which 'I didn't see anybody' is expressed as *No he visto a nadie*, literally 'I didn't see nobody'. Negative concord was formerly common in standard English, but today it is considered non-standard, and non-standard utterances like *I didn't see nobody*, though extremely common, are condemned.

negative evidence 1. In many branches of linguistics, the absence of evidence for something. For example, we have no evidence for a **Proto-Indo-European** word for 'sea', but it does not follow that there was none: perhaps the word was simply lost. 2. (also **correction**) In the study of child language acquisition, information presented to a child that its linguistic forms are wrong – most obviously, corrections by adults. This notion is interesting because (a) children rarely receive such evidence, and (b) when they do, they appear to ignore it.

negative polarity item A word or form which can only occur in certain types of contexts, especially negative contexts. An English example is *any*: *We don't have any wine*, but **We have any wine*.

negotiated input Bits of a foreign language which you learn by asking native speakers to clarify their utterances when you don't understand them.

Neogrammarian Hypothesis (also **regularity hypothesis**) The hypothesis that a change in pronunciation always affects all relevant words simultaneously, and hence that apparent exceptions require an explanation. Though enormously fruitful in historical work, this hypothesis is now known to be false, since **lexical diffusion** is well attested.

Neogrammarians A group of German historical linguists who, in the 1870s, put forward the **Neogrammarian Hypothesis** of sound change. The label is also extended to later linguists who accepted the hypothesis.

neologism (also **coinage**) A newly created word, such as (in recent years) *CD*, *Internet*, *yuppify* or *geopathic*.

neoteny Extended childhood. Neoteny is strongly characteristic of human beings: we are born while we are still fetuses, and for years we remain helpless and utterly dependent on our parents for survival. It is widely believed that this extended childhood is crucial in permitting our startling mental and cognitive development, including our language faculty.

Nepali The chief language of Nepal, an **Indo-Aryan** language.

nested dependency A grammatical construction in which two or more pairs of grammatical links between two points in a sentence are arranged as shown in Figure N1. Compare **cross-serial dependency**.

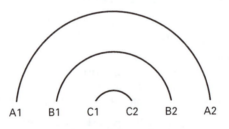

N1 A nested dependency

nesting An instance of **embedding** in which a category is embedded under, and interrupts, another instance of the same category. The following example shows a series of clauses, each smaller one nested within the next larger one: *The book [the professor [the students like] recommended] is good.*

network Any kind of system involving multiple connections among the elements of that system.

network accent The type of English accent used by television newsreaders in the USA: an educated variety of **General American**.

network grammar Another name for a **transition network**.

neurolinguistics The study of the relation between language and brain.

neuron (also **neurone**) A single nerve cell.

neuter In some languages with **gender,** a name given to a gender class which shows no correlation with sex, or sometimes no correlation with meaning at all. A neuter gender is found in ancient Greek, Latin, Russian and German, where it contrasts with masculine and feminine genders, and in Dutch and some varieties of Norwegian, where it contrasts with only one other gender, called the **common gender** (sense 2).

neutralization The disappearance in a certain position of a contrast between two or more phonemes which exists in other positions. For example, /p/ and /b/ contrast in English in most positions, but the contrast is neutralized after /s/ in the same syllable: there is no possibility of having different words /spɪt/ and /sbɪt/.

neutral position The position adopted by the vocal organs when they are not involved in an articulation.

neutral vowel Another name for **schwa**.

New Englishes The distinctive varieties of English spoken in the former British and American colonies, such as the Indian subcontinent, Malaysia, Singapore, the Philippines, Hong Kong and the West Indies.

newsgroup An electronic facility which allows people all over the world to exchange messages by means of the Internet. There are thousands of newsgroups, each devoted to a particular topic; a prominent newsgroup devoted to language is *sci.lang*. A newsgroup is more informal than a **list**; it is aimed chiefly at interested amateurs, rather than at professional specialists. Many newsgroups (including sci.lang) maintain a list of FAQs (frequently asked questions – with answers, of course) as a service to newcomers. If you join a newsgroup, follow it for a few days before jumping in with your own contributions, and be sure to read the FAQs before asking a question that may have been asked 600 times before. And be courteous – always.

NICE properties A mnemonic label for the distinctive properties of the English **auxiliaries**: *negation* (*John can't come*), *inversion* (*Can John come?*), *code* (*Yes, he can*) and *emphasis* (*John cán come*).

nickname An informal name given to a person, or sometimes to a place or a thing; use of a nickname usually expresses intimacy or affection, but sometimes contempt. Examples: *Ed, Ted* or *Eddie* for a man named *Edward*; *Babe* for the baseball player George Herman Ruth; *the Big Apple* for New York City; *Satchmo* for the jazz trumpeter Louis Armstrong; *the Misery Line* for the London Underground's Northern Line.

Nida, Eugene An American linguist (1914–), a missionary linguist who has contributed to **morphology**, to **lexical semantics**, and above all to the theory and practice of **translation**.

Niger-Congo A vast language family, with perhaps 1500 members, embracing most of the languages of Africa south of the Sahara. Among its numerous branches are **Kwa, Mande** and **Bantu**.

Niger-Kordofanian A proposed family of languages combining **Niger-Congo** and **Kordofanian**. Linguists are not sure if this is a valid grouping or not, though it seems to have majority support.

Nilo-Saharan A large language family whose members are spoken in a broad band running across the southern edge of the Sahara. Its classification is much disputed, and linguists are not certain it forms a single genetic family. Its best-known member is **Maasai**.

Nim Chimpsky A chimpanzee who was taught to use a version of **sign language** in an early experiment.

node Any labelled point in a **tree structure** for a sentence.

nomenclature A set of terms for naming the objects in some class.

nominal Pertaining to **nouns,** or to larger categories built upon nouns, such as **N-bars** and **noun phrases**.

nominalism 1. The view that the relation between the forms of words and their meanings is a purely arbitrary one, no more than an agreement among speakers. This view is universally accepted today, in spite of the existence of partial exceptions like **onomatopoeia**. The opposite view is **naturalism**. 2. The view that the various objects which can be referred to by a particular word, such as *dog*, have nothing in common except the name. Compare **realism, conceptualism, Platonism**.

nominalization A syntactic unit which behaves like a noun or a noun phrase but which is constructed from a verb, a verb phrase or a sentence. Examples (in brackets): *Her [arrival] startled us*; *[Smoking] is bad for you*; *[To err] is human*; *[Reading the literature] is essential*; *[That you are tired] is obvious*.

nominative In many languages with **case**, that particular case-form which is used to mark the subject of a sentence. English has such a form only for certain pronouns: *I, we, she*, and so on.

non- For any term of the form *non-X* with no entry of its own, see under *X*.

nonce form A word or form which is deliberately created on a particular occasion and which does not take root in the language.

non-configurational language A language in which the words of a sentence are not necessarily grouped into obvious units, and which therefore lacks **constituent structure**. Languages with **free word order** are often thought to be of this type.

non-finite A label applied to any verb-form which does not carry full marking for **tense** and **agreement** and which therefore cannot possibly be the only verb-form in a sentence. English has several non-finite forms: the **infinitive**, the **gerund** and two or three **participles**. See also the discussion under **finite**.

non-linear phonology Any theory of phonology in which the phonological structure of a word or phrase is held to be something different from a single linear sequence of elements. Such theories are currently the mainstream in phonology; prominent examples are **Autosegmental Phonology** and **Metrical Phonology**.

non-restrictive Of a modifier, not required to identify the entity being talked about. In *My adored mother, who made the best cakes in the county, always let us lick* *the bowl*, both the **adjective** *adored* and the **relative clause** *who made the best cakes in the county* are non-restrictive. Compare **restrictive**.

non-rhotic accent Any accent of English in which the historical /r/ has been lost everywhere except before a vowel. In such an accent, *farther* sounds like *father* and *tar* rhymes with *Shah*. Non-rhotic accents are typical of much of England, the eastern and southern USA, parts of the West Indies, and the Southern Hemisphere countries. Compare **rhotic accent**.

non-standard Not accepted as part of the **standard language**. The English sentence *I seen him yesterday, but I ain't seen him today* is very widely used by English-speakers but is considered non-standard.

non-terminal node A **node** in a tree which has more nodes below it.

non-U Not typical of upper-class British speech. The opposite is **U**.

non-verbal communication (also, informally, **body language**) Any aspect of communication which does not involve words, such as gestures, postures and expressions. See the note under **verbal** (sense 1).

NORM A *non-mobile, older, rural male* speaker. Such speakers tend to be conservative and to have speech which is more old-fashioned than that of most other speakers. In the early days of **dialectology**, these speakers were considered to be the most appropriate ones to collect data from, but today we realize that this policy conceals a large part of the real linguistic situation.

Norman French The distinctive variety of **French** spoken by the Normans, a group of Vikings who settled in Normandy (France) and learned French. Norman French was introduced into England by the Norman Conquest.

normative grammar A description of a language which is based upon **prescriptivism**, and which therefore tries to identify "correct" usage.

Norn A **Germanic** language formerly spoken in the Shetland and Orkney Islands of Scotland, where it was introduced by Vikings.

Norwegian The chief language of Norway, a member of the **Germanic** branch of **Indo-European**. Norwegian is unusual in having two different standard forms.

Nostratic hypothesis The hypothesis that the **Indo-European, Afro-Asiatic, Uralic, Altaic, Dravidian** and **Kartvelian** language families (and possibly others) are genetically related in a *Nostratic* family, all being descended from a *Proto-Nostratic* ancestor spoken perhaps 15,000 years ago. Chiefly developed by Russian linguists, the idea has won some support but is still deeply controversial.

notational convention Any notational device which, in some system, is understood as having some particular interpretation. For example, the notation C_0 may be understood as meaning 'a string of zero or more consonants', while the notation S → NP VP usually means 'a sentence may consist of a noun phrase followed by a verb phrase'.

notional grammar A description of a language in which linguistic categories are defined in terms of non-linguistic concepts. Traditional grammar was like this: it used attempted definitions like 'a noun is the name of a person, place or thing' and 'a sentence is a complete thought'. This doesn't work, and contemporary theories of grammar rely instead upon **formal** criteria.

noun A large **word class** found in all languages, or a word belonging to this class. In English, a noun typically has two grammatical forms called **singular** and **plural**: *dog/dogs; man/men*. (But there are exceptions: *furniture* has only a singular form, and *pants* has only a plural.) The central grammatical characteristic of a noun is that it can combine with certain other elements (most often a **determiner**) to produce a **noun phrase**. A simple test for nouns in English is a pair of frames like these: *This _____ is nice; These _____ are nice.* Any word which will go into one of the slots to make a grammatical sentence is a noun, since English grammar permits nouns, and only nouns, to appear there. English allows nouns to modify other nouns: in *maternity dress* and *bus station*, the nouns *maternity* and *bus* are modifying the nouns which follow them. Nouns in some other languages may exhibit other grammatical characteristics, such as **gender**, **case** and additional (or no) distinctions of **number**.

noun-complement clause A **complement clause** which is attached to a **noun**. Example (in brackets): *The rumour [that mobile phones cause cancer] is false.* Here the clause is attached to *rumour*.

noun phrase (NP) An important **syntactic category**. The most obvious characteristic of an NP is that it can perform certain functions in a sentence, such as acting as a **subject**, a **direct object**, or the object of a preposition. For example, anything which can fill the blank in the frame _____ *was/were nice* to give a grammatical sentence must be the subject of that sentence and hence must be an NP. Examples: *she, Susie, the spaghetti, most of my students, the south of France, those spicy little chicken things that Mike made*.

NP The abbreviation for **noun phrase**.

NP accessibility hierarchy A specific ordering of **grammatical relations** which turns out to be grammatically important in many languages. It looks like this: Subject > Direct Object > Indirect Object > Oblique Object.

Nubian A group of languages spoken along the river Nile and belonging to the **Nilo-Saharan** family.

nucleus The central and most sonorous part of a **syllable**, flanked by the **margins** (the **onset** and the **coda**) and usually consisting of a vowel or a diphthong. The vowel /e/ is the nucleus of the monosyllables *pest* and *spread*, of the first syllable of *medical*, and of the last syllable of *intend*.

null-subject language Another name for a **pro-drop language**.

number The **grammatical category** which, in the most straightforward cases, marks a grammatical distinction reflecting the number of countable things under discussion. Number is most usually marked on nouns and noun phrases, though there are other possibilities. English has a simple system which distinguishes only **singular** (typically representing a single object) and a **plural** (typically representing two or more objects). Examples: *dog/dogs, child/children, this book/these books*. Some languages add further number distinctions, such as a **dual** (two things) or a **paucal** (a few things); some other languages lack the category of number altogether, and make no distinction of form between one object and more than one object.

number of languages The number of languages currently spoken on earth, according to the most authoritative recent survey, is just over 6500; there is some uncertainty resulting partly from lack of information but mostly from the difficulty of deciding whether related language varieties should be counted as dialects of one language or as separate languages. Of these 6500, 52 per cent are spoken by fewer than 10,000 people, 28 per cent are spoken by fewer than 1000, and 10 per cent are spoken by fewer than 100. At the other extreme, just ten languages, each with well over 100 million speakers, are the mother tongues of 49 per cent of the earth's population.

number system In a particular language, the set of counting words equivalent to *one*, *two*, *three*, and so on, together with the principles used in that language for constructing these words.

numeral See **cardinal numeral** and **ordinal numeral**.

nursery word A word which is normally used only in talking to small children, such as *choo-choo* 'train' or *puddy-tat* 'cat'. Nursery words sometimes become more generally used, such as *wee* 'urinate'.

O

object Any noun phrase, other than a **subject**, which is an **argument** of a verb. We distinguish **direct objects**, **indirect objects** and **oblique objects**.

object language A language which we are talking about or describing. Compare **metalanguage**.

objective A label applied to that case-form of an English pronoun which is used for all purposes other than subjects of verbs, such as *me*, *him* and *them*.

oblique object A noun phrase which is an **argument** of a verb but which is not a **subject** or a **direct object** (or an **indirect object**, if these exist). In English, an oblique object is marked by a preposition: for example, *on the shelf* in *I put it on the shelf*. Some other languages mark oblique objects with postpositions or case-endings.

observer's paradox The problem that, when a linguist tries to observe speakers of a language in order to describe their spontaneous behaviour accurately, the speakers tend to modify their speech in self-conscious ways because they know they are being observed.

obstruent Any speech sound whose production involves an obstruction to the airflow sufficient at least to produce frication: a **plosive**, an **affricate** or a **fricative**. The opposite is **sonorant**.

obviative A grammatical form (usually a **pronoun**) found in certain languages and used to mark someone who is neither the speaker nor the hearer nor the person who is currently the centre of interest. Compare **proximate**.

Occitan A **Romance** language formerly spoken throughout most of southern France and still spoken in scattered communities today. Occitan is also called *Languedoc* and, inaccurately, *Provençal*.

occlusion A complete closure in the mouth, such as occurs during the pronunciation of a **plosive**, an **affricate** or a **nasal**.

occlusive An older name for a **plosive**, or sometimes for a **stop**.

OED See *Oxford English Dictionary*.

oesophagic airstream mechanism (also **esophagic**) A highly unusual way of producing a flow of air for speaking, essentially a controlled belch in which air from the stomach is forced up through the **oesophagus** and the **vocal tract**. This mechanism is used by people whose **larynx** has been surgically removed.

oesophagus (also **esophagus**) The tube which connects the **vocal tract** to the stomach, commonly called the *gullet*.

off-glide A **glide** occurring at the end of a **diphthong**, such as [j] in [aj]. Compare **on-glide**.

official language A language which, in some country or region, is recognized as a vehicle of official business: tax returns, birth certificates, identity cards, and the like. Multilingual countries like Belgium and Singapore may have two or more official languages. Compare **national language**.

ogam (also **ogham**) A distinctive **alphabet**, modelled on the Roman alphabet but having entirely different letters, formerly used by Celtic peoples in northern and western Europe.

Ogden, C(harles) K. An English classicist and critic (1889–1957), the co-author with **Richards** of a classic work on meaning, *The Meaning of Meaning*.

ogham Another name for **ogam**.

Old Church Slavonic The earliest **Slavic** language to be written down (in the ninth century) and the first to use the **Cyrillic alphabet**.

Old English (also **Anglo-Saxon**) The period in the history of English beginning with the Anglo-Saxon settlement of Britain and conventionally ending with the Norman Conquest in 1066, or sometimes in 1100. The vehicle of a large literature (such as *Beowulf*), Old English is vastly different from modern English and very similar to the older Germanic languages on the Continent.

Old European A hypothetical single language which some linguists believe was spoken in all or most of Europe in prehistoric times. The name is sometimes given more specifically to a language which appears to be the source of a large number of European river names. Linguists disagree strongly about whether such a language ever existed and, if it did, about whether it was an early form of **Indo-European** or some earlier language.

old language A meaningless expression. Except for **creoles**, all languages are equally "old" in that all are directly descended, without interruption, from the origins of human speech.

Old Norse The medieval language of the Vikings, a **Germanic** language recorded most importantly in the medieval literature of Iceland. Old Norse is the ancestor of the modern Scandinavian languages Icelandic, Norwegian, Danish and Swedish, and also of the extinct Norn.

Old Persian An early **Iranian** language, recorded in a number of **cuneiform**

inscriptions written during the time of the Old Persian Empire in the middle of the first millennium BC.

Omotic A small group of languages in eastern Africa, forming one branch of the **Afro-Asiatic** family.

one-word stage An early stage in child language acquisition, during which the child cannot produce any utterances longer than one word, such as *juice* or *doggie*.

on-glide A **glide** occurring at the beginning of a **diphthong**, such as [j] in [ja]. Compare **off-glide**.

onomastics The study of names, especially the origins of names.

onomatopoeia The coining or use of a word which attempts to represent a non-linguistic sound with ordinary speech sounds, such as English *buzz*, *clink*, *boom*, *cock-a-doodle-do* and *meow*.

onset The initial part of a **syllable**, preceding the **nucleus** (the vowel) and usually consisting of some number of consonants. The onsets of *splice*, *slice*, *lice* and *ice* are respectively /spl/, /sl/, /l/ and zero.

ontogeny The development of language in a single individual, from birth onwards. Compare **phylogeny**.

ontology The set of different kinds of things that exist, or that are posited in human minds or languages: people, animals, plants, lifeless objects, actions, events, states, and so on. Ontological categories are often important in languages: we say *Susie was struck by flying glass*, not *Flying glass struck Susie*, and we say *The cat is under the bed*, not *The bed is over the cat*.

opacity The property of a phonological rule, in some analysis, whose effect is not obvious from an examination of surface forms. The opposite is **transparency**.

open class A (large) **word class** to which new members are added readily and frequently, such as **noun**, **verb** and **adjective** in English. Compare **closed class**.

open-endedness (also **creativity**) The property of language by which there is no limit to the number of different things we can say. Open-endedness appears to be unique to human language: all other creatures are restricted to choosing from a short fixed list of possible "utterances".

open syllable A **syllable** which ends in a vowel, such as every one of the syllables in *banana*. Compare **closed syllable**.

open vowel Another name for a **low vowel**.

operating principles A set of principles which, in the view of some linguists, young children automatically follow in learning their first language. An example is 'pay attention to the ends of words'.

opposition A **contrast** between two or more speech sounds, such as that between [p] and [b] in English.

optative The **mood** category expressing a realizable wish, as in the somewhat archaic English *May you have a long life*. Some languages have a distinct set of verb-forms for this purpose.

Optimality Theory A theoretical approach to describing languages which holds that a language normally contains a number of conflicting requirements ('constraints'), some of which are more important than others. The form the language actually takes, then, will be *optimal*, in that the fewest constraints will be violated and the more important constraints will be violated less often than the less important ones. First developed for **phonology**, Optimality Theory is now being applied to **syntax**.

oracy The ability to use spoken language fluently and effectively, both in speaking and in comprehension.

oral 1. Pertaining to the mouth. 2. Of a speech sound, articulated in the mouth. In this sense, a **glottal** consonant is not oral, though **pharyngeal** consonants usually are considered oral. 3. Of a vowel, having no **nasalization**; not nasalized.

oral cavity The space inside the mouth.

oralism An educational policy designed to teach deaf children to speak and to master **lip-reading**. This policy does not work, and today it is considered more appropriate to teach **sign language**.

order of acquisition The sequence in which children learning a first language acquire particular sounds or particular forms or constructions. Certain universal tendencies can be observed in the order of acquisition.

ordinal numeral An adjectival form of a number: *first, second, tenth, twenty-seventh*. Compare **cardinal numeral**.

ordinary language philosophy (also **linguistic philosophy**) An approach to philosophy, sometimes especially to the **philosophy of language**, which rejects rigid formalization and focuses instead on the way in which language is actually used by human beings. This approach derives from the later work of **Wittgenstein**; among its leading proponents are **Ryle** and **Austin**.

organs of speech Another name for the **vocal organs**.

origin and evolution of language At present very little is known about the way in which human language came into existence. Some specialists think this occurred slowly and gradually, while others think language burst into existence very suddenly. Some think language evolved by natural selection, while others believe it was an accidental by-product of other developments. Some believe language arose millions of years ago in our remote non-human ancestors, others think it arose only with our own species just over 100,000 years ago, and still others believe it only came into existence around 40,000 years ago.

Orkhon inscriptions A group of inscriptions found in central Asia, dating from the eighth century AD. The language is a **Turkic** one, and these inscriptions represent the earliest known written form of a Turkic language. They are written in an indigenous alphabet.

oronym 1. The name of a mountain. 2. A formal name for a **pullet surprise**.

Orr, John A British Romanist and dialectologist (1885–1966).

orthoepy The study and teaching of "correct" (prestigious) pronunciation.

orthography A conventional and standardized way of writing a particular language, including a choice of letters (or other characters), spelling and punctuation.

Orton, Harold A British dialectologist (1898–1975), the leading figure in the preparation of the *Linguistic Atlas of England*.

Osthoff, Hermann A German linguist (1847–1909), a leading **Neogrammarian** and a major contributor to the study of Indo-European phonology and morphology.

OSV language A language in which the normal order of elements in a sentence is Object–Subject–Verb. Such languages are very rare, but one or two Amazonian languages are possibly of this type.

Oto-Manguean A family of languages spoken in southern Mexico.

out-of-Africa hypothesis The hypothesis that fully modern humans, *Homo sapiens sapiens*, originated solely in Africa and spread out from there to people the rest of the planet, displacing in the process the other hominids alive at the time, which therefore made little or no genetic contribution to today's humans. This view is supported by a majority of specialists, though others reject it in favour of the **parallel evolution hypothesis**. A linguistically interesting version of the out-of-Africa hypothesis is the **talking Eve hypothesis**.

overgeneralization 1. (also **overextension**) Especially in child language, the application of a word or other item to a wider range of things than it properly denotes, such as applying *daddy* to all men, *doggie* to all animals, or *moon* to all round things. The opposite is **undergeneralization**. 2. In child language, using morphological marking where it does not belong, producing things like *mens*, *foots* and even *footses*.

overgeneration In a **formal grammar**, the property of generating not only all the grammatical sentences but also a large number of ungrammatical ones, which must therefore be blocked ("filtered out") by some additional machinery.

overlap An occasion in a conversation in which one person begins speaking before another speaker has finished.

overt prestige The property of a language variety or a linguistic form which is generally accepted in the community as typical of educated usage. Compare **covert prestige**.

OVS language A language in which the normal order of elements in a sentence is Object–Verb–Subject. Such languages are very rare, but one or two Amazonian languages appear to be like this.

Oxford English Dictionary (*OED*) The great multi-volume dictionary of English, published early in the twentieth century, with a later *Supplement* and then a second edition in 1989. The *OED* attempts to record all words and senses recorded from AD 1000 to the present day. It is now available on CD-ROM.

oxymoron A phrase containing contradictory words, such as *cruel kindness*.

P

Pahlavi The name given to an ancestral form of **Persian** spoken from about the third century BC to the ninth century AD.

palaeography The study of ancient handwritten documents. Compare **epigraphy**.

palatal (A speech sound) produced by raising the front of the tongue toward the **palate**, such as the [j] of English *yes* and the [ɲ] of Spanish *cañon* 'canyon'.

palatalization 1. Raising the front of the tongue toward the **palate**, or moving the back of the tongue toward the palate, while producing a speech sound that does not otherwise involve the palate, one type of **secondary articulation**. The IPA represents palatalization with a superscript [ʲ]; hence [tʲ] is a palatalized version of [t]. Compare the palatalized [kʲ] in *key* with the unpalatalized [k] in *car*. 2. Any change in pronunciation in which a speech sound acquires such palatalization or in which a non-palatal sound is replaced by a palatal or palato-alveolar sound. An example is the change of original *$/k/$ to $/t\int/$ in English words like *cheese*, *child* and *church*. (Compare German *Käse*, *Kind*, *Kirche*, which preserve the original pronunciations better.)

palate The hard part of the roof of the mouth, just behind the **alveolar ridge**; it is traditionally called the *hard palate*.

palato-alveolar (A sound) produced with a constriction lying between the **alveolar ridge** and the **palate**, such as English [ʃ] (as in *shush*) or [dʒ] (as in *judge*). The name is unsystematic.

palatography A technique for finding out which areas of the roof of the mouth are touched by the tongue during an articulation. Either the roof of the mouth is coated with a coloured material or a false palate is inserted; the articulation is performed; and the mouth or the false palate is examined.

Pāli An early **Indo-Aryan** language in which many Buddhist scriptures are written, one of the **Prakrits**.

palimpsest A document from which one written text has been erased to make room for another.

palindrome A word or phrase which reads the same in both directions, such as *level* or *Madam, I'm Adam*. Punctuation is not counted.

Palmer, Harold A British applied linguist (1877–1949), a major figure in the **teaching of English as a foreign language**.

Palsgrave, John A British grammarian and cleric (?1480–1554), author of the first substantial grammar of **French**.

Pama-Nyungan A large group of related languages occupying all of Australia except for the northeastern corner. It is not clear whether Pama-Nyungan constitutes a single branch of a larger Australian family or whether it merely consists of those Australian languages which have not undergone the dramatic changes which have affected the *non-Pama-Nyungan* languages in that one corner.

Panglossian hypothesis A sarcastic label for the view that human language arose gradually by **natural selection**; the suggestion is that selectionists are claiming that our brains must have evolved specifically so that we could have language. Compare the **pop hypothesis**.

Pāṇini An Indian grammarian who probably lived around the fifth century BC. His great grammar of **Sanskrit**, which is clearly based on a long Indian grammatical tradition, is an outstandingly insightful piece of linguistic description, and it was not equalled anywhere in the world before the twentieth century.

Panjabi (also **Punjabi**) A major language of Pakistan and of western India, also widely spoken in Britain, a member of the **Indo-Aryan** branch of **Indo-European**. Panjabi is the language of the Sikh scriptures.

Papuan A large group of languages spoken on and near the island of New Guinea. Linguists are not sure if they are all related or not.

paradigm The full set of inflected forms exhibited by some class of lexical items, such as the case-forms of a class of nouns or the conjugated forms of a class of verbs. Often a paradigm is represented by a list of the forms of a single typical item.

paradigmatic relation Any relation between two or more linguistic items or forms which are competing possibilities, in that exactly one of them may be selected to fill some particular position in a structure. For example, all of the various inflected forms of a particular verb stand in a paradigmatic relation, since only one of them will be selected to appear whenever that verb is used. Compare **syntagmatic relation**.

paragrammatism Disordered grammar, a symptom of some kinds of **aphasia**.

paralanguage (also, informally, **tone of voice**) Any aspect of speaking other than the strictly linguistic content: pitch, loudness, tempo, timbre. Such factors carry information about the speaker's mood and attitude: angry, amused, frightened, or whatever.

parallel evolution hypothesis (also **multiregional hypothesis**) The hypothesis that human beings (*Homo sapiens*) evolved simultaneously from *Homo erectus* all over the Old World by continued interbreeding. Compare the **out-of-Africa hypothesis**.

parallel function strategy A proposed **perceptual strategy**, which says "assume that the subject of the main clause is also the subject of any subordinate clause". So, for example, when you hear *Lisa had a word with Susie before she left*, you are most likely to interpret *she* as meaning *Lisa*.

parallel processing A type of processing in which the task is divided up among many sub-parts of the system, all of them performing some part of the task at the same time. The processing of language in the brain appears to be of this type. This approach is used in the computer modelling called **connectionism**, where it is called *parallel distributed processing*. Compare **serial processing**.

parameter 1. In experimental work, a quantity which can take different values but for which a certain value may be chosen and held constant by the experimenter while the variation in something else is observed. 2. In certain theories of grammar, notably **Government-and-Binding Theory**, a particular feature of **universal grammar** which, in a given language, must take exactly one of a small number of possible values and which must be "set" appropriately by a child learning the language after exposure to an adequate range of data.

parameter-setting model A theoretical view of child language acquisition which holds that the child, upon exposure to the language it is learning, sets its innate **parameters** (sense 2) appropriately according to the data it hears. Proposed by **Chomsky**, this idea is intended to replace his earlier idea of a **language acquisition device**.

paraphrase Either of two sentences which are structurally or lexically different but which have approximately the same meaning. Example: *Jim bought a car from Sally*; *Sally sold a car to Jim*.

parataxis The use of **main clauses** side by side, with or without a connecting word like *and*, and without the use of **subordinate clauses**. Example: *She got up and she had a shower*. Compare **hypotaxis**.

parentheses 1. A notational device used in writing **rules** and **rule schemas** to show that some element is optionally present. For example, the rules n → Ø / V _____ V and n → Ø / V _____ hV can be combined into the schema n → Ø / V _____ (h)V, which states that /n/ is lost between two vowels whether or not it is followed by /h/. 2. A similar device used to show that some element is optional. For example, the pronunciation of the name *Deborah* may be given as /deb(ə)rə/, showing that the second syllable may be pronounced or not, indifferently. Compare **braces**.

parenthetical A word, phrase or sentence which interrupts a sentence and has no grammatical connection to the interrupted sentence. In the following examples, the parentheticals are set off by punctuation: *She was, in my opinion, the most desirable woman in England*; *The first international cricket match – this will probably surprise you – was played between Canada and the USA*.

parent language A language which is the direct ancestor of some other language(s), its **daughter language(s)**. For example, **Proto-Romance** (or **Vulgar Latin**) is the parent of the **Romance** languages.

parole The particular utterances produced by particular speakers on particular occasions; speech. The term **performance** means about the same. Compare *langue*.

parser A computer program which is capable of working out the structure, and hence the meaning, of sentences put into the computer by human beings, so that the computer can respond appropriately. The construction of good parsers is a major goal of **natural-language processing**.

parsing The process of assigning a syntactic structure to a string of words. This may be done either by a human being or by a **parser**. Parsing is a necessary first step in understanding anything you hear or read.

participant role A **semantic role** which represents an entity which participates more or less directly in the situation or action expressed in the clause, such as an Agent, a Patient, a Recipient or an Experiencer.

participle A name traditionally given to a **non-finite** verb-form which functions as a kind of adjective modifying a noun or a pronoun. English has at least two of these, the *-ing* participle (the 'imperfective' or 'present' participle) and the *-ed/-*

en participle (the 'perfective' or 'past' or 'passive' participle). The first is illustrated by examples like *The woman sitting next to Mike is Susie* and *Wanting to make a good impression, Susie chose her outfit carefully.* The second is illustrated by examples like *I can't read anything written in Dutch* and *Exhausted by her efforts, she decided to call it a day.* The label 'participle' is also given to a non-finite verb-form which combines with an auxiliary to construct a **periphrastic** verb-form. In English, both the *-ing* participle and the *-ed/-en* participle also do this, as shown in the following examples: *Susie is writing a letter; Susie has written a letter; Letters are being written; Letters have been written.* (The last two examples each contain two participles.) For syntactic purposes, it is often useful to make a distinction between the perfective/past participle (as in *We have finished the job*) and the passive participle (as in *The job has been finished*), even though the two are always identical in English. **Note:** do not confuse the *-ing* participle with the English **gerund**, which has the same form but behaves very differently.

particle 1. Broadly, and traditionally, almost any word in a language which is not derived from another word and which has a single unvarying form, such as *and, because, up,* or *with* in English. 2. Narrowly, and more usually today, one of a small class of items in English which can combine with simple verbs to make **phrasal verbs**, such as *up, off, on* and *down* (*make up, take off, turn on, write down*).

particle movement The phenomenon in English by which a **phrasal verb** can be split up. For example, instead of *She took off her dress*, we can say *She took her dress off*, with particle movement.

partitive A phrase or a form which expresses the notion of a part of a whole. Modern English has no special form for marking a partitive, though archaic English allows things like *He ate of my bread*, in which *of my bread* is a partitive (= 'some of my bread'). Many other languages have a distinct grammatical form for the partitive, as does Finnish: compare *Hän pani kirjat pöydälle* 'He put the books on the table' with *Hän pani kirjoja pöydälle* 'He put some books on the table', in which *kirjoja* is an overt partitive meaning '(some) books'.

part of speech A traditional label for **word class**.

Partridge, Eric A New Zealand-born British scholar and lexicographer (1894–1979), author of a large number of both scholarly and popular books, most of them dealing with the history of English.

Pashto (also **Pushtu**) A major language of Afghanistan, an **Iranian** language.

passive knowledge The knowledge which you have of a language which you can use in understanding it but which you don't use in speaking or writing it. For example, you might understand the words *nebbish, ersatz* and *eleemosynary* even if you never use them, and you might understand a phrase like *the authorization without which we cannot proceed* even if you never use such phrases. Your passive knowledge is always greater than your **active knowledge**.

passive voice A distinctive form of a verb (usually a **transitive verb**), or a construction involving such a form, with which the logical object of the verb becomes the surface subject and the logical subject is deleted or reduced to a peripheral phrase. A passive normally contrasts with an **active voice**. For example, the active sentence *The police arrested Janet*, in which the logical subject *the police* is also the surface subject, contrasts with two slightly different passive forms: the 'long passive' or 'passive with agent' *Janet was arrested by the* *police* and the 'short passive' or 'agentless passive' *Janet was arrested*, in which the logical object *Janet* is the surface subject. Some other languages permit an **impersonal** passive formed from an **intransitive verb**, in which the logical subject simply disappears; for example, the German intransitive verb *tanzen* 'dance' can appear in sentences like *Es wurde getanzt*, literally 'It was danced', in which the surface subject position is filled by the meaningless dummy item *es* (the sense is 'There was dancing').

Passy, Paul A French language-teacher and phonetician (1859–1940), the leading figure in the founding of the **International Phonetic Association**.

past A **tense** form which primarily serves to express past time. Almost every English verb has a distinct past-tense form, such as *killed* for *kill*, *saw* for *see* and *went* for *go*. When you say *I saw her*, you normally mean that the seeing took place earlier than the moment of speaking. But the correlation between past tense and past time is not perfect: in the sentences *It's time you went to bed* and *If I spoke better French, I could get a job in Paris*, the past-tense forms *went* and *spoke* do not express past time, but something different. Some languages with tense have two or more different past-tense forms expressing different degrees of remoteness in the past, while others have no separate past-tense form at all, distinguishing (for example) only future and non-future. (And some languages, of course, don't have tense at all.) **Note:** the English 'present perfect' forms, like *have finished* in *I have finished the wine*, are **not** past-tense forms but non-past ('present-tense') forms; confusion may arise here because identical-looking forms in several other European languages do indeed function as past-tense forms.

past perfect Another name for the **pluperfect**.

Patañjali An Indian grammarian (*c.* 150 BC), author of a major commentary of the grammar of **Pāṇini**.

patient The **semantic role** carried by a noun phrase expressing the entity which is undergoing an action, such as *the house* in *I'm painting the house*, *The house is being painted* and *The house collapsed*.

patois A regional speech-form of low prestige. The term is not used in linguistics.

patronymic An additional name carried by a person which indicates the name of his/her father or another male ancestor. In the name of the composer *Pyotr Ilyich Tchaikovsky*, the item *Ilyich* is a patronymic showing that his father's name was *Ilya*. The equivalent item for a mother's name is a *metronymic*.

paucal A distinctive **number** category found in some languages and denoting 'a few'. For example, nouns in the east African language Tigre have three forms: singular *färäs* 'horse', paucal *ʔäfras* 'a few horses', and plural *ʔäfresam* 'horses'. The paucal is sometimes called the 'little plural'.

Paul, Hermann A German linguist (1846–1921), a specialist in the history of **German**. Paul is best known for his insistence that linguistics should be regarded as a social science and for his great book *Principien der Sprachgeschichte*, a major synthesis of **Neogrammarian** ideas long regarded as the bible of historical linguistics.

pause A short interruption during the production of an utterance. A *silent pause* contains no sound; a *filled pause* is filled by a hesitation noise like *um* or *er*.

PC See **political correctness**.

Pedersen, Holger A Danish historical linguist (1867–1953), one of the foremost specialists in **Indo-European** of his day. He wrote the first popular book on the history of Indo-European studies and was the first to suggest the **Nostratic hypothesis**.

Peirce, C(harles) S. An American philosopher and logician (1839–1914); he did little work on language directly, but his emphasis on the role of language in philosophy has been very influential.

pejoration Any change in the meaning of a word by which the meaning becomes less respectful or more offensive. For example, *boor* and *knave* formerly meant merely 'farmer' and 'boy' respectively, but they have undergone pejoration. The opposite is **amelioration**.

pejorative Having a dismissive or insulting sense, as does *dump* in *This place is a dump*.

Penfield, Wilder An American-born Canadian neurosurgeon (1891–1976) who developed a technique for mapping out the specialist areas of the brain in great detail, including the language areas.

penult The next-to-last syllable of a word, such as *guis* in *linguistics*. Compare **antepenult, ultima**.

Penutian A major language family of western North America; its largest single branch is **Mayan**. Its precise membership is much debated, and some would include certain languages of South America.

perception Receiving and recognizing stimuli for the external world. In linguistics, we are chiefly interested in *speech perception*, the recognition of other people's utterances as utterances in a language we know; this is the first step in **comprehension**.

perceptual strategy (also **processing strategy**) Any one of a number of techniques which we may possibly use in comprehending utterances. A perceptual strategy is a kind of principled guess about how the words we are hearing fit together in a syntactic structure. Among the strategies which have been suggested as likely to be used are the **canonical sentoid strategy** and the principle of **late closure**, but there are many others. A **garden-path sentence** is difficult precisely because it is constructed so as to make the more obvious strategies lead to the wrong interpretation.

perfect The **aspect** category which describes a state of affairs resulting from an earlier action. English has a special form for this: the present-tense perfect ("present perfect") form *I have finished the wine* means, roughly, "There is no wine now because I drank the last of it earlier" – that is, it expresses a present state of affairs (no wine) resulting from an earlier action (my drinking). Note that this form is unambiguously present-tense: **I have finished the wine ten minutes ago* is ungrammatical. The corresponding past-tense form, the "past perfect" or "pluperfect", is *I had finished the wine*. In many other European languages, a form that looks identical to the English present perfect is functionally a simple past tense. **Note:** do not confuse the perfect with the **perfective**; even some textbooks make this mistake.

perfective An **aspect** category involving no reference to the internal temporal structure of an event. In English, the perfective is chiefly expressed by the simple past tense, as in *The hamster climbed the curtain* and *Lisa learned French in Caen*. The English simple present can also have a perfective meaning in certain circumstances, such as in stage directions: *Nellie draws a dagger and stabs herself.* (More commonly, though, the simple present has a **habitual** interpretation.) Compare **imperfective**. **Note:** do not confuse the perfective with the **perfect**.

performance The actual linguistic behaviour of particular individuals on particular occasions, including any hesitations, memory lapses, slips of the tongue or processing difficulties arising from long or complex structures. Compare **competence**.

performative An utterance which, all by itself, constitutes doing something. Examples (in suitable circumstances) include *I now pronounce you husband and wife*, *I promise to buy you a teddy bear* and *I accuse you of lying*. A verb used in such an utterance is a *performative verb*.

periphery In **Government-and-Binding Theory**, that part of the grammar of a language which is not determined by universal principles but which consists only of miscellaneous idiosyncrasies. Compare **core grammar**.

periphrasis The construction of grammatical forms by the use of additional words. For example, *has eaten* and *is eating* are periphrastic verb forms (compare *ate*), and *more beautiful* is a periphrastic comparative adjective (compare *lovelier*).

periphrastic Constructed by means of a **periphrasis**.

perseveration A **speech error** in which something that has already been said is erroneously repeated (usually only partially) later in the utterance. Examples: *bread and brutter* for *bread and butter*; *sometums* for *sometimes*.

Persian (also **Farsi**) The major language of Iran, also spoken in other parts of Asia, an **Iranian** language.

person The **grammatical category** which distinguishes individuals and entities according to their role in the conversation. All languages seem to distinguish **first person** (the speaker and possibly others associated with the speaker), **second person** (the addressee(s) and possibly others associated with the addressee(s)) and **third person** (everyone and everything else). Like most languages, English has a set of **personal pronouns** to express these distinctions.

personal pronoun A **pronoun** which chiefly serves to express differences in **person**, sometimes also with additional distinctions such as number, sex, gender or intimacy. English has the following personal pronouns: *I* (first-person singular), *we* (first plural), *you* (second-person singular and plural), *he, she, it* (third-singular, with additional sex-marking) and *they* (third plural). Other languages often have rather different systems.

PET scanner A device which can produce a detailed map of blood flow in the brain of a conscious person without damage. It can be used not only to identify areas of injury but also to observe activity in the brain of a healthy person performing various tasks, such as linguistic ones, thus aiding us in working out which parts of the brain are involved in performing which tasks. The initials stand for *positron emission tomography*.

pharyngeal (A speech sound) produced by a constriction in the **pharynx**, such as Arabic [ʕ] in [ʕali] *Ali*.

pharyngealized Produced with constriction of the **pharynx** accompanying another articulation. Pharyngealization is marked in the IPA with a following superscript [ʕ], as in [tˤ], a pharyngealized [t].

pharynx The space connecting the **larynx** to the **oral cavity** and the **nasal cavity**.

phatic communion The use of language purely to establish or maintain good social relations between people, such as comments about the weather between English-speakers who encounter one another but have nothing in particular to say.

Philippine languages A group of languages spoken in the Philippines, forming one group of the **Austronesian** family.

Philological Society A professional organization in Britain devoted to **historical linguistics**.

philology A label which has been applied to several different things. Originally, it was applied to the study of ancient documents, including literary texts, for such purposes as determining the date and place of origin or the identity of the writer, putting different copies of a text into historical order, correcting errors in a text, and commenting upon the language used. From about 1800, the term was applied to the new discipline of **comparative linguistics**; in this sense the names *comparative philology* or *the new philology* have sometimes been used. Today the term is most usually applied to that part of **historical linguistics** which is concerned with details, rather than with general principles, such as tracing the histories of particular words and names (**etymology** and **onomastics**).

philosophy of language The branch of philosophy dealing with the nature of language and its place in perception, thought and reasoning.

Phoenician The **Semitic** language, now extinct, anciently spoken in the eastern Mediterranean by the Phoenicians, a trading people who introduced the **alphabet** to the Greeks. The city of Carthage was a Phoenician colony, and the Phoenician spoken by the Carthaginians is called *Punic*.

Phoenician alphabet The particular **Semitic alphabet** used by the ancient Phoenicians. The Greeks took it over and added vowel letters (previously absent), thus producing the first complete alphabet.

phonaesthesia Another name for **sound symbolism**.

phonation The use of the **larynx** to modify air flowing through it so as to produce an audible source of acoustic energy which can be modified by the rest of the **vocal tract** to produce speech sounds.

phonation type Any one of the various types of activity in the **glottis** which can produce a stream of air for the organs of articulation to use in producing speech. There is disagreement as to what types should should be recognized; here is one classification: *nil phonation* (silent airflow through the open glottis), *breath* (noisy airflow through the open glottis, as in heavy breathing), *whisper* (noisy airflow through a partially closed glottis, as in a stage whisper), *creak* (very slow vibration of the vocal folds), *modal voice* (rapid vibration of the vocal folds) and *falsetto* (extremely rapid vibration of tensed vocal folds). Many combined phonation types are possible, such as *breathy voice* (the 'sighing' quality heard from certain actresses with little-girl voices) and *whispery voice* (a kind of murmur).

phone Another name for a **speech sound**.

phoneme Any one of the basic sound units found in a particular language, such as /k/, /t/ and /æ/ in English. Every word consists of a permitted sequence of the language's phonemes: *cat* is /kæt/, *tack* is /tæk/, *act* is /ækt/, *tact* and *tacked* are /tækt/, and so on. The number of phonemes varies from 10 in one Brazilian language to over 100 for one African language. English has 40-odd, the precise number depending on the accent.

phoneme monitoring An experimental technique in psycholinguistics in which a subject hearing a list of words is asked to listen for a particular sound: "Press this button when you hear a [p]." The purpose is usually to determine what characteristics of words in the list make the task more difficult.

phoneme system The complete set of **phonemes** found in some particular language or speech variety.

phonemic transcription A **transcription** of words or of connected speech in a particular speech variety in terms of the **phonemes** which have been set up by the analyst for that variety. Such a transcription provides the minimum information necessary to construct a complete pronunciation by rule; it omits all predictable phonetic detail. A phonemic transcription is enclosed in slashes, as with /flem/ and /lɪŋ'gwɪstɪks/ for English *phlegm* and *linguistics*. Compare **phonetic transcription**.

phonetic alphabet Any conventional system for representing speech sounds by providing a distinctive letter or symbol for each different sound. The most widely used one is the **International Phonetic Alphabet**, but **American transcription** is also used in the USA.

phonetics The study of speech sounds, conventionally divided into **articulatory**, **acoustic** and **auditory phonetics**. In *general phonetics*, we consider the entire range of possible speech sounds, without regard to whether or how these sounds may function in languages; in *linguistic phonetics*, we consider the ways in which languages exploit phonetic differences for linguistic (phonological) purposes. Phonetics deals with the physical nature of speech sounds, and not with their relations to other speech sounds in particular languages; this last is **phonology**.

phonetic transcription A type of **transcription** which merely represents the phonetic characteristics of the speech sounds used, in whatever degree of detail is considered desirable, without regard for the **phonemes** of the language. We use phonetic transcription mostly in two circumstances: (1) we haven't yet done a phonological analysis of the language, and hence we don't yet know which phonetic characteristics are contrastive and which are predictable; (2) we want to represent a pronunciation in more detail than a **phonemic transcription** can provide, in order to draw attention to some point. A phonetic transcription is enclosed in square brackets.

phonics A method of teaching children to read by the practice of associating particular letters or sequences of letters with particular sounds.

phonogram A symbol in some writing system which represents some unit of pronunciation, either a single speech sound (a **letter** in an **alphabet**) or a single syllable (a character in a **syllabary**). Compare **logogram**.

phonographic writing A writing system based on **phonograms**. Both **alphabets** and **syllabaries** constitute phonographic writing. Compare **logographic script**.

phonological recoding hypothesis The hypothesis that reading always involves converting the written words into sounds, even in silent reading. The idea is controversial.

phonology The branch of linguistics dealing with the way speech sounds behave in particular languages or in languages generally. Phonology examines *patterns of sounds*; it considers the relations between speech sounds from two points of view: **syntagmatically** (relations among sequences of sounds in morphemes, words or utterances) and **paradigmatically** (relations among the sounds making up the sound system of the language). Compare **phonetics**.

phonotactics In a particular language, the rules that determine which particular sequences of phonemes are allowed to occur in words. In English, for example, the rules allow both /blæk/ and /bræk/, though only the first happens to exist, but they prohibit /bnæk/, which is not a possible word. Languages differ greatly in their phonotactics.

phrasal category (also **maximal projection, double-bar category**) A **syntactic category** which constitutes a **phrase** (sense 2): a **noun phrase**, a **verb phrase**, an **adjective phrase**, an **adverb phrase** or a **prepositional phrase**.

phrasal verb A verb consisting of a simple verb plus one or more **particles** (sense 2); the meaning is not generally predictable from the meanings of the component parts. Examples: *make up, take off, put up with*.

phrase 1. Broadly, any sequence (in a sentence) of one or more words which constitutes a syntactic unit: a **constituent**. 2. Narrowly, and more usually, a particular kind of syntactic unit, with the following properties: (1) it is clearly built around a single word, such as a noun, a verb or a preposition, and (2) it is the largest unit built around that word occurring in that sentence. Only five types of phrase are widely recognized – **noun phrase, verb phrase, adjective phrase, adverb phrase, prepositional phrase** – though some linguists would add others. The sentence *The old man was staring gloomily out of the window* contains two noun phrases (*the old man*, built around *man*, and *the window*, built around *window*), one prepositional phrase (*out of the window*, built around *out of*), one adjective phrase (*old*, built around *old*), one adverb phrase (*gloomily*, built around *gloomily*), and two verb phrases (*staring gloomily out of the window*, built around *staring*, and *was staring gloomily out of the window*, built around *was*). (Some linguists would take a different view of the verb phrases.) Note that the sequence *old man* is a constituent, and hence a phrase in sense 1, but it is not a phrase in sense 2, since it is not the biggest unit built around *man*. The word around which a phrase is built is the **head** (or *lexical head*) of that phrase.

phrase marker Another name for a **tree structure** for a sentence.

phrase-structure grammar A type of **generative grammar** (sense 1) in which all the rules are of a particular type. There are two varieties. In the more familiar **context-free** phrase-structure **grammar**, every rule is a **context-free rule** of the form A → W, where A is a single category and W is a string of any number of categories, including zero. Examples: S → NP VP (a sentence may consist of a noun phrase followed by a verb phrase); NP → Det N′ (a noun phrase may consist of a determiner followed by an N-bar); VP → V NP NP (a verb phrase may consist of a verb followed by two noun phrases); S[INV +] → V[AUX +] NP VP[FIN −] (an inverted sentence may consist of an auxiliary verb followed by a noun phrase followed by a non-finite verb phrase); NP → e (a noun phrase may be empty). Such context-free grammars are very successful at accounting for most of the syntactic structures observed in natural languages. In the more powerful **context-sensitive** phrase-structure **grammars**, the rules differ in that a rule may be specified as applying only in a certain environment – that is, only when certain neighbouring categories are present. Examples: V → Vtr / _____ NP (a verb may be a transitive verb when immediately followed by a noun phrase); NP → NP[Dat] / V _____ NP (a noun phrase may be a dative noun phrase when immediately preceded by a verb and followed by another noun phrase). Context-sensitive grammars are far too powerful to provide plausible models for natural languages.

phylogeny The historical development of a language over time; the history of a particular language. Compare **ontogeny**.

phylum Another name for a **language family** or for a major branch of a family.

Piaget, Jean A Swiss psychologist (1896–1980), best known for his work on the development of cognition in children and for his claim that the development of language in children was merely an outgrowth of their general cognitive development, a position which brought him into conflict with the **innateness hypothesis** of Noam **Chomsky**.

pictogram A written symbol which is intended to be a recognizable picture of what it means. Pictograms are widely used in public signs; for example, a silhouette of a person holding a stick means "Be careful! Blind people crossing the road." Pictograms were used in some very early writing systems, in which, for example, the word for 'sun' was represented by a drawing of the sun, but such pictograms rapidly gave way to more abstract and convenient modes of representation. Pictograms are not part of any established writing system today, though it is still just about possible to pick out the pictographic ancestry of some Chinese characters. Do not confuse a pictogram with a **logogram**.

pidgin A crude and clumsy system of communication, with no recognizable grammar, stitched together out of bits and pieces of one or more natural languages and used by people who have no language in common. A pidgin may develop into a **creole**.

PIE Abbreviation for **Proto-Indo-European**.

pied-piping The construction in which a preposition is fronted along with its object, as in *To whom were you talking?* Compare *Who were you talking to?*, in which there is no pied-piping, but rather **preposition stranding**.

Pike, Kenneth L. An American linguist (1912–), the creator of **Tagmemics** and one of the founders of the **Summer Institute of Linguistics**. Though a contemporary of the **American structuralists**, and sometimes counted as one of them, he rejected many of their doctrines and made strenuous efforts to understand language in terms of human behaviour generally.

Pinker, Steven A Canadian psycholinguist (1954–), author of a celebrated book, *The Language Instinct*.

Pinyin A system for writing **Chinese** in the **Roman alphabet**. Now official in China, this system is regularly used in writing Chinese names in English and has replaced older systems, so that we now write, for example, *Mao Zedong* and *Beijing* instead of *Mao Tse-tung* and *Peking*.

pitch The quality of "highness" or "lowness" of a sound, as perceived by our ears. Generally speaking, the higher the **frequency** of a sound wave, the higher the pitch of a sound. The voices of women and children typically have a higher pitch than those of men; all languages make linguistic use of pitch for **intonation**, but some also use it for a **pitch accent** on words or in a **tone** system.

pitch accent A type of **word accent** found in certain languages in which some syllables in a word may have a higher **pitch** than others. For example, Japanese *hana* means 'nose' if it is pronounced with low pitch on both syllables, but 'flower' if it is pronounced with a low pitch on the first and a high pitch on the second. A pitch accent differs from a **tone** system in that, in a tone system, each syllable has its own independent tone, while, in a pitch accent, the pitch contour belongs to the whole word, and not to individual syllables.

pivot grammar A proposed grammatical analysis of the **two-word stage** in child language. In this view, the child has only two classes of words, called *pivot* and *open*, and only certain combinations of these are possible. This view is now known not be generally valid.

place of articulation The particular location in the vocal tract at which the **constriction** is made in producing a consonant. In principle, the place is named by a compound identifying the lower and upper organs involved in the constriction, as in *labio-dental* or *apico-alveolar*. In practice, we often use contracted and irregular forms like *velar*, *alveolar*, *palato-alveolar* and *retroflex*.

Platonism The view that the meaning of a generic word like *dog* is an abstract object (a *form*) which has a real existence in an abstract world. A real-world object which we call a dog is a dog merely because it bears a resemblance to the appropriate abstract form. Compare **nominalism** (sense 2), **conceptualism**, **realism**.

Plato's problem The problem of explaining how speakers can know so many things about their language which they have never been explicitly taught and which it seems unlikely they could have deduced from the speech they were exposed to.

pleonasm A linguistic form or expression in which the same information is given twice, as in *female woman*.

plosive A **consonant** produced by closing off the flow of air completely and then releasing it suddenly, such as [p], [d] or [k]. Compare **affricate**.

pluperfect (also **past perfect**) A name given to a verb form which is **past** in tense and **perfect** in aspect, such as *had finished* in *I had finished the job by ten o'clock*.

plural In English and many other languages, a **number** category which most typically expresses "two or more (of something)", like *dogs*, *men* and *people*. In a language with a **dual**, the plural means "three or more". Some languages, such as Chinese, do not have a distinct plural at all.

plurale tantum A noun which is plural in form but singular in meaning, such as *scissors*, *pants* or *binoculars*. The plural of this term is *pluralia tantum*.

poetics The analysis of poetry by the concepts and techniques of linguistics.

Pokorny, Julius A German historical linguist (1887–1970), a specialist in **Indo-European** and the author of the best-known dictionary of Indo-European roots.

Polish The chief language of Poland, a **Slavic** language.

politeness The use of linguistic features to maintain good relationships which are appropriate to the situation. Politeness phenomena include things like forms of **address**, appropriate use of markers like *please* and *excuse me*, and, in some languages, even vocabulary and verb-forms.

political correctness (**PC**) A political movement whose proponents seek to stamp out all linguistic forms and usages which they regard as discriminating against certain social groups.

polygenesis The hypothesis that human language arose independently on several different occasions. Compare **monogenesis**.

polyglot A person who speaks several languages.

Polynesian A group of languages spoken in the Pacific, forming one branch of the **Austronesian** family. Among them are Maori, Hawaiian and Samoan.

polysemy Multiple meanings for a single word, as with *foot*, which can mean 'bottom of the leg', 'unit of length' and 'bottom of a mountain'. It is not easy to distinguish polysemous words from **homophones**.

polysyllable A word containing two or more **syllables**, such as *lover*, *linguistics* or *polysyllabic*.

polysynthetic language A language in which **incorporation** is very highly developed. Sometimes the term is reserved more specifically for such a language in which the incorporated form of a word is quite different from its free form, such as the Australian language Tiwi, in which, for example, 'fire' is *yikwani* as an independent word but *-ki-* when it is incorporated into a verb.

pooh-pooh theory The conjecture that language arose out of cries of pain, fear, anger and excitement. There is no evidence to support this conjecture.

pop hypothesis A tongue-in-cheek label for the view that human language is an **emergent** phenomenon, that it just "popped" into existence when the brain had evolved a suitable level of complexity. Compare the **Panglossian hypothesis**.

portmanteau morph A single **morph** which represents two or more **morphemes**. An example is Latin *-ō* in *amō* 'I love', which simultaneously expresses first person, singular, present, active, indicative, most of which are usually marked by separate morphs in Latin.

Port Royal A name given to a group of seventeenth-century French grammarians who developed a remarkable view of grammar in terms of universal patterns of thought. Their major work, the *Grammaire générale et raisonnée*, is known as the *Port-Royal grammar*.

Portuguese The chief language of Portugal and Brazil, a **Romance** language.

possessive A form or construction indicating that somebody or something belongs to, or is associated with, somebody or something else. English has two different constructions for this: the -'s marker, as in *Susie's leg*, and the preposition *of*, as in *the leg of the table*.

possible-worlds semantics A type of **formal semantics** in which the analyst deals, not just with one "world", but with many different conceivable "worlds", and the truth value of a sentence is evaluated with respect to those various possibilities. For example, *All Irish women are female* is true in all possible worlds, but *All Irish women are blue-eyed* is true only in some possible worlds.

post-alveolar (A speech sound) produced with a constriction just behind the **alveolar ridge**, such as /r/ in the English of England (other speakers do not necessarily use this kind of /r/).

post-Bloomfieldians Another name for the **American structuralists**.

post-creole continuum The range of language varieties, from **acrolect** to **basilect**, which results when a **creole** undergoes some degree of **decreolization**.

postmodernism An intellectual movement which holds that no discoverable objective truth exists and that our version of reality is constructed by means of our language. Deeply fashionable in some quarters, postmodernism, or at least its application to scientific investigation, is dismissed by most working scientists, including linguists, as ignorant nonsense.

postposing Moving something to the end of the sentence. For example, *A book on the Chernobyl disaster has just come out* has a postposed counterpart *A book has just come out on the Chernobyl disaster*, in which the phrase *on the Chernobyl disaster* has been postposed. Compare **preposing**.

postposition An item which behaves just like a **preposition** except that it follows its object. An example is Basque *gainean* 'on top of', as in *mahai gainean* 'on top of the table'. English has one or two postpositions, including *ago*, as in *five years ago*.

postvocalic Occurring after a vowel, such as the /b/ and the /t/ in *about*.

Pott, August A German historical linguist (1802–87), one of the foremost specialists in **Indo-European** languages of his day; he worked especially on phonology and etymology.

poverty-of-the-stimulus argument The argument that the speech data available to a child learning its first language are inadequate to account for the knowledge of the language the child finally acquires, and hence that some version of the **innateness hypothesis** must be invoked.

power semantic An asymmetric arrangement in which a higher-ranking person addresses a lower-ranking one with an intimate (T) pronoun or otherwise with a lack of overt respect, but the lower-ranking person in turn addresses the higher-ranking one with a respectful (V) pronoun or otherwise with overt respect. Compare **solidarity semantic**.

PRAGMA A computer program which is capable not only of understanding questions put to it by a human being and of answering them appropriately, but also of guessing what the human being's intentions are and of providing additional relevant information which has not been asked for.

pragmatics The branch of linguistics which studies those aspects of meaning which derive from the **context** of an utterance, rather than being intrinsic to the linguistic material itself. For example, the utterance *Watch it! The hamster's out of his cage* can reasonably be interpreted as a request to close the door in certain contexts, but there is no possibility of claiming that the utterance actually *means* this.

Prague School The name usually given to the group of mostly east European linguists associated with the *Cercle Linguistique de Prague*, a body founded in 1926 to promote linguistic investigations. The Prague School's main theorists were **Mathesius**, **Trubetzkoy** and **Jakobson**, and its ideas have had a lasting effect upon the development of linguistics, not least because of Jakobson's later emigration to the USA, where he introduced and developed Praguian ideas.

Prakrits The various languages which developed from **Sanskrit** and which became the immediate ancestors of the modern **Indo-Aryan** languages. Some of the Prakrits are recorded in writing, such as **Pāli**.

pre-closing In conversation, an utterance by one speaker which offers to close the conversation. The offer need not be taken up, and may provide another speaker with a chance to change the subject.

predicate In the traditional two-way division of a sentence, all that part of the sentence which is not the **subject**. In English and many other languages, only a **verb phrase** can function as a predicate. In the following examples, *Susie* is the subject, and everything else is part of the predicate: *Susie is very pretty*; *Susie smokes*; *Susie smiled wickedly*; *Susie has always been interested in fossils*; *Susie wants to buy a new car*; *Susie was given a camera for her birthday*.

predicate nominal A **noun phrase** which follows a **copula** or a **quasi-copula**. The following bracketed examples are predicate nominals: *Susie is [a teacher]*; *Susie has become [a committed feminist]*; *Susie proved [an excellent sailor]*.

predicate position (also **predicative position**) The position occupied by a linguistic item which is inside a **predicate**, especially following a **copula** like *be*. **Adjectives** can occupy predicate position in English, as in *That dress is _____* (try it with adjectives like *red* and *new*). **Nouns** do not work in the same way: we can say *a maternity dress*, but we can't say **That dress is maternity*. Compare **attributive position**.

predication Asserting that somebody or something has some property. Such sentences as *Susie is clever, Susie smokes, Susie is my sister* and *Susie has blue eyes* all predicate some property of Susie (that is, they all assert that Susie has some property): being clever, being a smoker, being my sister, having blue eyes.

prefix An **affix** which must precede what it is attached to, such as *re-* in *rewrite* and *post-* in *post-war*.

prefix stripping A hypothesis about the **comprehension** of language which holds that people mentally remove prefixes from complex words during processing. For example, *inarticulate* would be mentally broken up into *in-* plus *articulate*, which would be "looked up" separately. This view is generally rejected.

prelinguistic Pertaining to the stage before full-blown language is achieved, either in connection with human origins or in connection with language acquisition by a child. The **cooing** and **babbling** stages of child language acquisition are often called *prelanguage*.

preposing (also **fronting**) Moving something to the beginning of the sentence. For example, the sentence *I saw a great film yesterday* has a preposed counterpart *Yesterday I saw a great film*, in which the adverb *yesterday* has been preposed. The term is also applied to cases in which the preposing is obligatory, as in *Have you finished your homework?*, in which the fronting of *have* is obligatory. Compare **postposing**.

preposition A smallish **word class** found in English and in many other languages (though not in all), or a word belonging to this class. An English preposition has an invariable form, and it most typically combines with a following **noun phrase** to form a **prepositional phrase** (but see also **preposition stranding**). The most frequent prepositions are little words like *of*, *to*, *in*, *on*, *at*, *from* and *with*, but some prepositions are much bigger, such as *underneath*, *notwithstanding*, *in front of* and *in spite of*.

prepositional phrase A syntactic unit consisting of a **preposition** followed by a **noun phrase**. Examples: *of the students* (as in *most of the students*), *in the box*, *under the bed*, *to London*, *without a hope*, *in front of our house*, *in spite of her protestations*.

preposition stranding The construction in which a **preposition** is not immediately followed by an object. In *Who were you talking to?* and *the guy I bought my car from*, the prepositions *to* and *from* are stranded. Compare **pied-piping**.

prescriptivism The approach to language which attaches priority to determining and teaching "correct" or "proper" usage and to identifying and eliminating "incorrect" usage. A degree of prescriptivism is usually held to be necessary in education, but most linguists reject prescriptivism as a basis for scientific investigation of language and espouse **descriptivism**.

present A **tense** form which includes as its major use, or one of its major uses, reference to the time of speaking. One of the two English tenses is called the "present" tense, but it might more accurately be called the "non-past" tense, since it covers both present and future time. Such English sentences as *She smokes*, *She is changing the oil*, *She has finished her dinner* and *She will be here soon* are all "present-tense", though some of them (especially the last) are rather confusingly given other names in many books.

presentative Any construction which serves to introduce a new person or object into the discourse, such as *There was a bus coming*, or *There was this bus coming*.

presupposition A proposition whose truth must be taken for granted if some utterance is to be regarded as sensible. For example, the utterance *Jim's wife runs a boutique* only makes sense if Jim is married; therefore *Jim is married* is a presupposition of this utterance. Presupposition survives negation: the utterance *Jim's wife doesn't run a boutique* still presupposes *Jim is married*. Compare **entailment**, **conversational implicature**.

preterite A simple **past**-tense form of a verb, such as *loved* or *took*.

preterminal node In a **tree structure** for a sentence, a **node** which has only one item below it – usually, a node naming a **word class** like Noun or Determiner, which has below it only a suitable word.

prevocalic Occurring before a vowel, such as the /b/ and the /t/ in *butter*.

primary articulation In the production of a speech sound, the point at which the **constriction** is greatest, and hence the point at which the airflow is most severely obstructed. A primary articulation may be accompanied by a **secondary articulation** at some other point in the vocal tract.

primary cardinal vowel In the traditional way of listing the **cardinal vowels**, any one of the vowels [i e ɛ a ɑ ɔ o u], selected because they are more frequent in the world's languages than the **secondary cardinal vowels**.

primary stress The strongest degree of stress in a word. In *education*, for example, the third syllable receives primary stress. Compare **secondary stress**.

primate The class of mammals to which human beings belong; it also includes apes, monkeys, lemurs, tarsiers and lorises. Primates have good vision and recognizable hands; they are unusual among mammals in their lack of specialization.

prime See **primitive** (sense 2).

priming An experimental technique in **psycholinguistics**, in which a subject is "prepared" for one word by first hearing a possibly related word. For example, a subject might be able to perform some task involving the word *ball* (such as deciding whether it is an English word) more rapidly after first hearing *tennis*. The object is usually to find out which words are closely related in the **mental lexicon**.

primitive 1. Ancient; early. When we speak of a "primitive" stage of some language, we mean only a stage which is earlier than other stages of that language, often particularly the earliest stage for which we can deduce any information at all; there is no suggestion that such an early stage was in any way cruder or less well developed than other languages or than later stages of that language. 2. (also **prime**) In a **formal grammar**, any one of the basic undefined notions in terms of which all the other concepts used in that grammar are defined.

primitive language A label which has nothing to refer to. Every human language ever discovered has a large vocabulary and a rich and complex grammatical system.

principal parts For a **verb**, a conventional listing of all those forms of the verb which a language-learner needs to know in order to correctly construct all the remaining forms of that verb. For modern English, these forms are the infinitive, the past tense and the past participle: *love, loved, loved; write, wrote, written; go, went, gone*. For other languages, such as Latin or Old English, a different list is required.

Principles-and-Parameters Approach Another name for the **Government-and-Binding Theory**.

Priscian A Roman grammarian (fifth century AD); his grammar of Latin represented a culmination of the Greek and Roman grammatical tradition, and it became the basis of Latin grammars down to the present day.

processing strategy Another name for a **perceptual strategy**.

proclitic A **clitic** which precedes the thing it is bound to. In the French sentence *Il te le donnera* 'He'll give it to you', the three pronouns *il* 'he', *te* 'you' and *le* 'it' are all proclitics bound to the following verb. Compare **enclitic**.

pro-drop language (also **null-subject language**) A language in which a verb does not need to be accompanied by an overt pronoun (especially a subject pronoun) if that pronoun is obvious from the context. In the pro-drop language Spanish, the verb-form *viene* 'comes' can make up a complete sentence: *Viene* 'He/she/it is coming'. English does not have pro-drop: we cannot say **Is coming*.

production Uttering speech. Speech production clearly involves a preliminary planning stage, during which content and structure are at least roughed out, followed by the retrieval of appropriate words and their insertion into the structure; there also appears to be some kind of "checking" or "editing" carried out before any sounds are uttered.

productivity The degree to which a grammatical pattern, often especially a pattern of **word-formation**, can be freely extended to new cases. For example, the English noun-forming suffix *-ness* is highly productive, while the noun-forming suffix *-th* (as in *warmth*) is totally unproductive today. The adverb-forming suffix *-wise* was formerly no more than weakly productive, but it has recently become very productive: *clotheswise, moneywise, healthwise, fitnesswise*.

pro-form Another name for an **anaphor**.

progressive (also **continuous**) An **aspect** form indicating that an action continues over some period of time. English uses its *be . . . -ing* form for this purpose, as in *She's washing the car* and *She was reading a book when the phone rang*.

Prolog A computer language which is particularly convenient for performing certain tasks involving language.

prominence The property of a linguistic element which stands out in comparison with neighbouring elements. For example, a stressed syllable is more prominent than an unstressed syllable.

pronoun A word class, or a word belonging to this class, whose members typically form **noun phrases** all by themselves, such as *you, she, something* or (in some circumstances) *this*.

pronunciation A particular way of uttering an individual word or (less usually) words in general. Speakers with different **accents** will typically use noticeably different pronunciations for many words, but, in addition, there are many particular words of English which are pronounced strikingly differently by different people even when they have similar accents: *economics, adult, advertisement, greasy, controversy, police, distribute, applicable, dispute* (noun), *kilometre, adversary, cervical*, and many, many others.

pronouncing dictionary A book which lists the words and names of a language together with their pronunciations. The standard pronouncing dictionary of English is *LPD*.

proper name A **noun** or a **noun phrase** whose only function is to pick out some individual person, place or thing. Examples: *Lisa, Abraham Lincoln, Spain, the Basque Country, the Golden Gate Bridge, the Roman Empire, the Eighteenth Dynasty*. Proper names conventionally take capital letters in English, but some words which are also conventionally capitalized are not proper names, such as *Frenchman*, *Tuesday* and *November*.

proper noun A **noun** which is a **proper name**, such as *Susie*, *Chicago* or *Finland*. Such a noun usually constitutes a **noun phrase** all by itself.

proposition A statement which is capable of being true or false. Consider the proposition *Susie is Irish*, and call this P. Now the English sentence *Susie is Irish* can reasonably be interpreted as asserting 'P is true'; the sentence *Susie is not Irish* can be interpreted as asserting 'P is false'; and the question *Is Susie Irish?* can be interpreted as asking 'Is P true or false?'

prose Ordinary writing; writing which is not poetic in nature.

Prosodic Analysis A theory of phonology developed in Britain by **Firth** and his students in the 1940s and 1950s. Unlike other theories of the day, it emphasized **syntagmatic relations** (the properties of *sequences* of speech sounds in speech). Its ideas have been revived within the contemporary **non-linear** theories of phonology.

prosody 1. The study of the structural features of poetry. 2. Another name for **suprasegmental**.

prospective An **aspect** form indicating that an action or event is viewed as likely to happen. English has no distinct form for this, and we use various constructions and adverbs for the purpose, such as *She'll (probably) be here soon* and *(I expect) she'll be arriving soon*.

protasis In an *if . . . (then)* sentence, the part that follows the *if*. Example (in brackets): *If [I drink any more wine,] (then) I'll have a hangover*. The other part is the **apodosis**.

prothesis The addition of a sound (usually a vowel) to the beginning of a word. For example, in the development of Latin into Spanish, all words beginning with *sp-*, *st-* or *sc-* acquired a prothetic *e-*: Latin *spiritus* 'spirit' but Spanish *espirito*; Latin *stannum* 'tin' but Spanish *estaño*; Latin *schola* 'school' but Spanish *escola*.

Proto-Indo-European (**PIE**) The hypothetical unrecorded ancestor of the **Indo-European** family of languages, thought by most specialists to have been spoken around 6000 years ago. See the **Indo-European homeland problem**.

proto-language An unrecorded language posited by linguists as the common ancestor of a group of languages which are genetically related. Such a language is named by prefixing *Proto-* to the name of the family, so that, for example, *Proto-Germanic* is the ancestor of the **Germanic** languages.

protolanguage A hypothetical primitive stage in the development of human language, characterized above all by a near-total absence of grammar and hence by a heavy use of clues from context to supplement a typically modest vocabulary. The linguist Derek **Bickerton** has proposed that full-blown language evolved (very suddenly!) from such an ancestral system, and further that protolanguage can be observed today in the speech of very young children, in the speech of individuals suffering from certain types of disability, in **pidgins**, and in the language behaviour of apes to which experimenters have tried to teach language. The idea is very controversial.

Proto-Romance The common ancestor of the **Romance** languages, **Vulgar Latin**.

prototype A particular example of something which is highly typical of its class and which may be taken as representing that class. For example, a sparrow is a prototypical bird, while a penguin or an ostrich is not. Compare **stereotype**.

"Proto-World" hypothesis (also *"Proto-Human"*, *"Proto-Sapiens"*) The hypothesis that all living and recorded languages are descended from a single ancestor, "Proto-World". Most linguists are inclined to think that such a language probably once existed. At the same time, we do not consider it possible to recover any information about it, since tens of thousands of years of divergence is more than enough to obliterate all traces of a common ancestry among related languages, or at least to ensure that any surviving traces of a common ancestry must be lost in the **background noise** of chance resemblances. A handful of linguists have recently been claiming that we *can* still discover fragments of the "**Mother Tongue**" in modern languages, but almost all others greet this suggestion with derision. **Note** that this hypothesis is technically distinct from **monogenesis**: it is possible that human language arose independently on several occasions (thus falsifying monogenesis), but that all varieties died out except one, which is the ancestor of all known languages (thus confirming the PW hypothesis).

Provençal A popular but inaccurate label for **Occitan**.

proverb A short and memorable saying which expresses a piece of experience, often in vivid language. Examples: *Look before you leap* (It is wise to investigate carefully before committing yourself to an irreversible course of action); *Faint heart ne'er won fair lady* (If you want something really badly, you should make every effort to get it, without fear of failure or embarrassment; otherwise, you probably won't get it.)

proxemics The study of how people arrange themselves in space when conversing, including how close together they stand or sit, which way they face, where they look, and whether and how they touch each other. Such things vary considerably among cultures and according to circumstances.

proximal Nearby. The term is applied to the closest **deictic position**, as represented by items like *this* and *here*. Compare **mesial, distal**.

proximate A grammatical form (usually a **pronoun**) found in certain languages and used to mark someone who is neither the speaker nor the hearer but is currently the centre of interest. Compare **obviative**.

pseudo-cleft sentence A particular sentence structure. The unmarked sentence *Susie bought a car yesterday* has the pseudo-cleft counterpart *What Susie bought yesterday was a car*. Compare **cleft sentence**.

psycholinguistics The discipline which studies the connections between language and mind, particularly **language processing**, the way in which utterances are produced and comprehended.

psychological reality The property of a linguistic theory or description which corresponds closely to the actual mental processes involved in using language. Some theories claim to embody a high degree of psychological reality; others make no such claims.

pullet surprise (also **oronym**) A phrase which has been amusingly misinterpreted, such as *pullet surprise* for *Pulitzer Prize*.

pulmonic airstream mechanism The use of lung air in speaking. A pulmonic **egressive** airstream is the chief source of air in speaking and the only source of air in most languages, including English.

pun A humorous play on words. An example is the hairdressing salon called *Curl Up and Dye*. Early writers like Shakespeare made heavy use of puns, often bawdy ones. For example, in *Twelfth Night*, Malvolio is trying to decide if a certain letter was written by the lady Viola; he declares 'These be her Cs, her Us, and her Ts; thus makes she her great Ps.' (In Shakespeare's time, *cut* was vulgar slang for the vulva.)

punctual An **aspect** form indicating that an action takes place at a particular moment. Some languages have a distinct verb-form for this; English does not, and we merely use the simplest possible verb-form with the correct tense-marking, as in *She sneezed*.

punctuation The use of special marks like commas, colons and full stops in writing to make clear the structure of a sentence.

Punjabi Another spelling of **Panjabi**.

pure vowel A vowel which retains the same quality from beginning to end, such as [u] or [a]; a vowel which is not a **diphthong** or anything more complex.

purism The view that **loan words** and other signs of influence from other languages constitute a kind of "contamination" sullying the 'purity' of a language, and hence that efforts should be made to get rid of them.

push chain See under **chain shift**.

Pushtu Another name for **Pashto**.

Putnam, Hilary An American philosopher (1926–), best known in linguistics for his studies of linguistic knowledge and for his criticisms of **truth-conditional semantics**.

Q

quality The most obvious property of a **vowel**, the characteristic which distinguishes it from other vowels, chiefly determined by the position of the jaw, tongue and lips during its production.

quantifier One of a group of items which grammatically behave like **determiners** but which have meanings expressing quantity, such as *many, most, some, no, few* and *lots of*. Examples: *most students, some American linguists, no women, lots of people*.

quantifier floating A construction in which a **quantifier** appears later in the sentence than its logical position. So, instead of *All the students have passed*, we can say *The students have all passed*, in which the quantifier *all* has "floated" out of its logical position.

quantitative approach A statistical approach to the study of **variation** in speech, introduced by William **Labov**. This has proved to be a powerful tool in uncovering regularities underlying the seemingly arbitrary variation in speech observed by only casual inspection.

quantitative linguistics The application of statistical methods to the linguistic properties of **corpora**.

quantity Another name for **length**.

quasi-copula A verb which resembles a **copula** but which has some semantic content. All the verbs in the following examples are quasi-copulas: *She remained calm*; *She became a teacher*; *She grew angry*.

Quechua A group of closely related languages spoken in and near the Andes. Quechua was the chief language of the Inca empire.

Queen's English An informal name given in Britain to **standard English**, or sometimes more particularly to **Received Pronunciation**. When a king is on the throne, the term is **King's English**.

question 1. An utterance that explicitly asks for a response, such as *Where are you going?* or *Are you ready?* 2. A sentence that has the typical form of such an utterance, such as a **rhetorical question**.

question word A special word used to ask a question requiring an answer other than *yes* or *no*, such as English *who*, *what*, *where* and *how*.

Quine, Willard V. O. An American philosopher of language (1908–); he has made many contributions, but is perhaps best known for his work on the logical problems of language learning and translation.

Quirk, (Sir) Randolph A British grammarian (1920–), director of the **Survey of English Usage** and co-author of a series of influential grammars of English.

R

radical obstruction In the articulation of speech sounds, an obstruction of the airstream which is great enough to interfere severely with the flow of air through the mouth and hence to produce an **obstruent**.

raising 1. Any change in pronunciation in which a vowel becomes higher than formerly, as when Middle English /e:/ changed to /i:/. 2. Any of several grammatical constructions in which some item appears in a higher clause than it logically belongs. In both the examples *Susie seems to be happy* and *I consider Susie to be perceptive*, the noun phrase *Susie* is the subject or the object of the verb in the main clause even though it is logically the subject of the verb *be* in the infinitival verb phrase.

raising verb A verb whose grammatical subject is the logical subject of a following verb, such as *seem* and *tend* in *Esther seems to enjoy gardening* and *Janet tends to drink too much at parties*.

Rajasthani An **Indo-Aryan** language spoken in west-central India.

Ramus, Petrus A French philosopher (1512–72), generally credited with introducing linguistic descriptions based entirely on **forms**, rather than on **meanings**.

Rask, Rasmus A Danish historical linguist (1787–1832), one of the founding fathers of **Indo-European** linguistics and a pioneer of the **comparative method**.

Raumer, Rudolf von A German linguist (1815–76), possibly the first linguist to distinguish clearly between spoken and written language in linguistic descriptions.

r-colouring (also **rhotacization**) Turning up the tip or the blade of the tongue while pronouncing a vowel, as occurs for example in a typical North American, Irish or West Country pronunciation of *bird*.

realism Any of several related but distinct views about the nature of the relation between perception and/or language on the one hand and the external world on the other, all of them united by the assumption that there really is something "out there". The version most relevant to the philosophy of language is the view that a generic word like *dog* refers to an entity which has a real existence of its own separate from that of all individual dogs. Compare **nominalism** (sense 2), **conceptualism**, **Platonism**.

realization Any representation of a linguistic form which is less abstract (closer to the surface) than some other representation of the same form. For example, the phonemic representation /ˈpʌti/ (*putty*) might be realized phonetically as [ˈpʰəɾi] by an American or as [ˈpʰati] by a Londoner.

reanalysis An important type of language change in which the syntactic structure assigned to a particular type of sentence is changed without affecting the surface form. For example, sentences like *It would be* [*desirable for you*] [*to take a holiday*] formerly had the structure shown, but this was reanalysed to *It would be desirable* [*for you to take a holiday*]. The fact that the reanalysis had taken place was not obvious until speakers began to say things like [*For you to take a holiday*] *would be desirable*; such utterances were formerly impossible.

rebus principle A device used in some early writing systems, especially those using **pictograms**, by which words are written by using sequences of characters with similar sounds but unrelated meanings. For example, English *son* might be written with the character for *sun*, which is easier to find a picture for, and *monkey* might be written with the character for *monk* plus the character for *key*.

recast A reformulation by an adult of a child's utterance. The child's *Doggie bark* may be followed by the adult recast *Yes, the dog's excited about something*. Compare **expansion** (sense 2).

Received Pronunciation (**RP**) A particular **accent** of English, considered the prestige norm in England but used by only a small minority of speakers. RP is the type of pronunciation most often described in reference books in England and most often taught to foreign learners of English in England. RP has at times been given various nicknames, such as "*BBC English*".

receptive aphasia Any type of **aphasia** which primarily disturbs comprehension. Compare **expressive aphasia**.

recessive Losing ground; becoming less frequent. The term is applied to a linguistic form which is disappearing as another form replaces it.

recessive accent The tendency, in English, to move the stress from the last to the first syllable of a word. Such words as *research, detail, cigarette, magazine* and *ice cream* were once stressed on the last syllable, but today many speakers stress the first syllable.

recipient The **semantic role** borne by a noun phrase which expresses the person who receives something, such as *Lisa* in *I sent Lisa a book* or *Lisa received a letter*.

reciprocal A form which indicates that two individuals are interacting in both directions, or that several individuals are interacting in various combinations. The usual English reciprocals are *each other* and *one another*, as in *We met each other in London* and *They were playing tricks on one another*.

reconstructed form A particular linguistic form or word which is nowhere recorded but which historical linguists believe must once have existed in some ancient language, on the basis of the evidence found in one or more descendants of that ancient language. For example, English *wheel* is descended from Old English *hweol*; this in turn is thought to derive from a Proto-Germanic **hwehula*, and this in turn from an earlier Proto-Indo-European **kwekwlo-*; both these last two are reconstructed forms. A reconstructed form is marked with an asterisk. Compare **attested form**.

reconstruction Any of various procedures used by historical linguists to work out the properties of an unrecorded earlier stage of a language or of an unrecorded language which is the ancestor of several recorded languages. The two chief methods are **comparative reconstruction** and **internal reconstruction**.

recursion (also **self-embedding**) The grammatical property by which a **constituent** can contain within it a smaller constituent of the same kind. For example, a sentence may contain a sentence, a noun phrase may contain a noun phrase, or a prepositional phrase may contain a prepositional phrase. The following example shows an NP containing an NP containing an NP containing an NP: [*a book about* [*the history of* [*the development of* [*personal computers*]]]]. Recursion is of crucial importance in language: its presence allows a language with a finite number of constructions and a finite number of words to produce an infinite number of sentences.

reduced clause A name sometimes given to a syntactic unit which looks quite a bit like a **clause** but lacks some of the material typically found in a complete clause. Here are some examples (in brackets): [*When in Rome*], *do as the Romans do*; [*Wanting to make a good impression*], *she chose her outfit carefully*.

reduction Any phonological process in which some sound is weakened or lost. For example, in the development of Old English *hūswīf* 'housewife' to modern *hussy*, the two long vowels were shortened and two consonants were lost, and the word has therefore undergone very considerable reduction.

redundancy The property of language by which an utterance typically contains more information than is strictly necessary to understand it. This property is crucial, since its presence means we can often understand an utterance even if we fail to hear bits of it.

reduplication The partial or complete repetition of a word for some grammatical purpose. For example, Malay uses reduplication to form adverbs (*baik* 'good', *baik-baik* 'well'), for plurality (*bunga* 'flower', *bunga-bunga* 'flowers'), and for word-formation (*mata* 'eye', *mata-mata* or *memata* 'policeman'). Tagalog uses it as part of its verbal inflection: *sulat* 'write', *susulat* 'will write'; *lapit* 'approach', *lalapit* 'will approach'.

Reed-Kellogg diagram A particular type of diagram which represents important features of the structure of a sentence. Such diagrams were formerly much used in the teaching of English grammar in American schools; constructing them was called "diagramming sentences". Figure R1 shows a Reed-Kellogg diagram for the sentence *The police trapped the frightened burglar just behind the house.*

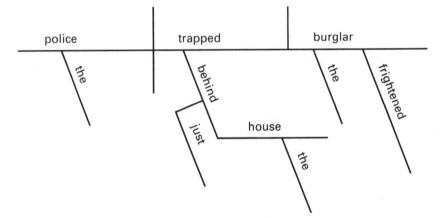

R1 A Reed-Kellogg diagram

referee A scholar who reads a piece of work submitted for publication, comments on it critically, and advises the editor on whether it deserves publication. This is usually done anonymously.

reference 1. The relation between a **noun phrase** and the person or thing it picks out in the world; see the examples under **referring expression**. 2. In a piece of scholarly work, an explicit mention of some other piece of work which you need to bring into the discussion. This is usually done by putting into your text at the relevant point something like '(Dixon 1994: 193)'; this tells your reader that you are drawing attention to something on page 193 of a work published by Dixon in 1994, and the list of references at the end of your work will give your reader full information about what that work is.

reference tracking Any device for keeping track of who or what is being referred to at some point in a discourse. For example, we can use *she* to pick out a woman already identified, providing certain conditions are met that will ensure no ambiguity if two or more women are already present in the discourse.

reference grammar A book containing a detailed and orderly description of the facts of a particular language, designed for looking things up rather than as a textbook for learning the language.

referent The object in the world which is picked out by a noun phrase serving as a **referring expression**.

referential index (plural **indices**) A notational device, usually a subscript letter, added to a noun phrase in a written sentence to indicate what it refers to. In *Susie$_i$ found her$_i$ book*, Susie found her own book; in *Susie$_i$ found her$_j$ book*, she found somebody else's book, as shown by the indices.

referring expression A **noun phrase** which picks out something in the world. Consider the following sentence: *Susie has decided that she will write a dissertation on the Minoan palaces of Crete*. This contains several referring expressions. It is quite clear what *Susie, Crete* and *the Minoan palaces of Crete* refer to, but *she* is potentially ambiguous: it probably refers to Susie, but it might refer to some other woman not identified here.

reflex A word or form which is descended from an ancestral word or form which is under consideration. For example, Latin *bonus* 'good' is continued as *bueno* in Spanish, *bon* in French, *buono* in Italian and *bun* in Romanian; all these are reflexes of *bonus*. Compare **etymon**.

reflexive A special grammatical item, usually a **pronoun**, which necessarily has the same interpretation as another **noun phrase** in the same sentence. The English reflexives are things like *herself* and *ourselves*: compare the meanings of *Susie injured herself* (one person involved) and *Susie injured her* (two people involved).

regional diffusion The spread of innovating linguistic forms from community to community across a country.

register 1. A particular style of language which is appropriate in certain circumstances. Murmuring to your lover, chatting with friends, writing an essay, being introduced to the Queen – all these require different registers of English. 2. The **pitch** range used in speech. Your voice may be naturally higher- or lower-pitched than some other voices; in addition, you may deliberately use a higher or lower part of your natural range in particular circumstances.

regression hypothesis The hypothesis that an adult who acquires a serious disorder of language "unlearns" features of language in the reverse order to that in which children learn them – that is, that the things learned last are lost first, and so on. This hypothesis is false.

regular A label applied to a particular word which takes all the grammatical forms which are usual for words of its class. For example, the verb *love* is regular: it has forms like *loves, loved, loved, loving*. But *take* is **irregular**: *takes, took, taken, taking*.

regular grammar Another name for a **finite-state grammar**.

regularity hypothesis Another name for the **Neogrammarian Hypothesis**.

Reichenbach, Hans A German philosopher (1891–1953), a **logical positivist** known particularly for his pioneering theory of **tense**.

reification fallacy The mistaken belief that, because we have invented a name, there must exist something "out there" for the name to refer to. Common in pseudo-sciences like astrology, this fallacy is by no means easy to avoid even in linguistics. On the one hand, **Chomsky** has seriously suggested that individual languages do not actually exist, and hence that the term **language** has nothing to denote; on the other, Chomsky's critics complain that the term **universal grammar**, beloved of Chomsky and his followers, does not correspond to any identifiable reality, but only to an article of faith.

relation Any linguistically significant connection between two objects or classes of objects. There are two main types: **syntagmatic** and **paradigmatic relations**.

relational adjective An **adjective** derived from a **noun** which has no meaning beyond that present in the noun and serving only to provide a form of the noun which can act as a **modifier**, such as *telephonic* from *telephone* and *Glaswegian* from *Glasgow*. These are little used in English: we prefer *Glasgow telephone system* to *Glaswegian telephonic system*. Languages which do not permit nouns to modify nouns, such as Spanish and Russian, make heavy use of such adjectives.

Relational Grammar A theory of grammar, developed by David Perlmutter and Paul Postal in the 1970s, in which the primitive notions are **grammatical relations** like Subject, Direct Object and Indirect Object; various processes are posited which shift noun phrases about from one relation to another.

relative clause A type of **subordinate clause** which is attached to a noun inside a **noun phrase** and which serves to provide information about the entity denoted by that noun phrase. There are two types. In a **restrictive** relative clause, the clause is essential in identifying what is being talked about. Examples (in brackets): *the woman [you were talking to]; any student [who needs advice]; the books [that I bought in London]*. In a **non-restrictive** relative clause, the clause is not required for identification but serves only to add extra information. Examples: *J. Edgar Hoover, [who had a fanatical fear of Communism]; these books, [which I bought in London]*. See also **headless relative clause**.

relative pronoun A **pronoun** which serves to introduce a **relative clause**. English uses *who, whom, whose* and *which* for this purpose. Examples (in brackets): *the woman [who] you were talking to; the woman to [whom] you were talking; any student [whose] work is unsatisfactory; the conclusions [which] we have reached*. Opinion is divided as to whether the item *that*, which can also introduce relative clauses, is a relative pronoun or a **complementizer**, as in *the books that I've been reading*. Relative pronouns are often optional in English: *the woman you were talking to*.

relative universal Another name for a **statistical universal**.

release In the production of a **stop** consonant, the point at which the complete closure is opened, allowing air to flow through again.

Relevance Theory A theory of **pragmatics** which holds that utterances are interpreted in such a way that they combine with the context so as to produce the maximum amount of new information with the minimum amount of processing effort. This theory has been extended to the totality of human **cognition**.

relexification The large-scale replacement of the **vocabulary** of a language by a new set of words, with little change in the grammar. The term is most often invoked in the study of **creoles**, since some scholars believe that a number of African and American creoles were historically derived from a single Portuguese-based creole used in west Africa by just such relexification, using words taken from other European languages.

relic form An older form which has dropped out of use in the language generally but which still survives in certain regions. For example, the verb-forms like *a'going* and *a'thinking* have disappeared from most varieties of English, but they survive in the Appalachians, where some people still say things like *I was a'shootin' at some squirrels*.

Renfrew, Colin An English archaeologist (1937–), a specialist in European prehistory who has argued that the **Indo-European** languages must have spread peacefully across Europe along with the spread of farming, rather than as a result of conquest. For this he requires that **Proto-Indo-European** must have been spoken around 10,000 years ago, a conclusion rejected by most linguists. Renfrew has also attempted to interpret the entire distribution of the world's languages in terms of just a few major economic events in the past.

repair A correction to a faulty utterance, either by the speaker or by the hearer.

replacement error Another name for a **selection error**.

reported speech Quoting what someone else has said. There are two types: **direct speech** and **indirect speech**.

representation Any way of putting a piece of language down on paper so as to show something about its linguistic structure.

resonance The physical phenomenon in which a body which can vibrate prefers to vibrate at certain frequencies. When such a body is caused to vibrate, it therefore favours and enhances those frequencies while suppressing others. As the configuration of the **vocal tract** is changed by moving the tongue, lips and jaw, its *resonant frequencies* also change; these show up as **formants** in speech.

resonant Another name for a **sonorant**.

REST The abbreviation for **Revised Extended Standard Theory**.

restricted code A style of language which uses a limited range of grammatical structures, which is of limited explicitness and depends heavily on context, which is only effective in communicating with people of similar background and experience, and which is acquired without formal education. According to the **deficit hypothesis**, restricted code is available to all speakers. Compare **elaborated code**.

restricted distribution The property of a linguistic item (especially a word) which does not occur in all the positions typically occupied by the members of its class. For example, English adjectives typically occur in at least two positions, illustrated by *She's a _____ girl* and *That girl is _____*; note the behaviour of *pretty*, *clever* and *tall*. But *mere* is possible only in the first position and *asleep* only in the second; these two adjectives have restricted distribution.

restricted language A variety of a language which is severely limited in its vocabulary and range of grammatical constructions. Important examples are the restricted varieties of English used in air-traffic control and in maritime navigation.

restrictive Of a modifier, required for identification. In *Please hand me the green scarf*, *green* is restrictive, since it is required to identify the scarf in question, but in *Please buy me this wonderful scarf, wonderful* is **non-restrictive**, since it is not required for identification. The distinction is most often applied to **relative clauses**.

resultative A piece of a sentence identifying the result of the action named in the sentence, such as *blue* in *I painted the bathroom blue*, or the entire sentence.

resumptive pronoun A label applied to a **pronoun** which, in some sense, marks a position from which something else has been removed. An example is *her* in *Susie, I like her*.

retracted Of a speech sound, produced a little farther back in the mouth than some point taken as a reference point. For example, English /t/ is often articulated a little farther back than usual when followed by /r/; we can say that the /t/ of *train* is retracted.

retreat problem The problem of how children manage to get rid of their overgeneralized forms, like *taked* for *took*, and to acquire instead the irregular adult forms.

retroflex (A speech sound) produced by curling the tip of the tongue up and back.

reversives A pair of words, especially **verbs**, which express opposing actions or positions, such as *raise/lower, tie/untie, dress/undress, lengthen/shorten*.

Revised Extended Standard Theory (REST) The version of **transformational grammar** current in the late 1970s, derived from the earlier **Extended Standard Theory**. Around 1980 the REST gave way to **Government-and-Binding Theory**.

rewrite rule The most familiar way of stating a rule in a **formal grammar**. In the most general form, a rewrite rule simply states that some sequence of items may be replaced by some other sequence of items: for example, A B A C → X W B. But the only rewrite rules of much linguistic use are *phrase-structure rules*, which have the restriction that the left side of the rule must contain exactly one item. Familiar rules like S → NP VP are of this type; this rule states that a sentence may consist of a noun phrase followed by a verb phrase.

Rhaeto-Romance A small branch of **Romance** spoken in Switzerland and Italy; its three members are **Romansh, Ladin** and **Friulian**.

rhetoric Writing or (more usually) public speaking which is intended to persuade readers or listeners to accept a particular point of view, or the study of how to do this effectively.

rhetorical question A question which does not expect an answer and which is asked merely for effect. An example occurs in Mark Antony's speech (in Shakespeare's play) defending the dead Julius Caesar against charges of excessive ambition: having reminded his audience that Caesar had three times refused the offer of a crown, Antony asks "Was this ambition?"

rhotacization Another word for *r*-colouring.

rhotic A convenient label for any **liquid** which is not a **lateral**; informally, an "R-sound". The very different speech sounds used for English /r/ in London, Glasgow and Chicago are all rhotics, as are the two Spanish sounds spelled <r> and <rr> in *pero* 'but' and *perro* 'dog'.

rhotic accent An accent of English in which the historical /r/ continues to be pronounced in all positions in which it was historically present, so that, for example, *farther* does not sound like *father* and *far* does not rhyme with *Shah*. Rhotic accents are typical of Scotland, Ireland, the southwest of England, parts of the West Indies, Canada, and all of the USA except for the east coast and the south. Compare **non-rhotic accent**.

rhyme 1. The relation between two or more words which are identical from the stressed vowel onward but different before the stressed vowel: *bear/care*; *plate/berate*; *utter/butter*; *vision/collision*. 2. That part of a **syllable** including everything but any consonants occurring before the vowel. For example, *eight*, *late* and *great* all have the rhyme /eɪt/.

rhyming slang A **language game** (sense 2) typical of the Cockney speech of London. A word is replaced by a two-word or longer phrase which rhymes with it, and then (usually) the second word of the phrase is deleted. For example, *head* is replaced by *loaf of bread*, which is then reduced to *loaf*, producing things like *Use your loaf!*

rhythm The pattern you perceive in speech or poetry as a result of the repetition at regular intervals of prominent elements, such as stressed syllables.

Richards, I. A. A British critic (1893–1979), co-author with **Ogden** of the influential book *The Meaning of Meaning*.

right-branching A type of syntactic structure in which modifiers follow their heads, so that recursion of the structure, when represented in a **tree structure**, produces a series of branches running down to the right. English is predominantly right-branching; try drawing a tree for *This is the dog that chased the cat that killed the rat that ate the malt that lay in the house that Jack built.*

right-dislocation A construction in which a **noun phrase** appears at the end of a sentence, its logical position being occupied by a **pronoun**. Example: *She's very clever, Lisa* (in the sense of *Lisa is very clever*).

right-ear advantage The observation that speech is perceived more effectively by the right ear than by the left (as shown by **dichotic listening** tests), reflecting the fact that the **language areas** are located, in most people, in the left hemisphere of the brain, which is directly connected to the right ear.

Robins, R(obert) H. An English linguist (1921–), a contributor to a number of areas but perhaps best known for his work on the **history of linguistics**.

Rohlfs, Gerhard A German descriptive and historical linguist (1892–1986), a specialist in **Romance** whose energies were directed primarily to studying the influence upon one another of the Romance and non-Romance languages throughout Europe; he was a severe critic of overenthusiastic appeals to **substrate** effects.

Role-and-Reference Grammar (RRG) A theory of grammar developed in the early 1980s by William Foley and Robert Van Valin. RRG is formulated in terms of the communicative purposes which need to be served and the grammatical devices available for serving them.

roll An old-fashioned name for a **trill**.

Roman alphabet An **alphabet** originally devised for writing **Latin** and today used, sometimes with local modifications, for writing the majority of European languages (including English) and a large number of other languages in parts of the world where European influence has been prominent. The Roman alphabet originated as a modification of an alphabet used by the **Etruscans**, who in turn had acquired it from the Greeks.

Romance The large family of languages all descended from the spoken **Latin** of the Roman Empire and hence the only survivors of the **Italic** branch of **Indo-European**. Among them are **Catalan**, **French**, **Friulian**, **Galician**, **Italian**, **Judaeo-Spanish**, **Ladin**, **Occitan**, **Portuguese**, **Romanian**, **Romansh**, **Sardinian** and **Spanish**.

Romanian The chief language of Romania and of Moldova (where it is often calld *Moldavian*), a **Romance** language.

Romanist A specialist in the **Romance** languages.

Romanization The process of representing in the Roman alphabet a language which is normally written in some other way.

Roman numerals A cumbersome way of writing **numerals** by using certain letters of the alphabet in a manner involving addition and subtraction, and crucially lacking a zero. For example, the year 1996 is written MCMXCVI in Roman numerals: (1000) + (100 from 1000) + (10 from 100) + (5) + (1). Invented by the Romans and used for centuries in Europe, the system finally gave way to **Arabic numerals** except for certain special purposes.

Romansh A **Rhaeto-Romance** language spoken in eastern Switzerland.

Romany (also **Romani**) The traditional language of the Travellers, or "Gypsies", an **Indo-Aryan** language brought originally from India. Few British or Irish Travellers can still speak Romany today, but it is still widely spoken in eastern Europe.

root In morphology, the simplest possible form of a **lexical morpheme**, from which all the other forms are built up. For example, the Latin verb meaning 'love' has the root *am-*; from this are formed the various **stems**, such as present *ama-* and perfect *amav-*, from which in turn are constructed complete word-forms like *amat* 'he loves' and *amavi* 'I have loved'.

Rosetta Stone A stone slab discovered in Egypt in 1799 and bearing the same text inscribed (in about 196 BC) in Egyptian **hieroglyphs**, in **demotic** Egyptian, and in Greek. Its discovery allowed **Champollion** to decipher the ancient Egyptian scripts and language.

rounded Of a speech sound, produced with **lip-rounding**. The term is most often applied to **vowels** like [u], [o] and [y], but it can also be applied to **consonants** like the [s^w] of *soon* and *swim*.

rounding 1. The property of a speech sound which is produced with rounded lips, such as [o]. 2. Any change in pronunciation in which lip-rounding is added to a speech sound which formerly lacked it, such as when [i] changes to [y]. For sense 2, the opposite is **unrounding**.

Rousseau, Jean-Jacques A French philosopher (1712–78), author of a celebrated essay on the origins of languages.

Rousselot, (l'Abbé) Pierre A French phonetician (1846–1924), a pioneer of **instrumental** and experimental **phonetics**.

RP The abbreviation for **Received Pronunciation**.

RRG See **Role-and-Reference Grammar**.

rule A statement expressing a linguistically significant generalization about the facts of a language, particularly when this is formulated within the formalism of some particular theory. It is possible for a rule to have some **exceptions**.

rule-governed Functioning in terms of a (typically small) number of explicit rules. Most linguists view language as rule-governed, and try to describe it accordingly. The alternative would be to see a language as a collection of miscellaneous and idiosyncratic facts held together by "tendencies" and "possibilities".

rule ordering In some theories of phonology and of grammar, the state of affairs in which the rules set up by the analyst must be applied in some particular order to get the right result; if the order is derived from general principles, the ordering is **intrinsic**, but if it is merely stipulated by the analyst, it is **extrinsic**.

rule schema In a formal grammar, the combination of two or more distinct rules which have elements in common into what looks like a single statement. For example, the two rules VP → V NP and VP → V NP PP can be combined in the schema VP → V NP (PP).

runic alphabet (also **futhark**) A distinctive **alphabet** used by Germanic peoples in northwestern Europe (including Britain) from about the third century AD. The alphabet was based upon the **Roman alphabet**, but its letters, or *runes*, are mostly different in shape.

Russell, Bertrand An English philosopher and mathematician (1872–1970); among numerous other achievements, he contributed to the development of **semantics**.

Russian The chief language of Russia, also widely spoken in the former Soviet Union, a **Slavic** language.

Ryle, Gilbert An English philosopher (1900–76), a proponent of **ordinary language philosophy** and an opponent of **mind–body dualism**.

S

S The symbol for **sentence** in a formal grammar.

Saami The **Finno-Ugric** language of the people of northern Scandinavia, commonly called *Lappish*, but this name is offensive.

Sacks, Harvey An American sociologist (1935–75), the founder of **conversation analysis**.

sagittal section A cut-away view of some part of the body running from front to back, as in the familiar diagram of the **vocal tract**.

Sajnovics, János A Hungarian astronomer (1735–85), the first person to note the existence of a **genetic relationship** between **Hungarian** and **Saami**.

Salish(an) A family of languages spoken along the northwest coast of North America.

saltation In genetics, a single large mutation which dramatically changes the nature of a species. It has sometimes been suggested that the human language faculty results from a saltation, but most specialists find this suggestion incredible.

Samoyed A group of languages spoken in Siberia, forming one group of the **Uralic** family.

Sanctus, Franciscus A Spanish grammarian (1523–1600), a proponent of "logical" or "universal" grammar, regarded by some Chomskyan linguists as an intellectual forebear.

sandhi Any phonological process which applies across a grammatical boundary. The change of /k/ to /s/ in going from *electric* to *electricity* is an example of sandhi across a morpheme boundary (*internal sandhi*), while the merger of /d/ and /j/ in the pronunciation of *did you* as /dɪdʒu/ is an example of sandhi across a word boundary (*external sandhi*).

Sanskrit An important ancient language of India, recorded in two forms: the earlier *Vedic Sanskrit*, the language of the Hindu scriptures, and the later *classical Sanskrit*, the language described in the grammar of **Pāṇini**. Sanskrit is an **Indo-European** language and the ancestor of the **Indo-Aryan** languages.

Sapir, Edward A German-born American linguist (1884–1939). A humanist with wide-ranging interests, Sapir studied under **Boas** and made important contributions to an astonishing number of fields: he championed the **phoneme** principle, studied and described a number of native American languages, proposed a number of genetic groupings, wrote a successful popular book on linguistics (*Language*), argued for a psychological basis of language, promulgated the first version of the **Sapir-Whorf hypothesis** (**Whorf** was his student), and helped to establish linguistics as an autonomous discipline. He is one of the greatest linguists of the twentieth century, and his works are still much read today.

Sapir-Whorf hypothesis (also **linguistic relativity hypothesis**) The hypothesis that the structure of our language significantly affects the way we perceive the world. This hypothesis is controversial.

Sardinian The indigenous language of Sardinia, a **Romance** language.

satellite A term which is used differently by different linguists, but always to name some kind of secondary or dependent item in a sentence, such as an **adjunct** or a **particle**.

satellite-framed language A language in which a verb of motion typically includes information about the *manner* of movement but not about the *path*. English is like this: it has lots of motion verbs like *walk, run, stroll, scurry, scramble, slink, sidle, ride, drive, coast* and *fly*, all expressing the manner of movement, while path usually has to be expressed by adding to one of these verbs a particle or preposition like *up, down, in, out, across* or *through*. Translating a description of movement from a satellite-framed language into a **verb-**

framed language like French or Spanish can be difficult. Compare the English sentence *The boy rode out of the courtyard* with its Spanish equivalent under this last entry.

satem language Any one of the ancient **Indo-European** languages in which the ancestral velar plosives were palatalized in certain circumstances. For example, the ancestral word **kmtom* '100' became *satem* in the satem language Old Persian. Compare **centum language** and see the remarks there.

Saussure, Ferdinand de A Swiss linguist (1857–1913). Though he began his career as a specialist in **Indo-European** studies, to which he made the important contribution of proposing what are now called the **laryngeals** (sense 2), Saussure went on to develop a wide-ranging general theory of language structure. He introduced his famous dichotomies between **synchronic** and **diachronic** approaches and between *langue* and *parole*, as well as the concept of the **linguistic sign**, and he effectively invented **structuralism** (in its original sense). His posthumous *Cours*, edited by his students and published in 1916, is probably the single most influential publication in linguistics of all time, and he is known as the "father of linguistics".

Saussurean paradox A puzzle resulting from two important observations. First, a language is a highly structured system. Second, every language is always changing. The paradox is this: how can a language continue to function effectively while it is in the middle of a number of changes? This paradox has only been resolved by the discovery (in the 1960s) of the relation between **variation** and **language change**.

savant A person who is severely mentally subnormal in most respects but who exhibits super-normal abilities in some particular area. **Christopher** is a linguistic savant.

S-bar In a **formal grammar**, the category to which a **complement clause** is assigned.

scalar feature A **distinctive feature** which may take one of three or more different values. For example, some people would treat vowel **height** as such a feature, with values ranging from [height 1] for a low vowel up to [height 4] for a high vowel. Compare **binary feature**.

Scale-and-Category Grammar The name given to an early version of **Systemic Linguistics**.

Scaliger, Joseph J. A French philologist (1540–1609). An outstanding practitioner of **philology** (in its older sense), he took a great interest in comparing languages, and he is regarded as one of the forerunners of **comparative linguistics**.

scan-copier A hypothetical mechanism in speech **production** which looks over the words selected for an utterance and then inserts them into their proper positions in the utterance. **Assemblage errors** are explained by invoking faults in the insertion process.

scansion The analysis of the metrical structure of verse, or, in some theories of phonology, of the metrical structure of natural languages.

schema (plural **schemata**) 1. A mental picture of some area of experience. A schema with no time element is a **frame** (sense 2); one with a time element is a **script** (sense 2). 2. See **rule schema**.

Schlegel, Friedrich von A German humanist and critic (1772–1829), one of the founders of **comparative linguistics**.

Schleicher, August A German linguist (1821–68), one of the outstanding specialists in **Indo-European** of his day; he introduced both the **tree model** for representing genetic relationships and the practice of **comparative reconstruction**.

Schmidt, Johannes A German linguist (1843–1901), a specialist in **Indo-European** best known for introducing the **wave theory** of genetic relationships.

Schuchardt, Hugo A German linguist (1842–1927). An eccentric and seemingly disorganized scholar, Schuchardt was the most prominent opponent of the **Neogrammarians**, whose "exceptionless sound laws" he could not find in the messiness of real language data. He single-handedly made the study of **pidgins** and **creoles** a serious part of linguistics and put the study of **Basque** on to a secure scholarly footing.

schwa The "neutral" vowel pronounced in the centre of the mouth, or the symbol [ə] used to represent it. Schwa is the commonest vowel in English, occurring, for example, in the first syllable of *about* and the last syllable of *carrot* and *circus*.

scope That part of a sentence which is affected by a **quantifier** or a **negative** contained in it. The string of words *Everybody doesn't have a car* has two readings, differing in the scope assigned to *every* and *not*: [everybody [not [have a car]]] ('Nobody has a car') and [not [everybody [have a car]]] ('Not everybody has a car').

Scots The distinctive variety of English spoken in the lowlands of Scotland, sometimes called *Lallans*. Scots must not be confused with **standard English** spoken with a Scottish accent.

Scottish Gaelic The traditional language of the Scottish highlands and islands, now giving way to English. It belongs to the **Goidelic** branch of the **Celtic** languages.

Scouse The distinctive variety of English spoken in and near the English city of Liverpool.

scrambling A label applied to the presence in sentences of highly variable word order in languages with **free word order**.

screeve A set of verb-forms in a language which differ in **person** and **number** but which are identical in **tense, aspect, mood** and **voice**. An example is the present imperfective indicative active of Latin *amāre* 'love': *amō* 'I love', *amās* 'you love' (singular), *amat* 's/he loves', *amāmus* 'we love', *amātis* 'you love' (plural), *amant* 'they love'. Traditional grammarians often refer to such a set as a "tense", but this is a misuse of the term 'tense'.

scribble talk Incomprehensible speech produced by young children, consisting of meaningless noises with an occasional recognizable word, but usually with good intonation.

script 1. A general term for any kind of writing system. 2. A mental picture of a typical series of events. For example, when you hear someone say *dinner party*, you immediately retrieve the sequence of events at a typical dinner party, which is of great assistance in understanding what is being said. Compare **frame** (sense 2).

Searle, John A British philosopher (1932–), a proponent of **speech act theory** and a critic of **artificial intelligence**, against which he devised the **Chinese room** thought-experiment.

Sebeok, Thomas A Hungarian-born American scholar (1920–), a leading proponent of **semiotics**, a major figure in the study of **animal communication**, and a tireless editor of compilations.

secondary articulation An articulation which accompanies another articulation (the **primary articulation**) so as to modify it in some way, such as **labialization**, **palatalization** or **nasalization**.

secondary cardinal vowel In the traditional system of **cardinal vowels**, any one of the eight vowels [y ø œ ɶ ɒ ʌ ɤ ɯ], which are conventionally regarded as being derived from the **primary cardinal vowels** by reversing the **lip-rounding**. Today it is more usual simply to group the cardinal vowels into rounded and unrounded vowels.

secondary stress A degree of stress which is less than **primary stress** but still greater than no stress. In the word *education*, the first syllable has secondary stress.

second language A language which you learn after puberty, and which is not your **mother tongue**.

second-language acquisition (SLA) The process of learning to speak a language which is not your mother tongue.

second person The category of **person** which includes reference to the addressee (and possibly others) but not to the speaker. English has only the pronoun *you* for this purpose, but many other languages make more elaborate distinctions.

secret language Another name for **argot**.

segment A single speech sound (consonant or vowel). Segments are psychologically real, and English-speakers have little difficulty in agreeing that, for example, the word *scream* consists of exactly five segments, commonly represented as /skriːm/ in a phonemic transcription (here the vowel /iː/ is a single segment). It is this agreement that makes alphabetic writing possible. We can talk about segments at either the phonetic or the phonemic level.

segmentation The analytical procedure of chopping up a word or an utterance into a linear sequence of **segments**.

selection The first step in **language planning**: choosing which language will be the basis of the planning.

selection error (also **replacement error**, **substitution error**) Any type of **speech error** in which a wrong word or form is used in place of the intended one.

selection(al) restriction A limitation on the ability of words to be combined in a sentence resulting from their meanings. Thus, *You have deceived my sister* is fine, but #*You have deceived my watermelon* is anomalous, because *deceive* selects for certain types of objects, and *watermelon* is not of the right category.

self-designation (also **autonym**) The name given to a language by its own speakers, such as *Cymraeg* for Welsh, *Euskara* for Basque or *Deutsch* for German.

self-embedding A type of **recursion** in which a syntactic unit is contained within another, larger, unit of the same kind; see the example under this last entry. If the smaller unit interrupts the larger one, the result is a **centre-embedding**; if not, it is a **left-branching** or a **right-branching**.

semantic anomaly See **anomaly, semantic**.

semantic component Another name for a **semantic feature**.

semantic differential A psychological technique for testing the emotional associations of words. Subjects are given some words one at a time and asked to rank each one along several numbered scales, such as *good* to *bad* or *relaxing* to *stressful*.

semantic feature (also **semantic component**) Any one of the basic elements into which the meaning of a word can be decomposed in **componential analysis**.

semantic field theory (also **lexical field theory**) An approach to the study of word-meanings which stresses the way such meanings are related within a particular area of the vocabulary, such as kinship terms or cooking terms; each of these areas is called a *semantic field*.

semantic network The connections in our minds which link words to other words of related meanings.

semantic relation (also **lexical relation**) Any one of several ways in which the meanings of particular words may be related, such as being **synonyms**, **antonyms**, **reversives**, or **hyponym** and **superordinate**.

semantic role (also **deep case, theta role**) Any one of the ways in which an entity represented by a noun phrase in a sentence may be involved in the action or state of affairs described by the sentence. Examples include Agent, Patient, Instrument, Place, Goal and Recipient.

semantics The branch of linguistics dealing with the study of **meaning**.

semiotics The study of sign systems in society. Though it is much influenced by **linguistics**, and though it takes language as the paradigm case of a social system of signs, semiotics in practice has chiefly been applied to such aspects of culture as literature, films, television and advertising.

semi-speaker A person who has a limited command of a language, often especially a language which is dying.

Semitic A group of languages forming one branch of the **Afro-Asiatic** family. Among them are **Arabic, Hebrew, Aramaic**, several languages of east Africa, and some extinct languages like **Akkadian** and **Phoenician**. The **alphabet** was invented by Semitic-speakers.

Semitic alphabets A group of **alphabets** all descended from a single alphabet invented several thousand years ago by **Semitic**-speakers in the Middle East. Most of these alphabets are defective in providing letters only for consonants, and not for vowels. Among them are the **Phoenician**, **Arabic** and **Hebrew** **alphabets**.

semi-vowel Another name for a **glide**.

Sen, Sukumar An Indian historical and comparative linguist (1900–92), a student of **Chatterji** and a specialist in **Indo-Aryan** languages and a major contributor to the study of their history.

sense The intrinsic meaning of a linguistic expression, most often a single word, often especially from the point of view of how this relates to the meanings of other words or expressions. Compare **reference**.

sense relation Any of the various ways in which the meanings of words may be related. For example, one word may be a **synonym**, an **antonym** or a **hyponym** of another.

sensory Pertaining to the input to our brains from our senses, such as vision and smell, or more generally to nervous impulses travelling toward the brain. Compare **motor**.

sensory aphasia A less usual name for **Wernicke's aphasia**.

sentence (**S**) The largest purely grammatical unit. The items in a sentence are linked by rather rigid grammatical rules about such things as the order of words, the endings on particular words, and the elements which particular words (especially verbs) require to be present or absent. So, for example, attempts like *Susie discovered, *Susie put the peanut butter, *Susie buyed good book, and *Fed Susie cat the all fail to be English sentences because they each violate one or more of these rules. (In contrast, the links between sentences in a discourse are much less rigid and only weakly grammatical.) It is important to note that a sentence, in linguistic usage, is an abstract object conforming to these rules. Many perfectly normal utterances are not sentences, such as *Sounds good* and *Susie* (the second in answer to a question like *Who's that?*)

sentence adverb An **adverb** which does not modify a verb or a verb phrase, but instead either modifies the entire sentence or describes the speaker's attitude towards the sentence. Among these are *probably, undoubtedly, maybe, frankly, hopefully* and *fortunately*. Examples of use: *Fortunately, I have a spare fan belt; Undoubtedly she has something up her sleeve; Frankly, you ought to stop seeing Bill; Hopefully, we'll be there in time for lunch.*

sentence stress The presence of strong **stress** on one particular word of an utterance, in order to emphasize it or to contrast it with something else. Using an accent to mark sentence stress, note the difference in interpretation of the following: *Jánet bought this book* (not Susie); *Janet bóught this book* (she didn't steal it); *Janet bought thís book* (not that one); *Janet díd buy this book* (you were wrong to deny it).

sentential subject A **subordinate clause** (in English, introduced by *that*) which stands in subject position. Example (in brackets): [*That she has given up smoking*] *surprises me.*

separation of levels An analytical procedure in describing a language. It requires that the phonological analysis must be completed before the morphology is examined, and that the morphological analysis must be completed before the syntax is examined. Defended by many **American structuralists** as a proper "scientific" procedure, this approach has long been rejected as unworkable.

sequence of tenses A grammatical restriction on the tense in a subordinate clause following a main clause, most usually the condition that a past tense must be followed by another past tense. This restriction applies only weakly in English, but note that *She said that she was coming* is at least more natural than *?She said that she is coming*.

Serbo-Croatian The chief language of Serbia, Bosnia and Croatia, a **Slavic** language. The Serbs write it in the **Cyrillic alphabet**, the Croats in the **Roman alphabet**. Since the war in the 1990s, both Serbs and Croats have maintained that Serbian and Croatian are separate languages.

serial processing Processing which is strictly linear: a sequence of items is processed one at a time. Compare **parallel processing**.

serial verb construction A grammatical pattern, found in some languages, in which a sequence of two or more verbs is typically used to express what might be expressed in another language with a single verb. For example, the west African language Yoruba says *ó mú ìwé wá* 'he took book [and] came' where English says *He brought the book*.

set theory A fundamental branch of mathematics which studies the properties of *sets*, where a set is a collection of things, such as the set of European capital cities or the set of positive whole numbers. Many varieties of **formal semantics** are based upon set theory.

sex differences in language Differences in the speech of men and women. In some languages these can be very large, involving different vocabulary or different pronunciations of certain words. Among the differences sometimes reported for English are the following: men and women talk about different things (undoubtedly); women's conversation is cooperative, while men's is competitive (apparently true); men interrupt more than women (true); women use more more **tag questions** than men (doubtful); men swear more than women (doubtful); women use certain words more often than men (*cute, divine,* colour terms like *burgundy* and *ecru*) (possibly true).

sexist language The use of language which betrays a patronizing or contemptuous attitude toward one sex (usually women), whether deliberately or unthinkingly.

shadowing An analytical technique in psycholinguistics in which a subject must repeat out loud whatever is heard through a set of earphones. This is used for studying **perception**; one interesting finding is that subjects often correct errors in what they hear.

Shelta A **creole**, based on English grammar with Irish vocabulary, used by Irish Travellers ("Gypsies").

shibboleth A linguistic form whose use or non-use is of crucial importance in gaining acceptance to a particular social group.

shift error Another term for **assemblage error**.

Shona The major language of Zimbabwe, a **Bantu** language.

short Of a **vowel** or a **consonant**, taking less time to pronounce than other vowels or consonants in the same language. The contrast between short and **long** segments is phonologically important in some languages; these are said to have contrasts of **quantity**.

shorthand Any of various systems for writing a language much faster than can be done with the conventional writing system, usually fast enough to keep up with speech of moderate tempo.

SHRDLU A computer program which can manipulate a "block world" consisting of blocks of various sizes, shapes and colours. It can understand and carry out instructions from a human being to move the blocks about and answer questions about where the blocks are at the moment.

Sībawayhi A Persian-born grammarian (eighth century AD), author of a famous and influential grammar of Arabic known as *al-Kitāb* 'The Book'.

sibilant A **consonant** whose production involves a hissing noise, especially [s].

Sievers, Eduard A German linguist (1850–1932), a specialist in **Indo-European**.

siglum An abbreviated name for a particularly important book in some specialist area, such as *SPE* (see that entry) in generative phonology or *REW* for Meyer-Lübke's *Romanisches Etymologisches Wörterbuch* in Romance linguistics. Use of such sigla is convenient for specialists but maddening for other readers when the sigla are not fully explained.

sign 1. See **linguistic sign**. 2. Any one of the individual meaningful elements in a **sign language**. For description and teaching, each sign may be decomposed into four *articulatory parameters*: *shape* (of the hand), *orientation* (of the hand), *location* (of the sign in space), and *movement* (of the hand).

Signed English (also **Manually Coded English**) A system for converting spoken English into gestures made with the hands, chiefly used for allowing deaf people to follow spoken English. Signed English is not a true **sign language**; it is slower and clumsier than a real sign language, but it is easier for hearing adults to learn than true sign language.

signified (French *signifié*) The meaning of a **linguistic sign**.

signifier (French *signifiant*) The form of a **linguistic sign**.

sign language Any of various systems used by deaf people to communicate and consisting of *signs* made chiefly with the hands and face which play roughly the same part as words in speech. Dozens of sign languages exist, including **American Sign Language** and **British Sign Language** (which are not closely related). Sign languages are typically highly sophisticated, and they possess all of the crucial features of spoken languages, including rich grammatical systems. A sign language normally bears no relation to the surrounding spoken language, and its grammatical system is usually very different. Some people learn a sign language as their first language.

signing space A certain space in front of a person using a **sign language**. The signer "places" people and things within this space so that they can be pointed to or used as points of reference for movement.

SIL See **Summer Institute of Linguistics**.

silent letter A letter in the conventional spelling of a word which corresponds to nothing in the pronunciation, such as *k* in *knife*, *p* in *pneumonia*, *g* in *gnu*, *b* in *doubt*, *gh* in *night*, *t* in *listen*, *mortgage* or *soften* or *n* in *autumn*. There is some variation among speakers: the *t* in *often*, the first *l* in *vulnerable* and the first *g* in *suggest* are pronounced by some speakers but are silent for others.

silent pause A hesitation in speech which is not filled by a noise like *um* or *er*.

simile A **figure of speech** in which one thing is explicitly compared to another using a word like *like* or *as*: *My love is like a red, red rose; He's as crazy as a loon.* Compare **metaphor**.

simple sentence A sentence which consists of a single **clause**. Compare **compound sentence**, **complex sentence**.

simplified spelling Any proposed system for making the spelling of English (or another language) more regular.

Sindhi An **Indo-Aryan** language spoken in southern Pakistan and western India.

sing-song theory Another name for the **la-la theory**.

singular In a language with the grammatical category of **number**, that form of a word (most often a **noun**) which is typically used to talk about a single object, such as English *dog*, *tree* or *idea*. In English, the singular contrasts only with a **plural** (*dogs*, *trees*, *ideas*), but some languages have other possibilities, such as a **dual**.

Sinhalese (also **Sinhala**) An **Indo-Aryan** language spoken in Sri Lanka.

Sinitic The branch of the **Sino-Tibetan** family which includes all of the **Chinese** languages.

Sino-Tibetan A vast language family in eastern and southeastern Asia. Its two main branches are **Sinitic** and **Tibeto-Burman**. The possible inclusion of the **Tai**, **Karen** and **Miao-Yao** languages is much disputed, a difficulty being that many of these languages have been so heavily influenced by **Chinese** that it is difficult to tell what they were like originally.

Siouan A family of languages chiefly spoken in north-central North America; its best-known members include Dakota and Crow. The Siouan languages are now thought to be related to the **Iroquoian** languages and perhaps to others.

sister In a **tree structure** for a sentence, the relation which holds between two **nodes** which have the same **mother**.

sister language One of two or more languages which have the same immediate ancestor, and which hence started out as nothing more than regional dialects of that ancestor. Among the sister languages of English are Dutch and German.

situation semantics An approach to the study of sentence meaning which takes a sentence as picking out a *situation* (this term has a technical sense in the theory). In contrast to most types of **formal semantics**, situation semantics considers the **context** of an utterance to be of crucial importance.

Skinner, B. F. An American psychologist (1904–90); a leading proponent of **behaviourism**, he developed in his 1957 book *Verbal Behavior* a behaviourist account of language acquisition which was fiercely criticized by **Chomsky**.

SLA See **second-language acquisition**.

slang Informal words and phrases which are not used in formal speech or writing but which may be used in relaxed conversation, especially with close friends or other people belonging to the same group as the speaker. Some slang words may persist for generations and become almost universally known, such as *booze* for 'alcoholic drinks'; more usually, though, slang words are replaced rather quickly by new ones, and use of the up-to-the-minute slang words may be an important marker of group identity. The boundary between slang and other in-group usages like **cant** and **jargon** (sense 1) is not at all sharp.

Slavic (also **Slavonic**) One of the major branches of the **Indo-European** family of languages; among its members are **Polish**, **Czech**, **Slovak**, **Sorbian**, **Russian**, **Ukrainian**, **Belorussian**, **Slovene**, **Serbo-Croatian**, **Bulgarian** and **Macedonian**. **Old Church Slavonic** is an important medieval Slavic language.

SLI See **Specific Language Impairment**.

slip of the ear A misunderstanding of what someone else has said, resulting from some error in processing it. An example is an American's mishearing of the name *Tariq Ali*, spoken with a British accent, as *Terry Kelly*. An amusing slip of the ear is a **pullet surprise**.

slip of the tongue Another name for a **speech error**.

slit fricative Any **fricative** produced with a broad, flat channel for airflow, such as [θ]. Compare **groove fricative**.

slot-and-filler grammar An approach to grammatical description which makes heavy use of **frames** (sense 1) (phrases or sentences with "holes" in them). The idea is that grammatical classes of words or phrases can be identified by their ability to fill particular holes successfully. For example, the frame *This _____ is nice* may be taken as defining the class of singular nouns in English.

Slovak The chief language of Slovakia, also spoken in neighbouring countries, a **Slavic** language.

Slovene The chief language of Slovenia, also spoken in neighbouring countries, a **Slavic** language.

Smith, Henry L. An American linguist (1913–72), a contributor to many areas, a highly influential language teacher, a successful promoter and publicizer of linguistics among the American public, and a co-author of the **Trager-Smith system** for analysing English vowels.

sobriquet An additional name or a nickname, often a humorous one, added to a person's name. For example, Geoffrey of Anjou was given the sobriquet *Plantagenet* from his habit of wearing a sprig of broom (French *plante genêt*) in his cap, and his descendants, kings of England, are consequently known as the House of Plantagenet. Many **surnames** derive from medieval sobriquets. Compare **epithet**.

social class Any one of the more-or-less identifiable groups into which the people in a community may be divided, particularly when these groups appear to be ranked in a hierarchy from highest to lowest. There are various factors which may be important in particular cases, such as the status of parents and ancestors, ethnic background, skin colour, religion, employment, language, accent or dialect, or money. Sociolinguists are often interested in identifying correlations between social class and linguistic behaviour.

social dialect Another name for a **sociolect**.

social network A way of describing and characterizing the closeness of relationships within a community, based on three questions: How many of the other people in the community do you interact with? How often do you interact with them? In how many different contexts do you interact with them? The answers to the first two questions are measures of the *density* of the network; the answer to the third is its *plexity*.

social semiotics An approach to **semiotics** (and **linguistics**) which holds that signalling systems (including language) cannot be usefully studied in isolation from their social functions. Compare the principle of **autonomy**.

social stratification of language The tendency, observable in most sizeable speech communities, for members of different **social classes** to speak differently. Very often we find that some particular form or usage is most frequent in the speech of the lowest class, becomes steadily less frequent as we move up through higher-ranking classes, and is rare or absent in the highest class, or else the other way round.

sociolect (also **social dialect**) A **dialect** used by a particular social group.

sociolinguistics The branch of linguistics which studies the relation between language and society; a central part of the subject is the study of **variation** in language.

sociolinguistic variable A choice between two or more different ways of saying something, such as different pronunciations or different grammatical forms, in the case in which members of different social groups rather consistently prefer different selections. In most cases, this social difference is visible only statistically: few people make the same choice every single time, but the frequency of a given choice is highly consistent for the members of each social group and differs between one social group and another. For example, every New Yorker can pronounce a word like *card* either with or without an *r*-constriction, but, the higher a New Yorker's social class, or the more formal the context, the more frequently s/he will use the constriction.

soft consonant An impressionistic label traditionally applied to certain correlations between spelling and pronunciation. For example, we say that English <c> is pronounced "soft" (as /s/) in *ceiling* but "hard" (as /k/) in *calling*. The term has no identifiable phonetic content. Compare **hard consonant**.

soft palate A traditional name for the **velum**.

solecism A form or usage which is normal for many or most speakers but which is considered to be non-standard or which is merely frowned upon by advocates of **prescriptivism**. English examples include the use of *ain't* and of the **split infinitive**.

solidarity semantic A symmetric arrangement in which two speakers address each other in the same manner, using an intimate (T) pronoun if they consider themselves members of the same group but the respectful (V) pronoun if not. Compare **power semantic**.

Somali A **Cushitic** language spoken in Somalia and in several neighbouring countries.

sonorant (also **resonant**) A **consonant** which is not an **obstruent** – that is, a consonant whose production does not involve a constriction of the vocal tract narrow enough to produce friction or to block the air completely. Among the sonorants are **nasals** like [n], **liquids** like [l] and [r] and **approximants** like [w].

sonority An important but elusive property of speech sounds. Roughly, the less obstructed the airstream is in the vocal tract, the more sonorous the sound. So, for example, [a] is very high in sonority, while [i], [l], [n], [s] and [t] show a steady decrease in sonority.

Sorbian (also **Lusatian, Wendish**) A **Slavic** language spoken in several localities in eastern Germany.

Sotho A **Bantu** language spoken in Lesotho and in parts of South Africa.

sound change Any more-or-less systematic change in pronunciation which takes place over time in some language. An example is the change of Middle English [i:] to [aɪ], which applied to every word containing [i:], such as *I, my, ice, mice, fly* and *line*.

sound law A statement describing a change in pronunciation which took place in some language at some time in the past and which appears to have been regular and exceptionless, or nearly so.

sound spectrograph An instrument that produces a record of a piece of speech in the form of inky lines on paper (a *sound spectrogram*); the horizontal axis represents time, the vertical axis represents **frequency** (and hence **pitch**), and the blackness of the lines represents **amplitude** (and hence loudness).

sound symbolism (also **phonaesthesia**) A relation between the sound of a word and its meaning which is not totally arbitrary, which shows some degree of **iconicity**. The most familiar type is **onomatopoeia**, but there are others.

source The **semantic role** representing the place from which movement begins, such as *the mountain* in *We walked down from the mountain* and *The mountain was spewing out clouds of smoke*. Compare *goal*.

SOV language A language in which the normal order of elements in a sentence is Subject–Object–Verb, such as Turkish, Japanese or Basque.

spandrel A structure which is pressed into service for a purpose for which it was not evolved, and hence a structure which did not arise by ordinary Darwinian **natural selection**. It has been suggested that the human language faculty is a spandrel – an accidental by-product of brain evolution which took place for other purposes. Few linguists are sympathetic to this idea: our language faculty seems so complex and so specialized that it can hardly have arisen by accident.

Spanish The chief language of Spain and of most of the countries of Latin America, a **Romance** language.

SPE (in full, *The Sound Pattern of English*) A famous book published by Noam **Chomsky** and Morris **Halle** in 1968. Though presented as a description of the phonology of English, the book in fact introduced the classical version of **generative phonology**, including the *SPE feature system*.

-speak A suffix used to label a particular way of speaking or writing. Sometimes the resulting formations are neutral, as in *Seaspeak*, a reduced variety of English used in maritime navigation, but more often they express contempt, as in *Pentagon-speak*, the wordy, pompous and dishonest way of speaking adopted by the US military, which prefers 'collateral damage' to 'dead civilians'. Compare **-ese**.

speaking in tongues (also **glossolalia**) The production, by a person placed in a kind of trance, of a stream of syllables which clearly do not represent a language known to the performer. Regarded by the devotees of certain religious sects as a God-given ability to speak an unknown foreign language, such performances in fact consist of nothing but the monotonous repetition of nonsense syllables.

specialization The property of language by which speech does not serve any non-linguistic purpose, such as eating or breathing.

Specific Language Impairment (**SLI**) A disability in which the sufferer, though otherwise speaking fairly normally, has extraordinary difficulty in using the right word-endings, producing things like *There's a trains coming* and *Yesterday I eat dinner late*. There is a certain amount of evidence suggesting that this results from a genetic defect.

specifier In some theories of grammar, a label given to a lexical item which occurs inside a **phrase** and which identifies or constrains the class of things to which the phrase refers. The specifier of a noun phrase is a **determiner**; that of an adjective phrase is a **degree modifier**. The identification of specifiers for verb phrases is controversial.

speculative grammar A medieval approach to the description of languages which tried to integrate the work of the Roman grammarians, the philosophy of Aristotle, and Christian theology. Its practitioners are called **Modistae**.

speech The production of meaningful utterances in a language. Speech has often been given such labels as *parole* and **performance**, in order to draw a contrast between actual linguistic behaviour and the abstract system underlying this behaviour, variously called *langue* or **competence** or just **language**; see the discussion under this last entry.

speech act A term which has been used in more than one sense. Most commonly today, this term simply means an **illocutionary act**: trying to do something by speaking, such as promising, threatening, persuading, ordering, apologizing, naming a ship, and so on. Note, though, that **Austin**, the originator of the term, uses it much more broadly to include other aspects of speaking.

speech act theory A theory of **pragmatics**, introduced by **Austin**, which holds that saying something is a way of doing something.

speech chain The entire sequence of events linking the speaker's brain to the hearer's brain during speech.

speech community A group of people, of whatever size, who interact with one another by speaking often enough that we can make generalizations about their linguistic behaviour as a group. The members of a speech community may or may not have a single language in common.

speech defect Any imperfection in speech which results not from a flaw in the language faculty but merely from a mechanical defect in the organs of speech or in the nerves or muscles controlling them, such as a **lisp**.

speech error (also **slip of the tongue**) A difference between what you intend to say and what you actually say, such as pronouncing a word wrongly or using a wrong word or a wrong grammatical form. This happens to everyone on occasion, and the study of such errors may tell us important things about speech **production**.

speech event A culturally significant event, with a recognizable beginning and end, which consists of speaking and which is conducted according to certain rules of procedure known to the participants. Examples include an after-dinner speech, a job interview, a classroom lesson, a sermon and a university lecture.

speech planning The initial stage in speaking, during which the speaker mentally works out what to say and how to say it.

speech recognition The first step in the **comprehension** of speech: identifying the speech sounds, words and grammatical forms present in a piece of speech you have just heard.

speech recognition system A computer program which is capable of understanding speech produced by human beings and of responding appropriately. Common in science-fiction films, such systems are just beginning to become a reality. A very simple system which can understand only a few commands is a *navigator*; a more sophisticated one which can convert speech into writing is a *dictation system*. At present these systems only work well with particular voices they have been trained with.

speech science The study of all aspects of the production, transmission and perception of speech; it includes not only **phonetics** but also anatomy, physiology, neurology and acoustics.

speech sound (also **phone**) The minimal phonetic unit of connected speech, a single consonant or vowel sound produced by some particular combination of airstream, glottal activity and position and/or movement of the organs of speech. In principle, a single speech sound is represented by a single phonetic symbol in square brackets, such as [u] or [k], but a shortage of symbols means that complex symbols and diacritics must often be used, as with [ã] and [tʷ].

speech synthesis The use of computer programs and electronic circuits to produce understandable "speech" in a human language, often by interpreting and processing written text typed into a computer.

speech therapy The diagnosis and treatment of disorders of spoken language.

***SPE* feature system** The system of **distinctive features** proposed in *SPE*. The features are mainly articulatory in nature and are binary. Examples are [continuant], [nasal], [coronal] and [high].

spelling In a particular language, the conventional way of representing an individual word in writing, particularly in a language written with an **alphabet**. A spelling system is subject to a number of competing pressures: representing the sounds of the language as consistently as possible, retaining traditional spellings even when the pronunciations of words have changed (as with English *knight*, *write* and *child*), retaining foreign spellings for words borrowed from other languages (as with *pizza* and *machine*), showing relationships among words which are in fact pronounced differently (as with *photograph* and *photography*), and distinguishing **homophones** (like *rite, right, write* and *wright*). Every spelling system represents a compromise among these pressures.

spelling pronunciation A pronunciation of a particular word which arises because of the influence of its spelling. For example, all the words like *missile, fertile* and *sterile* were formerly pronounced with short vowels in the last syllable, as they still are today in the USA. Since about 1900, though, these words have come to be pronounced in Britain with a last syllable rhyming with *mile,* because of the spelling. Similarly, the word *often,* which lost its [t] centuries ago, just like *soften, fasten, listen* and *castle,* has recently once again acquired a [t] for many speakers because of the spelling.

spelling reform Any programme for changing the conventional spelling of a language in order to make it simpler or more regular. Many such programmes have been put forward for English, which has a particularly messy spelling system, but none has made headway.

spirant An old-fashioned name for a **fricative**.

spirantization Any change in pronunciation in which another sound (usually a **plosive**) is converted into a **fricative**. An example is the change of ancestral *⋆p* into *f* in the Germanic languages.

split A type of language change in which the speech sounds that formerly belonged to one phoneme divide into two different phonemes. In *primary split,* some instances of the original phoneme merge with another existing phoneme, and the total number of phonemes is unchanged. Example: in early Latin, /s/ between vowels changed to [r], and these new [r]s joined the existing phoneme /r/. In *secondary split,* there is no such merger, and the number of phonemes increases. Example: in early Old English, /k/ became [tʃ] before front vowels; when some of these front vowels were later lost, /k/ and /tʃ/ became two distinct phonemes.

split brain The situation of a person whose **corpus callosum** has been cut for surgical reasons (usually to treat epilepsy), so that the two hemispheres of the brain are no longer connected.

split ergativity The phenomenon, occurring in most **ergative languages**, by which **ergativity** is present in certain circumstances but absent in others.

split infinitive A traditional name for the English construction in which the "infinitival" particle *to* is separated from a following verb by a word or phrase. Examples include *She decided to never touch another cigarette,* in which the sequence *to never touch* is the "split infinitive", and *Star Trek*'s famous *to boldly go.* The construction has been condemned by some people for generations as "ungrammatical" and "ignorant", but in fact it is the condemnation which is ignorant: the construction is a normal and unremarkable feature of English and is often more elegant than any alternative. Moreover, even the name is wrong, since nothing is "split": a sequence like *to touch* is not a grammatical unit.

spondee A metrical **foot** consisting of two stressed syllables, such as *feline, good news* or *spondee* itself.

spoonerism A **speech error** involving an amusing transposition of segments or syllables: *our queer old dean, a blushing crow,* and the classic *Mardon me, Padam, but you are occupewing my pie.*

Sprachbund Another name for a **linguistic area**.

Sprachgefühl A native speaker's intuitions about his or her language: for example, about what is "right" or "wrong", or about whether two words are related.

spreading activation model A model of **word recognition** and **word retrieval**, a simpler version of the **interactive activation model** in which the stimulation of words by other words only flows outward to new words, and never back toward words already stimulated.

S-structure The name given in **Government-and-Binding Theory** to a level of syntactic representation which is much less abstract than **D-structure** but still somewhat more abstract than the version of **surface structure** recognized in earlier theories of **transformational grammar**.

stacking Piling up two or more **modifiers** of the same kind, in such a way that no one of them is contained within another but all modify the same thing. The phrase *a pretty little white house* exhibits three stacked **adjectives**; the phrase *any card that is exposed by the dealer which is picked up* illustrates stacked **relative clauses**. Stacking must be distinguished from **self-embedding**, in which each item is contained within another, larger, item of the same kind.

stadialism The view that languages develop, in a predictable manner, through a sequence of distinct stages, each stage characterized by different structural (especially grammatical) properties. This view has the obvious consequence that some languages, at a given time, must be "more developed" than others. Once popular, such views are almost universally rejected today.

stammer Abnormal hesitation in speech; difficulty in speaking smoothly and continuously. Compare **stutter**.

standard English That particular variety ("dialect") of English which is considered to be appropriate in formal contexts and which is considered by many educated speakers to be appropriate in all contexts. Almost by definition, an educated English-speaker speaks standard English, since acquiring fluency in standard English is a large part of what we consider education. Note that (within certain limits) pronunciation is not considered part of standard English, and standard English may be spoken with almost any kind of regional accent. Compare **Received Pronunciation**. The written form of standard English is used for virtually all types of writing.

standardization The process of creating a **standard language** for a language which formerly lacked an agreed standard form.

standard language That particular variety of a language, usually both spoken and written, which is accepted as the norm for educated usage. The standard variety is taught in schools and used for almost all publication; educated speakers speak it in all circumstances, except possibly in speaking to relatives and close friends from the same background. Not every language has such a standard form.

Standard Theory The particular version of **transformational grammar** presented in Noam **Chomsky**'s 1965 book *Aspects of the Theory of Syntax*. With minor modifications, it remained the accepted version of the theory until the early 1970s, when, under pressure from **Generative Semantics**, it was replaced by the **Extended Standard Theory**.

starred form A form marked by an **asterisk**, for either of the purposes mentioned in that entry, but most often to indicate ungrammaticality.

statistical universal (also **relative universal**) A universal which is true for most languages but not for all. See further under **universal**.

stative An **aspect** form which expresses a state of affairs, rather than an event. For example, the verb *break* assumes a stative form in *The window is broken*.

stative verb A verb whose meaning is a state of affairs, rather than an event or an action. Examples are *know, love, exist* and *believe*. Stative verbs in English are reluctant to appear in the **progressive**: **I am knowing the answer*; **I am believing in God*. Compare **dynamic verb**.

Steele, Joshua An Irish phonetician (1700–91); he pioneered the study of the **suprasegmental** features of English.

stem In morphology, a form of a word which cannot stand alone but to which affixes can be added to produce grammatical word-forms. Most typically, a stem consists of a **root** plus some additional material. For example, the Latin verb meaning 'love' has the root *am-*; this takes further elements to produce stems, such as the present stem *ama-* and the perfect stem *amav-*; to these in turn are added personal endings to produce complete forms like *amat* 's/he loves' and *amavi* 'I have loved'.

stemmatology That branch of **philology** (sense 1) which deals with the relations among different copies of ancient manuscripts: which are older, which were copied from which others, and so on.

stereotype A description or a mental picture of the characteristics which are *typically* possessed by the things that can be referred to by some word. For example, a stereotypical *dog* has four legs, hair, a long snout, a tail, a distinctive barking noise, and so on, but a particular real dog might lack some of these characteristics and still count as a dog. Compare **prototype**.

stigmatized form A linguistic form which is considered non-standard and which, if used, makes a bad impression on many educated speakers. An English example is the verb form *ain't*.

stimulus-freedom The property of language which allows us to say anything at all in any circumstances. Animal signalling systems, in contrast, are largely *stimulus-bound*: an animal produces a particular call always and only in the presence of a suitable stimulus.

stock Another name for a **language family**, or for a major branch of a family.

stop A speech sound whose production involves a complete closure somewhere in the mouth or the throat, so that no air flows out of the mouth: a **plosive**, an **affricate** or a **nasal**.

story grammar The overall structure of a **text** (spoken or written, and not just a story in the familiar sense). A particular sort of text (a fairy tale, a political speech, the instructions for playing a game, a news article, or whatever) normally has some kind of consistent and identifiable structure, and a story grammar constructed by a linguist is an attempt to identify that structure as explicitly as possible.

stranding See **preposition stranding**.

stranding error A **speech error** in which a grammatical ending is attached to the wrong word, as in *Susie always does her homework verily quick* (intended . . . *very quickly*).

Stratificational Grammar A theory of phonology, grammar and semantics, proposed by Sidney Lamb in the 1960s, in which linguistic structure is seen as a set of distinct autonomous levels called *strata*.

strengthening Another name for **fortition**.

stress (also **accentuation**) Emphasis on a particular syllable (in comparison with others). Stress is typically produced by some combination of greater loudness, higher pitch and greater length.

stress-timing A type of speech rhythm in which stressed syllables occur at roughly equal intervals, regardless of the number of intervening unstressed syllables. Stress-timing is typical of all varieties of English except for some of those spoken in Africa, Asia and the Caribbean. Compare **syllable-timing**.

stricture In the articulation of a **consonant** sound, the point at which the **vocal tract** is narrowed most tightly.

strident Noisy. The term is chiefly applied to certain **fricatives**, such as [s] and [ʃ], which are noisier than other fricatives, such as [θ] and the bilabial [ɸ].

string A sequence of words considered without regard to its grammatical structure. The term is most often used in **formal grammars** of certain kinds.

strong form The way a grammatical word is pronounced when it is stressed, as opposed to the **weak form** it assumes when unstressed. Note the pronunciation of *can* in the following exchange; it is weak in the first occurrence and strong in the second: Bill: *I hear Lisa can teach ice-skating*; Susie: *Yes, she can*.

strong verb A verb in English or another **Germanic** language which inflects by changing the vowel of the stem, such as *sing/sang/sung* or *drive/drove/driven*. Compare **weak verb**.

structural ambiguity (also **constructional homonymy**) Two or more sharply distinct meanings for a string of words which differ only in the grammatical structures assigned, and do not depend on assigning different meanings to a single word. There are two types: **surface-structure ambiguities** and **deep-structure ambiguities**; see those entries for examples, and compare **lexical ambiguity**.

structural change In the traditional way of stating a **transformation**, a description of the structure which is produced by the action of the transformation.

structural description In the traditional way of stating a **transformation**, a description of the structure to which the transformation is allowed to apply.

structuralism An approach to the study of language which considers a language to be primarily a system of relations – that is, the place of every element in the language (speech sound, word or whatever) is defined by the way it relates to other elements in the language. Structuralism was introduced by **Saussure**, and almost all approaches to linguistics since Saussure have been structuralist, whereas before Saussure most approaches had been atomistic, regarding a language as primarily a collection of objects. **American structuralism** represents a distinctive and unusually narrow version of structuralism; note that some linguists apply the term 'structuralism' *only* to American structuralism, which is misleading. Structuralist ideas were imported from linguistics by **Lévi-Strauss** into anthropology, from where they have spread into the social sciences generally and even into literary criticism.

structural semantics Any approach to the study of meaning (especially word meaning) which is based upon the principles of **structuralism**.

structure Any particular way of arranging smaller linguistic units into larger ones, such as phonemes into syllables, words into phrases or phrases into sentences. Any given language typically permits only a small number of possible structures (that is, only a small number of legal arrangements), but languages differ somewhat in the structures they permit.

structure-dependence A fundamental property of the grammars of languages. The point is that the grammars of languages operate in terms of purely structural units like verbs, noun phrases and subordinate clauses; they do *not* operate in terms of things like 'the second word in the sentence' or 'words of two syllables'.

Sturtevant, Edgar H. An American linguist (1875–1952), a specialist in **Indo-European**; he helped to establish linguistics as an autonomous discipline and was a founder of the **Linguistic Society of America**. He proposed the **Indo-Hittite hypothesis**.

Sturtevant's paradox The observation that phonological change is regular but produces morphological irregularity (by disturbing previously regular patterns), while analogical change is irregular but produces morphological regularity (by levelling out alternations).

stutter The unintentional repetition of segments or syllables in speech, especially word-initial ones: *G-G-G-Good morning*. Compare **stammer**.

style Any particular and somewhat distinctive way of using a language. We may speak of the characteristic 'style' of an individual speaker or writer, or of the characteristic 'style' associated with particular circumstances, such as the writing of legal documents or commentating on football matches.

stylistics 1. Narrowly, the use of the concepts and techniques of linguistics in studying the language of literary texts like poetry and novels. 2. Broadly, the study of the aesthetic use of language, in all circumstances, not just in literature.

stylistic variation (also **contextual variation**) Variation in the kind of language used depending on the circumstances. For example, you would surely use different kinds of English when chatting to friends, when being interviewed for a job, when writing an essay for your teacher, and when writing a short story.

subcategorization Different grammatical behaviour by the various words belonging to a single **word class**. For example, English verbs are subcategorized according to whether they can or cannot appear in a number of constructions; a few examples are *Susie will _____*, *Susie will _____ that*, *Susie will _____ me the book*, and *Susie will _____ that she is too tired*. Try inserting into the blanks a number of different verbs, such as *go, buy, say, decide, give* and *tell*. The differences in behaviour that you find are instances of the subcategorization of verbs.

subjacency The central principle of the **bounding theory** of **Government-**

and-Binding Theory, proposed to account for the existence of **islands**. The full statement is complex and technical, but essentially it prevents two grammatical structures from being more than a certain distance apart within a sentence.

subject 1. A certain **grammatical relation**. In English, the subject is usually (not always) the first noun phrase in the sentence, and it is the only noun phrase the verb ever agrees with (English doesn't have much agreement, of course). Examples (in brackets): [*Susie*] *is clever*; [*These old clothes*] *need to be thrown out*; [*Drinking the water here*] *is a bad idea*; [*That she smokes*] *surprises me*. Like all grammatical relations, a subject is identified by its grammatical behaviour, not by its meaning, and it is not true that a subject necessarily represents the doer of an action. 2. A person who takes part in an experiment and whose behaviour is examined.

subjunctive A distinctive set of verb-forms found in some European languages and having some kind of connection with uncertainty or unreality. In Spanish, for example, 'I think it's true' is *Creo que es verdad*, with an ordinary verb-form *es* 'is', but 'I don't think it's true' is *No creo que sea verdad*, with subjunctive *sea*. English has mostly lost the subjunctive it once had, but the label 'subjunctive' is still sometimes applied to certain forms characteristic of conservative speech, such as the *leave* and *were* of *I suggest that she leave* and *if I were you*.

subordinate clause (also **dependent clause**) A **clause** which cannot stand alone to make a complete sentence by itself, but which must be attached to another clause in a complete sentence. There are several types; examples are bracketed: (1) an **adverbial clause** (*We left* [*before she arrived*]); (2) a **relative clause** (*The runner* [*who dropped the baton*] *was distraught*); (3) a **complement clause** (*She says* [*that she will come*]); (4) an **embedded question** (*I don't know* [*where she is*]); (5) a **sentential subject** ([*That she smokes*] *surprises me*).

subordinating conjunction A word which marks a **subordinate clause** as such, particularly an **adverbial clause**. English subordinating conjunctions come at the beginning of their clause: *if, when, because, although,* and so on. Traditional grammarians also counted the **complementizers** like *that* and *whether* as subordinating conjunctions; this is not usual today.

subordination The use of **subordinate clauses**.

subscript A letter, number or symbol written lower (and usually smaller) than normal and attached to a preceding item in order to mark it in some way or to provide a distinctive symbol for something. See **referential index** for a linguistic example, and compare **superscript**.

subset principle The hypothesis that a child learning its first language always sets up a rule as narrowly as possible and then expands it to cover more cases. This hypothesis runs into difficulty with **overgeneralization**.

substantive universal A **universal** of language which says something about the linguistic objects which can or must be present in languages. Example: all languages distinguish nouns and verbs. Compare **formal universal**.

substitution error Another name for a **selection error**.

substrate An **indigenous** language which comes under pressure from a more prestigious language moving into its territory, possibly to the extent of disappearing, but not before itself exerting a noticeable influence upon that other language. Historical linguists have often been fond of explaining away puzzling features of languages by appealing to substrate influence from known or unknown earlier languages, but such explanations must be treated cautiously. Compare **superstrate**.

subtraction An unusual morphological process in which a form is derived by removing part of the root. In Fijian, for example, a transitive verb is rendered intransitive by removing its final consonant, so that, for example, *kaut-* 'carry' and *saum-* 'repay' have intransitive forms *kau* and *sau*.

suffix An **affix** which follows the material it is attached to. Among English suffixes are the *-s* of *gives*, the *-ing* of *giving*, the *-ness* of *happiness*, and both the *-ful* and the *-ly* of *powerfully*.

Sumerian A language spoken in Sumer (southern Iraq) around 5000 years ago and for some time after, and used as a written language for much longer. So far as we know, Sumerian was the first language ever written down, since the Sumerians appear to have invented writing. Sumerian is not known to be related to any other language.

Summer Institute of Linguistics (**SIL**) An organization of missionary linguists which trains its members in linguistic fieldwork so that they can learn a local language effectively and (with the assistance of native speakers) translate the Bible into that language.

superfix An **affix** which consists entirely of a **suprasegmental** such as stress or tone. For example, some African languages mark the tense of a verb merely by using one or another tone on the verb; such tense-markers are superfixes.

superlative That form of an adjective or adverb indicating that a quality is present to the maximum degree: *biggest, most beautiful*.

superordinate With reference to a word A, a second word B which has the property that the meaning of A is a particular instance of the meaning of B. So, for example, *flower* is a superordinate of *rose* and *tulip*, because anything which is a rose or a tulip is necessarily a flower. Compare **hyponym**.

superscript A letter, number or symbol written higher (and usually smaller) than normal and attached to a preceding (or rarely following) item in order to mark it in some way or to provide a distinctive symbol for something. For example, linguists write [tʰ] to represent an aspirated version of [t] and [tʷ] to represent a labialized version of [t]. Compare **subscript**.

superstrate A more prestigious language which coexists with a less prestigious one and exerts a noticeable influence upon that less prestigious one. An example is French in France with respect to **minority languages** like Breton and Basque. Compare **substrate**.

suppletion The use of two or more entirely different **stems** in forming the inflections of a single lexical item, as in English *good/better, go/went, person/people*.

supraglottal vocal tract That part of the **vocal tract** lying above the **glottis**: the **pharynx**, the **oral cavity** and the **nasal cavity**.

suprasegmental (also **prosody** [as noun], *prosodic* [as adjective]) (Pertaining to) a phonological feature which can only be adequately described by referring to some unit longer than a single segment, such as a syllable or a word. The label is most often applied to **stress, tone** and **pitch accent**, but is sometimes also applied to **length, vowel harmony** and other phenomena.

surface structure A representation (usually a **tree structure**) of the structure of a sentence which is minimally abstract, which corresponds as closely as possible (within the particular theory of grammar being used) to the spoken form of the sentence. Compare **deep structure**.

surface-structure ambiguity The presence in a string of words of two (or more) distinct meanings which correspond to different **tree structures**. Examples: *Old men and women are easily frightened* (different groupings of the first four words); *Flying planes can be dangerous* (different category labels for *flying* and for *flying planes*). Compare **deep-structure ambiguity**.

surname A family name which is passed on from one generation to another.

Survey of English Usage A study of the grammatical features of English, based upon a corpus of spoken and written British English held at the University of London.

svarabhakti Another term for **anaptyxis**.

SVO language A language in which the normal order of elements in a sentence is Subject–Verb–Object, such as English, Spanish or Chinese.

Swadesh, Morris An American linguist (1909–67), a prominent **American structuralist** who did a good deal of work (both sober and eccentric) on comparing languages; he championed the use of **lexicostatistics** and **glotto-chronology** and developed the **Swadesh word list**.

Swadesh word list Any of several different lists of words, usually of either 100 or 200 words, consisting entirely of **basic vocabulary**. Such lists are widely used in comparing languages, either to estimate the degree of relatedness (if the languages are already known to be related) or to look for possible **genetic relationships** (if not).

Swahili (also *KiSwahili*) A major language of east Africa, a **Bantu** language much influenced by **Arabic**. It was formerly used as a trade language between Africans and Arabs.

swearing Using language which is considered vulgar, obscene or blasphemous by the community as a whole. Swear words may be used quite deliberately in ordinary speech, or they may be produced spontaneously by a speaker who receives an unpleasant shock. There is evidence that the second case is not controlled by the ordinary language areas of the brain, but by a deeper and more ancient part of the brain called the *limbic system*.

Swedish The chief language of Sweden, also spoken in parts of Finland, a **Germanic** language.

Sweet, Henry An English linguist and phonetician (1845–1912). Though he did important work on the history of English, he is best known for his work in phonetics: he made Britain the world's premier centre for phonetic research, taught Daniel **Jones**, and co-founded the **International Phonetic Association**. He is widely regarded as the model for Bernard Shaw's Henry Higgins in *Pygmalion* (and *My Fair Lady*), an identification always denied by Shaw.

Swiss German The distinctive variety of **German** spoken in Switzerland; several regional varieties exist.

switch-reference A grammatical device used in certain languages for keeping track of who's doing what to whom in a manner unfamiliar to speakers of European languages. Lakhota is such a language. In Lakhota, the two particles *na* and *ča* both correspond to English *and*, but there is an important difference. The verb-form *ʔí* means 'he arrived', while *kté* means 'he killed him', but note the difference between *ʔí na kté* 'he$_i$ arrived and killed him$_j$' (same person arriving and killing) and *ʔí ča kté* 'He$_i$ arrived and he$_j$ killed him$_i$' (same person arriving and being killed). That is, *ʔí* means 'same subject coming up', while *ča* means 'subject and object are about to be switched'.

syllabary A writing system in which each character represents a complete single syllable. Many such systems were used in the past (**Linear B** being a famous example), but only a very few languages are written with syllabaries today (Japanese is written with a combination of *two* syllabaries and Chinese characters).

syllabic consonant A consonant which makes up the nucleus of a syllable all by itself, such as *l* in Czech *vlk* 'wolf', or *n* in English *button* for most (not all) speakers.

syllabification Dividing a word into syllables.

syllable A fundamental but elusive unit in phonology. A syllable typically consists of one vowel or diphthong possibly preceded and/or followed by one or more consonants. Speakers usually find it easy to agree on the number of syllables in a word or a longer sequence; thus English-speakers agree that *salt*, *complete* and *testify* contain one, two and three syllables, respectively. Attempts have been made to define the syllable in terms of muscular contractions, in terms of neural programming, and in terms of peaks in **sonority**, but no completely satisfactory definition has been found; nevertheless, the syllable is a central unit in many contemporary theories of phonology.

syllable-timing A type of speech **rhythm** in which each syllable of an utterance takes roughly the same amount of time to produce. Spanish, for example, is a syllable-timed language, and spoken Spanish sounds rather staccato, or "rat-tat-tat", to English-speakers as a result. Compare **stress-timing**.

symbol A written mark which is used for some purpose other than writing out words in the ordinary way, such as 5, *, &, %, *ʃ* or the phonetic symbol θ.

symbolic system Any system consisting of a set of objects, called *signs*, such that each sign has a conventional and agreed meaning to the users of the system, most typically a meaning which cannot be guessed from the form of the sign and which must therefore be learned. Language is an outstanding example of a symbolic system.

synaesthesia The ability to perceive one kind of sensory stimulus as though it were another kind. A synaesthetic may report, for example, that white paint smells blue, that grass smells purple, that a hovering helicopter sounds green, that lemons taste pointy while chocolate tastes prickly, that the vowel [u] sounds yellow. Most notably, a synaesthetic sees speech in colour: individual sounds, individual words, individual names all have particular colours. The condition affects about one person in 25,000.

syncategorematic item A word which exhibits unique grammatical behaviour and which therefore cannot be assigned to any **word class**. English examples include *not*, the *please* of *Please pass the salt*, and the "infinitival" *to* of *I want to go home*.

synchronic Pertaining to a language at a particular point in time, often (but not necessarily) the present. A linguist might, for example, construct a synchronic description of present-day English or of the English of Shakespeare. Compare **diachronic**.

syncope The loss of a segment, especially a vowel, from the middle of a word, as in the British pronunciation of *medicine* as [medsɪn].

syncretism Identity in form between two grammatically different inflections. In Latin, for example, the genitive and dative singular are usually distinct, as with *filius* 'son', which has genitive *filii* and dative *filio*, but *filia* 'daughter' has genitive and dative *filiae*; this is syncretism.

synecdoche Any **figure of speech** in which a part is used to denote a whole, or vice versa: *hand* for 'employee' or 'sailor', or *Brazil* for the Brazilian national football team.

synonym One of two or more words which have identical or very similar meanings: *violin* and *fiddle*, *swamp* and *bog*, *fruitful* and *productive*.

syntactic category Any one of the various classes of object which may form part of the syntactic structure of a sentence. There are two main types: *lexical categories* (ordinary word-classes like *noun*, *verb* and *adjective*) and *phrasal categories* (larger units like *noun phrases*, *verb phrases* and *prepositional phrases*). Many theories of grammar also recognize certain *intermediate categories*, such as **N-bar**, and some theories treat *sentence* as a distinct syntactic category of its own type.

syntactic feature In some theories of grammar, one of a set of elementary syntactic units defined so that every **syntactic category** must consist of a permitted combination of these features. Very often each feature must take just one of a small set of possible *values*. For example, the noun phrase *those little kittens* might be analysed as [NOUN +] (it's a nouny category), [BAR 2] (it's a phrase, not a lexical item), [PERSON 3] (it's third-person), [PLURAL +] (it's plural). The particular features and values used vary from one theory to another. A well-designed feature system allows the analyst to pick out any required **natural class**, such as [BAR 2] (all phrasal categories) or [AUX +, FIN −] (all non-finite forms of auxiliaries).

syntagmatic relation A relation between two or more linguistic elements which are simultaneously present in a single structure: for example, between the phonemes making up a word, or between a verb and its object. Compare **paradigmatic relation**.

syntax Sentence structure, or the branch of linguistics which studies the structure of sentences.

synthetic A label applied to a grammatical form which is constructed entirely by affixing or modifying the word in question, without the use of any additional words. For example, the English verb *eat* forms a synthetic past tense *ate*; compare the **analytic** forms *has eaten* and *is eating*, in which an additional (auxiliary) word is used to construct the required grammatical form. Likewise, the adjectives *tall* and *good* form the synthetic comparative *taller* and *better*, while *beautiful* forms the analytic comparative *more beautiful*.

synthetic speech Something which sounds very much like human speech but is produced entirely by a machine, usually by a computer program controlling an electronic circuit (a *speech synthesizer*). Such a device may be able to take a piece of written English typed into the computer and produce an acceptably human-like pronunciation of it.

Syriac A dialect of **Aramaic** formerly much used by Christians as a **liturgical language**, still used today by certain Christian groups.

system A set of competing possibilities plus the rules for using them. For example, we speak of the *pronoun system* or the *verbal system* of a language, meaning the total set of pronouns or of verb-forms in the language plus the rules for using each one appropriately.

systematic correspondence A consistent correlation between the words of two languages, as follows: whenever a word W1 in language L1 contains a particular sound S1 in a particular position, then, with a high degree of consistency, a word W2 of the same or similar meaning in language L2 contains a particular sound S2 in the same position. For example, English /f/ and Latin /p/ show a systematic correspondence in word-initial position: English *fish* and Latin *piscis* 'fish'; English *father* and Latin *pater* 'father'; English *foot* and Latin *pes* 'foot'; English *for* and Latin *pro*; and so on. Moreover, this is just one of a large number of systematic correspondences linking English and Latin. When we find two languages linked by a number of such systematic correspondences, then, providing certain precautions are taken (see below), we may be confident that the languages are in **genetic relationship** to one another – that is, that they started off long ago as no more than two dialects of one language. In the case of English and Latin, that ancestral language is **Proto-Indo-European** (PIE), and the point is that all these words were present in PIE and began with the same sound, which has developed into /f/ in English but into /p/ in Latin. In identifying systematic correspondences, we must be careful to exclude from consideration several potentially misleading cases: **nursery words** like *mama* and instances of **sound symbolism** like *meow*, both of which occur all over the world in unrelated languages, and also **loan words**. For example, the apparent /p/–/p/ correspondence visible in English *pizza, pasta, piano* and Italian *pizza, pasta, piano* is not evidence of a genetic link: these words have simply been borrowed from Italian into English. These loans are easy to spot, but ancient loan words may be far more difficult to identify and may mislead us seriously.

Systemic Linguistics A highly distinctive approach to linguistic description which attempts to integrate grammatical facts with a range of communicative, pragmatic and sociolinguistic information. Originally called **Scale-and-Category Grammar**, the framework was first developed by Michael **Halliday**; its proponents particularly stress its utility in the analysis of **texts**.

Szemerényi, Oswald A Hungarian-British linguist (1913–), a leading specialist in **Indo-European**.

T

taboo A prohibition on the use of certain words or names in some or all circumstances. Among the taboo items in various societies are names of certain body parts, words pertaining to sex or excretion, names of certain relatives, names of certain animals, and names of gods.

tacit knowledge Another term for **competence**.

Tagalog A major language of the Philippines, an **Austronesian** language. It is the basis of the national language, sometimes called *Pilipino*.

Tagmemics A particular framework for grammatical description, a **slot-and-filler** approach which is designed to allow fieldworkers to reduce bodies of data to coherent descriptions efficiently.

tag question A question at the end of a statement, asking for confirmation, either explicitly (*She's Irish, isn't she?*) or rhetorically (*She's Irish, is she?*)

Tai A family of languages spoken in southeast Asia, including **Thai**.

talking drums A way of transmitting messages using drums whose pitch can be varied; intonation and rhythm can be represented so accurately that messages can be understood even without any words.

talking Eve hypothesis A version of the **African Eve hypothesis** which holds that the successful peopling of the earth by what was originally a small group of Africans came about because that group, uniquely, possessed language.

Tamil A major language of southern India and of Sri Lanka, a **Dravidian** language.

Tanoan A group of languages spoken in the southwestern USA. Tanoan is related to **Uto-Aztecan** in a larger **Aztec-Tanoan** family.

tap A speech sound produced by moving the tongue rapidly so that it briefly touches something else and then pulling it back where it started. An example is the tapped *r* of Spanish *pero* 'but'; another is the tapped *t* of American English *butter*. Compare **flap**. **Note:** many textbooks do not distinguish taps from flaps, but it seems preferable to make the distinction.

tapping The development in American English in which the consonants /t/ and /d/ in certain positions (especially between vowels) are pronounced as a tap, as in the typical American pronunciations of *butter*, *water*, *city*, *ready* and *muddy*. As a result of this, certain pairs of words, such as *wetting* and *wedding*, may be pronounced identically, while other pairs, such as *writer* and *rider*, may be distinguished only by the quality of the preceding vowel or diphthong. **Note:** textbooks often call this "flapping", but the label is not appropriate.

ta-ra-ra-boom-de-ay theory A speculative conjecture about the origin of language; it holds that language developed out of ritual dance and chanting. There is no evidence to support this conjecture.

target An utterance which a speaker intends to produce, as opposed to the faulty utterance produced when a **speech error** is made.

target language The foreign language you are trying to learn.

Tarski, Alfred A Polish logician (1902–83), a major figure in the development of **formal semantics**.

task-based learning A way of learning a foreign language in which a number of learners perform activities that require them to interact with one another.

ta-ta theory The conjecture that language arose from attempts at imitating hand gestures with the tongue and lips. There is no evidence to support this conjecture. This is a version of the **ding-dong theory**.

tautosyllabic Occurring in the same **syllable**. In *blister*, for example, the first three consonants (at least) are tautosyllabic.

taxonomic linguistics A term of abuse hurled at the **American structuralists** by the early proponents of **generative grammar** in the 1960s. The younger linguists were accusing the older ones of being excessively concerned with classification, at the expense of explanation.

taxonomy A classification. All linguistic description involves classification (for example, of words into **word classes**), but linguists have often disagreed over the proper balance, and the dividing line, between taxonomy and explanation.

TEFL (also **EFL**) The *teaching of English as a foreign language*.

telegraphic speech Speech which consists only of content words, with no grammatical words. The term is chiefly applied to children's utterances like *Daddy sock* and *No want juice*.

telic A label applied to an activity, or to a linguistic form (especially a **verb**) expressing that activity, which has a recognizable goal. Examples: *Lisa is cleaning the fridge*; *Susie is driving to Canterbury*. The opposite is **atelic**.

Telugu A major language of southern India, a **Dravidian** language.

template A general pattern for the formation of a certain class of morphological forms in a language. For example, a Swahili verb-form typically conforms to the template Subject–Tense–Object–Root–Mood, as in *utampenda* 'you will like him', which consists of *u*-'you' + *-ta* Future + *-m* 'him' + *-pend* 'like' + *-a* Indicative.

tempo The rate of speaking. We may distinguish between an individual's overall tempo (some people speak faster than others) and the tempo of a particular piece of speech (some stretches of speech are produced faster than others).

temporal Pertaining to time. Words, phrases and clauses like *yesterday, two years ago, after the race* and *when I was only six years old* are all temporal adverbials.

tense 1. A **grammatical category** which correlates fairly directly with time. Tense is usually, though not invariably, marked in the verb in those languages that have it. Some languages have only two tenses (usually past versus non-past, sometimes future versus non-future); some have three (usually past, present, future); and some have more (for example, they may distinguish recent past from remote past). The largest number of tenses so far reported is eleven, in the African language Bamileke-Dschang. English has only two tenses: past versus non-past ("present"), as in *loved/love, went/go, would/will*. **Note:** traditional grammarians often use the term 'tense' in a very loose way that includes also **aspect** and **mood**, but this usage is objectionable. See **screeve**. 2. A **distinc-**

tive feature sometimes invoked to distinguish two classes of vowels which are otherwise difficult to distinguish, such as /iː/ [+ tense] and /ɪ/ [− tense] in English. The feature **ATR** is now often used instead.

tensed Another word for **finite**.

terminal node In a **tree structure** for a sentence, a **node** which has nothing below it. Such a node is usually a lexical item.

TESL (also **ESL**) The *teaching of English as a second language*.

Tesnière, Lucien A French linguist (1893–1954), the leading figure in the development of **dependency grammar**.

TESOL The *teaching of English to speakers of other languages*.

text A continuous stretch of spoken or written language, but particularly one which forms a discrete unit by itself and has some recognizable internal structure.

text linguistics The application of linguistic techniques to the study of **texts**, often particularly in the hope of identifying the properties which distinguish one type of text from another.

TG The abbreviation for **transformational grammar**. The longer form **TGG** means *transformational generative grammar*.

Thai The chief language of Thailand, formerly called *Siamese*. It belongs to the **Tai** family.

thematic structure The structure of a sentence viewed from the way in which information is organized within it. Such notions as **topic** and **focus** are important in the study of thematic structure.

theme The **semantic role** carried by an entity which is passively involved in an action or a state of affairs without being strongly affected, such as *the ball* in *The ball is red* and *Susie tossed the ball to Mike*. Some linguists do not distinguish between a theme and a **patient**.

theoretical linguistics All of that part of linguistic activity which is chiefly concerned with identifying general principles of the structure and functioning of languages. The term contrasts most obviously with **applied linguistics**, but many linguists would also hold that purely descriptive work on particular languages is not theoretical in nature.

theory of mind (also **intentional stance**) The ability to recognize that other people have minds of their own and hence their own ideas, desires, needs, fears and so on. We are not born with this ability, but must acquire it in early childhood; failure to do so results in *mindblindness*, a feature of the disability called *autism*, which among other things is characterized by an inability to understand the speech of others or to communicate with them effectively.

thesaurus A reference book which groups together words of similar or related meaning. Such a book is chiefly intended to assist a writer looking for exactly the right word.

theta The symbol [θ], used to denote the voiceless dental fricative, as in *think*. Compare **eth**.

theta role The name used in **Government-and-Binding Theory** for what is otherwise called a **semantic role**.

theta theory That **module** of **Government-and-Binding Theory** which deals with the principles governing **theta roles**.

third person That category of **person** which includes no reference to the speaker or the addressee. English has the third-person pronouns *he*, *she*, *it* and *they*, but in fact practically all **noun phrases** are third-person: *Rome, my sister, the south of France, the outer planets of the solar system.*

thirteen-men rule Another name for **iambic reversal**.

Thomas, John J. A Trinidadian civil servant (1840–89), a pioneer in the study of **creoles** and perhaps the first outstanding African-American linguist.

Thomsen, Vilhelm A Danish comparative linguist (1842–1927), a specialist in the **Finno-Ugric** languages and the decipherer of the Old Turkish **Orkhon inscriptions**. Among his students were Karl **Verner**, Otto **Jespersen** and Holger **Pedersen**.

thorn The letter þ, often used in Old English for writing the sounds now spelled *th* (for example, Old English *þunor* is modern *thunder*). Since printers could not print this letter, the spelling *th* was introduced to replace it, though some printers used *y* instead, leading to the quaint early modern spellings like *y*ᵉ for *the*.

Thracian An ancient and very poorly recorded language of the Balkans; it seems to have been an **Indo-European** language.

throwing madonna hypothesis The conjecture that language arose as a by-product of the earlier development of the language areas of the brain for controlling rapid sequential muscular movement, as in throwing rocks. This conjecture has found little support.

Thurneysen, Rudolf A Swiss linguist (1857–1940), perhaps the greatest **Celtic** specialist of all time.

Tibetan The chief language of Tibet, a member of the **Tibeto-Burman** branch of **Sino-Tibetan**. The written form of Tibetan is very archaic and bears little resemblance to the spoken language.

Tibeto-Burman A group of languages spoken in southeast Asia and forming one branch of the **Sino-Tibetan** family. Among them are **Tibetan**, **Burmese** and the **Karen** languages.

tilde The diacritic ~, used in various orthographies and transcriptions for various purposes. In the IPA it indicates **nasalization**, so that [ã] represents a nasalized [a].

timbre The perceptual qualities which distinguish one sound from another, such as one vowel from another.

tip The frontmost point of the **tongue**. Compare **blade**.

tip-of-the-tongue phenomenon (also **TOT phenomenon**) The phenomenon in which you are speaking happily along, when all of a sudden you want a particular word or name, and you just can't find it.

TMA system The complete system for marking **tense, mood** and **aspect** in some language; these three categories are often intertwined in complex ways.

Tocharian (also **Tokharian**) Two extinct languages (*Tocharian A* and *B*) spoken in central Asia around AD 1000 and recorded in texts. Tocharian is now known to form one branch of **Indo-European**.

to-infinitive A label given to the English construction in which an **infinitive** is preceded by the particle *to*, as in *She wants to buy a Porsche*. The name is rather misleading, since a sequence like *to buy* is definitely not a grammatical unit; see under **split infinitive**.

token Any individual occurrence of a linguistic form in speech. For example, every time you utter the word *dog*, you are producing a different token of that word. Compare **type**.

Tokharian Another name for **Tocharian**.

Tok Pisin An English-based **pidgin** widely used in Papua New Guinea. It now has some native speakers; for these speakers, it is a **creole**.

tone A system, found in many languages, in which words consisting of identical consonants and vowels are distinguished in pronunciation and meaning entirely by the presence of different **pitches**. For example, Mandarin Chinese has four tones, and the syllable *shu* has different meanings depending on which tone is used: with a high-level tone, *shū* means 'write'; with a rising tone, *shú* means 'sorghum'; with a falling tone, *shù* means 'technique'; with a falling-rising tone, *shǔ* means 'category'. As you can see, the term 'tone' is also applied to each one of the contrasting patterns available in a tone language.

tone language A language in which **tone** is present. Tone languages are widespread, but are particularly common in southeast Asia and west Africa.

tone of voice An informal name for **paralanguage**.

tongue The flexible muscular body in the mouth, shaped like three-quarters of a tennis ball. The tongue is the single most important organ in producing speech sounds; it is conventionally divided into **tip, blade, front** and **dorsum** (**back**).

tongue twister A phrase which is deliberately constructed so as to make it difficult to pronounce accurately: *The sixth sheik's sixth sheep's sick.*

tonic Bearing the **stress**. For example, in the word *linguistics*, the second syllable is the tonic syllable.

Tooke, Horne (properly *John Horne Tooke*) An English philologist (1736–1812), a highly original if occasionally eccentric theorist of language, best known for his book *The Diversions of Purley*.

top-down A label applied to any kind of processing which begins with the largest units and successively decomposes these into ever smaller units, until the whole message has been processed. The opposite is **bottom-up**.

topic That part of a sentence which is presented as already existing in a discourse and which the rest of the sentence, the **comment**, is in some sense 'about'.

topicalization A construction in which some part of a sentence is made into a **topic**, usually by placing it at the beginning. In *This book I can't recommend*, the

NP *this book* is topicalized; compare the ordinary (unmarked) construction *I can't recommend this book*. Compare **left-dislocation**.

toponym A place name: the name of a city, town or village, of a river or lake, of a mountain or valley, a forest, a road, and so on.

TOT phenomenon See **tip-of-the-tongue phenomenon**

***tough*-movement** A name for the construction found in *John is easy to please*; compare *It is easy to please John*.

Tovar, Antonio A Spanish linguist (1911–85), perhaps the most talented Spanish linguist of the twentieth century. He had an astonishingly broad range of interests, including **Indo-European**, the ancient languages of Spain, **Basque** and **native American languages**.

Tower of Babel A myth found in the book of *Genesis* in the Old Testament. According to the story, all human beings originally had only a single language, but God, annoyed by their attempt to build a tower reaching up to heaven, scattered them and gave them different languages to prevent cooperation.

T pronoun An intimate or informal second-person pronoun, such as French *tu*, Spanish *tú* or German *du*, typically used in addressing a close friend or relative, a social inferior, or anyone whom the speaker regards as an intimate or as a member of the same group. Compare **V pronoun**.

trace theory A theoretical idea which is important in certain versions of **transformational grammar**, especially in the **Revised Extended Standard Theory**. The idea is that, every time a transformation moves some item to a different position, it leaves behind a *trace*, a kind of ghostly flag to mark the former presence of the moved item.

trachea (also, informally, **windpipe**) The tube connecting the lungs to the mouth and containing the **larynx**.

traditional grammar The entire body of grammatical description in Europe and America before the rise of modern linguistics in the twentieth century, often especially the type of grammar which has usually been taught in schools. Modern grammatical ideas are often derived directly from the traditional ones, but we have been forced to reject some traditional views as plainly inadequate or wrong, and the overtly **prescriptivist** orientation of most traditional grammar contrasts strongly with the **descriptivist** approach of modern linguistics.

Trager, George An American anthropological linguist (1906–92), a specialist in **native American languages** and in the structure of English. He worked closely with Bernard **Bloch**, and was a co-author of both the **Bloch and Trager system** and the **Trager–Smith system** for analysing English vowels.

Trager–Smith system A particular system for analysing the vowels and diphthongs of American English, a modification of the earlier **Bloch and Trager system**. Trager–Smith recognizes nine short vowels, and every long vowel and diphthong is regarded as a combination of one of these short vowels followed by *y* [j], *w* or *h*. For example, the vowels of *pit*, *put* and *cat* are taken as /i/, /u/ and /a/, respectively, while those of *beat*, *boon*, *buy* and *father* are analysed as /iy/, /uw/, /ay/ and /ah/, respectively. The system was once nearly universal in American textbooks and dictionaries, but it is little used today.

transactional function The use of language to communicate information and skills. Compare **interactional function**.

transcription Any system, but especially a linguistically sophisticated one, for representing speech on paper in a principled way, ignoring any conventional writing system (if there is one). The two principal types are **phonetic transcription** and **phonemic transcription**; these serve very different purposes.

transfer Carrying features of pronunciation and grammar from one language which you speak into another which you also speak or are trying to learn. If the feature being transferred is not typical of the second language, the result is *negative transfer*: a foreign accent or a grammatical mistake. If the feature being transferred *is* typical of the second language, the result is *positive transfer*: easier learning.

transformation In a **formal grammar**, a type of grammatical rule which has the power to change the structure of a sentence which is being generated by the grammar, for example by deleting something or by moving it to a different position.

transformational grammar (**TG**) A theory of grammar developed by Noam **Chomsky** in the 1950s and extensively modified by Chomsky and others in the succeeding decades. TG was the first type of **generative grammar** to be proposed; it was characterized by very abstract underlying representations for sentences which were acted upon by a number of powerful rules called **transformations**, which could modify the structures of sentences in important ways. Its first presentation (in *Syntactic Structures*, 1957) was only a sketch; Chomsky's 1965 book *Aspects of the Theory of Syntax* presented a more complete and extensively revised version, the **Standard Theory** (or the *Aspects* model). This was followed in turn by the **Extended Standard Theory** in the early 1970s and the **Revised Extended Standard Theory** in the late 1970s. Chomsky's 1981 book *Lectures on Government and Binding* introduced a radically different approach known as **Government-and-Binding Theory**, and the name 'transformational grammar' is no longer used for this framework or for the even newer **Minimalist Programme**.

transition A movement of the organs of speech from one fairly steady position to another during speech. Transitions are usually clearly visible in a *sound spectrogram* produced by a **sound spectrograph**.

transition network (also **network grammar**) A kind of graphical representation of possible sentences conceived only as strings of words. Such a network consists of a number of points connected by arrows; each arrow has a word on it; there is one start point and several finish points. You start at the start point and move along any available arrow to another point, and then continue in the same way until you reach an end point. Every time you follow an arrow, you write down the word attached to that arrow. When you have finished, the string of words you have obtained is one of the sentences permitted by the transition network. A transition network is exactly equivalent to a **finite-state grammar**. If you add certain extra machinery to a transition network, the result is an **augmented transition network**.

transitive verb A **verb** which takes a **direct object**, such as *hit, love, want, prefer, have* or *describe*. Examples of use: *She hit him, She wants a new car, She described the scene*. A strictly transitive verb cannot be used without a direct object: **She* *hit, *She wants, *She described carefully.* Some verbs, however, may be either transitive or **intransitive**, such as *understand: She understood the problem, She understood.* A **ditransitive verb** is a special type of transitive verb.

translation Taking a written text in one language and constructing an equivalent text in another language. Compare **interpreting**.

translation theory The application of the ideas and techniques of linguistics to general problems in **translation**.

transliteration Converting a written text from one alphabet to another, in such a way that each letter of the original is always rendered in the same way in the result. For example, the Russian word честолюбие, in the Cyrillic alphabet, might be transliterated into the Roman alphabet as *chestoljubije*. Compare **transcription**.

transparency The property of a phonological rule (in some analysis) whose effect is obvious from an examination of surface forms. The opposite is **opacity**.

transposition (also **exchange error**) A **speech error** in which two sounds or sequences of sounds are switched, as when someone says *our queer old dean* for the intended *our dear old queen.*

tree Another name for **tree structure**.

tree diagram Another name for **tree structure**.

tree model In historical linguistics, a conventional way of showing how the languages of a **language family** are grouped – that is, which are more closely related and which more distantly. See **family tree**.

tree structure (also **tree diagram, tree, phrase marker**) A particular way of representing the syntactic structure of a sentence. Every group of words making up a single syntactic unit (a **constituent**) is placed under one branch of the tree, and smaller branches which also make up larger grammatical units are likewise grouped together under larger branches; each branch, or **node**, carries a label to show what **syntactic category** it belongs to. Figure T1 shows a tree diagram for the sentence *Our new puppies are eating their dinner.*

trigraph A sequence of three letters used to represent a single sound, such as German *sch* for /ʃ/, as in *schön* 'beautiful'.

trill A speech sound produced by allowing some flexible organ to vibrate, such as the alveolar trill spelled <rr> in Spanish *perro* 'dog' or the bilabial trill used by some English-speakers to mean "It's cold", commonly written *Brrr*.

triphthong A single vowel which changes its quality twice – like a **diphthong**, but more complicated. Triphthongs are not common in English, but some speakers in England and in the eastern USA may pronounce *fire* as [faɪə].

trisyllable A word consisting of exactly three syllables, such as *kangaroo* or *linguistics*.

Trnka, Bohumil A Czech linguist (1895–1984), a scholar with wide-ranging interests and one of the founders of the **Prague School**.

trochee A metrical foot consisting of a stressed syllable followed by an

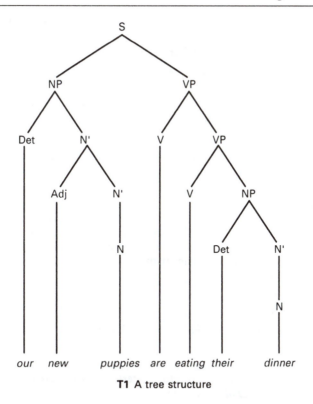

T1 A tree structure

unstressed one, as in the words *better* and *money*, or in the verse *Peter Piper picked a peck of pickled peppers.*

Trubetzkoy, (Prince) Nikolai A Russian linguist (1890–1938), one of the leading theorists of the **Prague School**, best known for his enormously influential book *Principles of Phonology*, which elaborated Prague School thinking in this domain.

truth-conditional semantics An approach to **formal semantics** which holds that the meaning of a sentence may be analysed in terms of the conditions which have to be satisfied for that sentence to be true. Highly influential in recent years, this approach makes no appeal to such factors as people's intentions and expectations or the context of an utterance.

Tswana A **Bantu** language chiefly spoken in Botswana and in adjacent parts of South Africa.

tune In some analyses of **intonation**, any one of the pitch sequences which are regarded as the building blocks from which complex intonation patterns are constructed.

Tungusic A group of languages, also called *Manchu-Tungus*, spoken in northeast Asia and forming one branch of the **Altaic** family. Its chief members are **Manchu** and **Evenki**.

Turing machine An abstract computing device, the most powerful type of **automaton**. A Turing machine can perform any computation which can be performed at all.

Turkic A group of mostly closely related languages spoken from the Balkans across central Asia into western China and forming one branch of the **Altaic** family. Its best-known member is **Turkish**.

Turkish The chief language of Turkey, also spoken in some neighbouring areas, a **Turkic** language.

turn In a conversation, a particular stretch of time during which one person is speaking and the others are listening. A turn ends when a different person begins to speak.

turn-taking The conversational behaviour in which each participant speaks for a while and then gives way to another speaker. Turn-taking is governed by rules, and a child learning its first language must learn those rules.

T/V pronouns In some languages, a pair of words meaning 'you' and both used to address one person, but differing in formality: the T pronoun is intimate, informal or condescending; the V pronoun is distant, formal or respectful. Examples: French *tu* and *vous*, European Spanish *tú* and *usted*; German *du* and *Sie*. A few languages carry the distinction over into the plural, as does German: *ihr* and *Sie*.

Twaddell, W. Freeman An American linguist (1906–82), a leading member of the **American structuralists**.

twang An informal label for a speech quality characterized by persistent **nasalization**.

two-word stage A particular stage in the **acquisition** of a first language by a child, during which the child can produce utterances which are two words long, such as *Gimme juice* or *Daddy sock*, but no longer.

type An abstract linguistic object. Every time you utter the word *dog*, you are producing another instance of a single type. Compare **token**.

typology The classification of languages according to their structural features, and not according to their ancestry. Any structural feature might in principle serve as the basis of a typology, but the only interesting classifications are those in which the languages in each category turn out to have other properties in common than the one chosen in the first place. Classification in terms of **basic word order** has proved to be particularly fruitful.

U

U Typical of upper-class British speech. The opposite is **non-U**.

UG See **universal grammar**.

Ugaritic An ancient **Semitic** language recorded from the fifteenth to the thirteenth centuries BC in what is now Syria.

Ukrainian The chief language of Ukraine, a **Slavic** language.

Uldall, Hans A Danish linguist (1907–57), a colleague of **Hjelmslev** in the development of **Glossematics**.

Ullmann, Stephen A Hungarian-born British linguist (1914–76); he was largely responsible for making **semantics** a central part of linguistics.

ultima (also **ult**) The last syllable in a word, such as *tics* in *linguistics*. Compare **penult, antepenult**.

umlaut (also **metaphony**) A change in the vowel of a word for grammatical purposes resulting from an ancient **assimilation**, as in English *goose/geese* and *mouse/mice*. Umlaut differs from **ablaut** only in its historical source.

un- For any term of the form *un-X* lacking an entry of its own, see under *X*.

unaccusative verb An **intransitive verb** whose subject is not an **agent**, such as *die, melt, sink* or *explode*. Many such verbs can also be used transitively: *The ice melted; The sun melted the ice.* Compare **unergative verb**.

unbounded dependency A grammatical link between two points in a sentence which can be any distance apart. For example, the link between a **WH-word** which introduces a question and the corresponding **gap** is an unbounded dependency. Example: *Who$_i$ did Alice say that Bill thought that Cynthia claimed that Dave discovered that Edna was going to marry e$_i$?* An unbounded dependency is the result of an **extraction**. Compare **local dependency**.

uncials A way of writing the **Roman alphabet** which uses only capital letters with a conspicuously rounded shape. Uncials were widely used in the early Middle Ages.

undergeneralization Especially in child language, the application of a word or other item to a narrower range of things than it properly denotes, such as applying *man* only to the child's father or *doggie* only to one dog. The opposite is **overgeneralization**.

underlying form An abstract representation of a word or a sentence which is posited by a linguist in order to allow certain generalizations to be expressed more readily.

understander system A computer program which is capable of understanding sentences typed in by a human being and of responding appropriately. Three famous examples are **ELIZA, SHRDLU** and **PRAGMA**.

unergative verb An **intransitive verb** whose subject is an **agent**, such as *dance, run, sing* or *jump*. Compare **unaccusative verb**.

ungrammatical Another term for **ill-formed**. **Note:** linguistically unsophisticated people often use 'ungrammatical' to mean merely **non-standard**, but the term is not so used in linguistics.

uniformity, principle of A fundamental principle of all scientific investigation. It may be stated as follows: the same physical laws apply everywhere, all the time, whether we're looking or not. We recognize a version of uniformity in linguistics: ancient languages were not different in nature from modern ones, and remote and unfamiliar languages are not different in nature from familiar ones.

uniqueness, principle of Another name for the principle of **contrast**.

univerbation A type of language change in which a phrase consisting of two (or more) words is reanalysed as a single word. An example is the change of Latin *clara mente* 'with a clear mind' into Spanish *claramente* 'clearly'.

universal Any property which is present in all languages (an **absolute universal**), or in *nearly* all languages (a **statistical universal**, or **relative universal**). An example of the first is 'All languages distinguish nouns and verbs'; an example of the second is 'All languages have at least one nasal consonant' (there are a few exceptions to this one). An **implicational universal** is any statement of the form 'If a language has property P, then it will also have property Q'; an example is 'If a language has front rounded vowels, then it also has back rounded vowels'. All those just cited are examples of **substantive universals**, statements about linguistic objects like verbs and vowels. Some linguists also recognize **formal universals**, statements about the form the grammar of a human language can take; such universals can only be stated within the framework of some particular theory of grammar, and they constitute most of the content of such a theory.

universal grammar (**UG**) The hypothetical structural properties which are necessarily common to all human languages, both real and possible, presumably because these properties are part of the human **language faculty**. The term is particularly associated with the work of Noam **Chomsky** and his followers; not all linguists are convinced that UG exists.

universal language Another name for an **artificial language**, or sometimes more specifically for an artificial language which is supposedly designed so as to avoid the ambiguity and inexplicitness of natural languages.

universal translator A hypothetical computer program which is capable of translating a language totally unknown to it into a familiar language. Because of **arbitrariness**, such a device is quite impossible.

unmarked form The opposite of a **marked form**; see the discussion and examples under that entry.

unpacking A change in pronunciation in which a single segment is converted into a sequence of two segments, such as when the palatal nasal [ɲ] is converted to the sequence [nj]. The opposite is **coalescence**.

unproductive Not available for forming new words. For example, the English noun-forming suffix *-th* is unproductive: we have cases like *warm* and *warmth*, but we cannot derive *coldth from *cold*.

unrounded Of a speech sound, pronounced without **lip-rounding**. For example, the vowels [i] and [a] are unrounded, and so are both of the consonants in *seat*. The opposite is **rounded**.

unrounding Any change in pronunciation in which a **rounded** vowel becomes **unrounded**, as when [y] changes to [i]. The opposite is **rounding** (sense 2).

Uralic A major language family of northern Eurasia, divided into a smaller **Samoyed** branch and a much larger **Finno-Ugric** branch. Some linguists think the **Yukaghir** languages are distantly related.

Urdu A major language of Pakistan, an **Indo-Aryan** language. At the spoken level, Urdu is the same language as **Hindi**, but it is written in a different alphabet and uses different technical and abstract words.

usage The linguistic habits of the people in a speech community, both in speech and in writing. Usage varies from person to person, from group to group, and according to context; both dictionaries and linguistic descriptions may show this by labelling particular words or forms as *slang, formal, old-fashioned, offensive, technical, informal,* and so on. All modern linguistic description is based upon **descriptivism**, careful observation of the usage of native speakers; **prescriptivism**, in contrast, frequently rejects observed usage in favour of uncommon or non-existent forms which are held to be superior for some reason.

Uto-Aztecan A family of languages spoken in Mexico and the southwestern USA; it includes **Hopi** and **Nahuatl**.

utterance A single particular piece of speech produced by somebody on a particular occasion.

uvula The very back of the roof of the mouth, where a little blob of flesh hangs down.

uvular (A speech sound) produced by pulling the back of the tongue toward the **uvula**, such as the [χ] in Dutch *Groningen*, Hebrew *chaim* 'life' and European Spanish *jota* (a dance).

uvularized Of a speech sound, produced with the back of the tongue pulled back toward the **uvula** while the principal articulation is being made somewhere else. The so-called 'emphatic' consonants of Arabic are uvularized.

V

Vachek, Josef A Czech linguist (1909–), the most prominent recent member of the **Prague School**.

vacuous rule application In a description of a language using **rules**, the case in which a rule applies to a representation so as to produce no change at all. Such vacuous application is permitted because it makes the overall description more economical.

valency The number of **arguments** required by a verb. The verb *smile* takes only one argument (it is *monovalent*), as in *Susie smiled*; *buy* takes two (it is *divalent*), as in *Susie bought a new car*; *give* takes three (it is *trivalent*), as in *Susie gave her niece a book token*. Certain processes, such as the **passive voice**, change the valency of a verb.

value 1. One of the two or more possibilities for a **distinctive feature** or a **syntactic feature**. For example, English nouns distinguish only two numbers, singular and plural; if we treat this difference in a grammar with a feature [plural], then the value [+ plural] means 'plurality is present', hence 'this form is plural', while the value [− plural] means 'plurality is absent', 'this form is singular'. 2. Any one of the possibilities covered by the use of a **variable** (sense 1) in a formal grammar.

variable 1. In many theories of grammar, a general symbol which can represent any of several competing possibilities, the **values** of that variable. For example, the symbol X″ (or X-double-bar, or XP) may be used to represent 'any phrasal category', including such possibilities as **noun phrase**, **verb phrase** and **prepositional phrase**. 2. In sociolinguistics, a convenient label for the existence of two or more competing **variants**, commonly written with some convenient symbol enclosed in parentheses. For example, *-ing* forms of verbs like *going* may be pronounced in two different ways: with a velar nasal (*going*) or with a coronal nasal (*goin'*). If we want to talk about this variation, we may introduce a variable such as '(ng)' to label it; this symbol simply denotes the range of possibilities.

variant One of two or more slightly different forms which exist in a single speech community and have equivalent meanings and/or functions but which may possibly (though not necessarily) differ in prestige or formality or merely in geographical preference. For example, English *I will not do it*, *I won't do it* and *I'll not do it* are variants differing in both formality and geography; Basque *ardao*, *ardo*, *ardú* and *arno* are regional variants of the word for 'wine'; the two pronunciations of *economics*, with /iː/ and with /e/, are variants which perhaps do not differ at all in social status or geography.

variation The existence of observable differences in the way a language is used in a speech community. There may be differences between one geographical area and another, between one social group and another, between one person and another, or even in the speech of a single person in different contexts. Some of this variation may be socially significant, in that certain choices are characteristic of some social groups but not of others. Variation was once dismissed by most linguists as peripheral and a nuisance; today, however, we recognize that variation is a central characteristic of language, one which is vital both in maintaining and expressing group membership and in serving as the vehicle of linguistic change (see the **Saussurean paradox**).

variety Any one of the distinguishable forms of a language, such as that used in a particular region, by a particular social group, or in a particular context.

Varro, Marcus Terentius A Roman humanist and linguist (116–27 BC), a brilliant and vastly erudite scholar who wrote an enormous number of books on language and other topics, only some of which still survive.

Vaugelas, Claude A French grammarian (1585–1650), author of a famous and influential grammar of French.

velar (A speech sound) produced by raising the back of the tongue toward the **velum**, such as [g] or [x].

velaric airstream mechanism One way of producing a flow of air for speaking. The back of the tongue is pressed against the **velum**, a second closure is made further forward in the mouth, and the tongue body is moved either down or up to change the pressure of the trapped air. When the front closure is released, air therefore flows either into the mouth or out of the mouth. Only the first of these occurs in speech, and it produces the velaric **ingressive** airstream used in making **clicks**.

velic closure The raising of the **velum** so that it closes off the **nasal cavity** from the **oral cavity**, thus preventing air from flowing through the nose. This is necessary for producing all speech sounds except those which are **nasal** or **nasalized**.

velum The soft, fleshy rear part of the roof of the mouth, informally called the *soft palate*.

Vendryes, Joseph A French historical linguist (1875–1960), author of a famous textbook of linguistics.

Ventris, Michael An English architect and amateur linguist (1922–56), the decipherer of the **Linear B** inscriptions.

verb A large **word class** found in all languages, or a word belonging to this class. The most obvious property of a verb is that it requires some minimum number of **noun phrases** to occur with it in a sentence and to serve as its **arguments**. An **intransitive verb** requires one argument, a **subject** (such as *smile* in *Jackie smiled*); a **transitive verb** requires two, a subject and an **object** (such as *kiss* in *Jackie kissed Mike*); a **ditransitive verb** requires three, a subject and two objects (such as *give* in *Jackie gave Mike a cuddle*). In many (but not all) languages, verbs are inflected for some or all of **tense, aspect** and **mood**; often they also exhibit **agreement** with their subjects and possibly with other arguments. In many (but not all) languages, verbs have two types of forms: **finite** forms (which are marked for tense and agreement) and **non-finite** forms (which are not). Some languages, including English, have a special subclass of **auxiliary** verbs with grammatical functions.

verbal 1. Expressed in words, either spoken or written. Compare **non-verbal communication. Note:** this term is used loosely in everyday speech to mean 'oral, spoken', as opposed to 'written', but this is *not* the sense it has in language studies. 2. Pertaining to **verbs**.

verbal complexity hypothesis The hypothesis that the **comprehension** of utterances is more difficult when those utterances contain verbs which can appear in a number of different constructions. So, for example, an utterance involving *prefer*, which can appear in at least five constructions, should be harder to process than one involving *take*, which can appear only in one construction. This hypothesis finds no support.

verbal noun A **noun** which is derived from a **verb** by some morphological process. Traditionally, this term is applied only to an item which behaves syntactically like a noun, such as *arrival* (from *arrive*) or *killing* (from *kill*) in cases like *this killing of baby seals* and *these senseless killings*. A similar item which behaves like a verb, such as *killing* in *deliberately killing prisoners*, is a **gerund**, not a verbal noun, but many people no longer make this distinction.

verb-complement clause A **complement clause** which follows a verb.

Examples (in brackets): *She suspects [that we're up to something]*; *I don't know [whether she's coming]*.

verb-framed language A language in which a verb of motion typically incorporates information about the *path* of movement, but not about the *manner*. Spanish is like this: it has lots of verbs like *entrar* 'go in', *salir* 'go out', *ascender* 'go up', *subir* 'go down', *pasar* 'go across', *penetrar* 'go through' and *circular* 'go about', but hardly any verbs corresponding to English *walk, scurry, stroll, limp, drive, ride* and *fly*. An English sentence like *The boy rode out of the courtyard* is rendered in Spanish as *El chico salió montando a caballo del patio*, literally 'The boy exited, on a horse, from the courtyard'. That is, the Spanish verb *salir* includes the notion of 'out' but not the notion of 'on horseback', while English *ride* does the reverse. Compare **satellite-framed language**.

verb phrase (VP) An important **syntactic category**. A VP in a sentence consists of a verb together with its obligatory objects and complements and its optional modifiers, but it excludes the **subject** of the sentence. Most typically, a VP functions as the **predicate** of a sentence. Examples (in brackets): *Susie [smiled]*; *Susie [opened a pack of cigarettes]*; *Susie [spread the peanut butter carefully over the bread]*; *Susie [wants to go home]*; *Susie [has decided that she needs a new car]*. A VP may also function as the complement of a verb, which means that it is contained within a larger VP; note the VPs *go home* and *needs a new car* in the last two examples. The treatment of **auxiliaries** in English is somewhat controversial; consider a sentence like *Susie has been writing letters*. Perhaps a majority of linguists would analyse this sentence as containing three VPs: *writing letters, been writing letters*, and *has been writing letters*. Some linguists, though, prefer other analyses which recognize only one VP in the sentence. A verb phrase may also function as a noun phrase. In the sentence *Carefully counting your top tricks is essential in bridge*, the phrase *carefully counting your top tricks* is a VP in its internal structure (it contains a verb with a direct object and an adverb), but it is a noun phrase with respect to the rest of the sentence (it is the subject of the sentence). It is the presence of the **gerund** ending *-ing* which allows a VP to do this.

verb serialization The use of a **serial verb construction**.

vernacular The ordinary, everyday spoken language of the people in a community, as opposed to a different variety of the same language, or to a different language, which is used in the same community for official purposes, for education or for high culture.

Verner, Karl A Danish historical linguist (1846–96), known above all for his discovery of **Verner's Law**.

Verner's Law An important change in the pronunciation of certain consonants which occurred very early in the history of the **Germanic** languages (which include English). Normally, the ancestral consonants */p t k/ developed into the fricatives /f θ x/ in Germanic (this is part of **Grimm's Law**), but sometimes they developed instead into /b d g/. What **Verner** discovered was that this second change happened whenever original */p t k/ were followed by the word-stress (and not word-initial). This discovery removed all the outstanding exceptions to Grimm's Law and made the history of the Germanic consonants absolutely regular; it also convinced the **Neogrammarians** that sound change was always absolutely regular.

vertical bilingualism An unusual arrangement found in certain mountainous areas. Several different languages are distributed by altitude, and each group of people speaks its own language and the language of the next lower group, but not the language of the next higher group.

Victor (also the **Wild Boy of Aveyron**) A French boy who was discovered living wild in the eighteenth century; he had seemingly had no contact with other people for years, and he had no language, nor was he able to learn much French after being discovered and rescued.

Vietnamese The chief language of Vietnam. Its genetic affiliations are uncertain, though a majority view assigns it to the **Mon-Khmer** branch of the **Austro-Asiatic** family.

virtual library An electronic service which allows specialists to distribute copies of their work over the Internet; these may be either finished versions for circulation or preliminary drafts intended to solicit criticism and discussion. The principal such service in linguistics is the *Applied Linguistics Virtual Library*, based at Birkbeck College in London; in spite of its name, this now caters also for theoretical linguistics.

visible speech Any system for representing the articulatory or acoustic characteristics of speech on paper, such as a *sound spectrogram* produced on a **sound spectrograph** or a graphical device used in teaching deaf people to speak.

Visser, F. Th. A Dutch linguist (1886–1976), author of a monumental study of the history of English syntax.

vocabulary (also **lexis, lexicon**) The words which exist in a particular language, or the words known to a particular speaker.

vocal-auditory channel The ordinary medium of speech: the production of sounds in the **vocal tract**, the transmission of those sounds through the air, and the reception and interpretation of those sounds by the ears and the brain.

vocal folds (also **vocal cords**) A symmetrical pair of tissues in the **larynx**. They can be tightly closed (as in straining or in producing a **glottal stop**), they can be opened wide (as in breathing), they can be opened narrowly (as in **whisper**), and they can be brought just together so that air from the lungs flowing up through them forces them to vibrate; this is **voicing. Note:** the spelling 'vocal chords' is an error.

vocal grooming The conjecture that language arose as a replacement for the elaborate grooming activity seen among our closest relatives, the apes, and hence as a way of providing social bonding among members of a group.

vocalic 1. Pertaining to **vowels**. 2. Having the nature of a vowel.

vocalism The quality of the vowels in a particular word. For example, the vocalism of Latin *porrum* 'leek' is much better preserved in Basque *porru* (a loan word) than in Spanish *puerro* or French *poireau*.

vocalization 1. The production of speech sounds. 2. Any change in pronunciation in which a **consonant** is converted into a **vowel** or a **glide**, such as when English *field* is pronounced as [fiwd].

vocal organs (also **organs of speech**) All those parts of the body which are used in producing speech. Sometimes the term is used more specifically to denote only the **supraglottal vocal tract**, those parts from the **larynx** up, excluding the lungs, the diaphragm, and so on.

vocal tract The entire passageway through which air can flow during speech, from the lungs to the lips and the nostrils. See the **supraglottal vocal tract**.

vocative A noun phrase used in addressing someone, such as *Lisa* in *Lisa, can you have a look at this?* Some languages have a distinct grammatical form for this purpose; this too is called a *vocative*.

vocoid Another name for a **vowel** in the phonetic sense (sense 1). Compare **contoid**.

Voegelin, Carl (1906–84) and **Voegelin, Florence** (1927–89) An American husband-and-wife team of anthropological linguists who almost invariably worked together. Specialists in **native American languages**, they founded or edited a number of important journals, and they produced the first attempt at listing and classifying the languages of the world.

voice 1. In grammar, any one of the various ways that may exist in a language for attaching the various **participant roles** (such as agent, patient, recipient) to the various **grammatical relations** (such as subject, direct object, indirect object). English distinguishes only an **active voice** (as in *Susie kissed Bill*) and a **passive voice** (as in *Bill was kissed (by Susie)*), but some languages have a larger range of possibilities. 2. In phonetics, another name for **voicing** (sense 1).

voice box An informal name for the **larynx**.

voiced Of a speech sound, produced with vibration of the vocal folds, such as [z], [g] or [a]. The opposite is **voiceless**.

voice dynamics A cover term for a range of vocal effects in speech other than the phonological characteristics of the language being spoken, including such factors as **tempo, rhythm, register** and **loudness**, but usually excluding **voice quality**.

voiceless Of a speech sound, produced without vibration of the vocal folds, as in [s] and [k]. Sometimes the term *unvoiced* is used with the same meaning, but note that it is wrong to use *devoiced* in this sense; see **devoicing**. The opposite is **voiced**.

voice mutation (also **breaking of the voice**) The process by which an individual's voice changes from a child's voice to an adult's. This happens around the onset of puberty.

voice onset time (**VOT**) In the production of a **plosive**, the time delay between the release of the plosive and the beginning of **voicing**.

voiceprint An informal name for a *sound spectrogram* produced by a **sound spectrograph**; this shows a detailed picture of a particular utterance by a particular individual, and may be helpful in identifying the individual whose voice is recorded.

voice quality The impression made on our ears by the voice of a particular individual, resulting partly from the size and shape of that individual's vocal organs, but mostly from individual habits in setting the vocal folds, the velum, and other organs during speech. Everybody's voice has a somewhat distinctive quality; that's how we can tell one voice from another.

voicing 1. (also **voice**) Vibration of the **vocal folds**, such as occurs in producing a **voiced** sound like [a], [m], [z] or [b]. 2. Any change in pronunciation in which a formerly **voiceless** sound becomes **voiced**.

Voltaic Another name for the **Gur** languages.

VOS language A language in which the normal order of elements in a sentence is Verb–Object–Subject, such as Malagasy in Madagascar. Such languages are not common.

VOT See **voice onset time**.

vowel 1. In phonetics, a speech sound whose production involves no significant obstruction of the airstream, such as [i], [u] or [a]. A **glide** like [j] or [w] is a (rather brief) vowel in this sense. 2. In phonology, a segment of high **sonority** which occupies the **nucleus** of a syllable, such as the /iː/ of English *seat*. A glide is not a vowel in this sense. The opposing term (in both senses) is **consonant**. **Note:** some people prefer to use the term **vocoid** for sense 1, reserving 'vowel' for sense 2.

vowel gradation Another name for **ablaut**.

vowel harmony A constraint applying in certain languages, by which only certain combinations of vowels are allowed to occur in a single word. In Turkish, for example, a word may contain either front vowels or back vowels, but not both. Compare **consonant harmony**.

vowel quadrilateral The familiar four-sided figure which represents (rather abstractly) the space inside the mouth within which vowels can be produced. A vowel pronounced with the tongue high (like [i]) is represented on the vowel quadrilateral by a symbol placed near the top; a vowel pronounced with the high part of the tongue pulled back (like [u]) is represented by a symbol placed near the right edge of the quadrilateral; and so on.

vowel shift A complex type of language change in which several different vowel phonemes in a language all change their phonetic quality at roughly the same time. A vowel shift is usually a **chain shift**, with each vowel moving into the space being vacated by another. The **Great Vowel Shift** of late medieval English is an example; this involved the changes [iː] > [aɪ], [eː] > [iː], [ɛː] > [eː], and [aː] > [ɛː] (among others).

vowel space An imaginary space of several dimensions, each dimension representing one of the possible ways in which one vowel can be different from another. The familiar **vowel quadrilateral** shows just two of those dimensions, **height** (vertical axis) and **backness** (horizontal axis), but the true vowel space has additional dimensions not easily represented on paper, such as **rounding** (sense 1) (the difference between [i] and [y]), **nasalization** (the difference between [a] and [ã]), **length** (the difference between [e] and [eː]), and others.

VP See **verb phrase**.

V pronoun A polite or respectful second-person pronoun, such as French *vous*, European Spanish *usted* or German *Sie*, typically used in addressing a stranger, a social superior, or anyone who the speaker does not regard as an intimate or as a member of the same social group. Compare **T pronoun**.

VSO language A language in which the normal order of elements in a sentence is Verb–Subject–Object, such as Irish or Welsh.

Vulgar Latin The spoken Latin of the Roman Empire, the direct ancestor of the **Romance** languages. It was significantly different from the *classical Latin* of most Roman literature, the sort of Latin studied in schools.

W

wabbit **phenomenon** Another name for the ***fis* phenomenon**.

Wackernagel's Law The statement that **clitics** tend universally to appear in the second position in a sentence, which is called *Wackernagel's position*. For example, French clitic pronouns do this, as in *Marie te le donnera* 'Mary will give it to you', literally 'Mary you it will-give'.

Wallis, John An English mathematician and polymath (1616–1703), a pioneer in **phonetics** and the author of a startlingly original grammar of English.

Wartburg, Walther von A Swiss historical linguist (1888–1971), best known for his etymological dictionary of French.

Washoe The first and most famous of a series of chimpanzees to which investigators attempted to teach a scaled-down version of **American Sign Language**, with controversial results.

Watkins, Calvert An American historical linguist (1933–), a leading specialist in **Indo-European**.

wave A periodic disturbance in something. A *sound wave* in air consists of periodic changes in the density of the air through which the sound is travelling. The **amplitude** of the wave is the size of the density change; the **wavelength** is the distance between successive points of maximum density, and hence the length of one *cycle*; the **frequency** is the number of cycles per unit time.

wavelength In a **wave**, the distance from one point of maximum disturbance to the next, the length of one *cycle*. Other things being equal, the greater the wavelength, the lower the **frequency**.

wave theory A way of looking at change in language and at regional differences in a language or a language family. Wave theory sees a language as a continuum occupying a certain area; every time a change is introduced at some location, that change spreads out across some part of the whole area occupied by the language, something like a ripple spreading across a pool of water. Since there are many changes being introduced at many different locations, after a while we find a complex pattern of overlapping changes, each of which has affected some areas but not others. Eventually, the regional differences become so great that we can no longer regard all the local varieties as constituting a single language; however – and this is the crucial point – the boundaries between the newly emerged regional languages are not at all sharp. Instead, we find only a continuum of regional forms, and the decision as to where to put the boundaries separating individual languages is a largely arbitrary one. Wave theory is undoubtedly realistic, and it conforms entirely to the findings of **dialect geo-**

graphy; nevertheless, the less realistic but more vivid **tree model** is usually preferred for displaying the structure of a language family.

weakening Another name for **lenition**.

weak form The way a grammatical word is pronounced when it is unstressed, as opposed to the **strong form** it assumes when stressed; see the example under this last entry.

weak verb In English and other **Germanic** languages, a verb which does not inflect by changing its stem-vowel, such as *love, loved, loved* or *put, put, put.* Compare **strong verb**.

Web site A document stored on a computer and linked to the Internet, so that it can be read (and printed) by everyone on the Internet. Thousands of individuals and organizations maintain *home pages* providing information about themselves and their work. Many people also maintain additional pages containing information on topics of interest to them; these pages often contain *links* to other people's sites dealing with the same or related topics. Quite a few of these sites are devoted to language, to linguistics or to particular languages. To find and read these sites, you need access to the Internet and a piece of software called a *browser*. If you know the *URL* (address) of a particular site, you can go straight to it. Otherwise, you can ask your browser to search for sites dealing with the topic you're interested in; once you've found an interesting site, you can *bookmark* it, so that you can go to it directly in the future. Some sites allow you to e-mail the owner with comments and questions; before trying this, be sure you have a very good reason.

Webster, Noah An American lexicographer (1758–1843), author of a famous and influential dictionary of American English (1828).

Weinreich, Uriel A Lithuanian-born American linguist (1926–67), a founder of **sociolinguistics** known especially for his pioneering study of **language contact** and for contributing to the development of our ideas about language change and variation.

well-formedness (also **grammaticality**) The state of being grammatical. A well-formed sentence in a language is a sentence which is consistent with all the grammatical rules of that language. Note two things. First, many perfectly normal utterances do not represent well-formed sentences. For example, consider this exchange: Bob: *Where are you going?* Susie: *To the library.* Here Susie's response is not a well-formed sentence. Second, there are well-formed sentences which do not represent normal utterances, because they are too long or too complex to be produced or comprehended. For example, *The book the professor the students who are doing linguistics like recommended is good* is a well-formed sentence, but it is intolerably difficult to understand, and it is not likely ever to be produced spontaneously. The opposite is **ill-formedness**.

Welsh The indigenous language of Wales, a member of the **Brythonic** branch of **Celtic**. Welsh is recorded from the early seventh century, though substantial texts exist only from several centuries later.

Wendish Another name for **Sorbian**.

Wenker, Georg A German dialectologist (1852–1911), the editor of the first **dialect atlas** of Germany.

Wernicke, Carl A German neurologist (1848–1905); he identified both **Wernicke's area** and **Wernicke's aphasia**.

Wernicke's aphasia (rarely also **sensory aphasia**) A type of **aphasia** resulting from damage to **Wernicke's area**. The sufferer is unable to understand speech and produces speech which is fluent but senseless.

Wernicke's area A localized area of the cerebral cortex of the brain, usually located just above and behind the left ear. One of the **language areas**, it appears to be largely responsible for comprehension and for access to ordinary vocabulary; damage to it produces **Wernicke's aphasia**.

whale songs Remarkable vocal displays produced by certain species of whale at certain times of the year; a typical performance lasts around half an hour, and all members of a group sing the same song. Remarkably, the song changes from year to year.

whisper A simple **phonation type** in which the front part of the **glottis** is closed but the back part is wide open. Air flowing through the opening produces friction noise and hence the familiar quality of a whisper. Whisper is much noisier than **breath**.

whispery voice (also **murmur**) A compound **phonation type** in which the vocal folds produce **voicing** and **whisper** simultaneously. Whispery voice is used contrastively in many languages of India, for example in the consonants spelled *bh*, *dh*, *jh* and *gh*, as in the name *Gandhi*. **Important note:** many textbooks call this *breathy voice*, but this term is inappropriate.

Whitney, William Dwight An American linguist (1827–94), a specialist in **Sanskrit** and the most influential American linguist of his day.

Whorf, Benjamin Lee An American linguist (1897–1941), a student of **Sapir** who produced some highly original descriptions of native American languages. He stressed (and probably exaggerated) the structural differences between these and European languages and developed a robust version of the **Sapir-Whorf hypothesis**.

WH-question A **question** which involves a question word like *who, what, where* or *how*, such as *Where are they?* Compare **yes–no question**.

WH-word A special word used for asking questions, such as English *who, what, where* and *how*.

Wild Boy of Aveyron See **Victor**.

wild child Another name for a **feral child**.

Wilkins, John An English polymath (1614–72); he pioneered the idea of a 'philosophical language', an artificial and universal language free of the limitations and ambiguities of natural languages.

Williams syndrome A disability afflicting some children at birth; it produces severe mental subnormality in many respects but leaves the language faculties unaffected and even "hyper-normal": sufferers speak fluently and enthusiastically and take great delight in unusual words, but may have trouble with reality and chatter about non-existent friends and happenings. This syndrome provides support for the **modular** view of mental and cognitive abilities.

windpipe An informal name for the **trachea**.

Wittgenstein, Ludwig An Austrian philosopher (1889–1951); he attached great importance to the study of language, and argued that many philosophical problems arise purely from insufficient attention to the nature and use of language.

word A term which is used in several different senses; the differences are important. An *orthographic word* is anything which is written with white spaces at both ends and no white space in the middle. This is of little linguistic interest, since the decision is partly arbitrary: we can write *land owners*, *land-owners* or *landowners*, and it doesn't matter. A *phonological word* is a sequence which is pronounced as a unit. A **lexical item** is a dictionary word: it's something you'd expect to find a separate entry for in a dictionary, such as DOG or TAKE. A **word-form** (or *grammatical word-form*) is a particular form assumed by a lexical item for particular grammatical purposes; for example, the lexical item DOG has the word-forms *dog* and *dogs*, and the lexical item TAKE has the word-forms *take, takes, took, taken, taking*. Consider the sentence *Our cat's been killing birds.* Here we find the lexical item CAT in the particular word-form *cat*. The sequence *cat's* (= *cat has*) is a single phonological word (it's pronounced as a unit) and a single orthographic word (it has no internal white spaces), but it nevertheless represents two lexical items (CAT and HAVE) and two word-forms (*cat* and *has*). When you use the term 'word', therefore, it is often essential to make clear just which sense you have in mind, and it may be preferable to use one of the more specific terms instead.

word-accent Any linguistic system for making some syllables in a word more prominent than others. There are two main types: **word stress** (as in English) and **pitch accent** (as in Japanese). Some languages (such as French) have no word-accent.

word-and-paradigm (**WP**) A label applied to a particular way of describing the grammar of a language, one which focuses on identifying all the classes and subclasses of words in a language and giving a complete set of grammatical forms for one example of each. This approach was much used by traditional grammarians, and even today most grammars of Latin adopt this approach. It is little used in linguistics.

word association Links between words in the mind, or a technique for revealing these links: a subject is given a word and must produce the first related word that comes to mind.

word blindness Another name for **dyslexia**.

word class (also **part of speech, lexical category**) Any one of the small number of grammatical classes into which the words of any language naturally fall, such as **noun, verb, adjective, determiner**. Languages differ in the particular classes they distinguish, and only the noun and verb classes appear to be universal. English has about fifteen classes.

word-form Any one of the several different forms which may be assumed by a single **lexical item** for different grammatical purposes. For example, the English lexical item DOG has only the two word-forms *dog* and *dogs*, while TAKE has at least five word-forms (*take, takes, took, taken, taking*). In some other languages, a single lexical item may have dozens or even hundreds of different word-forms: just think of all the different word-forms of a German adjective, a Latin noun or a French verb.

word-formation (also **lexical morphology**) Any process for creating new **lexical items** in a language. Among those used in English are **compounding**, **derivation** (sense 1), **clipping**, **blending**, and **back-formation**.

Word Grammar A theory of grammar proposed and developed by Richard Hudson in the 1980s. Word Grammar is unusual among theories of grammar in that almost all aspects of sentence structure are treated as properties of individual words.

word order The order in which words occur within a phrase or a sentence, or, more broadly, the order in which phrases occur in a sentence. Languages differ considerably both in the word order they prefer and in the degree of rigidity with which these preferences are enforced. See also **basic word order** and **free word order**.

word recognition Identifying a particular word which has been heard or read, the necessary first step in **comprehension**.

word retrieval Finding a particular word which is needed in speaking. This usually happens almost instantly; the **tip-of-the-tongue phenomenon** and **anomia** represent different degrees of difficulty in doing it.

word stress The presence of a characteristic **stress** on a particular syllable of a particular word. For example, English *ruminate, linguistics* and *kangaroo* have their word-stress on the first, the second and the third syllables respectively. Not all languages have word-stress.

working papers A periodical publication resembling a **journal** but containing preliminary drafts of papers being circulated for discussion.

Wörter und Sachen An approach to studying the origins and histories of words which stresses that knowledge of the society speaking the language is often of crucial importance. For example, the origin of the word *southpaw* 'left-handed person' can only be understood by realizing that, in the game of baseball, the pitcher always has the south on his left.

WP See **word-and-paradigm**.

Wright, Joseph An English historical linguist (1855–1930), a specialist in the **Germanic** languages and the author of a number of standard works on them, most notably his grammar of **Gothic**.

writing The representation of speech by means of permanent marks on a solid surface using an agreed and conventional system for doing so, a **writing system**. We apply the term 'writing' only to a complete system in which any utterance of the language can be adequately written down. Certain forerunners of writing allowed only certain types of information to be written down, such as taxes due and paid, and hence these were not true writing.

writing system Any conventional system for representing speech as marks on paper (or another solid surface). There are three main ways of constructing writing systems: using an **alphabet**, using a **syllabary**, or using **logograms**. The first two types represent speech sounds (or sequences of speech sounds) directly, and typically require only a small number of characters; the third does not represent speech sounds at all, but uses a different character for every word, thus requiring a huge number of different characters. Many writing systems consist of mixtures of these three types, such as the Japanese writing system and the Egyptian **hieroglyphs**; such mixed systems can be exceedingly complex.

wug test A procedure for testing whether young children have learned the rules for making regular English plurals. A child is shown a cute little figure and told "Look, here's a wug." A second, similar, figure is introduced, and the examiner says "Look, here's another wug. Now there are two . . ." A child who says *wugs*, with ending correctly pronounced [z], and who succeeds also with other nonsense words, has learned to form English plurals.

wynn The letter <ƿ>, borrowed from the **runic alphabet** and used in **Old English** to represent /w/, for which the **Roman alphabet** formerly had no letter.

X

X-bar system A particular theory of the way **syntactic categories** are constructed in languages. It holds that every syntactic category must either be a *lexical category* (a **word class**, like Noun or Verb) or be built up ("projected") from one of these lexical categories according to certain highly restrictive rules.

Xhosa A major language of South Africa, a **Bantu** language which exceptionally has **click** consonants.

Y

Yeniseian A family of languages spoken in Siberia. All but one of them (**Ket**) are now extinct, though others are recorded.

Yerkish A facetious name for the invented language taught to **Lana**.

yes–no question A question which expects the answer *yes* or *no*, such as *Are you going to Heather's wedding?* Compare **WH-question**.

Yiddish A language traditionally used by Jews in central and eastern Europe, a **Germanic** language closely related to **German**.

yogh The letter <ȝ>, used in writing **Middle English** in places where we would now write <g>, <gh> or <y>.

yo-he-ho theory The conjecture that language arose from rhythmic grunts emitted by groups of people doing heavy work. There is no evidence to support this conjecture.

Yonah, R. Another name for **Ibn Janah**.

Yoruba A major language of southwestern Nigeria, a member of the **Kwa** branch of **Niger-Congo**.

Young, Thomas An English scientist and linguist (1773–1829); he took the first steps in deciphering the Egyptian **hieroglyphs**, whose nature he was the first to understand, and he deciphered the **demotic** written form of Egyptian.

Yukaghir A group of languages spoken in Siberia, believed by some linguists to be distantly related to the **Uralic** languages.

Z

zero Any linguistic element which, in some analysis, is posited as being present but which has no phonetic realization. An example is the English zero plural. The plural of an English noun is usually distinguished from its singular by an overt marking, as with *dogs/dog* and *children/child*. But there are exceptions, such as *sheep*: *That sheep is hungry*, but *Those sheep are hungry*. We may say that the plural of *sheep* is marked by a zero.

zero-derivation Another name for **conversion**.

zeugma 1. A construction in which a word which needs to be combined with two other words can in fact only be combined with one of them. Example: *Have you ever wanted to learn French but didn't know how to go about it?*, in which the combination of *have you ever wanted* and *have you didn't know* is a zeugma. 2. A **coordinate structure** each part of which bears a different semantic relation to the rest of the sentence, as in *He took his hat and his leave* and *He watched the battle with interest and a telescope*. (The second type is more technically called a *syllepsis*.)

Zulu A major language of South Africa, a **Bantu** language which exceptionally has **click** consonants.

Further Reading

Below is an annotated list of selected books which you might like to read in order to learn more about language and linguistics. The list is grouped into categories; so far as possible, each category is arranged from briefest and most elementary to most comprehensive.

General Introductions

Trask, R. L. 1995. *Language: The Basics*. London: Routledge. A lively and entertaining popular introduction to the study of language.

Hudson, Richard. 1984. *Introduction to Linguistics*. Oxford: Blackwell. A brief introduction to what linguists do and how they go about it.

Miller, George A. 1996. *The Science of Words*. New York: Scientific American Library. An exceptionally attractive and well-illustrated survey of many of the chief areas of linguistics.

Aitchison, Jean. 1992. *Linguistics: An Introduction*. 4th edn. (also published as *Teach Yourself Linguistics*). London: Hodder & Stoughton. A very elementary textbook of linguistics.

Yule, George. 1996. *The Study of Language*. 2nd edn. Cambridge: Cambridge University Press. A slightly more detailed textbook, but still elementary.

Fromkin, Victoria and Robert Rodman. 1993. *An Introduction to Language*. 5th edn. New York: Harcourt Brace Jovanovich. A much more substantial textbook, but easy to read.

Language and Mind

Aitchison, Jean. 1989. *The Articulate Mammal*. 3rd edn. London: Routledge. A very readable introduction to psycholinguistics and especially to child language acquisition.

Aitchison, Jean. 1987. *Words in the Mind*. Oxford: Blackwell. An elementary introduction to how words are stored in the mind and used.

Peccei, Jean Stilwell. 1994. *Child Language*. London: Routledge. A very basic introduction to child language.

Jackendoff, Ray. 1993. *Patterns in the Mind*. New York: Harvester Wheatsheaf. A highly readable introduction to language and cognition.

Pinker, Steven. 1994. *The Language Instinct*. London: Allen Lane/Penguin. A famous collection of essays on language and mind, some very readable, some a little more demanding.

Steinberg, Danny. 1993. *An Introduction to Psycholinguistics*. London: Longman. A university-level textbook.

Language and Society

Trudgill, Peter. 1995. *Sociolinguistics*. 2nd edn. London: Penguin.

Romaine, Suzanne. 1994. *Language in Society*. Oxford: Oxford University Press.

Holmes, Janet. 1992. *An Introduction to Sociolinguistics*. London: Longman. These are three of the best introductions, in order of increasing size and coverage.

Bonvillain, Nancy. 1993. *Language, Culture, and Communication*. Englewood Cliffs, NJ: Prentice-Hall. A textbook of social and anthropological linguistics.

Coates, Jennifer. 1993. *Women, Men and Language*. 2nd edn. London: Longman. Perhaps the best of the many introductions to sex and language.

Edwards, John. 1994. *Multilingualism*. London: Penguin. A readable introduction to multilingualism, including educational issues.

Wardhaugh, Ronald. 1987. *Languages in Competition*. Oxford: Blackwell. An easy-to-read introduction to the politics of multilingual societies.

Pronunciation

Ashby, Patricia. 1995. *Speech Sounds*. London: Routledge. A very elementary introduction to phonetics.

O'Connor, J. D. 1973. *Phonetics*. Harmondsworth: Penguin.

Ladefoged, Peter. 1993. *A Course in Phonetics*. 3rd edn. Fort Worth: Harcourt Brace Jovanovich. These last two are university-level textbooks.

Knowles, Gerald. 1987. *Patterns of Spoken English*. London: Longman.

Roach, Peter. 1991. *English Phonetics and Phonology*. 2nd edn. Cambridge: Cambridge University Press. These last two books treat all aspects of the pronunciation of English.

Hawkins, Peter. 1984. *Introducing Phonology*. London: Hutchinson. Easier to read than most textbooks of phonology.

Grammar

Crystal, David. 1996. *Rediscover Grammar*. 2nd edn. London: Longman. A refresher course in the grammar you didn't learn at school.

Hurford, James R. 1994. *Grammar: A Student's Guide*. Cambridge: Cambridge University Press. Like the preceding, but more detailed and with exercises.

Fabb, Nigel. 1994. *Sentence Structure*. London: Routledge. A very elementary introduction to sentence structure.

Brown, Keith and Jim Miller. 1991. *Syntax: A Linguistic Introduction to Sentence Structure*. 2nd edn. London: HarperCollins. Easier to read than most textbooks of syntax.

Meaning

Hurford, James R. and Brendan Heasley. 1983. *Semantics: A Coursebook*. Cambridge: Cambridge University Press. An exceptionally readable elementary introduction.

Hofmann, Th. R. 1993. *Realms of Meaning*. London: Longman. Slightly more demanding than the preceding, but still very readable.

Jackson, Howard. 1988. *Words and Their Meaning*. London: Longman. Focuses on word-meanings and dictionary-writing.

Thomas, Jenny. 1995. *Meaning in Interaction*. London: Longman. The most readable textbook of pragmatics, the relation between meaning and context.

Language Change and Historical Linguistics

Trask, R. L. 1994. *Language Change*. London: Routledge. A brief and very elementary introduction.

Aitchison, Jean. 1991. *Language Change: Progress or Decay?* 2nd edn. Cambridge: Cambridge University Press. More substantial than the preceding, but still elementary.

McMahon, April M. S. 1994. *Understanding Language Change*. Cambridge: Cambridge University Press. A university-level textbook, but an outstandingly good one. Covers only language change, and not other aspects of historical linguistics.

Milroy, James. 1992. *Linguistic Variation and Change*. Oxford: Blackwell. A sociolinguistic approach to language change.

Trask, R. L. 1996. *Historical Linguistics*. London: Edward Arnold. A substantial textbook, but a particularly lively and readable one.

Crowley, Terry. 1992. *An Introduction to Historical Linguistics*. 2nd edn. Oxford: Oxford University Press. Another well-written textbook, particularly suitable for readers in Australia, New Zealand and the Pacific.

English

Crystal, David. 1988. *The English Language*. London: Penguin. A light-hearted introduction to many aspects of English.

Crystal, David. 1995. *The Cambridge Encyclopedia of the English Language*. Cambridge: Cambridge University Press. A lavishly illustrated popular book on all aspects of English.

Graddol, David, Dick Leith and Joan Swann. 1996. *English: History, Diversity and Change*. London: Open University/Routledge. An exceptionally attractive book on the history of English and on variation in English around the world.

McCrum, Robert, William Cran and Robert MacNeil. 1992. *The Story of English*. 2nd edn. London: Faber and Faber/BBC Books. An unusual history of English which focuses more on people than on linguistic data.

Leith, Dick. 1983. *A Social History of English*. London: Routledge. Another unusual history of English which focuses on social and political factors.

Pyles, Thomas and John Algeo. 1993. *The Origin and Development of the English Language*. 4th edn. Fort Worth: Harcourt Brace Jovanovich. This is one of several excellent books describing the linguistic changes which have affected English since the Old English period.

Hughes, Arthur and Peter Trudgill. 1996. *English Accents and Dialects*. 3rd edn. London: Edward Arnold.

Trudgill, Peter and Jean Hannah. 1994. *International English*. 3rd edn. London: Edward Arnold. These two books provide brief linguistic descriptions of the major regional varieties of English; the first deals with the British Isles, the second with the rest of the world. They require some knowledge of phonetics.

Wells, John. 1982. *Accents of English*. 3 vols. Cambridge: Cambridge University Press. A comprehensive description of the major types of English pronunciation all over the world. Requires a knowledge of phonetics.

Katamba, Francis. 1994. *English Words*. London: Routledge. Explains where English words come from, how they are built and how they behave.

Gramley, Stephan and Kurt-Michael Pätzold. 1992. *A Survey of Modern English*. London: Routledge. A big book covering all aspects of contemporary English; it has a large number of references to specialist work on particular topics.

Anyone interested in English should own a *good* English dictionary and know how to use it. In addition, you should be familiar with the great *Oxford English Dictionary* and know how to use that; it is available both in printed form and on CD-ROM.

Miscellaneous

Ingram, Jay. 1992. *Talk Talk Talk*. Toronto: Viking/Penguin. A collection of entertaining essays on selected aspects of language.

Smith, Neil. 1989. *The Twitter Machine*. Oxford: Blackwell. A stimulating collection of essays on many aspects of language.

Aitchison, Jean. 1996. *The Seeds of Speech*. Cambridge: Cambridge University Press. A popular introduction to the origin and evolution of human language.

Wallman, Joel. 1992. *Aping Language*. Cambridge: Cambridge University Press. A critical examination of the various attempts at teaching apes to use language. Not always easy reading.

Sampson, Geoffrey. 1985. *Writing Systems*. London: Hutchinson. There are many recent books on writing systems; most are catalogues, but this one focuses on the different ways in which a writing system can be constructed.

Pullum, Geoffrey K. 1991. *The Great Eskimo Vocabulary Hoax*. Chicago: University of Chicago Press. A delightful collection of humorous essays on the foibles of linguists, entertaining and enlightening. One or two require some background in linguistics, but most can be read by anyone.

Dictionaries and Encyclopedias

Penguin publish a number of brief and elementary dictionaries with titles like *Introducing Linguistics*, *Introducing Phonetics* and *Introducing Language and Society*; there are too many to list separately.

Crystal, David. 1992. *An Encyclopedic Dictionary of Language and Languages*. Oxford: Blackwell. A very general dictionary; it includes some straight linguistics but also treats languages and language families, the countries of the world and their languages, writing systems, language teaching, dictionary-writing, publishing, disability and other topics.

Crystal, David. 1997. *The Cambridge Encyclopedia of Language*. 2nd edn. Cambridge: Cambridge University Press. A lavishly illustrated popular book introducing virtually all aspects of the study of language.

Crystal, David. 1997. *A Dictionary of Linguistics and Phonetics*. 4th edn. Oxford: Blackwell. A more substantial dictionary than the one in your hand; it is aimed chiefly at university students and lecturers.

Malmkjær, Kirsten (ed.) 1991. *The Linguistics Encyclopedia*. London: Routledge. This one-volume encyclopedia contains several dozen entries each dealing with a major area of linguistics; further reading is suggested for each topic.

Newmeyer, Frederick J. (ed.) 1988. *Linguistics: The Cambridge Survey*. 4 vols. Cambridge: Cambridge University Press. This is a large collection of articles covering most areas of linguistics; each article provides a brief and up-to-date survey of the topic plus lots of further reading – very useful for getting started on a particular topic.

Bright, William (ed.) 1992. *International Encyclopedia of Linguistics*. 4 vols. New York: Oxford University Press. This is an encyclopedia of general linguistics; it provides particularly detailed information on the world's language families.

Asher, R. E. and J. M. Y. Simpson (eds). 1994. *The Encyclopedia of Language and Linguistics*. 10 vols. Oxford: Pergamon. This huge encyclopedia treats almost everything imaginable; you can almost always find a good introduction to the topic you're interested in.

Trask, R. L. 1996. *A Dictionary of Phonetics and Phonology*. London: Routledge. This book provides very detailed coverage of the terminology of phonetics (the study of speech sounds) and phonology (the study of sound systems in languages). It is aimed at university students and lecturers.

Trask, R. L. 1993. *A Dictionary of Grammatical Terms in Linguistics*. London: Routledge. This book provides very detailed coverage of the terminology of grammar, both traditional and contemporary, including both syntax (sentence structure) and morphology (word structure). It is aimed at university students and lecturers.

Electronic Resources

If you have access to the Internet, there are a number of services and information sources available in the area of language and linguistics; most of them are free, apart from the ordinary charges for being connected to the Net. They are of several types: **Web sites, databases, newsgroups, lists** and **virtual libraries**. See these entries in this dictionary for further information, and be *sure* to read and follow the advice given there. The *Oxford English Dictionary* and some other databases are available on CD-ROM; some are cheap, others expensive.

Professional Bodies

Many countries have national professional bodies devoted to general linguistics or to specific areas like applied linguistics and historical linguistics. Membership is usually open to everyone; there is an annual fee (usually reduced for students) which may possibly include a subscription to a journal. Most of these bodies organize conferences once or twice a year at which members can present their latest work for discussion; others hold more frequent but smaller meetings with only a single speaker at each. Britain has the *Linguistics Association of Great Britain* (general linguistics), the *British Association of Applied Linguistics* (applied linguistics) and the *Philological Society* (historical linguistics). The USA has a number of such bodies, the largest of which are the *Linguistic Society of America* (general linguistics) and the *American Association for Applied Linguistics* (applied linguistics). Many of these organizations maintain Web sites or can easily be tracked down on the Internet; otherwise a university linguistics department may be able to tell you which organizations exist in your area and how to get in touch with them. Note, however, that these bodies cater for professional specialists and students, not for beginners.

Courses

Many universities offer courses and degrees in linguistics and related areas, at both undergraduate and post-graduate level. Undergraduate degrees often combine linguistics with another subject, such as anthropology, cognitive science or a foreign language. The standard sources of information about university courses in your country will provide details, though note again that many linguistics departments maintain Web sites with full information. In many large cities it is possible to find evening classes in various areas of linguistics, and some universities put on summer schools lasting several weeks. The Linguistic Society of America and the Summer Institute of Linguistics both put on large-scale summer schools, but these are aimed at advanced students, not at beginners.